MY SiDEWALKS ON
SCOTT FORESMAN
READING STREET
Teacher's Guide

Level B
Volume 2

PEARSON
Scott
Foresman

Editorial Offices: Glenview, Illinois • Parsippany, New Jersey • New York, New York
Sales Offices: Boston, Massachusetts • Duluth, Georgia • Glenview, Illinois
Coppell, Texas • Sacramento, California • Mesa, Arizona

ISBN: 0-328-24790-1

4 5 6 7 8 9 10 V064 15 14 13 12 11 10 09 08 07
CC1

A Safe Place to Learn

MY SIDEWALKS ON
SCOTT FORESMAN
READING STREET
Intensive Reading Intervention

What can you do when a core reading program with small group instruction isn't enough for your struggling students? You can give them someplace safe where they can learn. Someplace where you can focus your instruction on their specific needs. Someplace where your students feel comfortable and confident as they accelerate and progress to on-level reading. Someplace like *My Sidewalks*.

My Sidewalks is a research-based, intensive reading intervention program that follows the Response to Intervention model. It works side-by-side with *Scott Foresman Reading Street* or any core reading program. It is designed to provide the most effective intervention for students who are struggling to read, with special consideration for English Language Learners. With daily instruction written specifically for Tier III students, you can help struggling readers steadily take steps to become proficient and confident readers.

3-TIER MODEL

TIER I
Core Program

TIER II
Core Plus
Strategic Intervention

TIER III
Intensive
Intervention ← *My Sidewalks*

Three Steps Toward Creating a Safe Place to Learn

1 SUSTAINED INSTRUCTION

My Sidewalks contains lesson plans for 30 full weeks. Every day, for 30–45 minutes, you can put your struggling readers—monolingual and English Language Learners— on solid footing. With instruction that is systematic and explicit, *My Sidewalks* helps you create a learning environment that is both consistent and predictable so your students can sustain progress every day. Your students will make strides with:

- Increased time on task
- Explicit teacher modeling
- Multiple response opportunities
- Tasks broken down into smaller steps

2 INTENSIVE LANGUAGE AND CONCEPT DEVELOPMENT

Research shows that a child's vocabulary entering first grade is a strong predictor of comprehension at eleventh grade. This is a critical area where Tier III students are deficient. *My Sidewalks* helps build a foundation for future comprehension success with daily, intensive language and concept development:

- Unit themes organized around science and social studies concepts
- Five to seven new vocabulary words tied directly to the week's theme
- Four weekly selections that build on the unit concept
- Concepts that connect from week to week

3 CRITICAL COMPREHENSION SKILLS

Along with daily vocabulary instruction, *My Sidewalks* provides explicit and systematic instruction on the comprehension skills and strategies researchers have identified as being the most critical for developing reading success:

- Drawing Conclusions
- Compare/Contrast
- Sequence
- Main Idea and Supporting Details

Components

Student Readers

My Sidewalks takes high-interest reading selections and puts them in an engaging magazine format. Every week, your Tier III students read four different selections that work together to develop a science or social studies concept. Week in and week out, these fiction and nonfiction selections help your students get a better understanding of the overall unit theme (the same themes and concepts found in *Scott Foresman Reading Street!*). 30 lessons, organized into 6 units. (5 units at Level A)

Teacher's Guides

My Sidewalks keeps your intervention instruction running smoothly. The Teacher's Guides contain everything you need for Tier III instruction. Complete lesson plans focus on high priority skills and provide daily routines with suggested time frames to help you keep your instruction focused and on time.
2 Volumes per level

Practice Books

Finally, a practice book written specifically for Tier III students. These consumable workbooks/blackline masters give your students additional practice in phonics, comprehension, vocabulary, and writing. Books are available for each level and have multiple practice selections for every lesson. Plus, each page contains a Home Activity to strengthen the school-home connection. *A Teacher's Manual with answer key is also available.*

Benchmark Readers

What's working for your students? Which students need more targeted instruction? Accurately assess your Tier III students' progress with these unit readers. Each 8-page book contains examples of all the skills targeted in the unit so you can find out instantly whether a student is ready to transition out of *My Sidewalks* or still needs additional intervention.

Alphabet Cards

Help your Tier III students practice letter names and sounds with these colorful cards. *(Level A)*

Assessment Book

All your assessment needs, all in one book. Along with assessment instruction, you'll find progress-monitoring forms, placement tests, unit assessments in individual and group formats, and guidelines for students to exit *My Sidewalks*.

Finger Tracing Cards

Hands-on Tracing Cards allow students to connect sounds to letters while they learn their letter shapes. *(Level A)*

Manipulative Letter Tiles

Sturdy, plastic, manipulative tiles are easy for little fingers to practice word building. *(Levels A–B)*

AudioText CD

Recordings of the Student Readers read at a fluent pace give Tier III students complete access to every selection.

Sing with Me Big Book

Large, illustrated Big Books develop oral vocabulary and build background. Pages inspire small group discussions using vocabulary words and include songs that demonstrate the words in context. *(Levels A–B)*

Sing with Me Audio CD

Song recordings accompany each Sing with Me Big Book. *(Levels A–B)*

Sound-Spelling Cards

Colorful cards with instructional routines introduce each sound-spelling in the intervention lesson. *(Levels A–C)*

Sound-Spelling Wall Charts

Large-size formats of the Sound-Spelling Cards are ideal for use in small-group instruction. *(Levels A–C)*

Tested Vocabulary Cards

Flash cards build important vocabulary knowledge and provide additional practice.

Welcome to *My Sidewalks*

This handy guide shows you how to provide effective instruction, manage your time, and help students catch up.

Write-On/Wipe-Off Cards

These cards have a write-on/wipe-off surface and writing lines for practicing letter forms, letter-sounds, spelling, and writing.

Level	Grade
A	1
B	2
C	3
D	4
E	5

MY SIDEWALKS ON
SCOTT FORESMAN
READING STREET
Intensive Reading Intervention

Authors

My Sidewalks was created by the leading researchers in the area of reading intervention instruction. Their work has helped struggling readers and is the basis for the 3-Tier model of instruction.

"Research shows that for students to make significant progress, they need systematic and intensive instruction that is tailored to their current instructional level."

Sharon Vaughn

Connie Juel, Ph.D.
Professor of Education
School of Education
Stanford University

Jeanne R. Paratore, Ed.D.
Associate Professor of Education
Department of Literacy and
Language Development
Boston University

Deborah Simmons, Ph.D.
Professor
College of Education and
Human Development
Texas A&M University

Sharon Vaughn, Ph.D.
H.E. Hartfelder/Southland
Corporation Regents
Professor
University of Texas

Contents

Unit 5 Responsibility

Unit 6 Traditions

Resources

Distinctions Between Levels

Understanding the Levels of *My Sidewalks*

The goal of the *My Sidewalks* program is to enable struggling readers to succeed with the reading material used in their regular classrooms. To achieve this, *My Sidewalks* focuses on accelerating students' acquisition of priority skills. Each level of *My Sidewalks* is designed to provide a year and a half of reading growth. Consequently there is an overlap of skills between one *My Sidewalks* level and the next.

These pages describe the skills students should have to successfully begin each level of *My Sidewalks* and what they will learn in that level. Use the Placement Tests to help you determine the correct level at which to enter each student.

To begin this level a child should know:	**In this level**, the instructional focus is on:
Early Reading Intervention (Grade K)	
	• Phonological and phonemic awareness • Letter names and sounds • Blending regular short-vowel words • Sentence reading
Level A (Grade 1)	
• Some phonological awareness	• Phonemic awareness • Letter names • Consonants: Individual letter-sounds, blends, and digraphs • Vowels: Short, long (CVCe), and *r*-controlled • Blending words and fluent word reading • High-frequency words • Oral vocabulary and concept development • Building fluency (40–60 WCPM) • Passage reading and retelling

To begin this level a student should know:	**In this level**, the instructional focus is on:

Level B (Grade 2)

• Letter names • Individual consonant letter-sounds • Some basic high-frequency words • And be able to read Benchmark Reader A2 with accuracy and comprehension	• Phonemic awareness • Letter names and sounds • Blending words and fluent word reading • High-frequency words • Oral vocabulary and concept development • Building fluency (70–90 WCPM) • Passage reading and retelling

Level C (Grade 3)

• Consonants: Individual letter-sounds, blends, and digraphs • Vowels: Short and long (CVCe) and be able to distinguish between them • A wider range of high-frequency words • And be able to read Benchmark Reader B2 with accuracy and comprehension	• Blending words and fluent word reading • Decoding multisyllabic words, including words with one or more affixes • Phonics: Vowels • Concept vocabulary • Building fluency (100–120 WCPM) • Passage reading and summarizing

Level D (Grade 4)

• Consonants: Individual letter-sounds, blends, and digraphs • Vowels: Short and long (CVCe) and be able to distinguish between them • How to decode regular VC/CV words with short and long (CVCe) vowels • Many high-frequency words • And be able to read Benchmark Reader C1 with accuracy and comprehension	• Decoding multisyllabic words, including words with one or more affixes • Phonics: Less frequent vowel patterns, such as vowel diphthongs • Concept vocabulary • Building fluency (110–130 WCPM) • Passage reading and summarizing

Level E (Grade 5)

• Consonants: Individual letter-sounds, blends, and digraphs • Vowels: Short and long (CVCe) and be able to distinguish between them • How to decode regular VC/CV words with short and long (CVCe) vowels • Many high-frequency words • And be able to read Benchmark Reader D1 with accuracy and comprehension	• Decoding multisyllabic words, including words with one or more affixes • Phonics: Less frequent vowel patterns, such as vowel diphthongs • Concept vocabulary • Building fluency (120–140 WCPM) • Passage reading and summarizing

Differentiating Instruction

The charts on these pages show instruction during a week in *My Sidewalks*. The charts can also be used as guides for **reteaching** or **accelerating** through parts of the lessons. In addition, the *If... then...* directions will help you identify how to customize instruction for your students.

Reteaching To meet the needs of the lowest performing readers, it may be necessary to modify the pacing and intensity of instruction. Activities shown in gray boxes on the charts may be repeated for these students.

Accelerating A child who shows mastery of skills following initial instruction may be ready for instruction at a faster pace with fewer repetitions. Activities shown in green boxes might be omitted for these students.

Levels A–B

	PHONEMIC AWARENESS	PHONICS	HIGH-FREQUENCY WORDS	CONCEPTS/ ORAL VOCABULARY	PASSAGE READING	FLUENCY	WRITING
Day 1	Phonemic Awareness	Blending Strategy	High-Frequency Words	Concepts/ Oral Vocabulary	Read a Passage	Reread for Fluency	
Day 2	Phonemic Awareness	Blending Strategy	High-Frequency Words		Read a Passage	Reread for Fluency	Write
Day 3	Phonemic Awareness	Blending Strategy	High-Frequency Words	Concepts/ Oral Vocabulary	Read a Passage	Reread for Fluency	
Day 4		Fluent Word Reading		Concepts/ Oral Vocabulary	Read Together	Reread for Fluency	Write
Day 5		Assess Word Reading	Assess Word/ Sentence Reading	Check Oral Vocabulary	Assess Passage Reading/ Reread		Write

■ **Reteach**   ☐ **Omit for acceleration**

If... a child is struggling with word reading,
then... reteach Word Work activities and include More Practice extensions.

If... a child lacks oral language,
then... elicit extended language from the child, provide ample opportunities for the child to respond when building concepts, and expand the structured picture walks before reading each selection.

If... a child's reading is so slow that it hinders comprehension,
then... provide additional models of fluent reading, give more corrective feedback during fluency practice, and include More Practice extensions when rereading for fluency.

If... an English learner struggles with sounds,
then... repeat appropriate practice activities.

Levels C–E

	VOCABULARY	COMPREHENSION	PASSAGE READING	PHONICS	FLUENCY	WRITING
Day 1	Vocabulary		Read a Passage	Blending Strategy (Level C)	**Reread for Fluency**	Write (Levels D–E)
Day 2	Vocabulary	Comprehension Skill	Read a Passage	Phonics	Reread for Fluency	**Write (Levels D–E)**
Day 3	Vocabulary	Comprehension Skill Assess (Levels D–E)	Read a Passage	Phonics	Reread for Fluency	Write
Day 4	Vocabulary	Comprehension Skill/Strategy Assess (Levels D–E)	Read Together (Level C) Read a Passage (Levels D–E)	Phonics Review (Level C)	Reread for Fluency	Write
Day 5	Vocabulary	Assess Comprehension	**Read Together (Levels D–E)** **Reread (Level C)**	Assess Sentence Reading (Level C)	Assess Fluency	Write

If... a student is struggling with word reading, **then...** reteach Vocabulary and Phonics activities and include More Practice extensions.

If... a student lacks oral language, **then...** elicit extended language from the student, provide ample opportunities for the student to respond when building concepts, and expand the After Reading discussion for each selection.

If... a student's reading is so disfluent that it hinders comprehension, **then...** provide additional models of fluent reading, give more corrective feedback during fluency practice, and include More Practice extensions for fluency.

If... a student lacks comprehension and is unable to retell or summarize, **then...** reteach comprehension skills and strategies, provide additional modeling of retelling and summarizing, and give more corrective feedback during practice.

If... an English learner lacks English vocabulary for known concepts, **then...** say the unknown English word, have the student repeat it, and ask questions that will allow the student to use the word in a meaningful context.

Meeting ELL Needs

My Sidewalks was developed to provide intensive reading intervention for Tier III students struggling to read and write. The program has been designed to reflect current research on literacy instruction for English language learners (ELLs)—not as additional notes, but integral to all elements of instruction. From its original conception, instruction to meet the needs of both native English speakers and English learners (who have some basic English conversational skills) has been integrated into the curriculum, teaching practices, and learning activities. Since English language learners acquire literacy skills in much the same way as their English-speaking peers, both will benefit from the same good instructional practices.

> **Research Says** "ELLs at risk for reading problems profit considerably in their literacy skills from systematic and explicit interventions that address the core reading skills of beginning reading: phonemic awareness, phonics, fluency, vocabulary, and comprehension. . . . Our work with ELLs suggests that postponing interventions to wait for language to become more proficient is not necessary, and supporting literacy acquisition in the language of instruction provided by the school for students at risk is beneficial." Vaughn, S., Linan-Thompson, S., *et al.* 2005. "Interventions for 1st Grade English Language Learners with Reading Difficulties." *Perspectives,* 31 (2), p. 31-35.

English language learners need. . .	My Sidewalks provides. . .
Phonemic Awareness	
• to develop familiarity with the sounds of English • to practice identifying, segmenting, and blending sounds in English words • to learn the sounds of English within words, in isolation and in meaningful contexts	• explicit and systematic modeling of sounds in words • scaffolded instruction that evokes active responses by children • ample practice identifying, counting, segmenting, blending, adding, and deleting sounds in words • clear lessons that tie phonemic awareness to phonics
Phonics	
• to learn the letters and letter-sound correspondences of English • to master identifying, segmenting, and blending the variety of sounds that letters represent in English words • to understand how to complete phonics activities • to use the phonics they learn—seeing, saying, reading, and writing words—with growing proficiency • to learn the sounds and spellings of written English words in meaningful contexts	• explicit phonics instruction with regular practice • routines for practicing the core English phonics elements • clear, step-by-step blending strategies understandable to students learning English as they learn to read • active learning—hearing, speaking, reading, and writing—that ties phonics to decodable text (Levels A–C) and to decoding of multisyllabic words in text (Levels D–E) • practice decoding and reading words related to concepts explored in oral language and texts

English language learners need. . .	My Sidewalks provides. . .

Vocabulary

• to develop oral vocabulary in English, including words already familiar to English-speaking children • to learn functional English vocabulary, including high-frequency words • to encounter new words in meaningful oral and written contexts • to hear, see, and use new words repeatedly • to learn academic English vocabulary	• multiple exposures to each vocabulary word • a routine for learning high-frequency words (at Levels A and B) • a routine for learning oral vocabulary (at Levels A and B) • a focus on words related to science and social studies concepts • multiple opportunities to practice using and producing oral and written vocabulary, including academic English • development of deep meaning for key concepts and words

Comprehension

• to continually improve their comprehension of oral English • to read comprehensible texts and develop abilities to interpret more complex written language • to use their prior knowledge in order to comprehend texts • to acquire understanding of sentence structures and text organizations of academic English • to learn about cultural concepts embodied in the readings	• an emphasis on oral language and concept development, to improve students' English proficiency and comprehension • an abundance of comprehensible reading materials focused on science and social studies concepts • modeling, instruction, and practice of priority comprehension skills and reading strategies, including prereading routines • explicit instructional routines that model new skills, build on students' prior knowledge, use visual elements to clarify ideas, and incorporate ample practice and review • exposure to the structures of English, text organization, and cultural concepts of the readings and lessons

Fluency

• to hear models of fluent reading of instructional-level texts • to practice and improve their fluent reading • corrective feedback on their reading	• teacher modeling to familiarize students with expressive, meaningful reading of instructional-level academic texts • engaging practice opportunities that include choral reading, paired reading, and reading with AudioText, which provide many models for building fluency • instruction in reading rate, accuracy, expression, and intonation • repeated readings and corrective feedback, to help students see words in context and pronounce them • progress monitoring and assessments to aid in fluency growth

Writing

• to develop their English proficiency by writing as well as reading • to write about ideas related to reading topics • to practice communicating their ideas in English through manageable, interesting writing activities	• opportunities to respond to literature about themes • scaffolded writing instruction including sentence frames for young children, manageable writing prompts for all students, and self-checking activities • feedback for writers from teacher and fellow students

Unit 4
Skills Overview

Why These Skills? *My Sidewalks* focuses on the priority skills children need in order to succeed at learning to read. **Priority skills** are the critical elements of early reading—phonemic awareness, phonics, fluency, vocabulary, and text comprehension. Scientifically based research has shown that these skills are the foundations of early reading and must be taught in a systematic sequence.

	WEEK 1 4–35 **When Things Change**	**WEEK 2** 36–63 **From Seed to Plant**
Phonemic Awareness	Segment and Count Sounds Segment Compounds into Words, Words into Sounds	Segment and Blend Sounds
Phonics — Blending Strategy	Sound of *a* in *ball*; Compound Words **REVIEW** Contractions	Long *a: ai, ay*; Long *e: e, ee, ea* **REVIEW** Vowel Sounds of *y*
Spelling	Words with Sound of *a* in *ball*	Words with Long *a: ai, ay*
High-Frequency Words	*gone, group, move, neighbor, promise*	*above, almost, change, often, straight*
Vocabulary — Concept	How can familiar things help us with changes?	How do plants change as they grow?
Oral Vocabulary	*familiar, keepsake, preserve, represent, valuable*	*adapt, annual, nutrients, soil, sprout*
Comprehension — Skill	Compare/Contrast	Compare/Contrast
Strategies	Preview, Ask Questions, Use Story Structure, Summarize	Preview, Ask Questions, Use Story Structure, Summarize
Writing	Response to Literature	Response to Literature
Fluency	Reread for Fluency Practice	Reread for Fluency Practice

WEEK 3	WEEK 4	WEEK 5
64–95 **Animals**	96–125 **What Changes Are Hard?**	126–159 **Weather Changes**
Add and Delete Ending Sounds Segment and Blend Sounds	Segment and Count Sounds	Segment Words into Syllables, Syllables into Sounds
Endings *-er, -est;* Long *o: o, oa, ow* **REVIEW** Base Words and Endings	Long *i: igh, ie* **REVIEW** Long Vowel Digraphs	Syllables V/CV and VC/V **REVIEW** Reading Longer Words
Words with Endings *-er, -est*	Words with Long *i: igh, ie*	Words with Syllables V/CV and VC/V
animal, country, cover, field, warm	*below, child, children, full, important*	*head, large, poor, though, wash*
How do animals change as they grow?	Why are some changes difficult?	How do changes in the weather affect us?
appearance, nursery, stage, tend, transform	*adjust, ancestor, courage, landmark, unexpected*	*blizzard, condition, forecast, predict, terrifying*
Compare/Contrast	Main Idea	Compare/Contrast
Preview, Ask Questions, Use Story Structure, Summarize	Preview, Ask Questions, Use Story Structure, Summarize	Preview, Ask Questions, Use Story Structure, Summarize
Response to Literature	Response to Literature	Response to Literature
Reread for Fluency Practice	Reread for Fluency Practice	Reread for Fluency Practice

Unit 5
Skills Overview

Why These Skills? *My Sidewalks* focuses on the priority skills children need in order to succeed at learning to read. **Priority skills** are the critical elements of early reading—phonemic awareness, phonics, fluency, vocabulary, and text comprehension. Scientifically based research has shown that these skills are the foundations of early reading and must be taught in a systematic sequence.

	WEEK 1 4–33 **Good Job!**	**WEEK 2** 34–67 **Taking Care of Animals**	
Phonemic Awareness	Segment Compounds into Words, Words into Sounds	Segment Words into Syllables, Syllables into Sounds	
Phonics Blending Strategy	Compound Words **REVIEW** Contractions	Syllables: Consonant + *le* **REVIEW** Reading Longer Words	
Spelling	Compound Words	Syllables with Consonant + *le*	
High-Frequency Words	*book, heard, hold, listen, piece*	*boy, either, hundred, several, you're*	
Vocabulary Concept	Why is it important to do a good job?	Why should we take care of animals?	
Oral Vocabulary	*career, community, employee, responsible, teamwork*	*concern, growth, litter, protection, veterinarian*	
Comprehension Skill	Main Idea	Sequence	
Strategies	Preview, Ask Questions, Use Story Structure, Summarize	Preview, Ask Questions, Use Story Structure, Summarize	
Writing	Response to Literature	Response to Literature	
Fluency	Reread for Fluency Practice	Reread for Fluency Practice	

WEEK 3	WEEK 4	WEEK 5
68–103 **Family Jobs**	104–127 **My Neighbors, My Friends**	128–159 **Doing the Right Thing**
Segment and Blend Sounds Add Phonemes	Segment and Blend Sounds Add Phonemes	Segment and Blend Sounds Segment and Count Sounds
Diphthongs *ou, ow*/ou/; Suffixes *-ly, -ful* **REVIEW** Endings and Suffixes	Sound of *oo* in *moon*; Prefixes *un-, re-* **REVIEW** Reading Longer Words	Diphthongs *oi, oy*; Silent Consonants *kn*/n/, *wr*/r/, *mb*/m/ **REVIEW** Diphthongs *ou, ow*; *oi, oy*
Words with Diphthongs *ou, ow*/ou/	Words with Sound of *oo* in *moon*	Words with Diphthongs *oi, oy*
ago, break, certain, probably, since	*been, brother, course, special, whole*	*hour, leave, minute, sorry, watch*
How can we be responsible family members?	What do good friends and neighbors do?	What happens when we do the wrong thing?
assign, behavior, cooperate, obedient, properly	*acquaintance, appreciate, communicate, local, respect*	*apologize, citizen, judgment, law, scold*
Draw Conclusions	Draw Conclusions	Compare/Contrast
Preview, Ask Questions, Use Story Structure, Summarize	Preview, Ask Questions, Use Story Structure, Summarize	Preview, Ask Questions, Use Story Structure, Summarize
Response to Literature	Response to Literature	Response to Literature
Reread for Fluency Practice	Reread for Fluency Practice	Reread for Fluency Practice

Unit 6
Skills Overview

Why These Skills? *My Sidewalks* focuses on the priority skills children need in order to succeed at learning to read. **Priority skills** are the critical elements of early reading—phonemic awareness, phonics, fluency, vocabulary, and text comprehension. Scientifically based research has shown that these skills are the foundations of early reading and must be taught in a systematic sequence.

		WEEK 1 4–35 **Sports**	**WEEK 2** 36–65 **The American Flag**
Phonemic Awareness		Segment and Blend Sounds Add Phonemes	Segment and Blend Sounds Add Phonemes
Phonics	**Blending Strategy**	Sound of *oo* in *book*; Suffixes *-er, -or* REVIEW Compound Words	Vowel Patterns *ew, ue*; Prefixes *pre-, dis-* REVIEW Vowel Patterns *ew, ue, oo*
	Spelling	Words with Sound of *oo* in *book*	Words with Vowel Patterns *ew, ue*
	High-Frequency Words	*bought, buy, clothes, won, worst*	*air, America, beautiful, Earth, world*
Vocabulary	**Concept**	Why are sports important in our country?	What does our flag mean?
	Oral Vocabulary	*athlete, challenge, champion, effort, rival*	*anthem, history, independence, patriotic, symbol*
Comprehension	**Skill**	Compare/Contrast	Sequence
	Strategies	Preview, Ask Questions, Use Story Structure, Summarize	Preview, Ask Questions, Use Story Structure, Summarize
	Writing	Response to Literature	Response to Literature
Fluency		Reread for Fluency Practice	Reread for Fluency Practice

WEEK 3	WEEK 4	WEEK 5
66–97	98–127	128–159
Family Celebrations	**A Cowboy's Life**	**Celebrations for Everyone**
Delete Phonemes Segment and Count Sounds	Segment and Blend Sounds Add Phonemes	Segment and Blend Sounds Add Phonemes
Contractions 're, 've, 'd; ph/f/, dge/j/ REVIEW Silent Consonants; ph/f/, dge/j/	Short e: ea; Base Words and Affixes REVIEW Read Longer Words	Vowel Patterns aw, au, au(gh); Base Words and Affixes REVIEW Read Longer Words
Contractions 're, 've, 'd	Words with Short e: ea	Words with Vowel Patterns aw, au, au(gh)
believe, company, everybody, money, young	alone, between, notice, question, woman	cold, finally, half, tomorrow, word
Why are family celebrations special?	Why should we learn about cowboys?	How do different people celebrate?
celebration, custom, occasion, sibling, tradition	climate, herd, livestock, occupation, rodeo	ceremony, culture, festival, international, regional
Draw Conclusions	Compare/Contrast	Main Idea
Preview, Ask Questions, Use Story Structure, Summarize	Preview, Ask Questions, Use Story Structure, Summarize	Preview, Ask Questions, Use Story Structure, Summarize
Response to Literature	Response to Literature	Response to Literature
Reread for Fluency Practice	Reread for Fluency Practice	Reread for Fluency Practice

Unit 4

Concept Development
to Foster Reading Comprehension

Theme Question: How do things change? How do they stay the same?

Concept: Our Changing World

EXPAND THE CONCEPT

Week 1	Week 2	Week 3	Week 4	Week 5
Lesson Focus How can familiar things help us with changes?	**Lesson Focus** How do plants change as they grow?	**Lesson Focus** How do animals change as they grow?	**Lesson Focus** Why are some changes difficult?	**Lesson Focus** How do changes in the weather affect us?

DEVELOP LANGUAGE

Oral Vocabulary familiar keepsake preserve represent valuable	**Oral Vocabulary** adapt annual nutrients soil sprout	**Oral Vocabulary** appearance nursery stage tend transform	**Oral Vocabulary** adjust ancestor courage landmark unexpected	**Oral Vocabulary** blizzard condition forecast predict terrifying
Background Reading "Let's Find Out: When Things Change"	**Background Reading** "Let's Find Out: From Seed to Plant"	**Background Reading** "Let's Find Out: Animals"	**Background Reading** "Let's Find Out: What Changes Are Hard?"	**Background Reading** "Let's Find Out: Weather Changes"

READ THE LITERATURE

Expository Nonfiction "Taking Pictures" **Realistic Fiction** "A New Tune for Tim" **Song** "My Favorite Things"	**Expository Nonfiction** "What Plant Will This Be?" **Realistic Fiction** "Garden Art" **Jokes** "Riddle Time"	**Expository Nonfiction** "A Safe Place for Animals" **Animal Fantasy** "A Tadpole's Tale" **Reference Sources** "Animal Family Names"	**Expository Nonfiction** "The Great Chicago Fire!" **Animal Fantasy** "Coal's New Home" **Cartoon** "I Miss My Old Friends"	**Narrative Nonfiction** "What Will You Need?" **Fable** "North Wind and Sun" **Poem** "The Telephone Call"

TEACH CONTENT

Time for SOCIAL STUDIES	TIME FOR Science	TIME FOR Science	Time for SOCIAL STUDIES	TIME FOR Science
• Family • Changes: Moving • Technology	• Plants • Farming • Growth and Change	• Life Cycle • Amphibians • Environment	• Home: Shelter • Urban, Suburban, Rural • History: Rebuilding	• Wind/Air • Weather • Clothing

Unit 4 develops the same concepts, vocabulary, and content-area knowledge as in Scott Foresman's *Reading Street*, Grade 2, Unit 4.

Unit 5

Concept Development

to Foster Reading Comprehension

Theme Question: What does it mean to be responsible?

Concept: Responsibility

EXPAND THE CONCEPT

Week 1
Lesson Focus
Why is it important to do a good job?

Week 2
Lesson Focus
Why should we take care of animals?

Week 3
Lesson Focus
How can we be responsible family members?

Week 4
Lesson Focus
What do good friends and neighbors do?

Week 5
Lesson Focus
What happens when we do the wrong thing?

DEVELOP LANGUAGE

Oral Vocabulary
career
community
employee
responsible
teamwork

Background Reading
"Let's Find Out: Good Job!"

Oral Vocabulary
concern
growth
litter
protection
veterinarian

Background Reading
"Let's Find Out: Taking Care of Animals"

Oral Vocabulary
assign
behavior
cooperate
obedient
properly

Background Reading
"Let's Find Out: Family Jobs"

Oral Vocabulary
acquaintance
appreciate
communicate
local
respect

Background Reading
"Let's Find Out: My Neighbors, My Friends"

Oral Vocabulary
apologize
citizen
judgment
law
scold

Background Reading
"Let's Find Out: Doing the Right Thing"

READ THE LITERATURE

Expository Nonfiction
"Soaring Skyscrapers"

Animal Fantasy
"Three Small Frogs"

Riddles
"Rhyme and Riddle"

Expository Nonfiction
"Safe Places for Strays"

Realistic Fiction
"Snuggles and Cuddles"

Poem
"The Monster's Pet"

Expository Nonfiction
"Tools for You and Me"

Realistic Fiction
"Counting on Tess"

Instructions
"Make a Chores Calendar"

Narrative Nonfiction
"What Makes a Nice Neighbor?"

Realistic Fiction
"The Twins Next Door"

Map
"How Does Jack Get to School?"

Expository Nonfiction
"Who Teaches Us Rules?"

Fantasy
"No Rules Day"

Article
"Funny Laws"

TEACH CONTENT

Time for **SOCIAL STUDIES**
- Job Responsibility
- Service
- Teamwork

TIME FOR **Science**
- Animals
- Shelter/Survival
- Pet Care

Time for **SOCIAL STUDIES**
- Cooperation
- Family Responsibility
- Tools/Equipment

Time for **SOCIAL STUDIES**
- Friendship
- Groups
- Communities

Time for **SOCIAL STUDIES**
- Rights and Responsibilities
- Laws
- Rules

Unit 5 develops the same concepts, vocabulary, and content-area knowledge as in Scott Foresman's *Reading Street*, Grade 2, Unit 5.

Concept Development
to Foster Reading Comprehension

Theme Question: How are traditions and celebrations important to our lives?

Concept: Traditions

EXPAND THE CONCEPT

Week 1	Week 2	Week 3	Week 4	Week 5
Lesson Focus Why are sports important in our country?	**Lesson Focus** What does our flag mean?	**Lesson Focus** Why are family celebrations special?	**Lesson Focus** Why should we learn about cowboys?	**Lesson Focus** How do different people celebrate?

DEVELOP LANGUAGE

Oral Vocabulary athlete challenge champion effort rival	**Oral Vocabulary** anthem history independence patriotic symbol	**Oral Vocabulary** celebration custom occasion sibling tradition	**Oral Vocabulary** climate herd livestock occupation rodeo	**Oral Vocabulary** ceremony culture festival international regional
Background Reading "Let's Find Out: Sports"	**Background Reading** "Let's Find Out: The American Flag"	**Background Reading** "Let's Find Out: Family Celebrations"	**Background Reading** "Let's Find Out: A Cowboy's Life"	**Background Reading** "Let's Find Out: Celebrations for Everyone"

READ THE LITERATURE

Expository Nonfiction "Play Ball!"	**Expository Nonfiction** "Taking Care of Our Flag"	**Narrative Nonfiction** "Angel Food Bakery"	**Biography** "Nat Love: A Great Cowboy"	**Narrative Nonfiction** "The Sweet Stink of Success"
Realistic Fiction "THAT'S a Football?"	**Realistic Fiction** "Broad Stripes and Bright Stars"	**Realistic Fiction** "Twice as Nice"	**Realistic Fiction** "Heather at the Rodeo"	**Fantasy** "Austin P. Crawler's Naughty Pig"
Diagram "Get Ready to Play Ice Hockey!"	**Song** "Old Glory"	**Cartoon** "Watch Where You Sit!"	**Expository Article** "Did You Know?"	**Instructions** "Piñata Game"

TEACH CONTENT

Time for **SOCIAL STUDIES**	Time for **SOCIAL STUDIES**	Time for **SOCIAL STUDIES**	Time for **SOCIAL STUDIES**	Time for **SOCIAL STUDIES**
• Cultural Traditions • Sports • Teamwork	• U.S. History: 13 Colonies • U.S. Symbols • U.S. Holidays	• Family • Celebrations • Goods and Services	• American West • Geography • Cowboys	• National Celebrations • International Celebrations • Geography

Unit 6 develops the same concepts, vocabulary, and content-area knowledge as in Scott Foresman's *Reading Street*, Grade 2, Unit 6.

Unit 4 Week 1 *When Things Change*

How can familiar things help us with changes?

Objectives *This week students will . . .*

Phonemic Awareness
- segment and count sounds in words
- segment compound words

Phonics
- blend and read words with the sound of *a* in *ball* and *walk*; compound words
- apply knowledge of letter-sounds to decode unknown words when reading
- recognize high-frequency words *gone, group, move, neighbor, promise*

Fluency
- practice fluency with oral rereading

Vocabulary
- build concepts and oral vocabulary: *familiar, keepsake, preserve, represent, valuable*

Text Comprehension
- read connected text
- compare and contrast to improve comprehension
- write in response to literature

Word Work *This week's phonics focus is . . .*

Sound of *a* in *ball*   Compound Words

High-Frequency Words *Tested Vocabulary*

The first appearance of each word in the Student Reader is noted below.

gone	He has **gone** to a movie. (p. 11)
group	A **group** is a number of people or things together. (p. 12)
move	When you **move,** you go from one place to another. (p. 6)
neighbor	A **neighbor** is someone who lives near you. (p. 6)
promise	To **promise** is to say that you will or will not do something. (p. 13)

Amazing Words *Oral Vocabulary*

The week's vocabulary is related to the concept of how familiar things help us cope with change.

familiar	well-known or common
keepsake	something kept to remind you of someone or something
preserve	to protect something or keep it safe from harm or change
represent	to stand for something
valuable	worth a lot of money or very important in some other way

Student Reader Unit 4 *This week students will read the following selections.*

Daily Lesson Plan

	ACTIVITIES	MATERIALS
Day 1	**Word Work** Phonemic Awareness: Segment and Count Sounds Phonics: Blend Words with the Sound of *a* in *ball*, *walk* High-Frequency Words *gone, group, move, neighbor, promise* **Build Concepts** *preserve, represent, valuable* **Read a Passage** "When Things Change," pp. 6–13 Comprehension: Use Strategies Reread for Fluency	Student White Boards Sound-Spelling Card 4 Tested Vocabulary Cards *Sing with Me Big Book* and Audio CD Student Reader: Unit 4 Routine Cards 1, 2, 3, 4, 6, 7 AudioText Practice Book, p. 75, Sound of *a* in *ball, walk*
Day 2	**Reread for Fluency** **Word Work** Phonemic Awareness: Segment Compound Words Phonics: Blend Compound Words High-Frequency Words *gone, group, move, neighbor, promise* **Read a Passage** "Taking Pictures," pp. 14–21 Comprehension: Use Strategies **Write** Response to Literature: Shared Writing	Student Reader: Unit 4 Student White Boards Tested Vocabulary Cards Routine Cards 1, 2, 3, 4, 6, 7 AudioText Word Cards Practice Book, p. 76, Compound Words
Day 3	**Reread for Fluency** **Word Work** Phonemic Awareness: Segment and Count Sounds Phonics: Fluent Word Reading High-Frequency Words *gone, group, move, neighbor, promise* **Build Concepts** *familiar, keepsake* **Read a Passage** "A New Tune for Tim," pp. 22–33 Comprehension: Compare/Contrast	Student Reader: Unit 4 Student White Boards Tested Vocabulary Cards Routine Cards 1, 2, 3, 4, 6 AudioText Practice Book, p. 77, Compare and Contrast
Day 4	**Reread for Fluency** **Word Work** Phonics: Spiral Review Phonological and Phonemic Awareness Activities, pp. 280–283 **Read Together** "My Favorite Things," p. 34 Comprehension: Listening **Build Concepts** *familiar, keepsake, preserve, represent, valuable* **Write** Response to Literature: Interactive Writing	Student Reader: Unit 4 Routine Cards 1, 4 AudioText Student White Boards Practice Book, p. 78, High-Frequency Words
Day 5	**Assessment Options** Fluency, Comprehension Sentence Reading; Passage Reading Phonological and Phonemic Awareness Activities, pp. 280–283 **Use Concepts** *familiar, keepsake, preserve, represent, valuable* **Read to Connect** "When Things Change," pp. 6–13 Comprehension: Compare/Contrast **Write** Response to Literature: Independent Writing	Reproducible p. 247 Sentence Reading Chart, p. 252 Student White Boards Fluency Progress Chart, p. 245 Student Reader: Unit 4 Routine Card 5 Practice Book, p. 79, Writing

See pp. xvi–xvii for how *My Sidewalks* integrates instructional practices for ELL.

Phonemic Awareness Segment and Count Sounds

To Do	To Say	2 minutes

Scaffold instruction.

Distribute white boards.
Write *wall*.

Model Listen to the sounds in *wall*. Stretch the sounds /www/ /òòò/ /lll/ as you write *w, a, ll*. Repeat. This time have children write the letters as you write. Now let's count the sounds in *wall*. I will say the word slowly and hold up a finger for each sound: /w/ /ò/ /l/. There are three sounds in *wall*.

Lead children in counting sounds as they write.

Teach and Practice Have children say the sounds with you as you point to the letters. (/w/ /ò/ /l/) Hold up a finger for each sound. How many sounds in *wall*? (3) How many letters in *wall*? (4) Continue counting sounds with these words:

all (2)   walk (3)   salt (4)   small (4)   chalk (3)   called (4)

Blending Strategy Sound of *a* in *ball, walk*

To Do	To Say	5–10 minutes

Use the blending routine.

Write *bat* and *wag*.

1 Connect You already can read words like these. What are the words? What is the middle sound in *bat* and *wag*? (/a/) Today we'll learn another sound the letter *a* has when *l* comes after it.

Display Sound-Spelling Card 4.

2 Use Sound-Spelling Card This is an audience. What sound do you hear at the beginning of *audience*? (/ò/) Say it with me: /ò/. When *a* is followed by *l* or *ll*, the *a* usually stands for the sound /ò/.

Scaffold instruction.

3 Listen and Write Write the letter *a* for /ò/. As you write, say the sound to yourself: /ò/. Now say the sound aloud.

Write *ball*.

4 Model When *a* is followed by *l* or *ll*, the *a* often stands for /ò/. This is how I blend this word: /b/ /ò/ /l/, *ball*.

Write *walk*.

Repeat with *walk*. Point out that you don't hear the sound /l/ in *walk*. In some words, the two letters *al* stand for the sound /ò/.

$$b \underset{\rightarrow}{a} \underset{\rightarrow}{l} \underset{\rightarrow}{l} \qquad w \underset{\rightarrow}{a} \underset{\rightarrow}{l} \underset{\rightarrow}{k}$$

CORRECTIVE FEEDBACK

Write each practice word. Monitor student practice.

5 Group Practice Let's try the same thing with these words. Give feedback, using the *if . . . then* statements on Routine Card 1.

fall   talk   halt*   call   scald*   stalk*

6 Individual Practice Write the words; have each child blend two of them.

bald   tall   halls   stall*   small   chalk

Check understanding of practice words.

*Children need to make sense of words that they segment and blend. If needed, help children with meanings. *Halt* means to stop. (Hold up your hand.) When you *scald* something, you burn it with liquid or steam. Hot cocoa might *scald* your mouth. A *stalk* is the tall stem of some plants. (Draw a cornstalk.) A *stall* is a place for an animal in a barn.

MORE PRACTICE

Build words with *all* and *alk*.

Build Words Have children write *all* and *alk* at the tops of their boards. Have them build new words by adding the letters *m, c, t, h,* and *sm* to the front of *all* and *t, w, ch,* and *st* to the front of *alk*. Model by adding *m* to *all* to form *mall*. Call on children to read each word and use it in a sentence or tell its meaning.

High-Frequency Words *gone, group, move, neighbor, promise*

	To Do	To Say
Teach high-frequency words.	Display *gone*.	**1 Say, Spell, Write** Use the Tested Vocabulary Cards. Display *gone*. Here are some words that we won't sound out. We'll spell them. This word is *gone*: *g, o, n, e* (point to each letter), *gone*. What is this word? What are the letters in the word? Now you write *gone*.
	Point to the *g* and *n* in *gone*.	**2 Identify Letter-Sounds** Let's look at the sounds in *gone* that you do know. What is this letter? *(g)* What is the sound for this letter? *(/g/)* Continue with *n*/n/.
		3 Demonstrate Meaning Tell me a sentence using *gone*. Model a sentence if children need help.
	Display *group, move, neighbor,* and *promise*.	Repeat the Routine with *group, move, neighbor,* and *promise*. Children can identify these letter-sounds and word parts: *group* (*gr*/gr/, *p*/p/), *move* (*m*/m/, *v*/v/), *neighbor* (*n*/n/, *b*/b/), and *promise* (*prom, s*/s/). Have children write the words in their word banks. Add the words to the Word Wall. Point out that the words they are learning are on p. 35.

ACTIVITY 2 Build Concepts

Oral Vocabulary *preserve, valuable, represent*

	To Do	To Say
Introduce oral vocabulary.	Display p. 16 of *Sing with Me Big Book*. Play audio CD.	This week you will learn about how familiar things help us when things change. Listen for the Amazing Words *preserve, valuable,* and *represent* as I sing this song. Play or sing the song. Then have children sing it with you.

1 Introduce, Demonstrate, and Apply |
| **Scaffold instruction.** | Follow the Routine to teach *preserve, valuable,* and *represent*. | ***preserve*** The song mentions *preserving* old things that belong to family members. When you *preserve* something, you protect it or keep it safe from harm or change. Have children say the word. You could *preserve* a photo by putting it in a frame. How do you *preserve* favorite drawings?

valuable The song suggests that old objects are more *valuable* than gold. Something *valuable* is worth a lot of money or is very important in some other way. Have children say the word. A string bracelet is *valuable* when a friend makes it for you. Name some things that are *valuable* to you. Tell why they are *valuable*.

represent All the treasures in the song *represent* a memory. *Represent* means to stand for something. Have children say the word. A seashell can *represent* a beach vacation. A stone can *represent* someone's longest hike. Name some things that *represent* special times for you. |
	Display the words on the Amazing Words board.	**2 Display the Words** Have children say each word as they look at it. You can find sounds and word parts you know in big words. Read *pre/serve* as you run your hand under the syllables. Children can identify *pr*/pr/ and *serve*. For *valuable* and *represent*, children can identify these letter-sounds and word parts: *valuable* (*val, b*/b/), *represent* (*rep, sent*/zent/).
	Monitor understanding.	**3 Use the Words** Ask children to use each word in a sentence. Model a sentence if children need help.
MORE PRACTICE		Use oral vocabulary to discuss the song. Where is a good place to *preserve* old things? What might Mommy's sled *represent*? Why does the speaker think these old things are *valuable*? Do you think they are *valuable*?

ACTIVITY **3** Read a Passage

Build Background "When Things Change," pp. 6–13

	To Do	**To Say**	
			10 minutes

Develop language and concepts.

See Routine Card 7.* Read aloud pp. 1–5 of the student book.

Preview the Book Read aloud the title on p. 1. The selections in this book are about things changing. Use pp. 2–3 to preview the weeks in this unit and p. 5 to preview the selections in this week. Ask children what they think each selection will be about.

Scaffold instruction.

See Routine Card 6. Display pp. 6–13.

Ask questions and elaborate on answers to develop language.

Key concepts: *valuable, familiar, patches, quilt, locket, photo, camera, preserve, album, snap*

Before Reading Read the title aloud. Do a structured picture walk with children.

pp. 6–7 This family is moving to a new place. What is the boy taking? (a dog) What is the girl taking? (a ball and bat) These things are valuable because they are familiar, or well-known, to the children.

pp. 8–9 This family is using patches, or pieces of cloth, to make a quilt. The patches are made of old, familiar clothing. How could the quilt help this family feel better about moving to a new place?

pp. 10–11 What is this? (a necklace) Yes, this necklace has a case called a locket on it. Point to the locket. What does the locket hold? (a photo) The locket holds a photo, or picture, that was taken with a camera. How does the locket preserve the photo?

pp. 12–13 Where are the photos? (in an album) Yes, the photo album has lots of photos. Why might kids snap and save photos like these?

Teach story words.

Write *photo.*

You will read this word in the story. It is *photo.* Have children say the word and spell it. Review its meaning. Let's read to find out how photos and other familiar things can help make changes easier.

Guide comprehension.

Monitor independent reading.

Model strategic reading. Use Routine Cards 2 and 3.

During Reading Read the page in a whisper. Raise your hand if you need help with a word. Stop at the end of each page to model asking questions. For example, for p. 7: After I read, I ask myself: What is this mainly about? The author tells that the kids are moving to a new home. The boy's dog makes him smile. I read that the girl plans to use her ball and bat to play games with new friends she will meet. I think this page is mainly about how familiar things can make a move easier.

Summarize.

Use oral vocabulary to develop the concept.

After Reading Do you think the boy's dog and the girl's bat and ball are *valuable?* Why or why not? What does the quilt *represent* to the family? Why are lockets *valuable?* What can a locket with a pal's photo *represent?* How can you *preserve* lots of photos?

Reread for Fluency "When Things Change," pp. 6–9

	To Do	**To Say**	
			5–10 minutes

CORRECTIVE FEEDBACK

Monitor oral reading.

Read pp. 6–9 aloud. Read them three or four times so your reading gets better each time. Give feedback on children's oral reading and use of the blending strategy. Use Routine Cards 1 and 4.

MORE PRACTICE

Instead of rereading just pp. 6–9, have children reread the entire selection three or four times. You may want to have children read along with the AudioText.

Homework

Practice Book, p. 75, Sound of *a* in *ball, walk*

*Routine Cards can be found at the back of this Teacher's Guide.

ACTIVITY 1 Reread for Fluency

Paired Reading "When Things Change," pp. 10–13

5–10 minutes

	To Do	**To Say**
CORRECTIVE FEEDBACK	Pair children. Monitor paired reading.	Children read pp. 10–13 orally, switching readers at the end of the first page. Have partners reread; now the other partner begins. For optimal fluency, children should reread three or four times. Give feedback on children's oral reading and use of the blending strategy. See Routine Cards 1 and 4.
MORE PRACTICE		Instead of rereading just pp. 10–13, have children reread the entire selection three or four times. You may want to have children read along with the AudioText.

ACTIVITY 2 Word Work

Phonemic Awareness Segment Compound Words

2 minutes

	To Do	**To Say**
Scaffold instruction.	Distribute white boards. Write *sunshine*.	**Model** Listen to the syllables in *sunshine*. Stretch the sounds in each syllable as you write the word part that goes with it: /sss/ /uuu/ /nnn/ as you write *sun* and /shshsh/ /ī ī ī/ /nnn/ as you write *sh, i, n, e*. Repeat. This time have children write the letters as you write.
	Lead children in blending sounds as they write.	**Teach and Practice** Have children say each word part as you point to the syllables *(sun, shine)* and then blend the syllables together to say the word. *(sunshine)* Continue with these words.
		sunset lunchbox granddad classmate homework sidewalk

Blending Strategy Compound Words

5–10 minutes

	To Do	To Say

Use the blending routine.

Write *sun* and *set*.

1 Connect You already can read words like these. What are the words? Today we'll learn about combining two words, such as *sun* and *set*, to make a compound word.

Scaffold instruction.

Write *sunset*.

2 Model A compound word is made up of two shorter words. The meaning of the compound word is often made up of the meanings of the two shorter words. What two words do you hear in *sunset?* (*sun* and *set*) What does *sunset* mean? (the time when the sun sets)

To read compound words, first I read the two words and then blend them into one word: /sun/ /set/, *sunset*.

s u n s e t

3 Listen and Write Write the word *sun*. Write the word *set* after it. As you write, say each small word to yourself: *sun, set.* Now say the compound word aloud. (*sunset*)

CORRECTIVE FEEDBACK

Write each practice word. Monitor student practice.

4 Group Practice Let's try the same thing with these words. Discuss word meanings and point out that compound words, such as *something* and *eyeball*, can also be made with words from the Word Wall. Give feedback, using the *if . . . then* statements on Routine Card 1.

campfire   baseball   inside   pigpen   backpack   something

5 Individual Practice Write the words; have each child blend two of them.

sandbox   bathtub   popcorn   eyeball   pancake   anthill   nickname

MORE PRACTICE

Model sorting compound words.

Sort Words Write *Compound Word, First Word,* and *Second Word* as headings. List compound words under the first heading. Discuss the meaning of each compound. The first time, model writing the two words that form the compound. Have children continue the activity, copying the compound words on their white boards and writing two words for each compound. Then call on children to read the compound words and use them in sentences.

Compound Word	First Word	Second Word
cupcake	cup	cake
himself	him	self
sunrise	sun	rise
laptop	lap	top

High-Frequency Words *gone, group, move, neighbor, promise*

3 minutes

	To Do	To Say

Teach high-frequency words.

Display *gone, group, move, neighbor,* and *promise.*

Use the Tested Vocabulary Cards. Point to a word. Say and spell it. Have children say and spell the word. Ask children to identify familiar letter-sounds and word parts. Have them take turns reading the words.

Lead cumulative review.

Use the Tested Vocabulary Cards to review high-frequency words from previous weeks.

ACTIVITY **3** Read a Passage

Reading "Taking Pictures," pp. 14–21

	To Do	To Say	*5–10 minutes*
Develop language and concepts.	See Routine Cards 6 and 7. Display pp. 14–21.	**Before Reading** Have children recall what they learned about snapping and saving photos. Read the title. Do a structured picture walk.	
Scaffold instruction.	Ask questions and elaborate on answers to develop language.	**pp. 14–15** What is the man doing? (taking a photo) Today it is easy to take a photo with a camera. Before cameras were invented, artists painted pictures.	
	Key concepts: *photo, camera, past, invented, artists, painted, copper plates*	**pp. 16–17** In the past, people used sunshine to help make a picture. What do you think happened to this picture when the sun set?	
		pp. 18-19 Point to the photos. The first photos were made on thin copper plates, or sheets of metal. Point to the camera on p. 19.	
		pp. 20–21 Today people can take photos with different kinds of cameras. Read the labels. Why do you think kids took these photos?	
Teach story words.	Write *camera* and *photo*.	You will read these words in the story: *camera* and *photo*. Point to each word. Have children say and spell each word. Review meanings. Now let's read to learn more about cameras of long ago and today.	
Guide comprehension.	Monitor independent reading.	**During Reading** Read the pages in a whisper. Raise your hand if you need help with a word. As you read, ask yourself: What am I learning about taking pictures? What is this mainly about?	
	Use Routine Cards 2 and 3.	**pp. 14–19** What did you learn about taking pictures in the past? (At first, people couldn't take photos. Then pictures wouldn't last long. The first photos were made on thin copper plates.)	
		pp. 20–21 What did you learn about photo-taking today? (Today you can take photos with different kinds of cameras to remember fun times.)	
Model summarizing.	Think aloud.	**After Reading** What did you learn about taking pictures? What was the selection mainly about? Model how to summarize. I read how artists painted pictures before cameras where invented. Then I read how cameras needed sunshine. First photos were made on copper plates. Today people use different kinds of cameras. I pick the most important ideas. The selection is mainly about how taking pictures has changed over time.	
MORE PRACTICE	Develop oral vocabulary.	Sunshine could help make pictures, but these pictures could not be *preserved.* Why? Why are photos *valuable?* What do they *represent?*	

ACTIVITY **4** Write

Response to Literature Shared Writing

	To Do	To Say	*5 minutes*
Guide shared writing.	Write sentence frames. Read the questions.	How did people take photos in the past? In the past, people _____. How do people take photos today? Today people _____.	
		Invite children to suggest answers. Discuss and record answers to complete the sentence frames. While writing, model connecting sounds to letters and forming letters (see pp. 257–259). Have children read answers aloud as you track print.	
Homework		Practice Book, p. 76, Compound Words	

ACTIVITY 1 Reread for Fluency

Oral Reading "Taking Pictures," pp. 14–17

5–10 minutes

	To Do	To Say
CORRECTIVE FEEDBACK	Monitor oral reading.	Read pp. 14–17 aloud. Read them three or four times so your reading gets better each time. Give feedback on children's oral reading and use of the blending strategy. See Routine Cards 1 and 4.
MORE PRACTICE		Instead of rereading just pp. 14–17, have children reread the entire selection three or four times. You may want to have children read along with the AudioText.

ACTIVITY 2 Word Work

Phonemic Awareness Segment and Count Sounds

2 minutes

	To Do	To Say
Scaffold instruction.	Distribute white boards. Write *sidewalk*.	**Model** There are two smaller words in *sidewalk, side* and *walk.* Stretch the sounds /sss/ /ī ī ī/ /d/ as you write *s, i, d, e.* Repeat. Have children write the letters as you write. Now let's count the sounds in *side.* I will say the word slowly and hold up a finger for each sound: /s/ /ī/ /d/.
	Lead children in segmenting and counting sounds as they write.	**Teach and Practice** Have children say the sounds as you point to the letters. (/s/ /ī/ /d/) Hold up a finger for each sound. How many sounds in *side?* (3) How many letters? (4) Repeat for *walk.* (3 sounds; 4 letters) Continue with these words: kickball baseball crosswalk fireplace pothole

Fluent Word Reading Sound of *a* in *ball, walk;* Compound Words

5–10 minutes

	To Do	To Say
Use the word-reading routine.	Write *kickball.*	**1 Connect** You can read this word because you know how to read compound words and words with the vowel sound /o̊/. What two smaller words are in this word? *(kick, ball)* What sound does *a* make in this word? (/o̊/) Remember, when you see *a* followed by *l* or *ll*, you know *a* usually stands for /o̊/. Now blend the two smaller words together. What is the compound word? *(kickball)*
Scaffold instruction.	Write *salt, chalk,* and *inside.*	**2 Model** When you come to a new word, look at all the letters in the word and think about its vowel sound or sounds and its parts. Say the sounds and word parts to yourself and then read the word. Model reading *salt, chalk,* and *inside.* When you come to a new word, what will you do?
	Write each practice word.	**3 Group Practice** Let's read these words. Look at all the letters, think about the vowel sounds and word parts, and say the sounds to yourself. We will read words with the vowel sound /o̊/ and compound words. When I point to the word, let's read it together. Allow 2–3 seconds previewing time for each word. barnyard small dishpan halt falls landform talked bald fishpond
CORRECTIVE FEEDBACK	**MONITOR PROGRESS**	*If . . .* children have difficulty previewing and reading whole words, *then . . .* have them use sound-by-sound blending. *If . . .* children can't read the words fluently at a rate of 1–2 seconds per word, *then . . .* continue practicing the list.

| MORE PRACTICE | Model reading words in sentences. | When I read a sentence, I read each word without stopping between the words. If I come to a word I don't know, I blend it. Then I read the sentence again. Model reading this sentence, stopping to blend *halt: The tall man at the crosswalk called out, "Halt!"* |
| | Write practice sentences. | Have each child read a sentence. **Use salt on popcorn but not on pancakes.** **Miss Hall spotted a small blackbird in her backyard.** **His granddad talked about baseball from sunrise to sunset.** |

High-Frequency Words *gone, group, move, neighbor, promise*

	To Do	To Say	3 minutes
Teach high-frequency words.	Display *gone, group, move, neighbor*, and *promise*.	Use the Tested Vocabulary Cards. Point to a word. Say and spell it. Have children say and spell the word. Ask children to identify familiar letter-sounds and word parts. Have them take turns reading the words.	

ACTIVITY **3** ## Build Concepts

Oral Vocabulary *familiar, keepsake*

	To Do	To Say	5–10 minutes
Teach oral vocabulary.	Display pp. 22–23 of the student book.	Today you will read a story about how a boy's *familiar* classmates give him an unusual *keepsake*. **1 Introduce, Demonstrate, and Apply**	*Routine*
Scaffold instruction.	Follow the Routine to teach *familiar* and *keepsake*.	**familiar** This story is about a boy who is moving. The boy takes something *familiar* with him to his new home. If something is *familiar*, it is well-known or common. Have children say the word. It's always good to see a *familiar* face when you come home. If you moved to a different school, would anything be *familiar?* Explain.	
		keepsake Before the boy moves, his classmates want to give him a *keepsake.* A *keepsake* is something kept to remind you of someone or something. Have children say the word. I enjoyed the ballgame so much that I kept the ticket as a *keepsake.* Describe a time when you kept something as a *keepsake.* What did the *keepsake* remind you of?	
	Display the words on the Amazing Words board.	**2 Display the Words** Have children say each word as they look at it. You can find sounds and word parts you know in bigger words. Read *fa/mil/iar* as you run your hand under the syllables. What letter do you see at the beginning of *familiar?* (f) What sound does it make? (/f/) Point to the second syllable. How do you say this word part? (/mil/) Read *keep/sake.* Children can identify k/k/, p/p/, and *sake.*	
	Monitor understanding.	**3 Use the Words** Ask children to use each word in a sentence. Model a sentence if children need help.	
MORE PRACTICE		Use oral vocabulary to discuss changes. If a new friend asks you to play a *familiar* game, would you know the rules or have to read the rules? Why? Would a locket with a pal's picture in it be a good *keepsake* for someone going away to college?	

ACTIVITY **4** Read a Passage

Reading "A New Tune for Tim," pp. 22–33

| To Do | To Say | *10 minutes* |

Teach compare/ contrast.

Scaffold instruction.

Introduce the skill.

Model the skill. Display pp. 19–20.

Apply the skill.

Today you will compare and contrast. Remember, when you compare and contrast, you tell how two or more things are alike and how they are different. For example, I can compare cameras used long ago with cameras used today. One way cameras long ago and cameras today are alike is that both take photos. One way they are different is that cameras long ago were big, but cameras today can be small.

You can also compare characters. Ana's pal Trish moves away. Ana and Trish both feel sad. Then Ana looks at a photo and remembers fun times with Trish. Now Ana smiles. **How are Ana's and Trish's feelings alike?** (Both are sad.) **How are Ana's feelings different after she looks at the photo?** (Now Ana feels happier.)

Develop language and concepts.

See Routine Card 6. Display pp. 22–33.

Model using key words and concepts.

Key concepts: *familiar, band class, preserve, valuable, neighbors, jams*

Before Reading Read the title. Do a structured picture walk.

pp. 22–23 Tim is moving, so he wants to take something familiar to his new home. **What will Tim bring?** (a trumpet) He'll bring a trumpet.

pp. 24–25 This is Tim's band class.

pp. 26–27 The band class plays a tune, or song, for Tim. Look at Tim's face. **How do you think he feels when he hears the tune?** (very happy)

pp. 28–29 It's moving day. Boxes help preserve the things that are valuable to Tim's family. **What is valuable to Tim?** (his trumpet)

pp. 30–33 Tim looks sad. Then he hears his new neighbors making music. Now Tim jams, or makes tunes, with his new friends. Compare how Tim looks on p. 30 with how he looks on p. 33. **How does he feel at the end—the same or different?** (different; Now he's happy.)

Monitor children's use of vocabulary.

Now turn to your partner and talk about the pictures, using the same words I did.

Guide com- prehension.

Monitor independent reading.

Use Routine Cards 2 and 3.

During Reading Read the pages in a whisper. Raise your hand if you need help with a word. As you read, compare Tim's feelings at different parts of the story.

pp. 22–23 **How does Tim feel about moving? Why?** (sad; He'll miss playing songs with his pals.)

pp. 24–27 **What keepsake does the band class give to Tim?** (They give him a song that they made up just for Tim.) **What will the keepsake remind Tim of?** (his pals in band class)

pp. 28–29 **Why is Tim feeling less sad?** (He can hum his tune and think of his pals.)

pp. 30–33 Compare Tim's feelings at the beginning of the story with his feelings and the end. **How have Tim's feelings changed?** (Tim was sad, but now he is happy.) **Why?** (He uses his song to make new friends.)

Guide retelling.

Prompt children as they retell the story.

After Reading Have one child retell the story while the others assist. **Who is the main character? What happens in the beginning of the story? in the middle? at the end?** See Monitoring Retelling, p. 246.

Homework

Practice Book, p. 77, Compare and Contrast

ACTIVITY 1   Reread for Fluency

Paired Reading "A New Tune for Tim," pp. 22–26

To Do	To Say	
		5–10 minutes

CORRECTIVE FEEDBACK

Pair children. Monitor paired reading.

Children read pp. 22–26 orally, switching readers at the end of the first page. Have partners reread; now the other partner begins. For optimal fluency, children should reread three or four times. Give feedback on children's oral reading and use of the blending strategy. See Routine Cards 1 and 4.

MORE PRACTICE

Instead of rereading just pp. 22–26, have children reread the entire selection three or four times. You may want to have children read along with the AudioText.

ACTIVITY 2   Word Work

Spiral Review Contractions

To Do	To Say	
		5–10 minutes

Review contractions and compound words.

Scaffold instruction.

Write *it's*.

You can read this word because you know how to read contractions. Remember, a contraction is a short way of writing two words as one word. An apostrophe takes the place of letters that are left out. What two words make up this contraction? *(it is)* What is the contraction? *(it's)*

Write *inside*.

You can read this word because you know how to read compound words. Remember, a compound word shows two smaller words joined together. What are the two smaller words? *(in, side)* What is the compound word? *(inside)*

Have children make a comparison.

How are contractions and compound words alike? (Both contractions and compound words are two words joined together.) **How are they different?** (A contraction has an apostrophe that takes the place of letters that are left out. It makes the new word shorter. A compound word does not have an apostrophe. The new word is not shorter. It is two smaller words put together with no letters left out.)

Distribute white boards. Write *it's* and *inside* at the top of a T-chart.

Sort Words Point to and read *it's* and *inside.* Then display this list of words: *aren't, sandbox, you'll, flagpole, I'm, homemade, can't, lipstick.* Call on children to read each word and tell whether it is a contraction or a compound word and why. Write the word in an appropriate column in a class chart as children write on their boards.

it's	inside
aren't	sandbox
you'll	flagpole
I'm	homemade
can't	lipstick

CORRECTIVE FEEDBACK

MONITOR PROGRESS

If . . . children have difficulty reading the words,
then . . . have them use sound-by-sound blending.

For more practice, see next page

MORE PRACTICE	Model reading words in sentences.	When I read a sentence, I read each word without stopping between the words. If I come to a word I don't know, I blend it. Then I read the sentence again. Model reading this sentence, stopping to blend *didn't: The baseball didn't go over the tall wall.*
	Write practice sentences.	Have each child read a sentence.
		Granddad won't walk in the pigpen because he'll get dirty. We'll use chalk to make a hopscotch game on the sidewalk. I'm packing a small pen and my homework in my backpack.

Phonological and Phonemic Awareness	Optional practice activities, pp. 280–283

ACTIVITY 3 Read Together

Choral Reading "My Favorite Things," p. 34

To Do	**To Say**	*10 minutes*

Develop language and concepts.	Display p. 34.	**Before Reading** One at a time, point to and identify each item in the picture that the girl is thinking about. Why might someone like these things? Allow children to share their ideas.
Model fluent reading.		Read the title of the song. Ask children to predict what it is about. **Listen to my voice as I sing this song. When I come to the end of each line, I'll emphasize the last word—the words that rhyme. I'll try to keep a rhythm as I sing.** Sing or read the song with expression, keeping a steady rhythm. You may wish to tap the beat with your foot. Sing it a second time, having children point to each word.
	Build fluency through choral reading.	**Choral Reading Now sing the song aloud with me. Try to make your voice sound like mine as we sing.** Reread the song several times with children.
Develop concepts.	Monitor listening comprehension.	**After Reading** How would you feel "when the dog bites" or "when the bee stings"? If you are scared or sad, how can remembering favorite things change your feelings? What favorite things make you feel less bad?

ACTIVITY 4 Build Concepts

Oral Vocabulary *familiar, keepsake, preserve, represent, valuable*

To Do	**To Say**	*5–10 minutes*

Review oral vocabulary.	Read the words on the Amazing Words board.	**Focus on Letter-Sounds** Remember, you can find sounds you know in big words.
		• **What word has the word part *mil* in it?** *val? sake?*
		• **Which word ends with the sounds /nt/? What letters stand for /nt/?**
		• **In which words does the letter *s* have the sound /z/?**

To Do	To Say
Encourage discussion.	**Provide Multiple Contexts** Review the meanings of the words. Then ask questions to place the words in diverse contexts. • If you hike in a *familiar* park, do you need a trail map? Why or why not? • What kind of a *keepsake* would you give to a friend who is moving? • If you want to *preserve* peaches, do you freeze them or eat them? • In sign language, what can your hands *represent?* (letters and words) • Describe someone who is a *valuable* friend to you.

	To Do	To Say
MORE PRACTICE	Apply oral vocabulary to new situations.	• Is a *familiar* story one you know or one you've never heard? (know) • Is a *keepsake* something you throw away or save? (save) • When you *preserve* something, do you want it to stay the same or change? (stay the same) • Does the U.S. flag *represent* our school or our country? (country) • If something is *valuable,* is it important or not important? (important)

ACTIVITY 5 Write

Response to Literature Interactive Writing

5–10 minutes

	To Do	To Say
Generate ideas.	Review the story "A New Tune for Tim."	**Why do you think Tim wanted to bring his trumpet to his new home?** Discuss ways the trumpet might remind Tim of his old home.
Share the pen.	Have children participate in writing about things that remind them of home.	Write *When I think of home, I think of _____.* Have children read the words you wrote. Then have them supply endings for the sentence. Invite individuals to write familiar letter-sounds, word parts, and high-frequency words. Have them find the spelling of high-frequency words on the Word Wall. Ask questions such as: • What is the first sound in *wall?* (/w/) What is the letter for /w/? *(w)* • What is the vowel sound in *wall?* (/o̊/) How do you know? (The letter *a* is followed by the letters *ll*.) • What is the last sound in *wall?* (/l/) What are the letters for /l/? *(ll)*
	Writing elements: conventions	Frequently reread what has been written while tracking the print. Point out that each sentence starts with a capital letter and ends with a period. Point out the extra space between words. Read the completed sentences aloud, having children read with you. (For example, *When I think of home, I think of family pictures on the wall. When I think of home, I think of my granddad. When I think of home, I think of the backyard.*)
MORE PRACTICE	Prompt independent writing.	**Journal Writing** Tell about something you would take with you if you had to move.
	Homework	Practice Book, p. 78, High-Frequency Words

ACTIVITY 1 — Assessment Options

Sentence Reading

To Do	To Say
	5 minutes

Assess sentence reading.

Use reproducible p. 247.

Have each child read the sentences. Record scores on the Sentence Reading Chart, p. 252. Work with one child as others complete Write Sentences below.

My granddad has gone walking with a group of neighbors.
There is a sandbox for small kids inside the mall.
When classmates move, I promise to call and talk to them.

CORRECTIVE FEEDBACK

MONITOR PROGRESS

If . . . children have trouble reading words with the sound of *a* in *ball* and *walk* and compound words,
then . . . reteach the blending strategy lessons on pp. 4 and 8.

If . . . children cannot read a high-frequency word,
then . . . mark the missed word or words on a high-frequency word list and send the list home for additional practice or have them practice with a fluent reader.

If . . . children misread a word in the sentence,
then . . . correct the error and have them reread the word and then the sentence.

Practice sentence writing.

Provide white boards.

Write Sentences Have children copy the sentences from reproducible p. 247 on white boards. Have them confirm spellings by comparing the words they wrote to the words in the sentences.

Phonological and Phonemic Awareness

Optional practice activities, pp. 280–283

Passage Reading

To Do	To Say
	5–10 minutes

Assess fluency and comprehension.

Determine which children to assess this week.

Choose from these options: monitoring fluency (see pp. 244–245) and/or monitoring retelling (see p. 246). Have children reread "A New Tune for Tim." Be sure each child is assessed every other week.

If you have time, assess every child.

ACTIVITY 2 — Use Concepts

Oral Vocabulary *familiar, keepsake, preserve, represent, valuable*

To Do	To Say
	5 minutes

Check understanding of oral vocabulary.

Preview next week's concept.

Use the Amazing Words to wrap up the week's concept.

Monitor understanding of oral vocabulary, using Routine Card 5.

As time allows, ask questions such as these.

- Tell me about the pictures on pp. 6–13 using some of the week's Amazing Words.
- How do you feel when you hear a favorite *familiar* song? Why?
- If you made a *valuable keepsake* for someone, what would it be?
- Why might you want to *preserve* your class photo each year?
- What items, such as birthday cards, can *represent* happy memories?

Next week you will read about how plants change as they grow.

ACTIVITY 3 Read to Connect

Reread "When Things Change," pp. 6–13

| | **To Do** | **To Say** | *10 minutes* |

Monitor comprehension: compare/contrast.

Have children reread "When Things Change" silently.

As you read, think about how the kids in the selection are alike and different. After rereading, ask:

- **How are the kids in this selection alike?** (They are all going through a tough change. They are all moving to new places. They are all bringing familiar things to the new places. These things remind them of home.)
- **How are the kids different?** (Each kid uses a different thing to remember pals and fun times.)

What are some familiar things that helped make the kids' moves easier? Record children's ideas in a list on the board. (dog, bat and ball, quilt, locket, photos) Children will use the list for Activity 4.

Make connections.

Have children make connections across texts.

We also read "Taking Pictures." **Find that. Look at the photos on p. 21 that kids snapped with today's cameras. How are they like the photos on p. 12 of "When Things Change?"** (Possible answer: The photos show kids having fun times with their pals. They show kids having fun at familiar places, such as parks, ballgames, school, campfires, and parties.) **How do these photos remind you of photos you have snapped?** Record these ideas in a chart.

We also read "A New Tune for Tim," **about a boy who must move to a new home. Before he moves, Tim's band class gives Tim a keepsake. What is Tim's keepsake?** (a song) **How is Tim's keepsake like the familiar things in "When Things Change"?** (The song helps Tim think about fun times.) **How is Tim's keepsake different from the familiar things?** (Tim can't see or hold the song, but he hums it and plays it on his trumpet.) Record children's ideas on a chart.

What did all the selections we read this week show us about changes? What is the big idea? (Sometimes changes are hard. Familiar things can help us with changes.)

ACTIVITY 4 Write

Response to Literature Independent Writing

| | **To Do** | **To Say** | *5–10 minutes* |

Assign descriptive writing.

Today you will write about how you can help a friend who is moving feel better. Describe how your friend might feel before, during, and after the move. Use words that describe your friend's feelings. Encourage children to use words you wrote on the board for Activity 3 as they write.

Guide sentence correction.

Writing elements: conventions, support

Have children check their writing by asking themselves these questions.

- **Does each sentence begin with a capital letter? end with the correct mark?**
- **Does each contraction have the apostrophe in the correct place?**
- **Did you use describing words?**

MORE PRACTICE

Have children share their sentences with the group. Write them on the board and have children practice reading and writing each other's sentences.

Homework   Practice Book, p. 79, Writing

Unit 4 Week 2 *From Seed to Plant*

How do plants change as they grow?

Objectives *This week students will . . .*

Phonemic Awareness
- segment and blend sounds in words

Phonics
- blend and read words with long *a: ai, ay* and long *e: e, ee, ea*
- apply knowledge of letter-sounds to decode unknown words when reading
- recognize high-frequency words *above, almost, change, often, straight*

Fluency
- practice fluency with oral rereading

Vocabulary
- build concepts and oral vocabulary: *adapt, annual, nutrients, soil, sprout*

Text Comprehension
- read connected text
- compare and contrast to improve comprehension
- write in response to literature

Word Work *This week's phonics focus is . . .*

Long *a: ai, ay*   Long *e: e, ee, ea*

High-Frequency Words *Tested Vocabulary*

The first appearance of each word in the Student Reader is noted below.

above   The sun is **above** the trees. (p. 41)

almost   I **almost** missed the bus. (p. 41)

change   To **change** means to make or become different. (p. 39)

often   It snows **often** in January. (p. 39)

straight   If something is **straight,** it does not bend, turn, or curve. (p. 42)

Amazing Words *Oral Vocabulary*

The week's vocabulary is related to the concept of how plants change as they grow.

adapt   to change to fit new situations or surroundings

annual   happening every year

nutrients   things that people, animals, or plants need to grow and be healthy

soil   the top layer of the Earth

sprout   to start to grow

Student Reader Unit 4 *This week students will read the following selections.*

Daily Lesson Plan

	ACTIVITIES	MATERIALS
Day 1	**Word Work** Phonemic Awareness: Segment and Blend Sounds Phonics: Blend Words with Long *a: ai, ay* High-Frequency Words *above, almost, change, often, straight* **Build Concepts** *adapt, annual, nutrients* **Read a Passage** "From Seed to Plant," pp. 38–43 Comprehension: Use Strategies Reread for Fluency	Student White Boards Sound-Spelling Card 2 Tested Vocabulary Cards *Sing with Me Big Book* and Audio CD Student Reader: Unit 4 Routine Cards 1, 2, 3, 4, 6, 7 AudioText Practice Book, p. 80, Long *a: ai, ay*
Day 2	**Reread for Fluency** **Word Work** Phonemic Awareness: Segment and Blend Sounds Phonics: Blend Words with Long *e: e, ee, ea* High-Frequency Words *above, almost, change, often, straight* **Read a Passage** "What Plant Will This Be?" pp. 44–51 Comprehension: Use Strategies **Write** Response to Literature: Shared Writing	Student Reader: Unit 4 Student White Boards Sound-Spelling Card 10 Tested Vocabulary Cards Routine Cards 1, 2, 3, 4, 6, 7 AudioText Practice Book, p. 81, Long *e: e, ee, ea*
Day 3	**Reread for Fluency** **Word Work** Phonemic Awareness: Segment and Blend Sounds Phonics: Fluent Word Reading High-Frequency Words *above, almost, change, often, straight* **Build Concepts** *soil, sprout* **Read a Passage** "Garden Art," pp. 52–61 Comprehension: Compare/Contrast	Student Reader: Unit 4 Student White Boards Tested Vocabulary Cards Routine Cards 1, 2, 3, 4, 6 AudioText Practice Book, p. 82, Compare and Contrast
Day 4	**Reread for Fluency** **Word Work** Phonics: Spiral Review Phonological and Phonemic Awareness Activities, pp. 280–283 **Read Together** "Riddle Time," p. 62 Comprehension: Listening **Build Concepts** *adapt, annual, nutrients, soil, sprout* **Write** Response to Literature: Interactive Writing	Student Reader: Unit 4 Routine Cards 1, 4 AudioText Student White Boards Practice Book, p. 83, High-Frequency Words
Day 5	**Assessment Options** Fluency, Comprehension Sentence Reading; Passage Reading Phonological and Phonemic Awareness Activities, pp. 280–283 **Use Concepts** *adapt, annual, nutrients, soil, sprout* **Read to Connect** "From Seed to Plant," pp. 38–43 Comprehension: Compare/Contrast **Write** Response to Literature: Independent Writing	Reproducible p. 247 Sentence Reading Chart, p. 252 Student White Boards Fluency Progress Chart, p. 245 Student Reader: Unit 4 Routine Card 5 Practice Book, p. 84, Writing

See pp. xvi–xvii for how *My Sidewalks* integrates instructional practices for ELL.

Word Work

Phonemic Awareness Segment and Blend Sounds

To Do	To Say	2 minutes

Scaffold instruction.

Distribute white boards.
Write *nail*.

Write *way*.

Lead children in blending sounds as they write.

Model Listen to the sounds in *nail*. Stretch the sounds /nnn/ /āāā/ /lll/ as you write *n, ai, l*. Repeat. Have children write letters as you write.

Teach and Practice Have children say the sounds with you as you point to the letters (/n/ /ā/ /l/) and blend the sounds to say the word. *(nail)* Listen to the sounds in *way*. Say /www/ /āāā/ as you write *w, ay*. Repeat. Have children write letters as you write. Have them say sounds as you point to letters and blend sounds to say the word. Continue with these words.

sail   say   paid   lay   train   spray

Blending Strategy Long *a: ai, ay*

To Do	To Say	5–10 minutes

Use the blending routine.

Write *rake* and *date*.

1 Connect You already can read these words. What are the words? *(rake, date)* What vowel sound do you hear in these words? (the long *a* sound) Today we'll learn about words with the long *a* sound spelled *ai* and *ay*.

Display Sound-Spelling Card 2.

2 Use Sound-Spelling Card This is an apron. What sound do you hear at the beginning of *apron?* (/ā/) Say it with me: /ā/. /ā/ is the long *a* sound: /ā/. It says its name: *a*/ā/. The two letters *ai* can stand for the long *a* sound when they are together.

Scaffold instruction.

3 Listen and Write Write the letters *ai* for /ā/. As you write, say the sound to yourself: /ā/. Now say the sound aloud.

Write *rain*.

4 Model The letters *ai* can stand for /ā/. This is how I blend this word: /r/ /ā/ /n/, *rain*. Now you try it: /r/ /ā/ /n/, *rain*.

Write *day*.

Repeat steps 2 and 3 for long *a: ay*. Model blending *day*: /d/ /ā/, *day*.

r a i n   d a y

CORRECTIVE FEEDBACK

Write each practice word. Monitor student practice.

5 Group Practice Let's try the same thing with these words. Give feedback, using the *if . . . then* statements on Routine Card 1.

wait   hay   plains*   play   frail*   tray

6 Individual Practice Write the words; have each child blend two of them.

day   pain   way   trails   sway*   waist   stray*   brain

Check understanding of practice words.

*Children need to make sense of words that they segment and blend. If needed, help children with meanings. *Plains* are flat areas of land. Corn is grown on the *plains.* If something is *frail*, it is not very strong. When you *sway*, you move slowly back and forth. (Model.) A *stray* is a lost animal.

MORE PRACTICE

Build words with *ail, ain*, and *ay*.

Build Words Have children write *ail, ain*, and *ay* at the tops of their boards. Have them add *m, n, p, sn*, and *tr* in front of *ail*; *m, dr, st*, and *tr* in front of *ain*; and *l, m, p, cl*, and *st* in front of *ay*. Model blending using bigger word chunks: *m, ail, mail*. Call on children to read each word and use it in a sentence or tell what it means.

High-Frequency Words *above, almost, change, often, straight*

To Do	To Say	
		3 minutes

Teach high-frequency words.

Display *above*.

1 Say, Spell, Write Use the Tested Vocabulary Cards. Display *above*. Here are some words that we won't sound out. We'll spell them. This word is *above*: *a, b, o, v, e* (point to each letter), *above*. What is this word? What are the letters in the word? Now you write *above*.

Point to the *b* and *v* in *above*.

2 Identify Letter-Sounds Read *a/bove* as you run your hand under the syllables. Let's look at the sounds in *above* that you do know. What is this letter? *(b)* What is the sound for this letter? (/b/) Continue with *v*/v/.

3 Demonstrate Meaning Tell me a sentence using *above*. Model a sentence if children need help.

Display *almost, change, often,* and *straight*.

Repeat the Routine with *almost, change, often,* and *straight*. Children can identify these letter-sounds and word parts: *almost* (al/ôl/, m/m/, st/st/), *change* (ch/ch/, n/n/, g/j/), *often* (f/f/, n/n/) and *straight* (str/str/, ai/ā/, t/t/). Have children write the words in their word banks. Add the words to the Word Wall. Point out that the words they are learning are on p. 63.

 ACTIVITY **2** Build Concepts

Oral Vocabulary *annual, adapt, nutrients*

To Do	To Say	
		5–10 minutes

Introduce oral vocabulary.

Display p. 17 of *Sing with Me Big Book.* Play audio CD.

This week you will learn about how plants change as they grow. Listen for the Amazing Words *annual, adapt,* and *nutrients* as I sing this song. Play or sing the song. Then have children sing it with you.

1 Introduce, Demonstrate, and Apply

Scaffold instruction.

Follow the Routine to teach *annual, adapt,* and *nutrients.*

annual In this song, watching plants grow every summer is an *annual* event. Something is *annual* if it happens every year. Have children say the word. Snow falling is an *annual* winter event in some places. What is an *annual* fall event? an *annual* spring event?

adapt We heard in the song that plants *adapt* to all conditions. When things *adapt*, they change to fit new situations or surroundings. Have children say the word. Some plants *adapt* to windy weather by growing large roots so they don't blow away. How do you *adapt* to windy weather? How do you *adapt* to rainy weather?

nutrients The song tells us plants need rain, sunlight, air, and *nutrients. Nutrients* are things that people, animals, or plants need to grow and be healthy. Have children say the word. Plants get *nutrients* from soil or dirt. What might happen if a plant didn't get the *nutrients* it needed?

Display the words on the Amazing Words board.

2 Display the Words Have children say each word as they look at it. You can find sounds and word parts you know in big words. Read *an/nu/al* as you run your hand under the syllables. What is the first syllable of *annual?* (an/an/) For *adapt* and *nutrients,* children can identify these letter-sounds and word parts: *adapt* (dapt), *nutrients* (n/n/, tr/tr/, nt/nt/, s/s/).

Monitor understanding.

3 Use the Words Ask children to use each word in a sentence. Model a sentence if children need help.

MORE PRACTICE

Use oral vocabulary to discuss the song. What might you see in the plants' *annual* summer show? Why do plants need *nutrients?* Can plants *adapt* to freezing conditions? How do you know?

ACTIVITY 3 Read a Passage

Build Background "From Seed to Plant," pp. 38–43

To Do	To Say	

10 minutes

Develop language and concepts.

See Routine Card 7. Read aloud p. 37 of the student book.

Preview the Week Use the photograph on p. 36 to introduce this week's concept of how plants change as they grow. **Lemons grow from these seeds. What changes do you think happen as the lemons grow?** Read aloud the titles and descriptions on p. 37. Ask children what they think each selection will be about.

Scaffold instruction.

See Routine Card 6. Display pp. 38–43.

Ask questions and elaborate on answers to develop language.

Key concepts: *flowers, pansies, seeds, nutrients, stems, buds, kernels, frail, adapt, cornstalks, cobs of corn, tassels, husks, vines, railings, ripe*

Before Reading Read the title aloud. Do a structured picture walk with children.

pp. 38–39 What do these pictures show? (kids planting seeds) **Yes, these pictures show kids planting flowers called pansies.** Point to details as you describe each step. **First, put seeds in a clay pot full of dirt. Next, put the pot in a sunny place. Then, water the dirt. Dirt, sunlight, and water are nutrients that help plants grow. Soon, small green stems start to grow. Then buds, or small flowers, grow on the stems. The buds change into pansies.**

pp. 40–41 What plants do you see growing? (corn) **The corn seeds, or kernels, grow to frail stems. The plants adapt and, over time, grow into tall, stronger cornstalks.** Point to a cornstalk. **Cobs of corn grow inside husks on the stalks. Tassels form on top.** Point out the tassels, husks, and cob. **Have you ever eaten a cob, or ear, of corn?**

pp. 42–43 What plants are growing? (grapes) **Grapes start out as seeds. They are planted in dirt. Then long, thin stems called vines grow. Farmers plant the vines next to wire railings. As the vines grow, they twist around the railings. When the grapes grow big and ripe, farmers snip bunches off of the vines. Let's read to learn how plants grow.**

Guide comprehension.

Monitor independent reading. Model strategic reading. Use Routine Cards 2 and 3.

During Reading Read the page in a whisper. Raise your hand if you need help with a word. Stop at the end of each page to model asking questions. For example, for p. 38: **After I read, I ask myself: What did I learn about planting pansies? What is the page mainly about? The author tells to get a pot and fill it with dirt. Then put pansy seeds in the dirt. Then put the pot in a sunny place. These are all steps for planting pansies, so this page is mainly about how to grow pansies.**

Summarize.

Use oral vocabulary to develop the concept.

After Reading What kinds of *nutrients* do pansies need to grow? Do pansies and corn need some of the same *nutrients?* Explain. Could picking ripe corn be an *annual* event? Why? How do grape plants *adapt* to being planted next to wire railings?

Reread for Fluency "From Seed to Plant," pp. 38–41

To Do	To Say	

5–10 minutes

CORRECTIVE FEEDBACK

Monitor oral reading.

Read pp. 38–41 aloud. Read them three or four times so your reading gets better each time. Give feedback on children's oral reading and use of the blending strategy. See Routine Cards 1 and 4.

MORE PRACTICE

Instead of rereading just pp. 38–41, have children reread the entire selection three or four times. You may want to have children read along with the AudioText.

Homework Practice Book, p. 80, Phonics: Long *a: ai, ay*

DAY

ACTIVITY 1 Reread for Fluency

Paired Reading "From Seed to Plant," pp. 40–43

| To Do | To Say | 5–10 minutes |

CORRECTIVE FEEDBACK

To Do: Pair children. Monitor paired reading.

To Say: Children read pp. 40–43 orally, switching readers at the end of the first page. Have partners reread; now the other partner begins. For optimal fluency, children should reread three or four times. Give feedback on children's oral reading and use of the blending strategy. See Routine Cards 1 and 4.

MORE PRACTICE

Instead of rereading just pp. 40–43, have children reread the entire selection three or four times. You may want to have children read along with the AudioText.

ACTIVITY 2 Word Work

Phonemic Awareness Segment and Blend Sounds

| To Do | To Say | 2 minutes |

Scaffold instruction.

To Do: Distribute white boards.
Write *me.*
Write *seed.*
Write *meat.*
Lead children in blending sounds as they write.

To Say:

Model Listen to the sounds in *me.* Stretch the sounds /mmm/ /ēēē/ as you write *m, e.* Repeat. This time have children write the letters as you write.

Teach and Practice Have children say the sounds with you as you point to the letters (/m/ /ē/) and blend the sounds to say the word. *(me)* Now listen to the sounds in *seed.* Say /sss/ /ēēē/ /d/ as you write *s, ee, d.* Have children say sounds as you point to letters and then blend the sounds to say the word. Repeat with *meat:* /m/ /ē/ /t/, *m, ea, t, meat.* Then continue with these words.

we feel neat she beach green

Blending Strategy Long e: e, ee, ea

5–10 minutes

To Do	To Say
Use the blending routine.	
Scaffold instruction.	
Write *these* and *Pete*.	**1 Connect** You already can read words like these. What are the words? *(these, Pete)* What vowel sound do you hear in these words? (the long *e* sound) Today we'll learn about other ways to spell the long *e* sound.
Display Sound-Spelling Card 10.	**2 Use Sound-Spelling Card** This is an easel. What sound do you hear at the beginning of *easel*? (/ē/) Say it with me: /ē/. /ē/ is the long *e* sound: /ē/. It says its name: *e*/ē/. The letter *e* can stand for /ē/.
	3 Listen and Write Write the letter *e* for /ē/. As you write, say the sound to yourself: /ē/. Now say the sound aloud.
Write *we*.	**4 Model** In this word, the letter *e* stands for /ē/. This is how I blend this word: /w/ /ē/, *we.* Now you try it: /w/ /ē/, *we.* Point out that when *e* is the only vowel in a word and it comes at the end of a word, it usually has the long *e* sound, /ē/.
Write *need*.	Repeat steps 2 and 3 for long *e: ee*. Write and model blending *need:* /n/ /ē/ /d/, *need.* Point out that two *e*'s together usually stand for the long *e* sound.
Write *seat*.	Repeat steps 2 and 3 for long *e: ea*. Write and model blending *seat:* /s/ /ē/ /t/, *seat.* Explain that when the vowels *ea* are together in a word, they often stand for the long *e* sound, /ē/.

w e   n e e d   s e a t

CORRECTIVE FEEDBACK	
Write each practice word. Monitor student practice.	**5 Group Practice** Let's try the same thing with these words. Give feedback, using the *if . . . then* statements on Routine Card 1.
	he see eat dream feast* teeth
	6 Individual Practice Write the words; have each child blend two of them.
	be deep beat peach sweet stream* wheel leaf
Check understanding of practice words.	*Children need to make sense of words as they segment and blend. If needed, help children with meanings. A *feast* is a big meal for lots of people during a special time. People might have a *feast* at Thanksgiving. A very small river is called a *stream*. A *stream* can become dry during a hot summer.

MORE PRACTICE	
Build words with *e, eep,* and *eal*.	**Build Words** Have children write *e, eep,* and *eal* at the top of their boards. Have them add *b, w, m, h,* and *sh* in front of *e; k, j, d, sl,* and *sh* in front of *eep;* and *m, r, s, squ,* and *st* in front of *eal*. Model blending using bigger word chunks: *d, eep, deep.* Call on children to read each word and use it in a sentence or tell what it means.

High-Frequency Words *above, almost, change, often, straight*

3 minutes

To Do	To Say
Teach high-frequency words.	Display *above, almost, change, often,* and *straight*.	Use the Tested Vocabulary Cards. Point to a word. Say and spell it. Have children say and spell the word. Ask children to identify familiar letter-sounds and word parts. Have them take turns reading the words.
Lead cumulative review.		Use the Tested Vocabulary Cards to review high-frequency words from previous weeks.

ACTIVITY 3 Read a Passage

Reading "What Plant Will This Be?" pp. 44–51

	To Do	To Say	*5–10 minutes*
Develop language and concepts. **Scaffold instruction.**	See Routine Cards 6 and 7. Display pp. 44–51. Ask questions and elaborate on answers to develop language. Key concepts: *pumpkins, vines, pits, peach, leaves, lemon, watermelons*	**Before Reading** Have children recall what they learned about the growth of pansies, corn, and grapes. Read the title. Do a structured picture walk. **pp. 44–45** What will we get when these seeds change and grow? (pumpkins) Pumpkins grow on vines, but in a different way than grapes do. This is its stem. **pp. 46–47** These big seeds are called pits or stones. What do these pits become? (peach trees) Point to the leaves on the peach trees. **pp. 48–49** Point to the seeds. What do they become? (lemon trees) Lemon trees like lots of sun. They don't grow well in shade. **pp. 50–51** These seeds will become watermelons. Watermelons grow on vines the way pumpkins do.	
Guide comprehension.	Monitor independent reading. Use Routine Cards 2 and 3.	**During Reading** Read the pages in a whisper. Raise your hand if you need help with a word. As you read, ask yourself: What am I learning about plants? What is this mainly about? **pp. 44–45** What did you learn about pumpkins? (A pumpkin begins as a seed. It needs sun and rain. Over time, it becomes a pumpkin.) **pp. 46–47** What did you learn about peaches? (First, a peach is a pit or stone. Over time, the peach pit becomes a peach tree with peaches on it.) **pp. 48–49** What did you learn about lemons? (A lemon starts as a seed. It needs lots of sun. In time, it becomes a lemon tree with lemons.) **pp. 50–51** What did you learn about watermelons? (Leaves grow from black seeds. They change into vines. Watermelons grow on the vines.)	
Model summarizing.	Think aloud.	**After Reading** What did you learn about plants? What was the selection mainly about? Model how to summarize. Each pair of pages told about a seed and the plant that grows from it. The selection is mainly about how plants change as they grow from seeds.	
MORE PRACTICE	Develop oral vocabulary.	How could you tell if the pumpkin, peach, lemon, and watermelon seeds got the right *nutrients?* If you pick ripe peaches *annually,* how often do you do it? Do you think lemons could *adapt* to a shady place?	

ACTIVITY 4 Write

Response to Literature Shared Writing

	To Do	To Say	*5 minutes*
Guide shared writing.	Write sentence frames. Read the questions.	For a seed to change, what does it need? A seed needs _____. How do seeds change? Seeds change _____. Invite children to suggest answers. Discuss and record answers to complete the sentence frames. While writing, model connecting sounds to letters and forming letters. (See pp. 257–259.) Have children read answers aloud as you track print.	
Homework		Practice Book, p. 81, Phonics: Long *e: e, ee, ea*	

3

Reread for Fluency

Oral Reading "What Plant Will This Be?" pp. 44–47

5–10 minutes

	To Do	To Say
CORRECTIVE FEEDBACK	Monitor oral reading.	Read pp. 44–47 aloud. Read them three or four times so your reading gets better each time. Give feedback on children's oral reading and use of the blending strategy. See Routine Cards 1 and 4.
MORE PRACTICE		Instead of rereading just pp. 44–47, have children reread the entire selection three or four times. You may want to have children read along with the AudioText.

ACTIVITY **2**
Word Work

Phonemic Awareness Segment and Blend Sounds

2 minutes

	To Do	To Say
Scaffold instruction.	Distribute white boards. Write *wait*. Write *week*. Lead children in blending sounds as they write.	**Model** Listen to the sounds in *wait.* Stretch the sounds /www/ /āāā/ /t/ as you write *w, ai, t.* Repeat. Have children write the letters as you write. **Teach and Practice** Have children say the sounds with you as you point to the letters (/w/ /ā/ /t/) and blend the sounds to say the word. *(wait)* Listen to the sounds in *week.* Say /www/ /ēēē/ /k/ as you write *w, ee, k.* Have children say the sounds as you point to letters and blend sounds to say the word. *(week)* Continue with these words.

rain   say   we   tree   reach   way   me

Fluent Word Reading Long *a: ai, ay;* Long *e: e, ee, ea*

5–10 minutes

	To Do	To Say
Use the word-reading routine. **Scaffold instruction.**	Write *nail* and *stay*. Write *snail, play, he, seem,* and *teach*. Write each practice word.	**1 Connect** You can read these words because you know the letters *ai* and *ay* can stand for the long *a* sound. What are these words? *(nail, stay)* **2 Model** When you come to a new word, look at all the letters in the word and think about its vowel sound and its parts. Say the sounds and word parts to yourself, and then read the word. Model reading *snail, play, he, seem,* and *teach.* When you come to a new word, what will you do? **3 Group Practice** Let's read these words. Look at all the letters, think about the vowel sounds and parts, and say the sounds and parts to yourself. We will read long *a* and long *e* words. When I point to the word, let's read it together. Allow 2–3 seconds previewing time for each word.

paid   day   he   cheek   street   waist   sprays   queen   scream

CORRECTIVE FEEDBACK	**MONITOR PROGRESS**	*If . . .* children have difficulty previewing and reading whole words, *then . . .* have them use sound-by-sound blending. *If . . .* children can't read the words fluently at a rate of 1–2 seconds per word, *then . . .* continue practicing the list.

| **MORE PRACTICE** | Model reading words in sentences. | When I read a sentence, I read each word without stopping between the words. If I come to a word I don't know, I blend it. Then I read the sentence again. Model reading this sentence, stopping to blend *beans: He may eat some strained green beans.* |
| | Write practice sentences. | Have each child read a sentence.

She needs a pail and sunscreen for a day at the beach.
Ray will be sailing on the sea next Sunday.
Can we reach the frail blue jay in the tree? |

High-Frequency Words *above, almost, change, often, straight*

| | **To Do** | **To Say** | 3 minutes |
| **Review high-frequency words.** | Display *above, almost, change, often,* and *straight.* | Use the Tested Vocabulary Cards. Point to a word. Say and spell it. Have children say and spell the word. Ask children to identify familiar letter-sounds and word parts. Have them take turns reading the words. | |

ACTIVITY 3 Build Concepts

Oral Vocabulary *soil, sprout*

	To Do	**To Say**	5–10 minutes
Teach oral vocabulary.	Display p. 52 of the student book.	Today you will read a story about how a boy and his granddad see plants and trees *sprout* from *soil* in a special garden.	*Routine*
		1 Introduce, Demonstrate, and Apply	
Scaffold instruction.	Follow the Routine to teach *soil* and *sprout* (n., v.).	**soil** This story takes place in the spring. Plants pop out of the *soil* in the spring. *Soil* is the top layer of the Earth. Have children say the word. People plant rows of seeds in *soil*. Name a word that means the same as *soil*. *(dirt, ground)*	
		sprout The boy and his granddad see branches *sprout* on a small tree. When a plant *sprouts,* it starts to grow. The new growth is called a *sprout.* Have children say the word. A bean seed needs sun and water before it will *sprout.* The new bean *sprout* has little green leaves. Describe a time when you saw a plant *sprout.* What did the *sprout* look like?	
	Display the words on the Amazing Words board.	**2 Display the Words** Have children say each word as they look at it. You can find sounds you know in unknown words. What letter do you see at the beginning of *soil*? (s) What sound does it make? (/s/) at the end of *soil*? (/l/) Continue with *sprout.* Children can identify the blend *spr* and the high-frequency word *out* to read *sprout.*	
	Monitor understanding.	**3 Use the Words** Ask children to use each word in a sentence. Model a sentence if children need help.	
MORE PRACTICE		Use oral vocabulary to discuss changes in plants. If you wanted a seed in a flowerpot to grow, what might you do to the *soil*? (water it, put it in the sunlight, add nutrients) When is the best time to see plants *sprout* outdoors—in the winter or spring? Why?	

ACTIVITY 4 Read a Passage

Reading "Garden Art," pp. 52–61

To Do	To Say	
		10 minutes

Teach compare/contrast.

Scaffold instruction.

Introduce the skill.

Model the skill. Display pp. 44, 50.

Apply the skill. Display pp. 47, 49.

Today you are going to compare and contrast things in a story. When you compare and contrast, you tell how two or more things are alike or different. For example, we can compare pumpkin seeds and watermelon seeds. One way they are alike is that plants grow from these seeds, but the seeds are different in size, shape, and color.

Compare the ripe peaches and lemons in this selection. How are they alike? (Peaches and lemons both grow on trees.) How are they different? (The size, color, and skins of the fruits are different.)

Develop language and concepts.

See Routine Card 6. Display pp. 52–61.

Model using key words and concepts.

Key concepts: *Japanese garden, homeland, reeds, trimming, bonsai tree, stray, leaves, branches, trained, twine, wire, art*

Monitor children's use of vocabulary.

Before Reading Read the title. Do a structured picture walk.

pp. 52–55 Where are the boy and his granddad? (in a garden) Yes, this is a Japanese garden. In Granddad's homeland, Japan, you often see gardens like this with rocks, small hills, a stream with fish, and tall grass called reeds. Point to the stream and reeds.

pp. 56–57 Granddad is trimming a little tree called a bonsai tree. A bonsai tree grows in a pot. Granddad keeps the tree small by cutting stray leaves and branches that stick out. How is trimming a bonsai similar to cutting a person's hair?

pp. 58–59 Granddad has trained each branch so his bonsai tree has a special shape. He wraps twine and wire to make branches grow a certain way. Are you surprised that you can train a tree?

pp. 60–61 The boy calls the bonsai tree "garden art." Can a tree be art? How would you describe the bonsai tree?

Now turn to your partner and talk about the pictures, using the same words I did.

Guide comprehension.

Monitor independent reading.

Use Routine Cards 2 and 3.

During Reading Read the pages in a whisper. Raise your hand if you need help with a word. As you read, compare and contrast Granddad's garden and bonsai tree with gardens and trees you have seen.

pp. 52–55 How is Granddad's garden different from gardens you have seen? (Granddad's garden has rocks, hills, streams with fish, reeds, and a bonsai tree. Other gardens have flowers or vegetables.)

pp. 56–57 How are a bonsai tree and a pine tree alike? different? (Both grow in soil and have branches. The bonsai is much smaller than a pine tree. The bonsai will stay small, but the pine tree will grow taller.)

pp. 58–61 How are the branches on a bonsai different from the branches on trees you have seen? (The bonsai has only a few branches that fan out from the stem. Other trees have many branches.)

Guide retelling.

Prompt children as they retell the story.

After Reading Have one child retell the story while the others assist. Who are the characters in this story? Where does the story take place? What happens at the beginning? in the middle? at the end? See Monitor Retelling, p. 246.

Homework

Practice Book, p. 82, Compare and Contrast

ACTIVITY 1 Reread for Fluency

Paired Reading "Garden Art," pp. 52–55

5–10 minutes

	To Do	To Say
CORRECTIVE FEEDBACK	Pair children. Monitor paired reading.	Children read pp. 52–55 orally, switching readers at the end of the first page. Have partners reread; now the other partner begins. For optimal fluency, children should reread three or four times. Give feedback on children's oral reading and use of the blending strategy. See Routine Cards 1 and 4.
MORE PRACTICE		Instead of rereading just pp. 52–55, have children reread the entire selection three or four times. You may want to have children read along with the AudioText.

ACTIVITY 2 Word Work

Spiral Review Vowel Sounds of y (/ī/, /ē/)

5–10 minutes

	To Do	To Say
Review vowel sounds of y.	Write *why*.	You can read this word because you know when *y* is the last letter in a word that has only one syllable, it usually stands for /ī/. What sound does *y* in this word stand for? (/ī/) What is the word? *(why)*
Scaffold instruction.	Write *rainy*.	You can read this word because you know when *y* is at the end of a word that has two or more syllables, it usually stands for /ē/. What sound does *y* in this word stand for? (/ē/) Remember, when reading words with two or more syllables, divide the word into smaller parts and then blend the parts together. In this word, I see a smaller word I know, *rain*. I blend *rain* with the sound for y, /ē/: *rain*, /ē/, *rainy*. What is the word? *(rainy)*
	Distribute white boards. Write *Long e* and *Long i* at the top of a two-column T-chart.	**Sort Words** Sort words by the vowel sounds of *y*: Long *i*, Long *e*. Display these words: *muddy, pansy, sky, creepy, my, try, party, sneaky, shy, by, sleepy, cry*. Call on children to read each word and tell which column to write it in. Write the word in a class chart as children write on their boards. **How are the words in the first column alike?** (They have one syllable; *y* stands for /ī/.) **How are the words in the second column alike?** (They have two syllables; *y* stands for /ē/.)

Long *i*	Long *e*
sky	muddy
my	pansy
try	creepy
shy	party
by	sneaky
cry	sleepy

CORRECTIVE FEEDBACK	**MONITOR PROGRESS**	**If . . .** children have difficulty distinguishing the sound of *y* in words, **then . . .** have them blend the words sound-by-sound and compare them with sample words *why* and *rainy*.

For more practice, see next page.

**MORE
PRACTICE**

Model reading words in sentences.	When I read a sentence, I read each word without stopping between the words. If I come to a word I don't know, I blend it. Then I read the sentence again. Model reading this sentence, stopping to blend *sleepy: Why does my puppy seem so sleepy?*
Write practice sentences.	Have each child read a sentence. **Will the sky be sunny, or will it be gray and rainy?** **The sneaky bunny will try to eat the beans on my tray.** **Jean is way too shy to ask my granny for a yummy treat.**

Phonological and Phonemic Awareness   Optional practice activities, pp. 280–283

ACTIVITY 3   Read Together

Choral Reading "Riddle Time," p. 62

To Do	To Say	10 minutes

Develop language and concepts.

Display p. 62

Before Reading These are funny riddles. Why do people like to read riddles? (They are fun to figure out. They make you laugh.)

Read the title of the selection. Ask children to predict what the riddles are about. **Riddles use words in silly ways. Each riddle asks a question. When I read the riddle, I'll raise my voice at the end to show that it is a question. Then I'll pause to think about the answer before reading it. The answers to the riddles are upside down at the bottom of the page.** Read each riddle and answer with appropriate intonation and pacing. Read it a second time, having children point to each word.

Model fluent reading.

Build fluency through choral reading.

Choral Reading Read each riddle aloud with me. Try to make your voice sound like mine as we read. Reread the riddles several times with children.

Develop concepts.

Monitor listening comprehension.

After Reading Which word that means "father" made the first riddle funny? *(pop)* What are two very different kinds of paste? (paste that sticks like glue, tomato paste) Would the answer to riddle three be funny if the farmer wanted to grow pumpkins instead of watermelons? Why not? How are jellybeans different from other beans?

ACTIVITY 4   Build Concepts

Oral Vocabulary *adapt, annual, nutrients, soil, sprout*

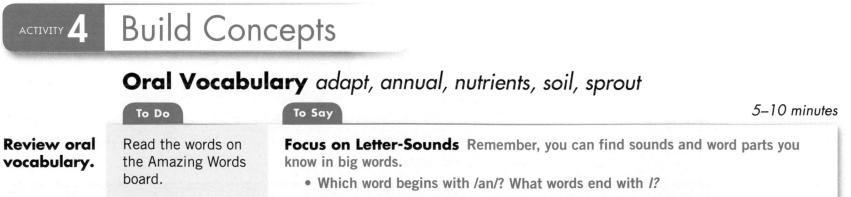

To Do	To Say	5–10 minutes

Review oral vocabulary.

Read the words on the Amazing Words board.

Focus on Letter-Sounds Remember, you can find sounds and word parts you know in big words.

- Which word begins with /an/? What words end with *l*?
- Which word has /tr/ in the middle? What letters stand for /tr/?
- Which word has *out* in it? Which word has the word part *dapt* in it?

To Do	To Say
Encourage discussion.	**Provide Multiple Contexts** Review the meanings of the words. Then ask questions to place the words in diverse contexts. • Why might someone dig in *soil?* • Which word goes with a Fourth of July parade? *(annual)* • If a child's pants are too short, we might say he is *sprouting.* Why? • How might you help a puppy *adapt* to its new home? • Does a person need *nutrients?* Why or why not? Do fruits and vegetables contain good *nutrients* for people?

MORE PRACTICE

Apply oral vocabulary to new situations.	• When people *adapt,* do they change or stay the same? (change) • Does an *annual* event happen every day or every year? (every year) • Would you put *soiled* clothes in a washing machine or a closet? Why? (washing machine; Something that has soil on it is dirty.) • If you gave a plant *nutrients,* would it get sick or grow? (grow) • Squat down. (Model) Now show how something *sprouts.*

ACTIVITY 5 Write

Response to Literature Interactive Writing

To Do	To Say	*5–10 minutes*

Generate ideas.

Review the story "Garden Art."	What did you learn about Granddad's little tree? Discuss what children learned about bonsai trees.	

Share the pen.

Have children participate in writing notes about Granddad's bonsai tree.	Write *Granddad's little tree _____.* Have children read the words you wrote. Then have them supply endings for each sentence. Invite individuals to write familiar letter-sounds, word parts, and high-frequency words. Have them find the spelling of high-frequency words on the Word Wall. Ask questions such as: • What are the first two sounds in *stay?* (/st/) What are the letters for /st/? *(st)* • What is the vowel sound in *stay?* (/ā/) What letters stand for the long *a* sound in *stay?* (ay)
Writing elements: conventions	Frequently reread what has been written while tracking the print. Point out that each sentence starts with a capital letter and ends with a period. Point out the extra space between words. Read the completed sentences aloud, having children read with you. (For example, *Granddad's little tree will stay small. Granddad's little tree has five branches. Granddad's little tree has branches that are trained to bend. Granddad's little tree is garden art.*)

MORE PRACTICE

Prompt independent wirting.	**Journal Writing** Tell about a tree you have seen in your neighborhood.

Homework	Practice Book, p. 83, High-Frequency Words

5

Assessment Options

Sentence Reading

To Do   **To Say**   *5 minutes*

Assess sentence reading.

Use reproducible p. 247.

Have each child read the sentences. Record scores on the Sentence Reading Chart, p. 252. Work with one child as others complete Write Sentences below.

We often wait for a sunny day to plant bean seeds.
Straight above the tree, a kite with a long tail sails by.
If it rains, almost all of these seeds may change to green plants.

CORRECTIVE FEEDBACK

MONITOR PROGRESS

If . . . children have trouble reading words with long *a: ai, ay* and long *e: e, ee, ea,* **then . . .** reteach the blending strategy lessons on pp. 20 and 24.

If . . . children cannot read a high-frequency word, **then . . .** mark the missed word or words on a high-frequency word list and send the list home for additional practice or have them practice with a fluent reader.

If . . . children misread a word in the sentence, **then . . .** correct the error and have them reread the word and then the sentence.

Practice sentence writing.

Provide white boards.

Write Sentences Have children copy the sentences from reproducible p. 247 on white boards. Have them confirm spellings by comparing the words they wrote to the words in the sentences.

Phonological and Phonemic Awareness   Optional practice activities, pp. 280–283

Passage Reading

To Do   **To Say**   *5–10 minutes*

Assess fluency and comprehension.

Determine which children to assess this week.

Choose from these options: monitoring fluency (see pp. 244–245) and/or monitoring retelling (see p. 246). Have children reread "Garden Art." Be sure each child is assessed every other week.

If you have time, assess every child.

Use Concepts

Oral Vocabulary *adapt, annual, nutrients, soil, sprout*

To Do   **To Say**   *5 minutes*

Check understanding of oral vocabulary.

Use the Amazing Words to wrap up the week's concept.

Monitor understanding of oral vocabulary, using Routine Card 5.

Preview next week's concept.

As time allows, ask questions such as these.
• Tell me about the pictures on pp. 38–43 using some of the week's Amazing Words.
• How might plants and animals *adapt* to life in a hot, dry desert? How are fish *adapted* to living in the water?
• Is your birthday an *annual* event? Explain.
• Explain how air and sun can be *nutrients*.
• If the things I name can be found in *soil*, say, "Soil." If not, say nothing. Worm *(soil)*, desk (not), seeds *(soil)*, roots *(soil)*, fish (not).
• Which word means a small stem springing out of the *soil?*

Next week you will read about things people and animals learn as they grow and change.

ACTIVITY 3 Read to Connect

Reread "From Seed to Plant," pp. 38–43

	To Do	**To Say** 10 minutes
Monitor comprehension: compare/contrast.	Have children reread "From Seed to Plant" silently.	As you read, think about how pansies, corn, and grapes are alike and different. After rereading, ask:

• **Tell some ways pansies, corn, and grapes are alike.** (possible answers: All start from seeds; all grow in soil; all change as they grow.)

• **Tell some ways pansies, corn, and grapes are different.** (Possible answers: You can eat corn and grapes, but you can't eat pansies; pansies grow in a pot, but corn and grapes grow on farms.)

Record children's responses on the board in a compare/contrast T-chart or in a Venn diagram. Children will use these ideas for Activity 4.

Make connections.	Have children make connections across texts.	**We also read "What Plant Will This Be?" Find that. What is one way that pumpkins and watermelons are like the grapes you read about in "From Seed to Plant"? How are they different from grapes?** (Alike: All grow on vines. You can make treats to eat from all of them. Different: Pumpkins and watermelons are big, but grapes are small. Pumpkins and watermelons have hard shells, but grapes do not.) Compare other types of plants across texts. Record ideas in a list.

We also read "Garden Art," about how Granddad grows a bonsai tree. In "From Seed to Plant," we found out how to grow pansies. How is growing a bonsai tree like growing pansies? How is it different? (Alike: Both grow in pots. Different: You trim and train the branches of the little trees, but you don't trim or train pansies.) Compare bonsai trees with peach and lemon trees or with grapevines on railings. Record ideas in a list.

What did all the selections we read this week show us about plants? What is the big idea? (Plants change as they grow.)

ACTIVITY 4 Write

Response to Literature Independent Writing

	To Do	**To Say** 5–10 minutes
Assign expository writing.		Today you will compare and contrast two plants that you learned about. Think about how these plants change as they grow. Tell how the plants are alike and how they are different. Encourage children to use words you wrote on the board for Activity 3 as they write.
Guide sentence correction.	Writing elements: conventions, organization, support	Have children check their writing by asking themselves these questions.

• **Does each sentence begin with a capital letter and end with a correct mark?**

• **Did I use *both* or *like* to show how the plants are alike? Did I use *but* or *not* to show how the plants are different?**

• **Did I describe each plant?**

MORE PRACTICE		Have children share their sentences with the group. Write them on the board and have children practice reading and writing each other's sentences.

Homework   Practice Book, p. 84, Writing

Unit 4 Week 3 *Animals*

How do animals change as they grow?

Objectives *This week students will . . .*

Phonemic Awareness
- add and delete ending sounds
- segment and blend sounds in words

Phonics
- blend and read words with endings *-er* and *-est* and words with long *o: o, oa, ow*
- apply knowledge of letter-sounds to decode unknown words when reading
- recognize high-frequency words *animal, country, cover, field, warm*

Fluency
- practice fluency with oral rereading

Vocabulary
- build concepts and oral vocabulary: *appearance, nursery, stage, tend, transform*

Text Comprehension
- read connected text
- compare and contrast to improve comprehension
- write in response to literature

Word Work *This week's phonics focus is . . .*

Endings *-er, -est*   Long *o: o, oa, ow*

High-Frequency Words *Tested Vocabulary*

The first appearance of each word in the Student Reader is noted below.

animal	Any living thing that can move about is an **animal.** (p. 72)
country	The **country** is the land outside the city. (p. 73) A **country** is also the land and a group of people with the same leader.
cover	When you **cover** something, you put something else over it. (p. 67) A **cover** is anything that protects or hides.
field	A **field** is a piece of land without trees. (p. 66)
warm	If something is **warm,** it is more hot than cold. (p. 67)

Amazing Words *Oral Vocabulary*

The week's vocabulary is related to the concept of how animals change as they grow.

appearance	the way something looks or the way it seems to look or be
nursery	a room or other place where babies and young children are cared for during the day
stage	a step or a certain time in a person's or animal's life
tend	to take care of or look after someone or something
transform	to change into something else

Student Reader Unit 4 — *This week students will read the following selections.*

Daily Lesson Plan

	ACTIVITIES	MATERIALS
Day 1	**Word Work** Phonemic Awareness: Add and Delete Ending Sounds Phonics: Blend Words with Endings *-er, -est* High-Frequency Words *animal, country, cover, field, warm* **Build Concepts** *appearance, stage, transform* **Read a Passage** "Animals," pp. 66–73 Comprehension: Use Strategies Reread for Fluency	Student White Boards Tested Vocabulary Cards *Sing with Me Big Book* and Audio CD Student Reader: Unit 4 Routine Cards 1, 2, 3, 4, 6, 7 AudioText Practice Book, p. 85, Endings *-er, -est*
Day 2	**Reread for Fluency** **Word Work** Phonemic Awareness: Segment and Blend Sounds Phonics: Blend Words with Long *o: o, oa, ow* High-Frequency Words *animal, country, cover, field, warm* **Read a Passage** "A Safe Place for Animals," pp. 74–81 Comprehension: Use Strategies **Write** Response to Literature: Shared Writing	Student Reader: Unit 4 Student White Boards Sound-Spelling Card 24 Tested Vocabulary Cards Routine Cards 1, 2, 3, 4, 6, 7 AudioText Practice Book, p. 86, Long *o: o, oa, ow*
Day 3	**Reread for Fluency** **Word Work** Phonemic Awareness: Segment and Blend Sounds Phonics: Fluent Word Reading High-Frequency Words *animal, country, cover, field, warm* **Build Concepts** *nursery, tend* **Read a Passage** "A Tadpole's Tale," pp. 82–93 Comprehension: Compare/Contrast	Student Reader: Unit 4 Student White Boards Tested Vocabulary Cards Routine Cards 1, 2, 3, 4, 6 AudioText Practice Book, p. 87, Compare and Contrast
Day 4	**Reread for Fluency** **Word Work** Phonics: Spiral Review Phonological and Phonemic Awareness Activities, pp. 280–283 **Read Together** "Animal Family Names," p. 94 Comprehension: Listening **Build Concepts** *appearance, nursery, stage, tend, transform* **Write** Response to Literature: Interactive Writing	Student Reader: Unit 4 Student White Boards Routine Cards 1, 4 AudioText Practice Book, p. 88, High-Frequency Words
Day 5	**Assessment Options** Fluency, Comprehension Sentence Reading; Mid-Unit Passage Reading Phonological and Phonemic Awareness Activities, pp. 280–283 **Use Concepts** *appearance, nursery, stage, tend, transform* **Read to Connect** "Animals," pp. 66–73 Comprehension: Compare/Contrast **Write** Response to Literature: Independent Writing	Reproducible p. 247 Sentence Reading Chart, p. 252 Assessment Book, p. 82 Fluency Progress Chart, p. 245 Student White Boards Student Reader: Unit 4 Routine Card 5 Practice Book, p. 89, Writing

See pp. xvi–xvii for how *My Sidewalks* integrates instructional practices for ELL.

ACTIVITY **1** Word Work

Phonemic Awareness Add and Delete Ending Sounds

2 minutes

	To Do	**To Say**
Scaffold instruction.	Distribute white boards. Write *fast*. Then add -*er* to form *faster*. Add -*est* to form *fastest*.	**Model** Listen to the sounds in *fast*. Stretch the sounds /fff/ /aaa/ /sss/ /t/ as you write *f, a, s, t*. Repeat. Have children write letters as you write. **Now listen as I add /èr/ to *fast*: *fast*, /èr/, *faster*.** Blend the base word with the ending as you write -*er*. Repeat. Have children add /èr/ as you write. **What new word do you make when you add /èr/ to *fast*? (faster)** Repeat for *fast, fastest*.
	Erase -*er* and -*est*. Lead children in adding and deleting sounds.	**Teach and Practice** What word do you make when you take away /èr/ from *faster*? *(fast)* Repeat. Have children erase letters with you. Repeat for *fastest, fast*. Add and delete -*er* and -*est* with these words: hot, hotter, hottest wide, wider, widest sunny, sunnier, sunniest

Blending Strategy Endings -*er*, -*est*

5–10 minutes

	To Do	**To Say**
Use the blending routine.	Write *cries, jogged,* and *smiling*.	**1 Connect** You studied words like these already. What are the words? Point to each word and have children say the word and then identify its base word and ending. **What happened to each base word before the endings were added?** Have children describe each type of spelling change. **Today we'll learn about words with the endings -*er* and -*est*.** *Routine*
Scaffold instruction.	Write *happy, happier,* and *happiest*.	**2 Model** The base word is *happy*. Point to *happier* and *happiest* and then cover each ending. The *y* in *happy* changed to *i* before -*er* and -*est* were added. Uncover each ending. **We add the ending -*er* to words to compare two things and -*est* to compare three or more things.** Give example sentences with *happier* and *happiest*. For words with endings, read the base word, then read the ending, and then blend the parts together. If the base word has two syllables, divide it into parts and then blend all the parts together. This is how I blend these words: *hap, pi, er—happier, hap, pi, est—happiest*. Remind children that when *y* changes to *i*, the *i* keeps the same sound as the *y* in the base word.
		h a p p i e r h a p p i e s t
		3 Listen and Write Write the word *happy*. Write the ending -*er* next to the *y*. Now erase the *y* and write *i* in its place. As you write, say the word to yourself: *happier*. Now say the word aloud. Repeat with *happiest*.
CORRECTIVE FEEDBACK	Write each practice word. Monitor student practice.	**4 Group Practice** Let's try the same thing with these words. Give feedback, using the *if . . . then* statements on Routine Card 1. longer biggest safer funnier bumpier sleepiest
		5 Individual Practice Write the words; have each child blend two of them. smallest sadder bravest muddiest sloppier rainiest
MORE PRACTICE	Model building words with -*er* and -*est*.	**Build Words** Have children write *Base Word*, -*er*, and -*est* at the tops of their boards. Have them add -*er* and -*est* to these base words: *dry, strong, thin, dirty, safe,* and *messy*. Model with *dry*. Call on children to use each -*er* and -*est* word in a sentence that compares two things or more than two things.

High-Frequency Words *animal, country, cover, field, warm*

To Do	To Say	3 minutes

Teach high-frequency words.

Display *animal.*

1 Say, Spell, Write Use the Tested Vocabulary Cards. Display *animal.* Here are some words that we won't sound out. We'll spell them. This word is *animal: a, n, i, m, a, l* (point to each letter), *animal.* What is this word? What are the letters in the word? Now you write *animal.*

Point to the *an, m,* and *l* in *animal.*

2 Identify Letter-Sounds Let's look at sounds and parts of *animal* that you do know. Read *an/i/mal.* What letters are in the first syllable of this word? *(an)* How do you say this word part? (/an/) Continue with *m*/m/ and *l*/l/.

Display *country, cover, field, warm.*

3 Demonstrate Meaning Tell me a sentence using *animal.* Model a sentence if children need help.

Repeat the Routine with *country, cover, field,* and *warm.* Children can identify these letter-sounds: *country* (*c*/k/, *n*/n/, *tr*/tr/, *y*/ē/), *cover* (*c*/k/, *v*/v/, *er*/èr/), *field* (*f*/f/, *ld*/ld/), and *warm* (*w*/w/, *m*/m/). Have children write the words in their word banks. Add the words to the Word Wall. Point out that the words they are learning are on p. 95.

ACTIVITY **2** Build Concepts

Oral Vocabulary *appearance, transform, stage*

To Do	To Say	5–10 minutes

Introduce oral vocabulary.

Display p. 18 of *Sing with Me Big Book.* Play audio CD.

This week you will learn about how animals change as they grow. Listen for the Amazing Words *appearance, transform,* and *stage* as I sing this song. Play or sing the song. Then have children sing it with you.

1 Introduce, Demonstrate, and Apply

Scaffold instruction.

Follow the Routine to teach *appearance, transform,* and *stage.*

appearance The song says a tadpole's *appearance* can fool you. An *appearance* is the way something looks or the way it seems to look or be. Have children say the word. A tadpole's *appearance* is more like a fish's than a frog's. Point to the first-stage tadpole, then the adult frog. Describe the *appearance* of this tadpole. Describe this frog's *appearance.*

transform We heard in the song that tadpoles *transform* as they grow up. When things *transform,* they change into something else. Have children say the word. How do tadpoles *transform* their *appearance* as they grow?

stage The song says that tadpoles are just in a *stage.* A *stage* is a step or a certain time in a person's or animal's life. Have children say the word. A tadpole goes through several *stages* before it becomes a frog. Use the picture to tell about the *stages* of a tadpole's *transformation.*

Display the words on the Amazing Words board.

2 Display the Words Have children say each word as they look at it. You can find sounds and parts you know in bigger words. Read *ap/pear/ance.* Children can identify *p*/p/, *r*/r/, *n*/n/, *c*/s/. They can decode *transform* and *stage.*

Monitor understanding.

3 Use the Words Ask children to use each word in a sentence. Model a sentence if children need help.

MORE PRACTICE

Use oral vocabulary to discuss the song. Does a baby frog have the same *appearance* as its parents? When is a tadpole finished *transforming?* Is the tadpole *stage* before or after the frog *stage?*

ACTIVITY 3 | Read a Passage

Build Background "Animals," pp. 66–73

	To Do	To Say	10 minutes
Develop language and concepts.	See Routine Card 7. Read aloud p. 65 of the student book.	**Preview the Week** Use the photograph on p. 64 to introduce this week's concept of how animals change as they grow. **How did this animal change as it grew?** Read aloud the titles and descriptions on p. 65. Ask children what they think each selection will be about.	
Scaffold instruction.	See Routine Card 6. Display pp. 66–73. Ask questions and elaborate on answers to develop language. Key concepts: *newborn, adult, transform, grows, down, grain, panda, appearance, cub, frisky, stage, joey, pocket*	**Before Reading** Read the title aloud. Do a structured picture walk with children. **pp. 66–67** These three pictures show a cat when it is a newborn, when it is young, and when it is a full-grown, or adult, cat. Point to the corresponding pictures. **What is a baby cat called?** (a kitten) **A kitten changes as it grows. It becomes an adult cat. Point to the adult cat.** **pp. 68–69** Point to the newborn animal. **What is a baby chicken called?** (a chick) **How does a chick transform, or change, as it grows? It gets bigger. It grows longer feathers on top of its fluffy down feathers. It learns to scratch for grain to eat. Over time, the chick becomes an adult chicken. Point to the adult chicken.** **pp. 70–71** Point to the adult panda. **This animal is a panda. What color is the panda?** (black and white) **How is a panda's appearance like a bear's appearance? A young panda is called a cub. Point to the panda cub. It is frisky, or playful. It eats plant stalks to grow big.** **pp. 72–73** Point to the newborn animal. **In this stage, the baby kangaroo, or joey, stays in its mother's pouch. The pouch is like a pocket for carrying things.**	
Teach story words.	Write *panda* and *pocket*.	You will read these words in the story: *panda* and *pocket.* Point to each word. Have children say and spell each word. Review meanings. **Let's read to find out how some animals change as they grow.**	
Guide comprehension.	Monitor independent reading. Model strategic reading. Use Routine Cards 2 and 3.	**During Reading** Read the page in a whisper. Raise your hand if you need help with a word. Stop at the end of each page to model asking questions. For example, for p. 66: After I read, I ask myself: What did I learn about how a kitten changes as it grows? The author tells how a newborn kitten can only eat, sleep, and cry. When the kitten changes and grows, it can run and play. This page is mostly about how a kitten changes over time.	
Summarize.	Use oral vocabulary to develop the concept.	**After Reading** Describe the chick's *appearance* when she first popped out of the egg. **How does eating lots of stalks help a panda cub *transform*?** (It gains weight. It grows bigger.) **In what *stage* did the kangaroo have pink skin?** (when it was a newborn kangaroo)	

Reread for Fluency "Animals," pp. 66–69

	To Do	To Say	5–10 minutes
CORRECTIVE FEEDBACK	Monitor oral reading.	Read pp. 66–69 aloud. Read them three or four times so your reading gets better each time. Give feedback on children's oral reading and use of the blending strategy. See Routine Cards 1 and 4.	
MORE PRACTICE		Instead of rereading just pp. 66–69, have children reread the entire selection three or four times. You may want to have children read along with the AudioText.	
Homework		Practice Book, p. 85, Phonics: Endings *-er, -est*	

ACTIVITY 1 Reread for Fluency

Paired Reading "Animals," pp. 70–73

To Do	To Say
	5–10 minutes

CORRECTIVE FEEDBACK

Pair children. Monitor paired reading.

Children read pp. 70–73 orally, switching readers at the end of the first page. Have partners reread; now the other partner begins. For optimal fluency, children should reread three or four times. Give feedback on children's oral reading and use of the blending strategy. See Routine Cards 1 and 4.

MORE PRACTICE

Instead of rereading just pp. 70–73, have children reread the entire selection three or four times. You may want to have children read along with the AudioText.

ACTIVITY 2 Word Work

Phonemic Awareness Segment and Blend Sounds

To Do	To Say
	2 minutes

Scaffold instruction.

Distribute white boards. Write *so*.

Write *soap*.

Write *slow*. Lead children in blending sounds.

Model Listen to the sounds in *so.* Stretch the sounds /sss/ /ōōō/ as you write *s, o.* Repeat. This time have children write the letters as you write.

Teach and Practice Have children say the sounds with you as you point to the letters (/s/ /ō/) and blend the sounds to say the word. *(so)* Now listen to the sounds in *soap.* Say /s/ /ō/ /p/ as you write *s, oa, p.* Have children say sounds as you point to letters and then blend the sounds to say the word. Repeat with *show*, /sh/ /ō/, *sh, ow.* Then continue with these words.

go	load	blow	coal	no	snow

Blending Strategy Long *o*: *o*, *oa*, *ow*

To Do	To Say	5–10 minutes

Use the blending routine.

Write *bone* and *those*.

1 Connect You already can read words like these. What are the words? (*bone, those*) What vowel sound do you hear in these words? (the long *o* sound) Yes, the words both have silent *e* at the end, so the *o* says its name. Today we'll learn other ways to spell the long *o* sound.

Scaffold instruction.

Display Sound-Spelling Card 24.

2 Use Sound-Spelling Card This is an ocean. What sound do you hear at the beginning of *ocean*? (/ō/) Say it with me: (/ō/). (/ō/) is the long *o* sound: (/ō/). It says its name: *o* (/ō/). The letter *o* can stand for (/ō/).

3 Listen and Write Write the letter *o* for /ō/. As you write, say the sound to yourself: /ō/. Now say the sound aloud.

Write *go*.

4 Model In each of these words, the letter *o* stands for /ō/. This is how I blend the first word: /g/ /ō/, *go*. Now you try it: /g/ /ō/, *go*. Point out that when a word or syllable ends with one vowel, the vowel is usually long.

Write *toast*.

Write *grow*.

Repeat steps 2 and 3 for the long *o*: *oa*. Write and model blending *toast*: /t/, /ō/, /st/, *toast*. Then repeat steps 2 and 3 for long *o*: *ow*. Write and model blending *grow*: /g/ /r/ /ō/, *grow*. Point out that the letters *oa* and *ow* often stand for the long *o* sound, /ō/.

g o   t o a s t   g r o w

CORRECTIVE FEEDBACK

Write each practice word. Monitor student practice.

5 Group Practice Let's try the same thing with these words. Give feedback, using the *if . . . then* statements on Routine Card 1.

so   low   roam*   foam*   flow*   slow   tow   loan*

Check understanding of practice words.

6 Individual Practice Write the words; have each child blend two of them.

no   crow   coach   own   moan*   float   toasty*   pillow   mow

*Children need to make sense of words as they segment and blend. If needed, help children with meanings. When animals or people *roam*, they wander around. My cat likes to *roam* around the house. *Foam* is a lot of very small bubbles stuck together. When something *flows*, it moves in a stream or current. To *loan* is to let someone borrow something. When you *moan*, you make a low sound in your throat that means you are sad or in pain. (Demonstrate.) Something *toasty* is nice and warm. My toes get *toasty* when I sit by the fire.

MORE PRACTICE

Build words with *o*, *oat*, and *ow*.

Build Words Have children write *o*, *oat*, and *ow* at the tops of their boards. Have them add *g*, *n*, and *s* in front of *o*; *b*, *c*, *fl*, and *thr* in front of *oat*; and *b*, *m*, *sn*, and *gl* in front of *ow*. Model building *g*, *o*, *go*. When finished, call on children to read each word and use it in a sentence or tell what it means.

High-Frequency Words *animal, country, cover, field, warm*

To Do	To Say	3 minutes

Teach high-frequency words.

Lead cumulative review.

Display *animal*, *country*, *cover*, *field*, and *warm*.

Use the Tested Vocabulary Cards. Point to a word. Say and spell it. Have children say and spell the word. Ask children to identify familiar letter-sounds and word parts. Have them take turns reading the words.

Use the Tested Vocabulary Cards to review high-frequency words from previous weeks.

ACTIVITY 3 Read a Passage

Reading "A Safe Place for Animals," pp. 74–81

To Do	To Say
	10–15 minutes

Develop language and concepts.

Scaffold instruction.

See Routine Cards 6 and 7. Display pp. 74–81.

Ask questions and elaborate on answers to develop language.

Key concepts: *wilderness, park, roam, forests, grizzly bear, fields, streams, vets, clinic, stage, appearance*

Before Reading Have children recall what they learned about baby animals changing as they grow. Read the title. Do a structured picture walk with children.

pp. 74–75 What kind of place is shown? This is a huge park in the wilderness, far away from cities. Point to the mountaintops. Wild animals roam in the forests and fields. Fish swim in the streams.

pp. 76–77 Park vets care for lost or hurt animals in the park. Point to the grizzly bear cub. This cub is hurt. How will the vets help him?

pp. 78–79 The park vets will take care of the cub at their clinic, or animal hospital. Then, at the stage when the cub is a little stronger, the vets will take him to this safe place in the park.

pp. 80–81 Look at the bear now. How has his appearance changed? Now the bear has grown strong and healthy.

Guide comprehension.

Monitor independent reading.

Use Routine Cards 2 and 3.

During Reading Read the pages in a whisper. Raise your hand if you need help with a word. As you read, ask yourself: What am I learning about the animals in the park? What is this mainly about?

pp. 74–76 What did you learn about the park? (The park is in the wilderness. It has many animals. Park vets take care of lost or hurt animals.)

pp. 77–79 What did you learn about the bear cub? (He is hurt. The vets will take care of him. When he gets stronger, they will take him to a safe place.)

pp. 80–81 How will the cub change over time? (He will grow to be a big, strong, healthy adult bear. He will be able to roam free in the park.)

Model summarizing.

Think aloud.

After Reading What did you learn about animals in the park? What was the selection mainly about? Model how to summarize. The first few pages tell about some of the wild animals in the park. The next pages tell how park vets take care of a hurt bear cub. They keep him safe until he grows big and strong. This selection is mainly about how park vets help a hurt cub as he grows into a strong bear.

MORE PRACTICE

Develop oral vocabulary.

Describe the *appearance* of a grizzly bear cub. What changes take place as the cub *transforms* into a full-grown grizzly bear? At what *stage* will the bear be free to roam in the park?

ACTIVITY 4 Write

Response to Literature Shared Writing

To Do	To Say
	5 minutes

Guide shared writing.

Write sentence frames. Read the questions.

How will park vets help the hurt cub get better? Park vets will _____.
How will the cub change? The cub will _____.

Invite children to suggest answers. Discuss and record answers to complete the sentence frames. While writing, model connecting sounds to letters and forming letters. (See pp. 257–259.) Have children read answers aloud as you track print.

Homework Practice Book, p. 86, Phonics: Long *o: o, oa, ow*

3

ACTIVITY 1 | Reread for Fluency

Oral Reading "A Safe Place for Animals," pp. 74–77

	To Do	To Say	
			5–10 minutes
CORRECTIVE FEEDBACK	Monitor oral reading.	Read pp. 74–77 aloud. Read them three or four times so your reading gets better each time. Give feedback on children's oral reading and use of the blending strategy. See Routine Cards 1 and 4.	
MORE PRACTICE		Instead of rereading just pp. 74–77, have children reread the entire selection three or four times. You may want to have children read along with the AudioText.	

ACTIVITY 2 | Word Work

Phonemic Awareness Segment and Blend Sounds

	To Do	To Say	
			2 minutes
Scaffold instruction.	Distribute white boards. Write *snowy*. Write *cleaner* and *soapiest*. Lead children in segmenting and blending sounds.	**Model** Listen to the sounds in *snowy.* Stretch the sounds in each syllable /sss/ /nnn/ /ōōō/ /ēēē/ as you write *snow, y.* Have children write the letters as you write. **Teach and Practice** Have children say the syllables with you as run your hand under each syllable *(snow, y)* and then blend the parts to say the word. *(snowy)* Repeat for *cleaner (clean, er)* and *soapiest (soap, i, est).* Continue with these words: **foamy slower snowiest soapier happiest sunniest**	

Fluent Word Reading Endings *-er, -est;* Long *o: o, oa, ow*

	To Do	To Say	
			5–10 minutes
Use the word-reading routine. **Scaffold instruction.**	Write *soapier* and *snowiest.*	**1 Connect** You can read these words because you know different spellings for long *o* and how to read words with the endings *-er* and *-est.* Remember, the letters *o, oa,* and *ow* can stand for the long *o* sound. When you read words with *-er* and *-est* endings, read the base word, then read the ending, and then blend the parts together. Keep in mind that the spellings of the base words may change before endings are added. What are the words? *(soapier, snowiest)*	*Routine*
	Write *go, crow, load, slower,* and *messiest.*	**2 Model** When you come to a new word, look at all the letters in the word and think about its vowel sounds and its parts. Say the sounds and word parts to yourself and then read the word. Model reading *go, crow, load, slower,* and *messiest.* When you come to a new word, what will you do?	
	Write each practice word.	**3 Group Practice** Let's read these words. Look at all the letters, think about the vowel sounds and word parts, and say the sounds and parts to yourself. We will read words with long *o* and the endings *-er* and *-est.* When I point to the word, let's read it together. Allow 2–3 seconds previewing time for each word. **no roast glow friskier slower throat shown dirtier sleepiest**	
CORRECTIVE FEEDBACK	**MONITOR PROGRESS**	**If . . .** children have difficulty previewing and reading whole words, **then . . .** have them use sound-by-sound blending. **If . . .** children can't read the words fluently at a rate of 1–2 seconds per word, **then . . .** continue practicing the list.	

MORE PRACTICE

Model reading words in sentences.	When I read a sentence, I read each word without stopping between the words. If I come to a word I don't know, I blend it. Then I read the sentence again. Model reading this sentence, stopping to blend *fastest: This toad has grown the fastest.*
Write practice sentences.	Have each child read a sentence.
	Joan acts sillier than Rose in this show.
	The boat was hard to row on the bumpiest waves.
	We gave the goats oats so they will grow bigger and stronger.

High-Frequency Words *animal, country, cover, field, warm*

To Do	To Say	3 minutes

Review high-frequency words.

| Display *animal, country, cover, field,* and *warm.* | Use the Tested Vocabulary Cards. Point to a word. Say and spell it. Have children say and spell the word. Ask children to identify familiar letter-sounds and word parts. Have them take turns reading the words. |

ACTIVITY **3** Build Concepts

Oral Vocabulary *nursery, tend*

To Do	To Say	10–15 minutes

Teach oral vocabulary.

| Display p. 82 of the student book. | Yesterday you read how park vets *tended* a hurt cub in a room that was like a *nursery* for baby animals. Today you will read a story about another baby animal—a baby frog. *Routine* |
| | **1 Introduce, Demonstrate, and Apply** |

Scaffold instruction.

Follow the Routine to teach *nursery* and *tend.*	***nursery*** In this story, the baby frog's pond is like a human baby's *nursery.* A *nursery* is a room or other place where babies and young children are cared for during the day. Have children say the word. You might see blankets and a playpen in a human baby's *nursery.* What else might you see? (a crib, diapers, rattles, bottles) How would a *nursery* at a zoo be different from a human baby's *nursery?*
	tend The father frog *tends* his baby in this story. He shows him how to leap. To *tend* means to "take care of or look after someone or something." Have children say the word. A mother dog *tends* her puppies. What does a mother cat tend? What does a father bear tend?
Display the words on the Amazing Words board.	**2 Display the Words** Have children say each word as they look at it. Look for sounds and word parts you know. Read *nurs/er/y* as you run your hand under the syllables. Children can identify these letter sounds and word parts: *nur*/nėr/, *s*/s/, *y*/ē/. They can decode *tend.*
Monitor understanding.	**3 Use the Words** Ask children to use each word in a sentence. Model a sentence if children need help.

MORE PRACTICE

| | Use oral vocabulary to discuss changes in animals. How do vets *tend* sick animals to help them get better? (They feed and clean them, check for cuts and broken bones, and make them beds.) Would a zoo nursery be filled with newborn or adult animals? Explain. |

ACTIVITY 4 | Read a Passage

Reading "A Tadpole's Tale," pp. 82–93

| To Do | To Say | 10 minutes |

Teach compare/ contrast.

Scaffold instruction.

Introduce the skill.

Model the skill.

Today you'll compare and contrast things in a story. When you compare and contrast, you tell how two or more things are alike or different. For example, we can compare and contrast bear cubs and adult bears. Make a two-column T-chart with the title *Bear Cubs and Adult Bears* and column headings *Same* and *Different*. One way a cub and an adult bear are the same is that both animals have fur. One way they are different is that a cub is smaller than an adult bear.

Apply the skill.

Compare and contrast the bear cub's park with a park where children play. How are the two parks alike? How are they different? Record children's responses in the chart.

Develop language and concepts.

See Routine Card 6. Display pp. 82–93.

Model using key words and concepts.

Key concepts: *tadpole, frogs, worries, stage, appearance, transformed*

Before Reading Read the title. Do a structured picture walk.

pp. 82–83 When a frog first hatches from its egg, it is a tadpole. Point to the tadpole. A tadpole's parents are frogs. Point to the frogs. How is this tadpole like the frogs? How is it different? The frogs and the tadpole live in a pond. The frogs have strong arms and legs, but the tadpole doesn't. The frogs can jump, but a tadpole can't.

pp. 84–85 Tad worries because he is not strong and fast like Dad.

pp. 86–87 Now Tad has grown. At this stage, Tad has teeth. Who are Tad's pals? How is Tad like his pals? How is he different?

pp. 88–89 Tad's appearance has changed again. What changed? Yes, now Tad has little legs. Tad still looks worried. Why?

pp. 90–91 Now Tad has strong arms and legs like his dad. He can leap on the leaf like his dad. Tad has transformed into a frog.

Monitor children's use of vocabulary.

pp. 92–93 Tad is in a Jumping Show. What do you think happens?

Now turn to your partner and talk about the pictures, using the same words I did.

Guide comprehen- sion.

Monitor independent reading.

Use Routine Cards 2 and 3.

During Reading Read the pages in a whisper. Raise your hand if you need help with a word. As you read, compare and contrast the appearance of Tad with the appearance of his parents.

pp. 82–85 Why is Tad sad? (Tad is sad because he doesn't look like his parents.) How is Tad different from his parents? (Tad is a tadpole and his parents are frogs. Tad doesn't have arms and legs. He has a tail.)

pp. 86–89 After two weeks, how does Tad change? (Tad has teeth.) After more weeks, how is Tad still growing? (Tad has legs, then arms.)

pp. 90–93 How is Tad like his parents now? (He has arms and legs. He is a frog.) Does Tad feel the same now as he did at the beginning of the story? Explain. (Tad was sad and worried, but now he's happy because he's a strong frog like his dad and he won the Jumping Show.)

Guide retelling.

Prompt children as they retell the story.

After Reading Have one child retell the story while the others assist. Where does this story take place? Who are the characters in this story? What happens at the beginning? in the middle? at the end? See Monitor Retelling, p. 246.

Homework

Practice Book, p. 87, Compare and Contrast

ACTIVITY **1** Reread for Fluency

Paired Reading "A Tadpole's Tale," pp. 82–85

5–10 minutes

To Do	To Say

CORRECTIVE FEEDBACK

Pair children. Monitor paired reading.

Children read pp. 82–85 orally, switching readers at the end of the first page. Have partners reread; now the other partner begins. For optimal fluency, children should reread three or four times. Give feedback on children's oral reading and use of the blending strategy. See Routine Cards 1 and 4.

MORE PRACTICE

Instead of rereading just pp. 82–85, have children reread the entire selection three or four times. You may want to have children read along with the AudioText.

ACTIVITY **2** Word Work

Spiral Review Base Words and Endings

5–10 minutes

To Do	To Say

Review base words and endings.

Scaffold instruction.

Write *soaks, brushes, floated, moaning, faster,* and *slowest.*

Look at these words. You can read these words because you know how to blend base words and endings. Remember, read the base word first, then read the ending, and then blend the parts together. What are these words? Point to each word and have children say the word aloud. Then have them identify the base word and its ending. Did the spelling of the base words change before the endings were added? (no)

Write *smiles, hurries, tried, grinning, snowier,* and *muddiest.*

Sometimes the spelling of the base word changes before an ending is added. You can cover the ending to help you figure out the base word. Then blend the base word and the ending together. If the base word has two syllables, divide it into smaller parts and then blend the parts with the ending. What are these words? Point to each word and have children say it aloud. Then have them identify the base word and the spelling change.

Distribute white boards.

Build Words Have children copy the base words and endings. Have them read the words and identify spelling changes. Discuss meanings, pointing out, for example, words describing past actions and words comparing two or more things.

Base Word	-s/-es	-ed	-ing		Base Word	-er	-est
cry	cries	cried	crying		wet	wetter	wettest
skip	skips	skipped	skipping		sloppy	sloppier	sloppiest
groan	groans	groaned	groaning		fluffy	fluffier	fluffiest

CORRECTIVE FEEDBACK

MONITOR PROGRESS

If . . . children have difficulty identifying the base word,
then . . . review possible spelling changes and have them locate changes in words.

For more practice, see next page

Continued Spiral Review

MORE PRACTICE	Model reading words in sentences.	When I read a sentence, I read each word without stopping between the words. If I come to a word I don't know, I blend it. Then I read the sentence again. Model reading this sentence, stopping to blend *happiest: Jo is happiest when she holds smaller puppies.*
	Write practice sentences.	Have each child read a sentence.
		The crow flies low and snatches the shiniest ring.
		Joan smiled as she hurried after the fastest jumping frog.
		The bunnies are friskier when they are not eating all day.

Phonological and Phonemic Awareness   Optional practice activities, pp. 280–283

ACTIVITY **3**   # Read Together

Echo Reading "Animal Family Names," p. 94

	To Do	**To Say**	*10 minutes*

Develop language and concepts. | Display p. 94. | **Before Reading** These are photos of adult animals. What are the names of these animals? (bear, deer, horse, sheep) What do you know about these animals? (Allow children to share what they know.)

Model fluent reading. | | Read the title of the feature. Ask children to predict what they will learn. Then point to the labels under the photos. **Photos in books often have labels. Labels are words that name things. Labels give information. I read each label carefully, one at a time. I use the photographs to help me understand the labels.** Read the labels at the appropriate rate, pausing after each boldfaced word and set of names. Read them a second time, having children point to each word.

| | Build fluency through echo reading. | **Echo Reading** Read each label aloud after me. Try to make your voice sound like mine when you read. Reread the labels several times with children echoing each label.

Develop concepts. | Monitor listening comprehension. | **After Reading** What information do the labels give about animal families? (father's name, mother's name, baby's name) Describe the *appearance* of a sheep. What is the father's name? the mother's name? the baby's name? Tell about other animal family names you know.

ACTIVITY **4**   # Build Concepts

Oral Vocabulary *appearance, nursery, stage, tend, transform*

	To Do	**To Say**	*5–10 minutes*

Review oral vocabulary. | Read the words on the Amazing Words board. | **Focus on Letter-Sounds** Remember, you can find sounds and word parts you know in big words.
- Which word has a *c* in it? What sound does *c* make in this word?
- Which word has *trans* and *form* in it? Which word has *end? age?*
- Which word has the sound /ėr/?

To Do	To Say
Encourage discussion.	**Ask for Examples and Reasons** Review the meanings of the words. Then ask questions that elicit examples and reasons from children. • How does a cake change in *appearance* from the time it is first mixed to the time it is decorated and ready to eat? • Would you find water, food, and beds in a zoo *nursery?* Why or why not? What else might you find in a zoo *nursery?* • During the two-year-old *stage,* a child might say *no* to everything. What else might a child do at this *stage?* (carry a blanket) • Would a farmer *tend* or *transform* cows? Why?

MORE PRACTICE

Apply oral vocabulary to new situations.	• If the things I say can be *transformed,* say, "*Transform.*" If not, say nothing. A dog into a cat. (not) A yard into a garden. (transform) A basement into a playroom. (transform) A kite into an airplane. (not) • Describe a classroom that has a neat and clean *appearance.* • If you want to see a zookeeper *tend* young monkeys, would you go to a *nursery* or a post office? Why? • Describe a *stage* you went through. Use *stage* when you tell about it.

ACTIVITY **5**   ## Write

Response to Literature Interactive Writing

5–10 minutes

	To Do	To Say
Generate ideas. **Share the pen.**	Review the story "A Tadpole's Tale."	**How does Tad win the Jumping Show?** Discuss how Tad changed as he grew until he was eventually able to perform well at the Jumping Show.
	Have children participate in writing to compare Tad with others at the Jumping Show.	Write *At the Jumping Show, Tad ___.* Have children read the words you wrote. Then have them supply endings for each sentence. Invite individuals to write familiar letter-sounds, word parts, and high-frequency words. Have them find the spelling of high-frequency words on the Word Wall. Ask questions such as: • What is the base word in *slowest?* (slow) What is the vowel sound in *slow?* (/ō/) • What letters stand for /ō/ in *slowest?* (ow) • What ending do you see on *slowest?* (-est)
	Writing elements: conventions	Frequently reread what has been written while tracking the print. Point out that each sentence starts with a capital letter and ends with a period. Point out the extra space between words. Read the completed sentences aloud, having children read with you. (For example, *At the Jumping Show, Tad is not the slowest. At the Jumping Show, Tad jumps faster than the others. At the Jumping Show, Tad has the longest jump.*)

MORE PRACTICE

Prompt independent writing.	**Journal Writing** Tell about something you have learned to do well.

Homework	Practice Book, p. 88, High-Frequency Words

ACTIVITY 1 — Assessment Options

Sentence Reading

To Do	To Say	5 minutes

Assess sentence reading.

Use reproducible p. 247.

Have each child read the sentences. Record scores on the Sentence Reading Chart, p. 252. Work with one child as others complete Write Sentences below.

Will vets cover this sick animal with a warm blanket?
The biggest goat roams in the field with yellow roses.
I feel happier when I go for a slow walk in the country.

CORRECTIVE FEEDBACK — **MONITOR PROGRESS**

If . . . children have trouble reading words with *-er* and *-est* and long *o: o, oa, ow,*
then . . . reteach the blending strategy lessons on pp. 36 and 40.

If . . . children cannot read a high-frequency word,
then . . . mark the missed word or words on a high-frequency word list and send the list home for additional practice or have them practice with a fluent reader.

If . . . children misread a word in the sentence,
then . . . correct the error and have them reread the word and then the sentence.

Practice sentence writing.

Provide white boards.

Write Sentences Have children copy the sentences from reproducible p. 247 on white boards. Have them confirm spellings by comparing the words they wrote to the words in the sentences.

Phonological and Phonemic Awareness — Optional practice activities, pp. 280–283

Mid-Unit Passage Reading

To Do	To Say	5–10 minutes

Assess fluency and comprehension.

Determine which children to assess. Use Assessment Book, p. 82.

Choose from these options: monitoring fluency (see pp. 244–245) and/or monitoring retelling (see p. 246). Have children read the Unit 4 Mid-Unit Fluency Passage in the Assessment Book. Be sure each child is assessed every other week.

If you have time, assess every child.

ACTIVITY 2 — Use Concepts

Oral Vocabulary *appearance, nursery, stage, tend, transform*

To Do	To Say	5 minutes

Check understanding of oral vocabulary.

Preview next week's concept.

Use the Amazing Words to wrap up the week's concept.

Monitor understanding of oral vocabulary, using Routine Card 5.

As time allows, ask questions such as these.

- Tell me about the pictures on pp. 66–73 using some of the week's Amazing Words.
- Describe the *appearance* of a frog in its baby *stage*.
- Is *transforming* more like changing or swimming? Why?
- Vets *tend* a hurt bear cub. Why would it be dangerous for you to *tend* a hurt bear cub?
- If you could plan a *nursery* for kittens, what would it look like? Why?

Next week you will read about some difficult changes for people and animals.

ACTIVITY 3 Read to Connect

Reread "Animals," pp. 66–73

	To Do	To Say	10 minutes

Monitor comprehension: compare/contrast.

To Do: Have children reread "Animals" silently.

To Say: **As you read, compare and contrast baby and adult animals. Ask yourself how baby animals and adult animals are alike and different.** After rereading, ask:

In what ways are a kitten and its mother alike? How is a kitten different from its mother? Record children's ideas on a two-column chart on the board. Write *Kitten and Cat* at the top of the chart. Write *Alike* and *Different* at the tops of the columns. (Possible answers: Alike: Both have fur. Both have four legs. Different: A kitten is smaller than a cat.) Children will use the list for Activity 4.

Ask similar questions for the other animals in the selection and record responses in compare/contrast charts for *Chick and Chicken, Cub and Panda, Joey and Kangaroo.*

Make connections.

To Do: Have children make connections across texts.

To Say: **We also read "A Safe Place for Animals." Find that. How is the grizzly bear cub in this selection the same as the panda cub in "Animals"? How is it different?** Record answers in a two-column T-chart or Venn diagram. (Possible answers: Both cubs look like their mothers. The panda cub is black and white. The grizzly cub is brown. The panda cub eats stalks. The grizzly cub eats fish.)

We also read "A Tadpole's Tale," about how a tadpole changed as he grew. Compare the changes Tad went through with the changes the kitten, chick, panda, and kangaroo went through as they grew. Which animal changed the most? Make lists of each animal's changes and then compare the lists. (Tad changed the most. He transformed into a frog. The other animals did not change as much.)

What did all the selections we read this week show us about changes in animals? What is the big idea? (Animals change as they grow.)

ACTIVITY 4 Write

Response to Literature Independent Writing

	To Do	To Say	5–10 minutes

Assign descriptive writing.

To Say: **Today you will write about your favorite animal. Describe how the animal changes as it grows.** Encourage children to use words you wrote on the board for Activity 3 as they write.

Guide sentence correction.

To Do: Writing elements: conventions, organization, support

To Say: Have children check their writing by asking themselves these questions.

- **Does each sentence begin with a capital letter?**
- **Does each sentence end with the correct mark?**
- **Does the order of the sentences make sense?**
- **Did I add details about my animal?**

MORE PRACTICE

Children can draw pictures that illustrate the main growth stages of the animal and then share their pictures and sentences with others. Children can take turns reading and writing each other's sentences. They can also write comparisons of each other's animals.

Homework   Practice Book, p. 89, Writing

Unit 4 Week 4 *What Changes Are Hard?*

Why are some changes difficult?

Objectives *This week students will . . .*

Phonemic Awareness
- segment and count sounds in words

Phonics
- blend and read words with long *i: igh, ie*
- apply knowledge of letter-sounds to decode unknown words when reading
- recognize high-frequency words *below, child, children, full, important*

Fluency
- practice fluency with oral rereading

Vocabulary
- build concepts and oral vocabulary: *adjust, ancestor, courage, landmark, unexpected*

Text Comprehension
- read connected text
- identify main idea to improve comprehension
- write in response to literature

Word Work *This week's phonics focus is . . .*

Long *i: igh, ie*

High-Frequency Words *Tested Vocabulary*

The first appearance of each word in the Student Reader is noted below.

below	His room is **below** mine. (p. 100)
child	A **child** is a young boy or girl. (p. 102)
children	**Children** are young boys and girls. (p. 99)
full	If something is **full,** it cannot hold any more. (p. 102)
important	Something that is **important** has a lot of meaning or worth. (p. 101)

Amazing Words *Oral Vocabulary*

The week's vocabulary is related to the concept of changes that are difficult.

adjust	to get used to a change
ancestor	a family member that lived before you
courage	doing the right thing even when it is hard or dangerous
landmark	something familiar or easily seen that helps people know where they are
unexpected	something that happens without warning that surprises you

Student Reader Unit 4 *This week students will read the following selections.*

Daily Lesson Plan

	ACTIVITIES	MATERIALS
Day 1	**Word Work** Phonemic Awareness: Segment and Count Sounds Phonics: Blend Words with Long *i: igh, ie* High-Frequency Words *below, child, children, full, important* **Build Concepts** *adjust, landmark, unexpected* **Read a Passage** "What Changes Are Hard?" pp. 98–105 Comprehension: Use Strategies Reread for Fluency	Student White Boards Sound-Spelling Card 16 Tested Vocabulary Cards *Sing with Me Big Book* and Audio CD Student Reader: Unit 4 Routine Cards 1, 2, 3, 4, 6, 7 AudioText Practice Book, p. 90, Long *i: igh, ie*
Day 2	**Reread for Fluency** **Word Work** Phonemic Awareness: Segment and Count Sounds Phonics: Blend and Build Words with Long *i: igh, ie* High-Frequency Words *below, child, children, full, important* **Read a Passage** "The Great Chicago Fire!" pp. 106–111 Comprehension: Use Strategies **Write** Response to Literature: Shared Writing	Student Reader: Unit 4 Student White Boards Letter Tiles *b, c, d, e, f, g, h, i, l, n, p, r, s, t* Tested Vocabulary Cards Routine Cards 1, 2, 3, 4, 6, 7 AudioText
Day 3	**Reread for Fluency** **Word Work** Phonemic Awareness: Segment and Count Sounds Phonics: Fluent Word Reading High-Frequency Words *below, child, children, full, important* **Build Concepts** *ancestor, courage* **Read a Passage** "Coal's New Home," pp. 112–123 Comprehension: Main Idea	Student Reader: Unit 4 Student White Boards Tested Vocabulary Cards Routine Cards 1, 2, 3, 6 AudioText Practice Book, p. 91, Main Idea and Details
Day 4	**Reread for Fluency** **Word Work** Phonics: Spiral Review Phonological and Phonemic Awareness Activities, pp. 280–283 **Read Together** "I Miss My Old Friends," p. 124 Comprehension: Listening **Build Concepts** *adjust, ancestor, courage, landmark, unexpected* **Write** Response to Literature: Interactive Writing	Student Reader: Unit 4 Student White Boards Routine Cards 1, 4 AudioText Practice Book, p. 92, High-Frequency Words
Day 5	**Assessment Options** Fluency, Comprehension Sentence Reading; Passage Reading Phonological and Phonemic Awareness Activities, pp. 280–283 **Use Concepts** *adjust, ancestor, courage, landmark, unexpected* **Read to Connect** "What Changes Are Hard?" pp. 98–105 Comprehension: Main Idea **Write** Response to Literature: Independent Writing	Reproducible p. 248 Sentence Reading Chart, p. 252 Student White Boards Fluency Progress Chart, p. 245 Student Reader: Unit 4 Routine Card 5 Practice Book, p. 93, Writing

See pp. xvi–xvii for how *My Sidewalks* integrates instructional practices for ELL.

ACTIVITY **1** | Word Work

Phonemic Awareness Segment and Count Sounds

To Do	To Say	
		2 minutes

Scaffold instruction.

Distribute white boards.
Write *light*.

Model Listen to the sounds in *light*. Stretch the sounds /lll/ /īīī/ /t/ as you write *l*, *igh*, *t*. Repeat. This time have children write the letters as you write. Now let's count the sounds in *light*. I will say the word slowly and hold up a finger for each sound: /l/ /ī/ /t/. There are three sounds in *light*.

Write *lie*. Lead children in counting sounds as they write.

Teach and Practice Have children say the sounds with you as you point to the letters. (/l/ /ī/ /t/) Hold up a finger for each sound. How many sounds in *light*? (3) How many letters? (5) Repeat for *lie*. (2 sounds; 3 letters) Then continue counting sounds with these words:

right (3)   tie (2)   bright (4)   flies (4)   flights (5)   tried (4)

Blending Strategy Long *i: igh, ie*

To Do	To Say	
		5–10 minutes

Use the blending routine.

Write *bite*.

1 Connect You already can read this word. What is the word? *(bite)* What vowel sound do you hear in *bite*? (long *i*) Today we will learn two other ways to write the long *i* sound.

Routine

Scaffold instruction.

Display Sound-Spelling Card 16.

2 Model This is ice cream. What sound do you hear at the beginning of *ice cream*? (/ī/) Say it with me: /ī/. /ī/ is the long *i* sound: /ī/. It says its name: *i*/ī/. The letters *igh* stand for the long *i* sound, /ī/, when they are together.

3 Listen and Write Write the letters *igh* for /ī/. As you write, say the sound to yourself: /ī/. Now say the sound aloud.

Write *right*.

4 Model When *i* is followed by *gh*, these letters usually stand for the long *i* sound. This is how I blend this word: /r/ /ī/ /t/, *right*. Now you try: /r/ /ī/ /t/, *right*.

Write *tries*.

Repeat steps 2 and 3 for long *i: ie*. Then model blending *tries*: /t/ /r/ /ī/ /z/, *tries*. Point out that when two vowels appear together in a word or syllable, the first usually stands for its long sound and the second is silent.

r i g h t   t r i e s

CORRECTIVE FEEDBACK

Monitor student practice.

5 Group Practice Let's try reading these words. Give feedback, using the *if . . . then* statements on Routine Card 1.

pie   sigh*   dries   fight   cried   sunlight

6 Individual Practice Write the words; have each child blend two of them.

die   high   ties   tight   spied   thigh*   brighter

*Children need to make sense of words that they segment and blend. If needed, help children with meanings. You might *sigh* when you are tired or sad. (Demonstrate.) Your *thigh* is between your hip and knee. (Point to it.)

MORE PRACTICE

Build words with *ight* and *ies*.

Build Words Have children write *ight* and *ies* at the tops of their boards. Have them add *f, m, n, s, fr,* and *br* in front of *ight*, and *d, l, p, cr, fl,* and *sk* in front of *ies*. Model blending using bigger word chunks: *n, ight, night*. Then call on children to read each word and use it in a sentence or tell what it means.

High-Frequency Words *below, child, children, full, important*

To Do	To Say	
		3 minutes

Teach high-frequency words.

Display *below.*

1 Say, Spell, Write Use the Tested Vocabulary Cards. Display *below.* Here are some words that we won't sound out. We'll spell them. This word is *below:* *b, e, l, o, w* (point to each letter), *below.* What is this word? What are the letters in the word? Now you write *below.*

Point to *be* and *low* in *below.*

2 Identify Letter-Sounds Let's look at the sounds and word parts in *below* that you do know. Read *be/low* as you run your hands under the syllables. What smaller word is in the first part of *below? (be)* What smaller word is in the second part? *(low)*

3 Demonstrate Meaning Tell me a sentence using *below.* Model a sentence if children need help.

Display *child, children, full,* and *important.*

Repeat the Routine with *child, children, full,* and *important.* Children can identify these letter-sounds and word parts: *child* (*ch*/ch/, *ld*/ld/), *children* (*chil, dr*/dr/, *n*/n/), *full* (*f*/f/, *ll*/l/), *important* (*im, port, nt*/nt/). Have children write the words in their word banks. Add the words to the Word Wall. Point out that the words they are learning are on p. 125.

ACTIVITY 2 | Build Concepts

Oral Vocabulary *adjust, landmark, unexpected*

To Do	To Say	
		5–10 minutes

Introduce oral vocabulary.

Display p. 19 of *Sing with Me Big Book.* Play audio CD.

This week you will learn about changes that are hard. Listen for the Amazing Words *unexpected, adjust,* and *landmark* as I sing this song. Play or sing the song. Then have children sing it with you.

1 Introduce, Demonstrate, and Apply

Scaffold instruction.

Follow the Routine to teach *adjust, landmark,* and *unexpected.*

adjust The family will have to *adjust* to many new things after they move. When you *adjust,* you get used to a change. Have children say the word. The family will have to *adjust* to a new town and a new home. What are some changes you have had to *adjust* to?

landmark A *landmark* guides the family on their way to their new home. A *landmark* is something familiar or easily seen that helps people know where they are. Have children say the word. A very big statue would be a good *landmark* in a city. What other things make good *landmarks?*

unexpected In the song, the family makes an *unexpected* move to a new home. When something *unexpected* happens, it happens without warning and surprises you. Have children say the word. If you all came to school in pajamas, that would be *unexpected.* I would be very surprised! What are some *unexpected* events that have surprised you?

Display the words on the Amazing Words board.

2 Display the Words Have children say each word as they look at it. You can find sounds and word parts you know in big words. Read *un/ex/pect/ed/.* How do you say the first syllable of *unexpected? (un)* Continue for additional syllables. For *adjust,* children can identify the word part *just.* Children can decode *landmark.*

Monitor understanding.

3 Use the Words Ask children to use each word in a sentence. Model a sentence if children need help.

MORE PRACTICE

Use oral vocabulary to discuss the song. Is it easy to *adjust* to *unexpected* changes? Why or why not? How might finding *landmarks* help the family adjust to a new town?

ACTIVITY **3** Read a Passage

Build Background "What Changes Are Hard?" pp. 98–105

To Do	To Say	

10 minutes

Develop language and concepts.

See Routine Card 7. Read aloud p. 97 of the student book.

Preview the Week Use the illustration on p. 96 to introduce this week's concept of difficult changes. **This girl is starting at a new school. Is that a hard change? What other kinds of changes are hard?** Read aloud the titles and descriptions on p. 97. Ask children what they think each selection will be about.

Scaffold instruction.

See Routine Card 6. Display pp. 98–105.

Ask questions and elaborate on answers to develop language.

Key concepts: *unhappy, worried, frown, adjust, nervous, shy, greets, introduces, welcomes*

Before Reading Read the title aloud. Do a structured picture walk with children.

pp. 98–99 What does this girl's expression tell us? (She's not happy.) **Daisy is unhappy because it is her first day at her new school. She is worried that the children will not like her.**

pp. 100–101 Point to Daisy's frown. **She still feels worried. Sometimes it is hard to adjust to a new school and new friends. Even though Daisy is feeling nervous and shy, she decides to smile and be nice. Is that a good plan?**

pp. 102–103 Grace greets Daisy. **How do you think this makes Daisy feel?** (relieved, happy)

p. 104 Grace introduces Daisy to their teacher, who welcomes Daisy to the class. **What might you say to welcome a new student?**

p. 105 Where is Daisy now? (at home in bed) **She made a friend and will soon adjust to her new school. Let's read more about Daisy's first day.**

Guide comprehension.

Monitor independent reading. Model strategic reading. Use Routine Cards 2 and 3.

During Reading Read each page in a whisper. Raise your hand if you need help with a word. Stop at the end of each page to model asking questions. For example, for p. 98: **After I read, I ask myself: What did I learn about Daisy? What problem does she have? I read that Daisy is not happy because she has to start at a new school. She says, "No one will like me!" This page is mostly about how worried Daisy is about starting classes at a new school.**

Summarize.

Use oral vocabulary to develop the concept.

After Reading Would the flagpole shown on p. 100 be a good *landmark* to help Daisy find her way to the school? What *unexpected* thing happens as Daisy steps into the hall of her new school? What things help Daisy *adjust* to her new school?

Reread for Fluency "What Changes Are Hard?" pp. 98–101

To Do	To Say	

5–10 minutes

CORRECTIVE FEEDBACK

Monitor oral reading.

Read pp. 98–101 aloud. **Read them three or four times so your reading gets better each time.** Give feedback on children's oral reading and use of the blending strategy. See Routine Cards 1 and 4.

MORE PRACTICE

Instead of rereading just pp. 98–101, have children reread the entire selection three or four times. You may want to have children read along with the AudioText.

Homework

Practice Book, p. 90, Phonics: Long *i: igh, ie*

ACTIVITY 1 Reread for Fluency

Paired Reading "What Changes Are Hard?" pp. 102–105

To Do	To Say
	5–10 minutes

CORRECTIVE FEEDBACK

Pair children. Monitor paired reading.

Children read pp. 102–105 orally, switching readers at the end of the first page. Have partners reread; now the other partner begins. For optimal fluency, children should reread three or four times. Give feedback on children's oral reading and use of the blending strategy. See Routine Cards 1 and 4.

MORE PRACTICE

Instead of rereading just pp. 102–105, have children reread the entire selection three or four times. You may want to have children read along with the AudioText.

ACTIVITY 2 Word Work

Phonemic Awareness Segment and Count Sounds

To Do	To Say
	2 minutes

Scaffold instruction.

Distribute white boards.
Write *flight*.

Model Listen to the sounds in *flight.* Stretch the sounds /fff/ /lll/ /īīī/ /t/ as you write *f, l, igh, t*. Repeat. This time have children write the letters as you write. **Now let's count the sounds in *flight*. I will say the word slowly and hold up a finger for each sound: /f/ /l/ /ī/ /t/. There are four sounds in *flight*.**

Write *pie*. Lead children in counting sounds as they write.

Teach and Practice Have children say the sounds with you as you point to the letters. (/f/ /l/ /ī/ /t/) **Hold up a finger for each sound. How many sounds in *flight*?** (4) **How many letters?** (6) **Repeat for *pie*.** (2 sounds; 3 letters) Then continue counting sounds with these words:

tie (2)   sighed (3)   lied (3)   tight (3)   cries (4)   high (2)

Blend and Build Words Long *i*: *igh, ie*

	To Do	**To Say**
Review blending words.	Write *fright* and *spies*.	Remember, when you see the letters *igh* or *ie* together, they usually stand for the long *i* sound, /ī/. When I blend words like these, I look for bigger chunks of each word. This is how I blend the first word: *fr, ight, fright.* Now you try it: *fr, ight, fright.* Let's do the same for the second word: *sp, ies, spies.* Now you try it: *sp, ies, spies.*
CORRECTIVE FEEDBACK	Write the practice words. Monitor student practice.	Write the words; have each child blend two of them. Give feedback, using the *if . . . then* statements on Routine Card 1.
		light die bright flights flies sighing tries tied
	Provide letter tiles *b, c, d, e, f, g, h, i, l, n, p, r, s,* and *t.*	**Build Words** Write *right.* **Can you blend this word?** *(right)* **Spell *right* with letter tiles. Now add *b* to the beginning of *right.* What is the new word?** *(bright)*

- **Change the *b* in *bright* to *f.* What is the new word?** *(fright)*
- **Change the *fr* in *fright* to *n.* What is the new word?** *(night)*
- **Change the *n* in *night* to *s.* What is the new word?** *(sight)*

Write *tie.* **Can you blend this word?** *(tie)* **Spell *tie* with letter tiles. Now add *d* to the end of *tie.* What is the new word?** *(tied)*

- **Change the *t* in *tied* to *l.* What is the new word?** *(lied)*
- **Change the *l* in *lied* to *cr.* What is the new word?** *(cried)*
- **Change the *cr* in *cried* to *sp.* What is the new word?** *(spied)*

	To Do	**To Say**
MORE PRACTICE	Sort *igh* and *ie* words.	**Sort Words** Have children write *igh* and *ie* at the tops of their boards. Then list these words on the board: *tight, pie, slight, lies, highest, brighter, tried, skies, mighty,* and *fried.* Have children read each word aloud and write it in the appropriate column. Discuss how words in each column are alike. (In the first column, *igh* stands for the long *i* sound. In the second column, *ie* also stands for the long *i* sound.)

igh	*ie*
tight	pie
slight	lies
highest	tried
brighter	skies
mighty	fried

High-Frequency Words *below, child, children, full, important*

	To Do	**To Say**
Teach high-frequency words.	Display *below, child, children, full,* and *important.*	Use the Tested Vocabulary Cards. Point to a word. Say and spell it. Have children say and spell the word. Ask children to identify familiar letter-sounds and word parts. Have them take turns reading the words.
Lead cumulative review.		Use the Tested Vocabulary Cards to review high-frequency words from previous weeks.

ACTIVITY **3** Read a Passage

Reading "The Great Chicago Fire!" pp. 106–111

| | To Do | To Say | *10–15 minutes* |

Develop language and concepts.

Scaffold instruction.

See Routine Cards 6 and 7. Display pp. 106–111.

Ask questions and elaborate on answers to develop language.

Key concepts: *Chicago, raging fire, quaked, flames, smoke, jammed, trunks, adjust, rebuild, skyscrapers*

Before Reading Have children recall what they learned about difficult changes. Read the title. Do a structured picture walk with children.

pp. 106–107 What does this picture show? (a big fire) A raging fire burned for days in the city of Chicago in 1871. Buildings burned. The land quaked, or shook. People ran from the flames and smoke.

pp. 108–109 People jammed, or crowded, the streets. Some dragged heavy trunks full of clothes and other things. After the fire, people had to adjust to many new things. They had to rebuild their stores and homes. Point out the workers' tasks in the background illustration.

pp. 110–111 When were these photographs taken? (shortly after the fire, 1890, today) By 1890, Chicago had rebuilt many new buildings. Today, it is even bigger with its tall skyscrapers.

Teach story words.

Write *Chicago*.

You will read this word in the story. It is *Chicago.* Have children say the word and spell it. Point to it on a map and explain it is a big city in Illinois. Now let's read to learn more about the Great Chicago Fire.

Guide comprehension.

Monitor independent reading.

Use Routine Cards 2 and 3.

During Reading Read the pages in a whisper. Raise your hand if you need help with a word. As you read, ask yourself: What did I learn about the Great Chicago Fire? What is this mainly about?

pp. 106–109 What did you learn about the Great Chicago Fire? (Buildings burned, land quaked, and people lost homes and things.)

pp. 110–111 What did you learn about what happened after the fire? (People helped those who had lost everything. People started to rebuild.) People did not give up. They started rebuilding the city right away.

Model summarizing.

Think aloud.

After Reading What did you learn about the Great Chicago Fire? What was the selection mainly about? Model how to summarize. The first few pages describe how terrible the fire was. The next pages explain how people started to rebuild the city right away. This selection is mainly about what happened during and right after the Great Chicago Fire.

MORE PRACTICE

Develop oral vocabulary.

Do you think the Great Chicago Fire was *unexpected?* What changes did people have to *adjust* to after the fire? Do you think the fire burned any *landmarks?*

ACTIVITY **4** Write

Response to Literature Shared Writing

| | To Do | To Say | *5 minutes* |

Guide shared writing.

Write sentence frames. Read the questions.

How does a big fire change a city? A big fire _____.
How does a big fire change people's lives? People _____.

Invite children to suggest answers. Discuss and record answers to complete the sentence frames. While writing, model connecting sounds to letters and forming letters. (See pp. 257–259.) Have children read answers aloud as you track print.

ACTIVITY **1** Reread for Fluency

Oral Reading "The Great Chicago Fire!" pp. 106–109

5–10 minutes

	To Do	To Say
CORRECTIVE FEEDBACK	Monitor oral reading.	Read pp. 106–109 aloud. Read them three or four times so your reading gets better each time. Give feedback on children's oral reading and use of the blending strategy. Use Routine Cards 1 and 4.
MORE PRACTICE		Instead of rereading just pp. 106–109, have children reread the entire selection three or four times. You may want to have children read along with the AudioText.

ACTIVITY **2** Word Work

Phonemic Awareness Segment and Count Sounds

2 minutes

	To Do	To Say
Scaffold instruction.	Distribute white boards. Write *cries.*	**Model** Listen to the sounds in *cries.* Stretch the sounds /k/ /rrr/ /ī ī ī/ /zzz/ as you write *c, r, ie, s.* Repeat. This time have children write the letters as you write. **Now let's count the sounds in *cries.* I will say the word slowly and hold up a finger for each sound: /k/ /rrr/ /ī ī ī/ /zzz/. There are four sounds in *cries.***
	Write *nights.* Lead children in counting sounds as they write.	**Teach and Practice** Have children say the sounds with you as you point to the letters. (/k/ /rrr/ /ī ī ī/ /zzz/) **Hold up a finger for each sound. How many sounds in *cries*? (4) How many letters? (5) Repeat for *nights.* (4 sounds, 6 letters) Then continue counting sounds with these words:** **sighs** (3) **skies** (4) **lied** (3) **flies** (4) **fight** (3) **lightest** (6)

Fluent Word Reading Long *i: igh, ie*

5–10 minutes

	To Do	To Say
Use the blending routine.	Write *tight, skies.*	**1 Connect** You can read these words because you know different spellings for the long *i* sound. Remember, when you see the letters *igh* or *ie* together, they usually stand for the long *i* sound, /ī/. What are these words? *(tight, skies)*
Scaffold instruction.	Write *sighed, lie.*	**2 Model** When you come to a new word, look at all the letters in the word and think about its vowel sounds and its parts. Say the sounds and word parts to yourself and then read the word. Model reading *sighed* and *lie* in this way. When you see a new word, what are you going to do?
		3 Group Practice Let's read these words. Look at all the letters, think about the vowel sounds and word parts, and say the sounds to yourself. We will read words in which *igh* and *ie* stand for the long *i* sound. When I point to the word, we will read it together. Allow 2–3 seconds previewing time for each word. pie sight spied flights lies highest tried tighter dries
CORRECTIVE FEEDBACK	**MONITOR PROGRESS**	*If . . .* children have difficulty previewing and reading whole words, *then . . .* have them use sound-by-sound blending. *If . . .* children can't read the words fluently at a rate of 1–2 seconds per word, *then . . .* continue practicing the list.

Routine

MORE PRACTICE

| Model reading words in sentences. | When I read a sentence, I read each word without stopping between the words. If I come to a word I don't know, I blend it. Then I read the sentence again. Model reading this sentence, stopping to blend *fright: The lost girl cried with fright.* |
| Write practice sentences. | Have each child read a sentence.
The kite flies high across the skies.
Justin spied lots of bright stars last night.
Ling gave a mighty sigh as she dried the last dish. |

High-Frequency Words *below, child, children, full, important*

| To Do | To Say | 3 minutes |

Review high-frequency words.

| Display *below, child, children, full,* and *important.* | Use the Tested Vocabulary Cards. Point to a word. Say and spell it. Have children say and spell the word. Ask children to identify familiar letter-sounds and word parts. Have them take turns reading the words. |

ACTIVITY **3** Build Concepts

Oral Vocabulary *ancestor, courage*

| To Do | To Say | 5–10 minutes |

Teach oral vocabulary.

| Display p. 106 of the student book. | You just read about the Great Chicago Fire of 1871. People showed a lot of *courage* during the fire. I wonder if any of us has an *ancestor* who lived through it. Today we'll read about a dog that shows *courage* when he has to move to a new home.

1 Introduce, Demonstrate, and Apply |

Scaffold instruction.

Follow the Routine to teach *ancestor* and *courage.*	**ancestor** The Great Chicago Fire took place more than 100 years ago when our *ancestors* were alive. An *ancestor* is a family member who lived before you. For example, your great-grandparents are your *ancestors*. Have children say the word. Some people are named after an *ancestor*. Do you know where your *ancestors* lived? **courage** The people of Chicago showed *courage* when they helped each other during and after the fire. Someone shows *courage* when he or she does the right thing even when it is hard or dangerous. Have children say the word. It takes *courage* to rescue someone from a fire. Does it take *courage* to move to a new home? Why or why not?
Display the words on the Amazing Words board.	**2 Display the Words** Have children say each word as they look at it. You can find sounds and word parts you know in big words. Read *an/ces/tor* as you run your hand under the syllables. How do you say the first syllable of *ancestor?* (*an*/an/) the second syllable? (*ces*/ses/) Read *cour/age* as you run your hand under the syllables. Children can identify *c*/k/, *r*/r/, and *g*/j/.
Monitor understanding.	**3 Use the Words** Ask children to use each word in a sentence. Model a sentence if children need help.

MORE PRACTICE

| | Use oral vocabulary to discuss facing hard changes. It takes *courage* to face hard changes. What are some hard changes your *ancestors* might have faced? How did your *ancestors* show *courage?* What kinds of hard changes take *courage* to face today? |

Read a Passage

Reading "Coal's New Home," pp. 112–123

To Do	To Say	10 minutes

Teach main idea and supporting details.

Scaffold instruction.

Introduce the skill.

Model the skill.

Apply the skill. Display p. 98.

Today you will find the main idea and details in a story. Remember, the main idea is the most important idea about the topic, what the selection is all about. Details are the smaller pieces of information that tell more about the main idea. For example, if I read about someone's party, the main idea might be that everyone had fun. Details might describe presents, games, and food.

The topic of "What Changes Are Hard?" is starting at a new school. What is the main idea of this story? (It is hard to start at a new school.) What details tell more about the main idea? (Daisy worries that the kids won't like her. She slows down when she sees the school.)

Develop language and concepts.

See Routine Card 6. Display pp. 112–123.

Model using key words and concepts.

Key concepts: *apartment building, owner, country, wagging, courage, scared, adjust*

Monitor children's use of vocabulary.

Before Reading Read the title. Do a structured picture walk.

pp. 112–113 This story is about a dog named Coal. Coal lives in an apartment building and gets walked in the park by his owner.

pp. 114–117 These pictures show Coal's owner, Joan. She is frowning and crying. She feels very sad. She has to move and can't have a dog. Coal will move to a new home with the man in the van.

pp. 118–121 This is Coal's new family. The kids are happy to see Coal. Coal's new home is in the country. It has a red barn, a lake, green hills, and hens. Coal is racing fast! His tail is wagging and the kids are cheering. This seems like a good change for Coal.

pp. 122–123 Coal tries swimming for the first time. At first he is scared, but he jumps in anyway. That takes courage! Now Coal loves to swim. Do you think Coal will adjust quickly to his new home?

Now turn to your partner and talk about the pictures, using the same words I did.

Guide comprehension.

Monitor independent reading.

Use Routine Cards 2 and 3.

During Reading Read the pages in a whisper. Raise your hand if you need help with a word. As you read, ask yourself: What is the main idea? What details tell more about the main idea?

pp. 112–116 What is the main idea of these pages? (Coal has to move to a new home.) What details tell more about the main idea? (Joan has to move and can't have pets. Joan and Coal are both sad.)

pp. 117–119 What is the main idea of these pages? (Coal's new family is happy to meet Coal.) What details tell more about the main idea? (The kids smile at Coal. They say they're happy to meet him.)

pp. 120–123 What is the main idea of the whole story? (Coal had to move, but he likes his new home.)

Monitor retelling.

Prompt children as they retell the story.

After Reading Have one child retell the story while the others assist. **What happens in the beginning of the story? in the middle? at the end?** See Monitoring Retelling, p. 246.

Homework Practice Book, p. 91, Main Idea and Details

ACTIVITY **1** Reread for Fluency

Paired Reading "Coal's New Home," pp. 112–115

	To Do	To Say	
			5–10 minutes

CORRECTIVE FEEDBACK

Pair children. Monitor paired reading.

Children read pp. 112–115 orally, switching readers at the end of the first page. Have partners reread; now the other partner begins. For optimal fluency, children should reread three or four times. Give feedback on children's oral reading and use of the blending strategy. See Routine Cards 1 and 4.

MORE PRACTICE

Instead of rereading just pp. 112–115, have children reread the entire selection three or four times. You may want to have children read along with the AudioText.

ACTIVITY **2** Word Work

Spiral Review Long Vowel Digraphs *(ai, ay, oa, ow, ea, ee, ie, igh)*

	To Do	To Say	
			5–10 minutes

Review long vowel digraphs.

Write *brain.*

You can read this word because you know how to blend words that have two vowels together. Remember, when two vowels appear together in a word or syllable, the first vowel usually stands for its long sound and the second vowel is silent. What sound do the letters *ai* stand for in this word? *(long a, /ā/)* What is the word? *(brain)*

Scaffold instruction.

Write *sigh.*

You can read this word because you know how to blend words that have *i* followed by *gh.* When you see the letters *igh* together, they usually stand for the long *i* sound. What is the word? *(sigh)*

Distribute white boards. Write column headings Long *a*, Long *o*, Long *e*, and Long *i*.

Sort Words Use a chart to sort words according to their long vowel sounds. Write the column headings on the board and make a separate list of these words: *float, grain, spray, light, slow, beach, flies, sheets.* Have children copy the headings on their boards and write each word in the correct column. Discuss how the words in each column are alike, and have children identify the long vowel spellings. Call on children to read the words aloud and use them in sentences.

Long *a*	Long *o*	Long *e*	Long *i*
grain	float	beach	light
spray	slow	sheets	flies

CORRECTIVE FEEDBACK

MONITOR PROGRESS

If . . . children have difficulty reading the words,
then . . . have them blend the words sound-by sound.

MORE PRACTICE

Model reading words in sentences.

When I read a sentence, I read each word without stopping between the words. If I come to a word I don't know, I blend it. Then I read the sentence again. Model reading this sentence, stopping to blend *stream: Joan might play by the stream.*

Write practice sentences.

Have each child read a sentence.

We may sleep on the train at night.
The gray goat tries to steal a peach pie.
Will Kay grow green beans?

Phonological and Phonemic Awareness

Optional practice activities, pp. 280–283

Read Together

Choral Reading "I Miss My Old Friends," p. 124

To Do	To Say	10 minutes

Develop language and concepts.

Display p. 124.

Before Reading Read the title and ask children to predict what the comic strip will be about. Look at the top of the page. How do you think the girls feel? Why? Allow children to share their conclusions. The girls just moved, so they are sad. They don't know each other. They don't have friends.

Model fluent reading.

Build fluency through choral reading.

Model prosody.

When I read comic strips, I look at the pictures in order. Point out the order of the pictures. When I read the words the characters say, I speak as though I'm talking to a friend. I also try to use my voice to show how the characters feel. Read the strip in a conversational tone that expresses the characters' feelings. Read it a second time, having children point to each word.

Choral Reading Now read the comic strip aloud with me. Try to make your voice sound like mine. Reread the strip several times with children.

Develop concepts.

Monitor listening comprehension.

After Reading How do the girls feel at the end? Why? Does it take *courage* to make a new friend? How can new friends help someone *adjust* to an *unexpected* move?

Build Concepts

Oral Vocabulary *adjust, ancestor, courage, landmark, unexpected*

To Do	To Say	5–10 minutes

Review oral vocabulary.

Read the words on the Amazing Words board.

Focus on Letter-Sounds You can find sounds you know in big words.

- Which word has *land* in it? Which word has *just* in it?
- Which word begins with *an*? Which word begins with *un*?
- In which words does the letter *c* stand for /k/?

Encourage discussion.

Ask for Examples Review the meanings of the words. Then ask children to give examples that demonstrate their understandings of the words.

- Describe some changes that are hard to *adjust* to. Is it always hard to *adjust* to a change? What changes might be easy to *adjust* to?
- Tell me something about one of your *ancestors.*
- Name someone who has shown *courage.* What did that person do?
- What *landmarks* would help visitors find their way to our school?
- Tell about an *unexpected* experience that made you feel good.

MORE PRACTICE

Apply oral vocabulary to new situations.

- When you *adjust,* do you get used to a change or try not to change? (get used to a change)
- Is an *ancestor* a relative or a friend? (a relative)
- Is a *landmark* easy to spot or hard to spot? (easy to spot)
- Is an *unexpected* event something planned or a surprise? (a surprise)

ACTIVITY **5** | **Write**

Response to Literature Interactive Writing

| To Do | To Say | *5–10 minutes* |

Generate ideas.

Review the story "Coal's New Home."

What change happened in Coal's life? How well did Coal adjust to this change? Discuss Coal's old and new homes and how quickly he adjusted to life in the country.

Share the pen.

Have children participate in writing sentences comparing Coal's old and new homes.

Write these sentence starters: *Coal's old home _____. Coal's new home _____.* Have children read the words you wrote. Then have them supply endings for the sentences. Invite individuals to write familiar letter-sounds, word parts, and high-frequency words. Have them find the spelling of high-frequency words on the Word Wall. Ask questions such as:

• **What is the first sound in** *lake?* (/l/) **What is the letter for /l/?** *(l)*

• **What is the vowel sound in** *lake?* (/ā/) **What letter stands for the long** *a* **sound in** *lake? (a)*

• **What is the last sound in** *lake?* (/k/) **What letter stands for /k/ in** *lake? (k)*

• **What letter do we add to the end of** *lake* **to make the** *a* **say its name?** *(e)* **Does this letter make a sound?** (No, it is silent.)

Writing elements: conventions

Frequently reread what has been written while tracking the print. Point out that each sentence starts with a capital letter and ends with a period. Point out the extra space between words.

Read the completed list aloud, having children read with you. (For example, *Coal's old home is in a tall building. Coal's old home is next to a park. Coal's old home had no children. Coal's new home is in the country. Coal's new home has three children. Coal's new home has high hills. Coal's new home has a big lake. Coal's new home has a red barn with hay.*)

MORE PRACTICE

Prompt independent writing.

Journal Writing Describe someone or something that has changed in your life.

Homework

Practice Book, p. 92, High-Frequency Words

ACTIVITY 1 Assessment Options

Sentence Reading

	To Do	To Say	5 minutes

Assess sentence reading.

Use reproducible p. 248.

Have each child read the sentences. Record scores on the Sentence Reading Chart, p. 252. Work with one child as others complete Write Sentences below.

It is important to tie the rope tight.
The children ate pie that was full of peaches.
High on the hill, one child spies a lake below him.

CORRECTIVE FEEDBACK

MONITOR PROGRESS

If . . . children have trouble reading words with long *i: igh, ie,*
then . . . reteach the blending strategy lesson on p. 52.

If . . . children cannot read a high-frequency word,
then . . . mark the missed word or words on a high-frequency word list and send the list home for additional practice or have them practice with a fluent reader.

If . . . children misread a word in the sentence,
then . . . correct the error and have them reread the word and then the sentence.

Practice sentence writing.

Provide white boards.

Write Sentences Have children copy the sentences from reproducible p. 248 on white boards. Have them confirm spellings by comparing the words they wrote to the words in the sentences.

Phonological and Phonemic Awareness

Optional practice activities, pp. 280–283

Passage Reading

	To Do	To Say	5–10 minutes

Assess fluency and comprehension.

Determine which children to assess this week.

Choose from these options: monitoring fluency (see pp. 244–245) and/or monitoring retelling (see p. 246). Have children reread "Coal's New Home." Be sure each child is assessed every other week.

If you have time, assess every child.

ACTIVITY 2 Use Concepts

Oral Vocabulary *adjust, ancestor, courage, landmark, unexpected*

	To Do	To Say	5 minutes

Check understanding of oral vocabulary.

Use the Amazing Words to wrap up the week's concept.

Monitor understanding of oral vocabulary, using Routine Card 5.

As time allows, ask questions such as these.

- Tell me about the pictures on pp. 98–105 using some of the week's Amazing Words.

- What is your favorite neighborhood *landmark?* What is special about this *landmark?* Is there anything *unexpected* about it?

- Do you think people who show *courage* may also feel scared at the same time?

- Why do you think some people *adjust* to changes more easily than other people do? What could you learn from someone who *adjusts* easily?

Preview next week's concept.

- How might your life be different from your *ancestor's* life?

Next week you will read about changes in the weather.

ACTIVITY 3 Read to Connect

Reread "What Changes Are Hard?" pp. 98–105

To Do	To Say	*10 minutes*

Monitor comprehension: main idea and supporting details.

To Do: Have children reread "What Changes Are Hard?" silently.

To Say: As you read, think about the story's main idea and important details. After rereading ask:

- **What is topic of the story?** (Daisy's first day at a new school)
- **What is the main idea of the story?** (Possible answers: The first day at a new school is a hard change. Making a friend can make you feel happier at a new school.)
- **What are some details that tell more about the main idea?** (Daisy worries that the kids won't like her. Grace greets Daisy and helps her. Daisy feels happier after she meets Grace.)

Record children's responses in a chart, identifying the topic, main idea, and supporting details.

Make connections.

To Do: Have children make connections across texts.

To Say: We also read "The Great Chicago Fire!" Find that. How did the fire change the lives of people in Chicago? How did people adjust to these changes? Record children's ideas in a list on the board. (For example, fire destroyed many homes and stores, so people had to build new buildings. People's belongings burned in the fire, so people in other places gave them new things.) Children will use the list for Activity 4.

We also read "Coal's New Home," about a dog who moves to a new home. How does Coal feel about his new home at the end of the story? What do Coal and Daisy both learn about moving to a new place? Record ideas in a chart.

What do all the selections we read this week show us about hard changes? What is the big idea? (Changes can be hard, but people can find a way to adjust to them.)

ACTIVITY 4 Write

Response to Literature Independent Writing

To Do	To Say	*5–10 minutes*

Assign narrative writing.

Guide sentence correction.

To Do: Writing elements: conventions, focus, organization

To Say: Today you will write a story about a second grader starting at a new school. Tell what makes this change hard and how the second grader handles the change. Encourage children to use words you wrote on the board for Activity 3 as they write.

Have children check their writing by asking themselves these questions.

- **Did I begin each sentence with a capital letter?**
- **Did I use correct marks at the ends of sentences?**
- **Did I include details that tell more about the main idea?**

MORE PRACTICE

Have children share their sentences with the group. Write their sentences on the board and have children practice reading and writing each other's sentences. Children can also suggest other ways to deal with the changes described.

Homework   Practice Book, p. 93, Writing

Unit 4 Week 5 *Weather Changes*

How do changes in weather affect us?

Objectives *This week students will . . .*

Phonemic Awareness
- segment words into syllables and syllables into sounds

Phonics
- blend and read words with syllables V/CV and VC/V
- apply knowledge of letter-sounds to decode unknown words when reading
- recognize high-frequency words *head, large, poor, though, wash*

Fluency
- practice fluency with oral rereading

Vocabulary
- build concepts and oral vocabulary:
  blizzard, condition, forecast, predict, terrifying

Text Comprehension
- read connected text
- compare and contrast to improve comprehension
- write in response to literature

Word Work *This week's phonics focus is . . .*

Syllables V/CV and VC/V

High-Frequency Words *Tested Vocabulary*

The first appearance of each word in the Student Reader is noted below.

head	Your **head** is where your eyes, ears, nose, mouth, and brain are. (p. 129)
large	Something that is **large** is big. (p. 129)
poor	This **poor** child is hurt. (p. 129)
though	**Though** it looked like rain, we went on our walk. (p. 129)
wash	When you **wash** something, you clean it with soap and water. (p. 130) To **wash** away means to carry along by water.

Amazing Words *Oral Vocabulary*

The week's vocabulary is related to the concept of weather changes.

blizzard	a huge snowstorm with lots of wind and blowing snow
condition	the way a thing or person is
forecast	a statement of what is going to happen
predict	to say what you think will happen in the future
terrifying	very frightening

Student Reader Unit 4 *This week students will read the following selections.*

Daily Lesson Plan

	ACTIVITIES	MATERIALS
Day 1	**Word Work** Phonemic Awareness: Segment Syllables and Sounds Phonics: Blend Words with Syllables V/CV and VC/V High-Frequency Words *head, large, poor, though, wash* **Build Concepts** *condition, predict, terrifying* **Read a Passage** "Weather Changes," pp. 128–135 Comprehension: Use Strategies Reread for Fluency	Student White Boards Tested Vocabulary Cards *Sing with Me Big Book* and Audio CD Student Reader: Unit 4 Routine Cards 1, 2, 3, 4, 6, 7 AudioText Practice Book, p. 94, Open and Closed Syllables
Day 2	**Reread for Fluency** **Word Work** Phonemic Awareness: Segment Syllables and Sounds Phonics: Blend and Sort Words with Syllables V/CV and VC/V High-Frequency Words *head, large, poor, though, wash* **Read a Passage** "What Will You Need?" pp. 136–145 Comprehension: Use Strategies **Write** Response to Literature: Shared Writing	Student Reader: Unit 4 Student White Boards Tested Vocabulary Cards Routine Cards 1, 2, 3, 4, 6, 7 AudioText Word Cards
Day 3	**Reread for Fluency** **Word Work** Phonemic Awareness: Segment Syllables Phonics: Fluent Word Reading High-Frequency Words *head, large, poor, though, wash* **Build Concepts** *blizzard, forecast* **Read a Passage** "North Wind and Sun," pp. 146–157 Comprehension: Compare/Contrast	Student Reader: Unit 4 Student White Boards Tested Vocabulary Cards Routine Cards 1, 2, 3, 4, 6 AudioText Practice Book, p. 95, Compare and Contrast
Day 4	**Reread for Fluency** **Word Work** Phonics: Spiral Review Phonological and Phonemic Awareness Activities, pp. 280–283 **Read Together** "The Telephone Call," p. 158 Comprehension: Listening **Build Concepts** *blizzard, condition, forecast, predict, terrifying* **Write** Response to Literature: Interactive Writing	Student Reader: Unit 4 Routine Cards 1, 4 AudioText Student White Boards Practice Book, p. 96, High-Frequency Words
Day 5	**Assessment Options** Fluency, Comprehension Sentence Reading; End-of-Unit Test Phonological and Phonemic Awareness Activities, pp. 280–283 **Use Concepts** *blizzard, condition, forecast, predict, terrifying* **Read to Connect** "Weather Changes," pp. 128–135 Comprehension: Compare/Contrast **Write** Response to Literature: Independent Writing	Reproducible p. 248 Sentence Reading Chart, p. 252 Student White Boards Assessment Book, p. 51 Student Reader: Unit 4 Routine Card 5 Practice Book, p. 97, Writing

See pp. xvi–xvii for how *My Sidewalks* integrates instructional practices for ELL.

Word Work

Phonemic Awareness Segment Words into Syllables, Syllables into Sounds

To Do	To Say
	2 minutes

Scaffold instruction.

Distribute white boards.
Write *robot*.

Model Listen to the sounds in *robot*. I hear two syllables in *robot*. Point to each syllable as you read *ro/bot*. **Listen to the sounds in each syllable.** Stretch the sounds /rrrōōō/, /booot/ as you write *ro*, *bot*. Repeat. This time have children write the letters as you write.

Lead children in segmenting words and syllables.

Teach and Practice Have children say the sounds in each syllable as you point to the letters. **How many syllables are there?** (two) **What are they?** *(ro, bot)* **What word does *ro/bot* make?** *(robot)* Continue with these words:

pa/per   riv/er   fro/zen   trav/els   la/dy   fin/ished

Blending Strategy Syllables V/CV (Open) and VC/V (Closed)

To Do	To Say
	5–10 minutes

Routine

Use the blending routine.

Write *napkin* and *puppy*.

1 Connect You can already read words like these. **Where do you divide words like these?** (between the two middle consonants) **What are the words?** *(napkin, puppy)* Today you will learn about words that have only one consonant between two vowels.

Scaffold instruction.

Write *paper*.

2 Model When a word has one consonant between two vowels, the consonant usually goes with the second syllable. Draw a line between *a* and *p*. This is how I blend this word: /pā/ /pər/, *paper*. **Does *a* have a long or short vowel sound?** Point out that a vowel at the end of a syllable is usually long.

Write *lemon*.

Now look at this word. Draw a line between *e* and *m*. If I divide the word after *e*, the vowel will stand for its long sound and I would say: /lē/ /mən/. That doesn't sound like a word. Erase the line and draw a line between *m* and *o*. If I divide the word after *m*, the *e* stands for its short sound. Let's blend it: /lem/ /ən/, lemon. I know that word!

$$p \ a \ p \ e \ r \longrightarrow \qquad l \ e \ m \ o \ n \longrightarrow$$

Write *seven*.

3 Listen and Write Write this word. Draw a line after the first vowel. Try blending it using a long vowel sound for the first syllable. **Is this a word?** (no) Erase the line and redraw it after *v*. Blend the word again using a short vowel sound for the first syllable. **What is the word?** *(seven)*

CORRECTIVE FEEDBACK

Write each practice word. Monitor student practice.

4 Group Practice Let's try the same thing with these words. Give feedback, using the *if . . . then* statements on Routine Card 1.

tiger   salad   never   babies   open   shadow

5 Individual Practice Write the words; have each child blend two of them.

closet   over   melon   cabin   siren   lizards   pony   visits

MORE PRACTICE

Model sorting two-syllable words by the vowel sound of the first syllable.

Sort Words Have children write *Long Vowel* and *Short Vowel* on their boards. List these words on the board: *hotel, camel, planet, silent, lazy, clever*. Have children decide if the first syllable of each word has a long or short vowel sound, then write the word in the appropriate column.

Long Vowel	Short Vowel
hotel	camel
silent	planet
lazy	clever

High-Frequency Words *head, large, poor, though, wash*

To Do	To Say	
Teach high-frequency words.	Display *head*.	**1 Say, Spell, Write** Use the Tested Vocabulary Cards. Display *head*. Here are some words that we won't sound out. We'll spell them. This word is *head: h, e, a, d* (point to each letter), *head.* What is this word? What are the letters in the word? Now you write *head.*
	Point to *h* and *d* in *head*.	**2 Identify Letter-Sounds** Let's look at the sounds in *head* that you do know. Point to *h.* What is this letter? *(h)* What is the sound for this letter? *(/h/)* Continue with *d/d/.*
		3 Demonstrate Meaning Tell me a sentence using *head.* Model a sentence if children need help.
	Display *large, poor, though,* and *wash*.	Repeat the Routine with *large, poor, though,* and *wash.* Children should be able to identify these letter-sounds and word parts: *large (lar), poor (p/p/, r/r/), though (th/th/), wash (w/w/, sh/sh/).* Have children write the words in their word banks. Add the words to the Word Wall. Point out that the words they are learning are on p. 159.

3 minutes

Routine

ACTIVITY **2** ## Build Concepts

Oral Vocabulary *condition, predict, terrifying*

To Do	To Say	
Introduce oral vocabulary.	Display p. 20 of *Sing with Me Big Book.* Play audio CD.	This week you will learn about weather changes. Listen for the Amazing Words *condition, predict,* and *terrifying* as I sing this song. Play or sing the song. Then have children sing it with you.
		1 Introduce, Demonstrate, and Apply
Scaffold instruction.	Follow the Routine to teach *condition, predict,* and *terrifying.*	***condition*** The song tells about changing weather *conditions.* A *condition* is the way a thing or person is. Weather *conditions* can be sunny, rainy, warm, and so on. Have children say the word. What weather *conditions* do we have today? Is your bedroom usually in a neat *condition?* Would you buy a used bike that was in poor *condition?*
		predict The song says that weather is hard to *predict.* When you *predict* something, you say what you think will happen in the future. Have children say the word. The weather people on TV *predict* it will rain tomorrow. What do you *predict* will happen in class this afternoon?
		terrifying The song describes a storm as *terrifying.* When something is *terrifying,* it is very frightening. Have children say the word. I think a *terrifying* storm would have lots of loud thunder and bright lightning. A grizzly bear would be *terrifying* to campers. What might *terrify* you?
	Display the words on the Amazing Words board.	**2 Display the Words** Have children say each word as they look at it. You can find sounds and word parts you know in big words. Read *con/di/tion* as you run your hand under the syllables. What sound does *c* make in *condition?* *(/k/)* Continue with *n/n/* and *di/di/.* Children can identify these letter-sounds and word parts: *terrifying (t/t/, fy/fī/, ing), predict (pr/pr/, dict).*
	Monitor understanding.	**3 Use the Words** Ask children to use each word in a sentence. Model a sentence if children need help.

5–10 minutes

Routine

MORE PRACTICE

Use oral vocabulary to discuss the song. What is strange about the weather *conditions* in the song? Do you agree that weather is hard to *predict?* What would you do during a *terrifying* storm?

Read a Passage

Build Background "Weather Changes," pp. 128–135

	To Do	To Say	*10 minutes*

Develop language and concepts.

See Routine Card 7. Read aloud p. 127 of the student book.

Preview the Week Use the picture on p. 126 to introduce this week's concept of weather changes. **Would you rather be inside or outside during this kind of weather? Why?** Read aloud the titles and descriptions on p. 127. Ask children what they think each selection will be about.

Scaffold instruction.

See Routine Card 6. Display pp. 128–135.

Ask questions and elaborate on answers to develop language.

Key concepts: *weather conditions, safe, funnel cloud, dangerous, flood, siren, cellar, cozy, blizzard, drifts, icy*

Before Reading Read the title aloud. Do a structured picture walk with children.

pp. 128–129 Where are these people? (at the beach) Beaches are fun when it is sunny and warm. What are the weather conditions at this beach? (stormy) Yes, big dark clouds usually mean a storm is coming. What should the people do? (leave) It isn't safe to be outside in a storm.

pp. 130–131 This is a funnel cloud. Point to it. When might you see a cloud like this? (during a tornado) A tornado has dangerous winds. Rivers may flood, or wash over, their banks. If you hear a tornado siren, go to a safe place. These people go into the cellar, a room under their home. They can stay cozy, or comfortable, until the storm is over.

pp. 132–133 Why is this storm dangerous? In a snowstorm, or blizzard, winds blow snow into piles called drifts. Cars can slide on icy roads.

pp. 134–135 There's a lot of work to do after a snowstorm. People have to shovel the snow away from cars, buildings, and sidewalks. But you can also have fun skating, sledding, or playing in the snow.

Teach story words.

Write *cloud*.

You will read this word in the story. It is *cloud*. Have children say the word and spell it. Review its meaning. **Let's read about weather changes.**

Guide comprehension.

Model independent reading. Model strategic reading. Use Routine Cards 2 and 3.

During Reading Read each page in a whisper. Raise your hand if you need help with a word. Stop at the end of each page to model asking questions. For example, for p. 131: After I read, I ask myself: What did I learn about big storms? What is this mainly about? The author says to run down to this safe, cozy place and wait for the storm to be over. This page is mainly about how to stay safe when there is a funnel cloud during a big storm.

Summarize.

Use oral vocabulary to develop the concept.

After Reading What weather *conditions* did you read about? How can listening to weather *predictions* help people stay safe from storms? What can happen when weather *conditions* change unexpectedly? What makes a tornado *terrifying*? Is driving in a snowstorm *terrifying*? Why?

Reread for Fluency "Weather Changes," pp. 128–131

	To Do	To Say	*5–10 minutes*

CORRECTIVE FEEDBACK

Monitor oral reading.

Read pp. 128–131 aloud. Read them three or four times so your reading gets better each time. Give feedback on children's oral reading and use of the blending strategy. See Routine Cards 1 and 4.

MORE PRACTICE

Instead of rereading just pp. 128–131, have children reread the entire selection three or four times. You may want to have children read along with the AudioText.

Homework Practice Book, p. 94, Phonics: Open and Closed Syllables

ACTIVITY 1 Reread for Fluency

Paired Reading "Weather Changes," pp. 132–135

5–10 minutes

	To Do	To Say
CORRECTIVE FEEDBACK	Pair children. Monitor paired reading.	Children read pp. 132–135 orally, switching readers at the end of the first page. Have partners reread; now the other partner begins. For optimal fluency, children should reread three or four times. Give feedback on children's oral reading and use of the blending strategy. See Routine Card 4.
MORE PRACTICE		Instead of rereading just pp. 132–135, have children reread the entire selection three or four times. You may want to have children read along with the AudioText.

ACTIVITY 2 Word Work

Phonemic Awareness Segment Words into Syllables, Syllables into Sounds

2 minutes

	To Do	To Say
Scaffold instruction.	Distribute white boards. Write *magic.*	**Model** Listen to the syllables in *magic.* I hear two syllables in *magic.* Point to each syllable as you read *mag/ic.* Listen to the sounds in each syllable. Stretch the sounds /mmmaaaj/ /iiik/ as you write *mag, ic.* Repeat. This time have children write the letters as you write them.
	Lead children in segmenting words and syllables as they write.	**Teach and Practice** Have children say the sounds in each syllable as you point to the letters. How many syllables are there? (two) What are they? *(mag, ic)* What word does *mag/ic* make? *(magic)* Continue with these words:
		a/corn pres/ent spi/ders la/bel drag/on com/ics

Blend and Sort Words Syllables V/CV and VC/V

To Do	To Say	
		5–10 minutes

Blend words with syllables V/CV and VC/V.

Scaffold instruction.

CORRECTIVE FEEDBACK

Write *acorn*.

This is how I blend this word: /ā/ /kôrn/, *acorn*. Now you try it: /ā/ /kôrn/, *acorn*.

Write *visit*.

This is how I blend this word: /viz/ /it/, *visit*. Now you try it: /viz/ /it/, *visit*.

Remember, if a word has one consonant between two vowels, you usually divide the word before the consonant and say a long vowel sound in the first syllable. If you don't say a word you know, then divide the word after the consonant and say a short vowel sound in the first syllable.

Write the practice words. Monitor student practice.

Write the words; have each child blend two of them. Give feedback, using the *if . . . then* statements on Routine Card 1.

shivers*   cozy   habit*   opens   metal   rapid*   babies   protect*

Check understanding of practice words.

*Children need to make sense of words they segment and blend. If needed, help children with meanings. Your body *shivers* when you feel cold. Demonstrate. A *habit* is something you do over and over again, often without thinking about it. *Rapid* means "very quick." Water flows fast in a *rapid* river. *Protect* means to keep something or someone safe.

Model sorting two-syllable words by the vowel sound of the first syllable.

Sort Words Have children write *Long Vowel* and *Short Vowel* on their boards. Then list these words: *robot, shadow, lemons, fever, lizard, moment, robins, pilot, music, never.* Have children decide if the first syllable of each word has a long or short vowel sound, and then write it in the appropriate column. Call on children to read the words and use them in sentences or tell what they mean.

Long Vowel	Short Vowel
robot	shadow
fever	lemons
moment	lizard
pilot	robins
music	never

MORE PRACTICE

Sort Words List these words on the board: *frozen, flavor, bacon, tulip, finished, travels.* Have children add the words to the chart they started above. Call on children to read these words and explain how they divided them. Discuss how the words in each column are alike.

High-Frequency Words *head, large, poor, though, wash*

To Do	To Say	
		3 minutes

Teach high-frequency words.

Lead cumulative review.

Display *head, large, poor, though,* and *wash*.

Use the Tested Vocabulary Cards. Point to a word. Say and spell it. Have children say and spell the word. Ask children to identify familiar letter-sounds and word parts. Have them take turns reading the words.

Use the Tested Vocabulary Cards to review high-frequency words from previous weeks.

ACTIVITY **3** Read a Passage

Reading "What Will You Need?" pp. 136–145

	To Do	To Say

10–15 minutes

Develop language and concepts.

Scaffold instruction.

See Routine Cards 6 and 7. Display pp. 136–145.

Ask questions and elaborate on answers to develop language.

Key concepts: *conditions, umbrella, wipers, sunscreen, protect*

Before Reading Have children recall what they learned about weather changes. Read the title. Do a structured picture walk with children.

pp. 136–137 This first window shows that it's raining outside. What weather conditions are shown in the other windows? (sunny, snowy)

pp. 138–139 It's raining, so the girl uses an umbrella to stay dry. Wipers sweep rain off the boy's glasses so he can see.

pp. 140–141 The girl is putting on sunscreen. The boy is drinking water. How can sunscreen and water protect you on sunny days?

pp. 142–145 The kids' warm clothes protect them on snowy days. You need different things to protect yourself in different kinds of weather. Do you need mittens on a sunny day? Why not?

Teach story words.

Write *umbrella*.

You will read the word *umbrella*. Have children say the word and spell it. Review its meaning. Let's read more about what people need.

Guide comprehension.

Monitor independent reading.

Use Routine Cards 2 and 3.

During Reading Read the pages in a whisper. Raise your hand if you need help with a word. As you read, ask yourself: What am I learning about different kinds of weather? What is this mainly about?

pp. 136–139 What do people need on rainy days? (umbrellas, wipers) Umbrellas and wipers protect you on rainy days.

pp. 140–145 What do people need on sunny days? (sunscreen, water) in snow? (warm clothes) The kids know what they need if they want to play outside in any kind of weather.

Model summarizing.

Think aloud.

After Reading What did you learn about how people protect themselves in different weather conditions? What was the selection mainly about? Model how to summarize. The selection shows what the kids need if they want to play outside. They need umbrellas when it rains, sunscreen and water on sunny days, and warm clothes when it snows. I pick the most important idea. The selection is mainly about what people need for different kinds of weather.

MORE PRACTICE

Develop oral vocabulary.

For what weather *condition* do you need an umbrella? If the weather forecasters *predict* a sunny day, what do you need if you want to play outside? Is it *terrifying* to be outside without a coat in a snowstorm? Explain.

ACTIVITY **4** Write

Response to Literature Shared Writing

	To Do	To Say

5 minutes

Guide shared writing.

Write sentence frames. Read the questions.

What do you need when it rains? You need _____.
What do you need when it is sunny? You need _____.
What do you need when it snows? You need _____.

Invite children to suggest answers. Discuss and record answers to complete the sentence frames. While writing, model connecting sounds to letters and forming letters. (See pp. 257–259.) Have children read answers aloud as you track print.

ACTIVITY **1** Reread for Fluency

Oral Reading "What Will You Need?" pp. 136–139

5–10 minutes

	To Do	To Say
CORRECTIVE FEEDBACK	Monitor oral reading.	Read pp. 136–139 aloud. Read them three or four times so your reading gets better each time. Give feedback on children's oral reading and use of the blending strategy. See Routine Cards 1 and 4.
MORE PRACTICE		Instead of rereading just pp. 136–139, have children reread the entire selection three or four times. You may want to have children read along with the AudioText.

ACTIVITY **2** Word Work

Phonemic Awareness Segment Words into Syllables

2 minutes

	To Do	To Say
Scaffold instruction.	Distribute white boards. Write *lady*.	**Model** Listen to the syllables in *lady*. I hear two syllables in *lady*. Point to each syllable as you read *la/dy*. Listen to the sounds in each syllable. Stretch the sounds /lllāāā/, /dēēē/ as you write *la, dy*. Repeat. This time have children write the letters as you write them.
	Lead children in segmenting words and syllables as they write.	**Teach and Practice** Have children say the sounds in each syllable as you point to the letters. **How many syllables are there?** (two) **What are they?** *(la, dy)* **What word does** *la/dy* **make?** *(lady)* Continue with these words: mu/sic plan/et mod/el rob/ins la/dies shiv/ered

Fluent Word Reading Syllables V/CV and VC/V

5–10 minutes

	To Do	To Say
Use the word-reading routine.	Write *spiders* and *river*.	**1 Connect** You can read these words because you know how to read two-syllable words that have one consonant between two vowels. Remember, you have to decide how to divide the word and whether the first syllable has a long or short vowel sound. What are these words? *(spiders, river)*
Scaffold instruction.	Write *student* and *closet*.	**2 Model** When you come to a new word, look at all the letters in the word and think about its vowel sounds and its parts. Say the sounds and word parts to yourself, and then read the word. Model reading *student* and *closet* in this way. When you see a new word, what are you going to do?
	Write each practice word.	**3 Group Practice** Let's read these words. Look at all the letters, think about the vowel sounds, and say the sounds to yourself. We will read words that have one consonant following the first vowel in the first syllable. When I point to the word, we will read it together. Allow 2–3 seconds previewing time for each word. tiger dragon fever human seventh shadows project major ponies
CORRECTIVE FEEDBACK	**MONITOR PROGRESS**	**If . . .** children have difficulty previewing and reading whole words, **then . . .** have them use sound-by-sound blending. **If . . .** children can't read the words fluently at a rate of 1–2 seconds per word, **then . . .** continue practicing the list.

MORE PRACTICE	Model reading words in sentences.	When I read a sentence, I read each word without stopping between the words. If I come to a word I don't know, I blend it. Then I read the sentence again. Model reading this sentence, stopping to blend *clever*: *Is it ever clever to stay silent?*
	Write practice sentences.	Have each child read a sentence.
		The lazy camel never traveled across a desert. **Did you finish hitching the pony to the wagon?** **A lizard is running in the tulips by the cabin!**

High-Frequency Words *head, large, poor, though, wash*

	To Do	**To Say**	*3 minutes*
Review high-frequency words.	Display *head, large, poor, though,* and *wash.*	Use the Tested Vocabulary Cards. Point to a word. Say and spell it. Have children say and spell the word. Ask children to identify familiar letter-sounds and word parts. Have them take turns reading the words.	

ACTIVITY 3 ## Build Concepts

Oral Vocabulary *blizzard, forecast*

	To Do	**To Say**	*5–10 minutes*
Teach oral vocabulary.	Display pp. 132–133 of the student book.	Earlier this week, we read about some dangerous weather changes. These pictures show a *blizzard.* If a blizzard is in the *forecast,* you should stay inside to be safe. Today we'll read a make-believe story about other kinds of weather changes.	*Routine*
		1 Introduce, Demonstrate, and Apply	
Scaffold instruction.	Follow the Routine to teach *blizzard* and *forecast.*	*blizzard* A *blizzard* is a big snowstorm with lots of wind and blowing snow. Sometimes school is cancelled after a *blizzard* because the roads and sidewalks have too much snow. **Have children say the word. Have you ever seen a *blizzard?* What makes *blizzards* dangerous?**	
		forecast TV news and newspapers give a weather *forecast* every day. A *forecast* tells what is going to happen. **Have children say the word. Scientists study weather patterns and then make *forecasts* about future weather. If the *forecast* for tomorrow is sunny, what might you wear?**	
	Display the words on the Amazing Words board.	**2 Display the Words** Have children say each word as they look at it. **You can find word parts and syllables you know in bigger words.** Read *bliz/zard* as you run your hand under the syllables. **What is the first syllable in *blizzard?*** *(bliz)* **What is the second syllable?** *(zard)* Repeat for *fore/cast.* Children can decode both words.	
	Monitor understanding.	**3 Use the Words** Ask children to use each word in a sentence. Model a sentence if children need help.	
MORE PRACTICE		Use oral vocabulary to discuss weather changes. **Why is it important to pay attention to weather *forecasts?* What would you do if the *forecast* called for a *blizzard?* What would you do if the *forecast* was wrong?**	

Read a Passage

Reading "North Wind and Sun," pp. 146–157

| To Do | To Say | 10 minutes |

Teach compare/contrast.

Scaffold instruction.

Introduce the skill.

Model the skill. Display pp. 142–143.

Apply the skill.

Today you will compare and contrast. Remember, when you compare and contrast, you tell how two or more things are alike and how they are different. For example, we can compare Katy and Alan on these pages. One way they are alike is they both wear hats to protect their heads. One way they are different is that Alan's hat covers his whole head and Katy's hat covers just the top of her head.

Let's compare and contrast the weather yesterday and the weather today. Think about what the weather was like yesterday. Is there one way the weather from yesterday and today is alike? What are some ways the weather is different?

Develop language and concepts.

See Routine Card 6. Display pp. 146–157.

Model using key words and concepts.

Key concepts: *bragging, contest, stronger, huffs, puffs, burns, hotter, not give up, force*

Monitor children's use of vocabulary.

Before Reading Read the title. Do a structured picture walk.

pp. 146–147 North Wind and Sun are bragging. When you brag, you tell others how great you are. Is it polite to brag? North Wind and Sun will have a contest to see who is stronger. The one who can make the lady take off her hat will win.

pp. 148–151 North Wind huffs and puffs. Demonstrate. Why? North Wind wants to blow the lady's hat off. Lemons blow off trees, but the lady holds her hat tightly.

pp. 152–155 North Wind gives up. Now it is Sun's turn. Sun shines brightly. What do you think Sun's plan is? Sun makes the lady feel hot. She takes off her coat. Sun burns hotter. Now the lady takes off her hat.

pp. 156–157 Sun did not give up, and he didn't use force, so he wins the contest. Now the lady is enjoying a nice picnic by the stream.

Now turn to your partner and talk about the pictures, using the same words I did.

Guide comprehension.

Monitor independent reading.

Use Routine Cards 2 and 3.

During Reading Read the pages in a whisper. Raise your hand if you need help. As you read, compare and contrast the characters.

pp. 146–147 What is one way that North Wind and Sun are alike? (Both brag about themselves.) They both think they are strong. Both of them like to brag. How is the lady different from North Wind and Sun? (The lady is human; North Wind and Sun represent things in nature.)

pp. 148–155 Compare and contrast North Wind's and Sun's actions during the contest. (Both try to get the lady to take her hat off. North Wind uses strong winds, but Sun uses heat. North Wind quits, but Sun doesn't. North Wind uses force, but Sun doesn't.)

pp. 156–157 How is the weather at the end of the story different from the weather during the contest? (The weather is nice at the end. During the contest, it was too windy or too hot.) Do North Wind and Sun both work hard to win the contest? (Yes, but North Wind uses force, and using force is not a good way to win.)

Guide retelling.

Prompt children as they retell the story.

After Reading Have a child retell the story while the others assist. What happens at the beginning? in the middle? at the end? See Monitor Retelling, p. 246.

Homework

Practice Book, p. 95, Compare and Contrast

ACTIVITY 1 Reread for Fluency

Paired Reading "North Wind and Sun," pp. 146–149

5–10 minutes

To Do	To Say
CORRECTIVE FEEDBACK	Pair children. Monitor paired reading.	Children read pp. 146–149 orally, switching readers at the end of the first page. Have partners reread; now the other partner begins. For optimal fluency, children should reread three or four times. Give feedback on children's oral reading and use of the blending strategy. See Routine Cards 1 and 4.
MORE PRACTICE		Instead of rereading just pp. 146–149, have children reread the entire selection three or four times. You may want to have children read along with the AudioText.

ACTIVITY 2 Word Work

Spiral Review Reading Longer Words (Syllables VCCV, VCV)

5–10 minutes

	To Do	To Say
Review reading two-syllable words VCCV and VCV.	Write *rabbit* and *basket*. Draw lines between *bb* and *sk*.	You can read these words because you know how to read two-syllable words with two consonants in the middle. Remember, divide the word between the two middle consonants, read each syllable, and then blend the syllables together. What are these words? (*rabbit, basket*)
	Write *spider*. Draw a line before *d*.	When two-syllable words have just one consonant between two vowels, you have to decide how to divide the word and whether the first syllable should have a long or short vowel. Usually, the consonant goes with the second syllable, making the first vowel stand for its long sound. What is the word? (*spider*)
Scaffold instruction.	Write *lemons*. Draw a line after *m*.	If you use a long vowel sound for the first syllable and the word you say doesn't make sense, then put the consonant with the first syllable and use a short vowel sound for the first syllable. What is the word? (*lemons*)
	Distribute white boards.	**Sort Words** Use a chart to sort words by their syllabication patterns. Have children write *rab/bit, spi/der,* and *lem/ons* at the tops of their boards. Then list these words on the board: *tennis, clover, trumpet, cabin, helmet, bacon, pilot, seven, winter, river, lazy, clever.* Have children decide how to divide each word and write it in the appropriate column. Call on children to read the sorted words and discuss how the words in each column are alike.

rab/bit	spi/der	lem/ons
tennis	clover	cabin
trumpet	bacon	seven
helmet	pilot	river
winter	lazy	clever

CORRECTIVE FEEDBACK	**MONITOR PROGRESS**	*If . . .* children have difficulty reading the words, *then . . .* have them compare the words to examples of the syllable patterns and blend the words sound-by-sound.

For more practice, see next page

Continued Spiral Review

MORE PRACTICE		
	Model reading words in sentences.	When I read a sentence, I read each word without stopping between the words. If I come to a word I don't know, I blend it. Then I read the sentence again. Model reading this sentence, stopping to blend *shivers: Corbin shivers by the frozen pond.*
		Have each child read a sentence.
	Write practice sentences.	**Get out the napkins, the butter, and the salad.** **Jason and his baby sister will stay at this hotel with their mom and dad.** **In a moment this shop will be open to the public.**
	Phonological and Phonemic Awareness	Optional practice activities, pp. 280–283

ACTIVITY 3 ## Read Together

Choral Reading "The Telephone Call," p. 158

	To Do	To Say	10 minutes
Develop language and concepts.	Display p. 158.	**Before Reading** How do you feel when it's raining outside? What do you do on rainy days? Allow children to share their thoughts. These kids are having a telephone conversation. Talking to a friend is a good way to spend time inside on a rainy day.	
Model fluent reading.	Model prosody.	Read the title of the poem. Ask children to predict what it is about. Poems often have rhythm, or a strong beat. When I read poems, I try to read with rhythm. I also try to use my voice to show how the speaker in the poem feels. Read the poem rhythmically and expressively. Read it a second time, having children point to each word. Have them identify rhyming words.	
	Build fluency through choral reading.	**Choral Reading** Now read the poem aloud with me. Try to make your voice sound like mine as we read. Reread the poem several times with children.	
Develop concepts.	Monitor listening comprehension.	**After Reading** How does the speaker feel at the beginning of the poem? Why? What makes the speaker feel "better right away"? What makes you feel better when you have to stay inside on a rainy day?	

ACTIVITY 4 ## Build Concepts

Oral Vocabulary *blizzard, condition, forecast, predict, terrifying*

	To Do	To Say	5–10 minutes
Review oral vocabulary.	Read the words on the Amazing Words board.	**Focus on Letter-Sounds** Remember, you can find sounds and word parts you know in big words. <ul><li>Which word has two *z*'s in the middle? How do you divide this word into syllables?</li><li>Which words have the sound /k/? Say each word part with /k/ in it.</li><li>Which word has a *y* in it? What sound does *y* stand for in this word?</li></ul>	
	Encourage discussion.	**Elicit Personal Experiences** Review the meanings of the words. Then ask questions to connect the words to children's personal experiences. <ul><li>When you watch a weather *forecast* on TV, what kinds of weather *conditions* do you hope the reporter will *predict?* Why?</li><li>Has a *blizzard* or some other kind of dangerous weather *condition* ever kept our school closed? Tell about the storm.</li><li>What weather *condition* do you think is the most *terrifying?* Why?</li></ul>	

MORE PRACTICE

Apply oral vocabulary to new situations.

- If I say something could happen in a *blizzard,* shiver and say, "Blizzard." If not, do nothing. Snow drifts. (blizzard) Strong winds. (blizzard) Hot temperatures. (not) Slippery roads. (blizzard)
- If I say something that is *terrifying,* make a scared face and say, "Terrifying." If not, do nothing. Tornadoes. (terrifying) Kittens. (not) Movie monsters. (terrifying) Chocolate cake. (not)
- If I say something that is in good condition, clap. If not, do nothing. A flat tire. (not) A bike with no scratches. (good condition) A book with a ripped cover. (not) A healthy pet. (good condition) A shiny coin. (good condition) A broken toy. (not)

ACTIVITY **5** | Write

Response to Literature Interactive Writing

| To Do | To Say | *5–10 minutes* |

Generate ideas.

Review the story "North Wind and Sun."

What can North Wind do? What can Sun do? Compare and contrast the abilities and traits of North Wind and Sun.

Share the pen.

Have children participate in writing a list of things North Wind and Sun can do.

Write these sentence starters: *North Wind can _____. Sun can _____.* Have children read the words you wrote. Then have them supply endings for each sentence. Invite individuals to write familiar letter-sounds, word parts, and high-frequency words. Have them find the spelling of high-frequency words on the Word Wall. Ask questions such as:

- **What letters are in the first syllable of** *lemons? (lem)* **How do you say this syllable?** (/lem/)

- **What letters are in the second syllable of** *lemons? (ons)* **How do you say this syllable?** (/ənz/)

Writing elements: conventions

Frequently reread what has been written while tracking the print. Point out that each sentence starts with a capital letter and ends with a period. Point out the extra space between words.

Read the completed list aloud, having children read with you. (For example, *North Wind can blow lemons off the trees. North Wind can blow robins from the branches. North Wind can make the lady shiver. Sun can burn bright and hot. Sun can make the lady take off her coat and hat.*)

MORE PRACTICE

Prompt independent writing.

Journal Writing Tell what type of weather is your favorite.

Homework

Practice Book, p. 96, High-Frequency Words

ACTIVITY 1 Assessment Options

Sentence Reading

| To Do | To Say | 5 minutes |

Assess sentence reading.

To Do: Use reproducible p. 248.

To Say: Have each child read the sentences. Record scores on the Sentence Reading Chart, p. 252. Work with one child as others complete Write Sentences below.

Never pet a tiger on its large head!
Take the poor camel to the river and wash the mud off it.
The clever robot cannot talk, even though it looks human.

CORRECTIVE FEEDBACK

MONITOR PROGRESS

If . . . children have trouble reading words with syllables V/CV and VC/V
then . . . reteach the blending strategy lesson on p. 68.

If . . . children cannot read a high-frequency word,
then . . . mark the missed word or words on a high-frequency word list and send the list home for additional practice or have them practice with a fluent reader.

If . . . children misread a word in the sentence,
then . . . correct the error and have them reread the word and then the sentence.

Practice sentence writing.

To Do: Provide white boards.

Write Sentences Have children copy the sentences from reproducible p. 248 on white boards. Have them confirm spellings by comparing the words they wrote to the words in the sentences.

Phonological and Phonemic Awareness

Optional practice activities, pp. 280–283

End-of-Unit Test

| To Do | To Say | 10 minutes |

Assess fluency and comprehension.

To Do: Use Assessment Book, p. 51.

To Say: Options for end-of-unit assessment are available in the Assessment Book.

ACTIVITY 2 Use Concepts

Oral Vocabulary *blizzard, condition, forecast, predict, terrifying*

| To Do | To Say | 5 minutes |

Check understanding of oral vocabulary.

To Do: Use the Amazing Words to wrap up the week's concept.

Monitor understanding of oral vocabulary, using Routine Card 5.

To Say: As time allows, ask questions such as these.

- Describe the pictures on pp. 128–135 using some of the week's Amazing Words.
- How do you feel when you see something *terrifying?*
- What do you *predict* will happen in class tomorrow?
- Do scientists make *predictions* when they give a *forecast?*
- Would the roads be in a dangerous *condition* during a *blizzard?* Why? Would you *predict* that the desert would have many *blizzards?* Why or why not?

Preview next week's concept.

Next week you will read about why it is important to do a good job.

ACTIVITY 3 Read to Connect

Reread "Weather Changes," pp. 128–135

| To Do | To Say | 5 minutes |

Monitor comprehension: compare/contrast.

Have children reread "Weather Changes" silently.

As you read, compare and contrast the different kinds of weather. Think about how the weather conditions are alike and different. After rereading, ask:

- **How are a big windstorm and a blizzard alike? How are they different?**
- **What is one way people can stay safe during all kinds of dangerous weather?**

Record children's comparisons on the board. (For example, both windstorms and blizzards have strong winds. A blizzard has snow, but a windstorm doesn't. People can stay safe in most kinds of bad weather by staying inside.) Children will use the list for Activity 4. Add ideas to the list as you review the selections below.

Make connections.

Have children make connections across texts.

Compare the weather described in "What Will You Need?" to the weather in "Weather Changes." Should Katy and Alan play outside during a blizzard? Why or why not? If they play outside after a blizzard, what do they need? (They should stay inside during a blizzard, but they can play outside after a blizzard if they wear warm hats, coats, mittens, and scarves.)

We also read "North Wind and Sun." Find that. Do you think Katy or Alan would wear a big hat like the lady's hat on a windy day? Why or why not? What would they wear if Sun was shining bright and hot? (They wouldn't wear a big hat on a windy day because it could blow off. On a hot day, they might wear T-shirts, shorts, sandals, and sunscreen.)

What do all the selections we read this week show us about weather changes? What is the big idea? (Weather can change quickly, so it is important to be prepared for these changes.)

ACTIVITY 4 Write

Response to Literature Independent Writing

| To Do | To Say | 5–10 minutes |

Assign expository writing.

Guide sentence correction.

Writing elements: conventions, organization

Today you will write about two different kinds of weather. Compare and contrast the two kinds of weather, telling how they are alike and different. Encourage children to use words you wrote on the board for Activity 3 as they write.

Have children check their writing by asking themselves these questions.

- Did I use a capital letter to begin each sentence and proper noun?
- Did I use correct marks at the ends of sentences?
- Did I include words such as *both* and *like* to show how two things are alike? Did I include words such as *not, but,* or *different* to show how two things are different?

MORE PRACTICE

Have children share their sentences with the group. Write them on the board and have children practice reading and writing each other's sentences.

Homework   Practice Book, p. 97, Writing

Unit 5 Week 1 *Good Job!*

Why is it important to do a good job?

Objectives *This week students will . . .*

Phonemic Awareness
- segment compounds into words and words into sounds

Phonics
- blend and read compound words
- apply knowledge of letter-sounds to decode unknown words when reading
- recognize high-frequency words *book, heard, hold, listen, piece*

Fluency
- practice fluency with oral rereading

Vocabulary
- build concepts and oral vocabulary: *career, community, employee, responsible, teamwork*

Text Comprehension
- read connected text
- identify main idea to improve comprehension
- write in response to literature

Word Work *This week's phonics focus is . . .*

Compound Words

High-Frequency Words *Tested Vocabulary*

The first appearance of each word in the Student Reader is noted below.

book	This **book** has many pictures. (p. 12)
heard	I **heard** the noise. (p. 10)
hold	Will you **hold** my hat? (p. 10) That jug can **hold** a lot of water.
listen	When you **listen,** you try to hear something or someone. (p. 10)
piece	I lost a **piece** of the puzzle. (p. 9)

Amazing Words *Oral Vocabulary*

The week's vocabulary is related to the concept of the importance of doing a good job.

career	the work or job a person does
community	the people who live around you
employee	someone who works for a person, a company, the government, or something else
responsible	expected to take care of something or someone
teamwork	when a group of people put a lot of effort into doing something together

Student Reader Unit 5 *This week students will read the following selections.*

6	**Let's Find Out: Good Job!**	Expository Nonfiction
14	**Soaring Skyscrapers**	Expository Nonfiction
22	**Three Small Frogs**	Animal Fantasy
32	**Rhyme and Riddle**	Riddle

Daily Lesson Plan

	ACTIVITIES	MATERIALS
Day 1	**Word Work** Phonemic Awareness: Segment Compound Words Phonics: Blend Compound Words High-Frequency Words *book, heard, hold, listen, piece* **Build Concepts** *community, responsible, teamwork* **Read a Passage** "Good Job!" pp. 6–13 Comprehension: Use Strategies Reread for Fluency	Student White Boards Tested Vocabulary Cards *Sing with Me Big Book* and Audio CD Student Reader: Unit 5 Routine Cards 1, 2, 3, 4, 6, 7 AudioText Practice Book, p. 98, Compound Words
Day 2	**Reread for Fluency** **Word Work** Phonemic Awareness: Segment Compound Words Phonics: Blend and Build Compound Words High-Frequency Words *book, heard, hold, listen, piece* **Read a Passage** "Soaring Skyscrapers," pp. 14–21 Comprehension: Use Strategies **Write** Response to Literature: Shared Writing	Student Reader: Unit 5 Routine Cards 1, 2, 3, 4, 6, 7 Tested Vocabulary Cards AudioText Student White Boards
Day 3	**Reread for Fluency** **Word Work** Phonemic Awareness: Segment Compound Words Phonics: Fluent Word Reading High-Frequency Words *book, heard, hold, listen, piece* **Build Concepts** *career, employee* **Read a Passage** "Three Small Frogs," pp. 22–31 Comprehension: Main Idea	Student Readers: Units 4 and 5 Routine Cards 1, 2, 3, 4, 6 Tested Vocabulary Cards AudioText Student White Boards Practice Book, p. 99, Main Idea and Details
Day 4	**Reread for Fluency** **Word Work** Phonics: Spiral Review Phonological and Phonemic Awareness Activities, pp. 280–283 **Read Together** "Rhyme and Riddle," p. 32 Comprehension: Listening **Build Concepts** *career, community, employee,* *responsible, teamwork* **Write** Response to Literature: Interactive Writing	Student Reader: Unit 5 Routine Cards 1, 4 AudioText Student White Boards Practice Book, p. 100, High-Frequency Words
Day 5	**Assessment Options** Fluency, Comprehension Sentence Reading; Passage Reading Phonological and Phonemic Awareness Activities, pp. 280–283 **Use Concepts** *career, community, employee,* *responsible, teamwork* **Read to Connect** "Good Job!" pp. 6–13 Comprehension: Main Idea **Write** Response to Literature: Independent Writing	Reproducible p. 248 Sentence Reading Chart, p. 253 Student White Boards Fluency Progress Chart, p. 245 Monitor Retelling, p. 246 Student Reader: Unit 5 Routine Card 5 Practice Book, p. 101, Writing

See pp. xvi–xvii for how *My Sidewalks* integrates instructional practices for ELL.

Phonemic Awareness Segment Compounds into Words, Words into Sounds

	To Do	**To Say**	*2 minutes*

Scaffold instruction.

Distribute white boards.
Write *baseball.*

Model Listen to the two shorter words that make up *baseball.* Segment and clap out *base, ball.* Listen to the sounds in the first word, *base.* Stretch the sounds /b/ /āāā/ /sss/ as you write *b, a, s, e.* Repeat. This time have children write the letters as you write. **Listen to the sounds in the second word, *ball.*** Stretch the sounds /b/ /ȯȯȯ/ /lll/ as you write *b, a, l, l.* Repeat. This time have children write the letters as you write.

Lead children in segmenting compounds into words and words into sounds.

Teach and Practice Have children segment and clap out the words in *baseball: base, ball.* Then have them say the sounds as you point to the letters in each of the shorter words. (/b/ /ā/ /s/, /b/ /ȯ/ /l/) Continue the activity with these words:

sandbox   bedtime   inside   weekend   rainbow   sunlight

Blending Strategy Compound Words

	To Do	**To Say**	*5–10 minutes*

Use the blending routine.

Scaffold instruction.

Write *bed* and *time.*

1 Connect You studied words like these already. What are these words? *(bed, time)* Today we will learn about combining two words, such as *bed* and *time,* to make a compound word.

Write *bedtime.*

2 Model *Bedtime* is a compound word. A compound word is made up of two shorter words. The meaning of a compound word is often made up of the meanings of the two shorter words. What two words do you hear in *bedtime? (bed* and *time)* What does *bedtime* mean? (the time to go to bed) To blend a compound word, read the two shorter words and then blend them together. This is how I blend this word: *bed, time, bedtime.*

b e d   t i m e

Write *bedtime.*

3 Listen and Write When you write compound words, write each of the shorter words with no space between them. First write *bed: b, e, d.* Write *time* after it: *t, i, m, e.* As you write, say the sounds of each shorter word to yourself. Say each shorter word aloud. Say the compound word aloud.

CORRECTIVE FEEDBACK

Write each practice word. Monitor student practice.

4 Group Practice Let's try reading these compound words. Then we'll say the two words that form each one. Give feedback, using the *if . . . then* statements on Routine Card 1.

lunchbox (lunch, box)   bathtub (bath, tub)   sunshine (sun, shine)
snowman (snow, man)   oatmeal (oat, meal)   kickball (kick, ball)

5 Individual Practice Write the words; have each child blend two of them.

classmate   popcorn   sidewalk   sailboat   flagpole   daylight

MORE PRACTICE

Model building compound words.

Build Words Write shorter words on a chart. Have children copy the chart, blend the shorter words, and write the compound word in the third column.

1st Word	2nd Word	Compound Word
ant	hill	anthill
back	yard	backyard
rain	coat	raincoat
fire	fly	firefly

High-Frequency Words *book, heard, hold, listen, piece*

To Do	To Say
Teach high-frequency words. Display *book*.	**1 Say, Spell, Write** Use the Tested Vocabulary Cards. Display *book*. Here are some words that we won't sound out. We'll spell them. This word is *book*: *b, o, o, k* (point to each letter), *book*. What is this word? What are the letters in the word? Now you write *book*. *Routine*
Point to the first and last letters in *book*.	**2 Identify Letter-Sounds** Let's look at the sounds in *book* that you do know. What is this letter? *(b)* What is the sound for this letter? *(/b/)* Continue with *k*.
	3 Demonstrate Meaning Tell me a sentence using *book*. Model a sentence if children need help.
Display *heard, hold, listen,* and *piece*.	Repeat the Routine with *heard, hold, listen,* and *piece*. Children can identify these letter-sounds and word parts: *heard* (*h*/h/, *d*/d/), *hold* (*h*/h/, *ld*/ld/), *listen* (*lis, n*/n/), and *piece* (*p*/p/, *c*/s/). Have children write the words in their word banks. Add the words to the Word Wall. Point out that the words they are learning are on p. 33.

ACTIVITY 2 Build Concepts

Oral Vocabulary *community, responsible, teamwork*

To Do	To Say
Introduce oral vocabulary. Display p. 21 of *Sing with Me Big Book*. Play audio CD.	This week you will learn about doing a good job. Listen for the Amazing Words *community, responsible,* and *teamwork* as I sing this song. Play or sing the song. Then have children sing it with you. *Routine*
	1 Introduce, Demonstrate, and Apply
Scaffold Instruction. Follow the Routine to teach *community, responsible,* and *teamwork*.	***community*** Because the firefighters do a good job, the whole *community* feels safe. The people who live around you are your *community*. The neighborhood you live in is also your *community*. Have children say the word. **Our *community* may pitch in to clean up an empty lot.** Which people in our *community* help us feel better when we are sick?
	responsible In the song, Anna is *responsible* for hooking up the hose. If someone is *responsible*, that person must do a job or take charge of something that others are counting on. Have children say the word. **I am *responsible* for teaching this class.** What are you *responsible* for in school?
	teamwork The firefighters must practice *teamwork* to get their job done right. It is *teamwork* when a group of people puts a lot of effort into doing something together. Have children say the word. **A class may earn money for a trip by using *teamwork* to wash cars.** When do we use *teamwork*?
Display the words on the Amazing Words board.	**2 Display the Words** Have children say each word as they look at it. **You can find sounds and word parts you know in big words.** Read *team/work*. Children can decode *team* and should know the high-frequency word *work*. For *responsible* and *community*, they can identify these letter-sounds and word parts: *responsible* (*r*/r/, *spon, s*/s/, *b*/b/), *community* (*c*/k/, *m*/m/, *n*/n/, *ty*/tē/).
Monitor understanding.	**3 Use the Words** Ask children to use each word in a sentence. Model a sentence if children need help.

MORE PRACTICE

Use oral vocabulary to discuss the song. **How do the firefighters keep the *community* safe? How do they use *teamwork* to put out a fire? What is Roger *responsible* for?**

Read a Passage

Build Background "Good Job!" pp. 6–13

To Do	To Say	10 minutes

Develop language and concepts.

See Routine Card 7. Read aloud pp. 1–5 of the student book.

Preview the Week Read aloud the title on p. 1. The selections in this book are about being responsible. Use pp. 2–3 to preview the weeks in this unit and p. 5 to preview the selections in this week. Ask children what they think each selection will be about.

Scaffold instruction.

See Routine Card 6. Display pp. 6–13.

Ask questions and elaborate on answers to develop language.

Key concepts: *jobs, responsible, worker, teamwork, community*

Before Reading Read the title aloud. Do a structured picture walk with children.

pp. 6–7 What jobs are shown on p. 6? If needed, point out picture details to help children identify each job. What do you know about these jobs? Point to the truck. What does the truck driver do? Yes, truck drivers drive big trucks across the country. They deliver food, machine parts, and other things.

pp. 8–9 What are these workers doing? (making cars and parts for cars) Each worker is responsible for making a different car part. What will they do with all the parts? (put them together to make a car) It takes teamwork to make a car!

pp. 10–11 What are most of these workers doing? (fixing the road) Why is this job important to the community? (roads need to be safe for drivers)

pp. 12–13 What kinds of jobs are these kids doing? If needed, point out details in each picture to help children identify each task. Do you do any of these jobs? Which jobs are you responsible for doing at home?

Teach story words.

Write *worker*.

You will read this word in the selection. It is *worker*. Have children say the word and spell it. Review its meaning. Let's read to find out more about jobs that workers do and why it's important that they do a good job.

Guide comprehension.

Monitor independent reading. Model strategic reading. Use Routine Cards 2 and 3.

During Reading Read the page in a whisper. Raise your hand if you need help with a word. Stop at the end of each page to model asking questions. For example, for p. 6: After I read, I ask myself: What did I learn about jobs? What is this page mainly about? The author says, "People work at lots and lots of jobs." I see pictures of different types of jobs people do. I learned that people work hard at many different kinds of jobs.

Summarize.

Use oral vocabulary to develop the concept.

After Reading How do workers use *teamwork* to make a car? How do workers who fix roads help keep their *community* safe? What other types of jobs keep a *community* safe? What kinds of jobs might a kid be *responsible* for at home? Do you use *teamwork* at home?

Reread for Fluency "Good Job!" pp. 6–9

To Do	To Say	5–10 minutes

CORRECTIVE FEEDBACK

Monitor oral reading.

Read pp. 6–9 aloud. Read them three or four times so your reading gets better each time. Give feedback on children's oral reading and use of the blending strategy. See Routine Cards 1 and 4.

MORE PRACTICE

Instead of rereading just pp. 6–9, have children reread the entire selection three or four times. You may want to have children read along with the AudioText.

Homework

Practice Book, p. 98, Phonics: Compound Words

ACTIVITY 1 Reread for Fluency

Paired Reading "Good Job!" pp. 10–13

To Do	To Say	

5–10 minutes

CORRECTIVE FEEDBACK

Pair children. Monitor paired reading.

Children read pp. 10–13 orally, switching readers at the end of the first page. Have partners reread; now the other partner begins. For optimal fluency, children should reread three or four times. Give feedback on children's oral reading and use of the blending strategy. See Routine Cards 1 and 4.

MORE PRACTICE

Instead of rereading just pp. 10–13, have children reread the entire selection three or four times. You may want to have children read along with the AudioText.

ACTIVITY 2 Word Work

Phonemic Awareness Segment Compounds into Words, Words into Sounds

To Do	To Say	

2 minutes

Scaffold instruction.

Distribute white boards.
Write *sailboat*.

Model Listen to the two shorter words that make up *sailboat.* Segment and clap out *sail, boat.* Listen to the sounds in the first word, *sail.* Stretch the sounds /sss/ /āāā/ /lll/ as you write *s, ai, l.* Repeat. This time have children write the letters as you write. Listen to the sounds in the second word, *boat.* Stretch the sounds /b/ /ōōō/ /t/ as you write *b, oa, t.* Repeat. This time have children write the letters as you write.

Lead children in segmenting compounds into words and words into sounds as they write.

Teach and Practice Have children segment and clap out the words in *sailboat: sail, boat.* Then have them say the sounds as you point to the letters in each of the shorter words. (/s/ /ā/ /l/, /b/ /ō/ /t/) Continue the activity with these words:

cannot   pancake   sunrise   snowflake   birthday   railroad

Blend and Build Words Compound Words

To Do	To Say	5–10 minutes

Review blending compound words.

CORRECTIVE FEEDBACK

Write *sunrise*.

You can read this word because you know how to read compound words. Remember, compound words are made up of two shorter words. Read each shorter word and then blend them together. Here's how I blend this word: *sun, rise, sunrise.* Now you try it: *sun, rise, sunrise.*

Write the practice words. Monitor student practice.

Write the words; have each child blend two of them. Give feedback, using the *if . . . then* statements on Routine Card 1.

backbone　　nighttime　　beehives*　　blueprint*　　tightrope*　　catfish

Check understanding of practice words.

*Remind children to think about each shorter word to try to figure out the meanings of compound words. If needed, help them with meanings. *Beehives* are nests or boxes where bees live. A *blueprint* is a drawing that shows the plan for making or building something. In a circus, people walk across a *tightrope* tied high above the ground on poles.

Distribute white boards.

Build Words List these shorter words on the board or on sets of index cards: *rain, sun, back, snow, mail* in one group; *bow, shine, pack, box, storm* in another group. Have children build compound words by combining pairs of listed words. Model choosing and blending *rain, bow, rainbow.* Then call on children to read the compound words, identify the two shorter words in each one, and use them in sentences or tell what they mean.

MORE PRACTICE

Display pp. 6–13. Model finding compound words.

Sort Words Find compound words in "Good Job!" Have children scan the selection and make a list of the compound words they find. Call on children to read the compound words, identify the two shorter words in each one, and use them in sentences or tell what they mean. Model the activity using *inside* on p. 6.

High-Frequency Words *book, heard, hold, listen, piece*

To Do	To Say	3 minutes

Teach high-frequency words.

Lead cumulative review.

Display *book, heard, hold, listen,* and *piece.*

Use the Tested Vocabulary Cards. Point to a word. Say and spell it. Have children say and spell the word. Ask children to identify familiar letter-sounds and word parts. Have them take turns reading the words.

Use the Tested Vocabulary Cards to review high-frequency words from previous weeks.

ACTIVITY **3** | Read a Passage

Reading "Soaring Skyscrapers," pp. 14–21

	To Do	**To Say**	*10–15 minutes*

Develop language and concepts.

Scaffold instruction.

See Routine Cards 6 and 7. Display pp. 14–21.

Ask questions and elaborate on answers to develop language.

Key concepts: *skyscraper, process, workers, blueprint, machines, steel beams, hard hats*

Before Reading Have children recall what they learned about different jobs. Read the title. Do a structured picture walk.

pp. 14–15 Very tall buildings are called skyscrapers because they seem to scrape the sky. Where do we usually find skyscrapers? (in big cities)

pp. 16–17 It takes a step-by-step process and many workers to build a skyscraper. First, workers look at a blueprint, a plan for making the building. Point to it. After they study the blueprint, they start building.

pp. 18–19 What is this machine called? (a bulldozer) Yes, bulldozers, dump trucks, cement trucks, cranes, and other machines are used to build a skyscraper. These steel beams make the floors of a skyscraper very strong. The workers walk carefully on beams high above the ground. They wear hard hats to protect their heads.

pp. 20–21 Why do you think these people like to watch the workers?

Teach story words.

Write *skyscraper* and *worker*.

You will read these words in the selection: *skyscraper* and *worker*. Have children say each word and spell it. Review meanings. Let's read more about workers who build a skyscraper.

Guide comprehension.

Monitor independent reading.

Use Routine Cards 2 and 3.

During Reading Read the pages in a whisper. Raise your hand if you need help with a word. As we read, ask yourself: What am I learning about workers who build a skyscraper? What is this mainly about?

pp. 14–17 What is a skyscraper? (a very tall building) What did you learn about building a skyscraper? (It is a big job. The first step is to make plans. Then the builders use the plans to start building.)

pp. 18–21 What are these pages mainly about? (It takes many workers and big machines to build a skyscraper.)

Model summarizing.

Think aloud.

After Reading What did you learn about building a skyscraper? What was the selection mainly about? Model how to summarize. The first two pages explain that building a skyscraper is a big job. The next pages tell about the steps for building a skyscraper and what workers do. I put that all together and pick the most important idea. The selection is mainly about how a skyscraper is built.

MORE PRACTICE

Develop oral vocabulary.

Does it take *teamwork* to build a skyscraper? What jobs might different workers be *responsible* for? Does everyone want a skyscraper built in their *community*? Why or why not?

ACTIVITY **4** | Write

Response to Literature Shared Writing

	To Do	**To Say**	*5 minutes*

Guide shared writing.

Write a sentence frame. Read the question.

How do workers build a skyscraper? Workers _____.

Invite children to suggest answers. Discuss and record answers to complete the sentence frame. While writing, model connecting sounds to letters and forming letters. (See pp. 257–259.) Have children read answers aloud as you track print.

ACTIVITY 1 — Reread for Fluency

Oral Reading "Soaring Skyscrapers," pp. 14–17

5–10 minutes

	To Do	To Say
CORRECTIVE FEEDBACK	Monitor oral reading.	Read pp. 14–17 aloud. Read them three or four times so your reading gets better each time. Give feedback on children's oral reading and use of the blending strategy. See Routine Cards 1 and 4.
MORE PRACTICE		Instead of rereading just pp. 14–17, have children reread the entire selection three or four times. You may want to have children read along with the AudioText.

ACTIVITY 2 — Word Work

Phonemic Awareness Segment Compounds into Words, Words into Sounds

2 minutes

	To Do	To Say
Scaffold instruction.	Distribute white boards. Write *flashlight*.	**Model** Listen to the two shorter words that make up *flashlight*. Segment and clap out *flash, light*. Listen to the sounds in the first word, *flash*. Stretch the sounds /fff/ /lll/ /aaa/ /shshsh/ as you write *fl, a, sh*. Repeat. This time have children write the letters as you write. Listen to the sounds in the second word, *light*. Stretch the sounds /lll/ /īīī/ /t/ as you write *l, igh, t*. Repeat. This time have children write the letters as you write.
	Lead children in segmenting compounds into words and words into sounds.	**Teach and Practice** Have children segment and clap out the words in *flashlight*. Then have them say the sounds as you point to the letters in each of the shorter words. (/f/ /l/ /a/ /sh/, /l/ /ī/ /t/) Continue with these words:
		nutshell campfire spaceship flagpole weekday backpack herself

Fluent Word Reading Compound Words

5–10 minutes

Routine

	To Do	To Say
Use the word-reading routine.	Write *homemade*.	**1 Connect** You can read this word because you know how to read compound words. Remember, read each shorter word and then blend them together. What two shorter words do you see? *(home, made)* What is the word? *(homemade)*
Scaffold instruction.	Write *bathtub, snowball,* and *mailbox*.	**2 Model** When you come to a new word, look at all the letters in the word and think about its vowel sounds and its parts. Say the sounds and word parts to yourself, and then read the word. Model reading *bathtub, snowball,* and *mailbox* in this way. When you come to a new word, what will you do?
	Write each practice word.	**3 Group Practice** Let's read these compound words. Look at all the letters, think about the vowel sounds and parts, and say the sounds and parts to yourself. When I point to the word, let's read it together. Allow 2–3 seconds previewing time per word.
		hallway cupcake rainfall fireplace highway barnyard grapevine sunburn
CORRECTIVE FEEDBACK	**MONITOR PROGRESS**	**If . . .** children have difficulty previewing and reading whole words, **then . . .** have them use sound-by-sound blending. **If . . .** children can't read the words fluently at a rate of 1–2 seconds per word, **then . . .** continue practicing the list.

MORE PRACTICE	Model reading words in sentences.	When I read a sentence, I read each word without stopping between the words. If I come to a word I don't know, I blend it. Then I read the sentence again. Model reading this sentence, stopping to blend *birthday: We had homemade cupcakes at my birthday party.*
	Write practice sentences.	Have each child read a sentence. **The sunscreen is inside my backpack.** **Do you like to play baseball or kickball?** **Look at that rainbow above the treetops!**

High-Frequency Words *book, heard, hold, listen, piece*

3 minutes

	To Do	**To Say**
Review high-frequency words.	Display *book, heard, hold, listen,* and *piece.*	Use the Tested Vocabulary Cards. Point to a word. Say and spell it. Have children say and spell the word. Ask children to identify familiar letter-sounds and word parts. Have them take turns reading the words.

ACTIVITY **3** Build Concepts

Oral Vocabulary *career, employee*

5–10 minutes

	To Do	**To Say**
Teach oral vocabulary.	Display pp. 6 and 16 of the student book.	This week we've read about different *careers* that workers can have. For example, this man has a *career* as a cab driver. He is an *employee* of a cab company. These workers have *careers* as builders. They are *employees* of a construction company. Today we'll read a make-believe story about some frogs who are builders.
		1 Introduce, Demonstrate, and Apply
Scaffold instruction.	Follow the Routine to teach *career* and *employee.*	**career** One *career* we've read about is a truck driver. A person's *career* is the work or job the person does. Have children say the word. My *career* is teaching. What *career* might you want some day?
		employee Workers who make parts of a car are *employees* of a car factory. An *employee* is someone who works for a person, a company, the government, or something else. Have children say the word. I am an *employee* of our school district. Who else is an *employee* of our school?
	Display the words on the Amazing Words board.	**2 Display the Words** Have children say each word as they look at it. You can find sounds and word parts you know in big words. What letter do you see at the beginning of *career? (c)* What sound does it stand for? (/k/) Repeat for *r*/r/. For *employee,* children can identify *em*/em/, *pl*/pl/, and *ee*/ē/.
	Monitor understanding.	**3 Use the Words** Ask children to use each word in a sentence. Model a sentence if children need help.
MORE PRACTICE		Use oral vocabulary to discuss different jobs. What is a *career* where people help animals feel better? Do you know an adult who is an *employee?* Who does that adult work for?

ACTIVITY **4** Read a Passage

Reading "Three Small Frogs," pp. 22–31

| To Do | To Say | 10 minutes |

Teach main idea and supporting details.

Scaffold instruction.

Develop language and concepts.

Introduce the skill.

Model the skill. Display p. 146 of the student book. Draw a web listing the main idea in the center and details as outer spokes.

Apply the skill.

See Routine Card 6.

Display pp. 22–31.

Model using key words and concepts.

Key concepts: *built, lily pads, blew down, house, cattails, brick, chimney, fireplace*

Monitor children's use of vocabulary.

Guide comprehension.

Monitor independent reading.

Use Routine Cards 2 and 3.

Guide retelling.

Prompt children as they retell the story.

Today you will find the main idea of a story. Remember, the main idea is the most important idea in a selection. Supporting details tell more about the main idea. For example, I can find the main idea of "North Wind and Sun," a story we read last week. North Wind and Sun have a contest to see who is stronger. North Wind tries to blow the hat off a lady's head, but it stays on. Sun shines hot, so the lady takes off her hat. The story is mainly about North Wind and Sun's contest to see who can make the lady take off her hat.

Listen to this short story. Kate has a new baby brother. The baby sleeps and cries a lot. He is very small. What is the main idea? (Kate has a baby brother.) What are some details? (The baby sleeps, cries, and is small.)

Before Reading Read the title. Do a structured picture walk.

pp. 22–23 The three frogs each built a home. The first frog made his home from lily pads. Lily pads are the floating leaves of water lily plants, plants that grow in the soil of the pond's floor.

pp. 24–25 Point to the destroyed lily pad house. Snake blew down the lily pad house. Now the first frog goes to the home of the second frog. What is this home made of? These are cattails, tall, thin plants with furry brown parts at their tops. What do you think will happen next?

pp. 26–27 Snake blew down the house made of cattails. The two frogs are going to the third frog's house. It is made of brick.

pp. 28–29 Can Snake blow down the brick house? No, the brick house is too strong for Snake to blow down.

pp. 30–31 Snake tries to slide down the chimney. The third frog puts a pot of hot water in the fireplace. Snake will fall in the water.

Now turn to your partner and talk about the pictures, using the same words I did.

During Reading Read the pages in a whisper. Raise your hand if you need help with a word. As you read, ask yourself: What is the story mainly about? What is the most important idea?

pp. 22–25 What are these pages mainly about? (Snake blows down the first two houses.) The houses weren't made of strong materials. The frogs didn't do a good job building their homes.

pp. 26–29 What are these pages mainly about? (Snake couldn't blow down the brick house.) The brick house is too strong for Snake. The last frog did a good job building his home. Brick is a strong material.

pp. 30–31 What happens at the end? (The third frog puts a pot of hot water at the bottom of the chimney. Snake will fall into it.) What is the story's main idea? (A strong house and a good plan keep the frogs safe.)

After Reading Have one child retell the story while the others assist. Who are the characters? What happened at the beginning? in the middle? at the end? See Monitoring Retelling, p. 246.

Homework   Practice Book, p. 99, Main Idea and Details

ACTIVITY 1 | Reread for Fluency

Paired Reading "Three Small Frogs," pp. 22–25

	To Do	To Say	
			5–10 minutes

CORRECTIVE FEEDBACK

To Do: Pair children. Monitor paired reading.

To Say: Children read pp. 22–25 orally, switching readers at the end of the first page. Have partners reread; now the other partner begins. For optimal fluency, children should reread three or four times. Give feedback on children's oral reading and use of the blending strategy. See Routine Cards 1 and 4.

MORE PRACTICE

Instead of rereading just pp. 22–25 orally, have children reread the entire selection three or four times. You may want to have children read along with the AudioText.

ACTIVITY 2 | Word Work

Spiral Review Contractions 's, n't, 'll, 'm

	To Do	To Say	
			5–10 minutes

Review contractions.

Scaffold instruction.

To Do: Write *he's, isn't, she'll,* and *I'm.*

To Say: These words are contractions. Remember, a contraction is a short way of writing two words as one. An apostrophe takes the place of a letter or letters. You can read these words by first reading the word part before the apostrophe and then blending it with the part that comes after the apostrophe. Point to *he's.* What two words make this contraction? *(he is)* What is the word? *(he's)* Repeat with *isn't, she'll,* and *I'm.*

To Do: Distribute white boards.

To Say: **Build Words** Use a chart to make new words. Write *it is, they will, I am, are not, do not, you will,* and *here is* under the heading *Two Words.* Write a second heading, *Contractions.* Have children copy the words and then combine each word pair to make a contraction. Call on individuals to read the listed contractions and use them in sentences. How are contractions and compound words alike? How are they different? (Both combine two words into one. Contractions use apostrophes in place of one or more letters, but compounds show all letters for both words.)

Two Words	Contractions
it is	it's
they will	they'll
I am	I'm
are not	aren't
do not	don't
you will	you'll
here is	here's

CORRECTIVE FEEDBACK

MONITOR PROGRESS

If . . . children have difficulty building contractions,
then . . . model combining words and have children repeat using their white boards.

For more practice, see next page.

MORE PRACTICE

Model reading words in sentences.	When I read a sentence, I read each word without stopping between the words. If I come to a word I don't know, I blend it. Then I read the sentence again. Model reading this sentence, stopping to blend *we'll: After school, we'll play baseball.*	
Write practice sentences.	Have each child read a sentence.	
	What's inside your backpack? I'm sad that she couldn't go on the sailboat. We'll bring cupcakes and you'll bring popcorn.	

Phonological and Phonemic Awareness   Optional practice activities, pp. 280–283

ACTIVITY 3 Read Together

Choral Reading "Rhyme and Riddle," p. 32

	To Do	To Say	10 minutes

Develop language and concepts.

Display p. 32.

Before Reading There are three riddles on this page. Each riddle is four lines long. Point to each riddle. What is a riddle? Allow children to share what they know. A *riddle* is a puzzle where you try to give the answer. The riddle gives you clues. The answers to the riddles on this page rhyme with words at the end of each riddle's second line. Remember, rhyming words have the same ending vowel and consonant sounds. For example, the words *hot* and *not* rhyme.

Model fluent reading.

Read the title of the selection. Have children look at the photos and predict what the riddles will be about. Look at the line at the end of each riddle. This line shows where the answer goes. Listen as I read the first riddle. Notice how I pause at the end of each line. Read the first riddle, making sure to pause after each line. Pause at the end of the riddle and have children provide the answer. The answer, *vet,* rhymes with *pet.* Read the riddle a second time, this time saying the answer at the end. Have children point to each word as you read. Repeat these steps with the remaining riddles.

Build fluency through choral reading.

Choral Reading Now read the riddles aloud with me. We'll say the answer at the end of each riddle. Try to make your voice sound like mine and pause when I do. Reread each riddle several times with children.

Develop concepts.

Monitor listening comprehension.

After Reading What jobs are described in the riddles? Who uses a ladder? Who makes your pet feel better? Who explores space?

ACTIVITY 4 Build Concepts

Oral Vocabulary *career, community, employee, responsible, teamwork*

	To Do	To Say	5–10 minutes

Review oral vocabulary.

Read the words on the Amazing Words board.

Focus on Letter-Sounds Remember, you can find sounds and word parts you know in big words.

- Which words begin with *c?* What sound does *c* stand for? (/k/)
- Which words end with the sound /ē/?
- Which word has the word part *spon* in it?
- Which word is a compound word? What two shorter words make up that word?

To Do	To Say
Encourage discussion.	**Provide One Context** Review the meanings of the words. Then ask questions that place all the words in the same context. • What is something a police officer is *responsible* for doing? How might police officers use *teamwork* in their jobs? • How does a person with a *career* as a police officer help the *community*? • Is a police officer an *employee*? Who does a police officer work for?

MORE PRACTICE

Apply oral vocabulary to new situations.	• If you have a *career* where you are an *employee,* do you work for yourself or for a company or other person? (company or other person) • If I use *teamwork,* do I work with a group or by myself? (group) • Name some jobs people have in our *community*.

ACTIVITY **5** Write

Response to Literature Interactive Writing

| To Do | To Say |
5–10 minutes

Generate ideas.

Review the story "Three Small Frogs."	Which houses did Snake blow down? What were those houses made of? Which house could he not blow down? Why? Discuss why Snake was able to blow the first two houses down but not the last house. It is important to do a good job when you build a house. A house needs to be strong.

Share the pen.

Have children participate in writing a list of ways they could build a strong house.	Write *We can build a strong house with* _____. Have children read the words you wrote. Then have them supply endings for the sentence. Invite individuals to write familiar letter-sounds, word parts, and high-frequency words. Have them find the spelling of high-frequency words on the Word Wall. Ask questions such as: • What two sounds do you hear at the beginning of *bricks?* (/br/) What letters stand for these sounds? *(br)* • What is the vowel sound in *bricks?* (/i/) What is the letter for /i/? *(i)* • What is the last sound in *bricks* before we add the ending *-s?* (/k/) What two letters can stand for /k/ in the middle or end of a word? *(ck)*
Writing elements: conventions	Frequently reread what has been written while tracking the print. Point out that each sentence ends with a period. Point out the extra space between words and between sentences. Read the completed list aloud, having children read with you. (For example, *We can build a strong house with bricks. We can build a strong house with pieces of wood. We can build a strong house with nails.*)

MORE PRACTICE

Prompt independent writing.	**Journal Writing** Tell about the place where you live.

| *Homework* | Practice Book, p. 100, High-Frequency Words |

ACTIVITY 1 Assessment Options

Sentence Reading

To Do **To Say**   *5 minutes*

Assess sentence reading.

Use reproducible p. 248.

Have each child read the sentences. Record scores on the Sentence Reading Chart, p. 253. Work with one child as others complete Write Sentences below.

Listen to the bluebirds sing from the treetops at sunrise!
I heard you ate a big piece of birthday cake.
My backpack can hold a baseball, a book, and my lunchbox.

CORRECTIVE FEEDBACK

MONITOR PROGRESS

If . . . children have trouble reading compound words,
then . . . reteach the blending strategy lesson on p. 84.

If . . . children cannot read a high-frequency word,
then . . . mark the missed word or words on a high-frequency word list and send the list home for additional practice or have them practice with a fluent reader.

If . . . children misread a word in the sentence,
then . . . correct the error and have them reread the word and then the sentence.

Practice sentence writing.

Provide white boards.

Write Sentences Have children copy the sentences from reproducible p. 248 on white boards. Have them confirm spellings by comparing the words they wrote to the words in the sentences.

Phonological and Phonemic Awareness

Optional practice activities, pp. 280–283

Passage Reading

To Do **To Say**   *5–10 minutes*

Assess fluency and comprehension.

Determine which children to assess this week.

Choose from these options: monitoring fluency (see pp. 244–245) and/or monitoring retelling (see p. 246). Have children reread "Three Small Frogs." Be sure each child is assessed every other week.

If you have time, assess every child.

ACTIVITY 2 Use Concepts

Oral Vocabulary *career, community, employee, responsible, teamwork*

To Do **To Say**   *5 minutes*

Check understanding of oral vocabulary.

Use the Amazing Words to wrap up the week's concept.

Monitor understanding of oral vocabulary, using Routine Card 5.

As time allows, ask questions such as these.
- Describe the pictures on pp. 6–13 using some of the week's Amazing Words.
- Tell about something you are *responsible* for doing at home. Do you like having this *responsibility?*
- Describe a time that your family used *teamwork* to complete a task or project.
- Name a person whose job is to help kids in your *community* learn. What *career* does that person have?
- Name a kind of company that has more than one *employee.* What do the *employees* at that company do?

Preview next week's concept.

Next week you will read about taking care of animals.

ACTIVITY 3 Read to Connect

Reread "Good Job!" pp. 6–13

| To Do | To Say | *10 minutes* |

Monitor comprehension: main idea and supporting details.

To Do: Have children reread "Good Job!" silently.

To Say: As you read, think about what the selection is mainly about and smaller details that tell more about the main idea. After rereading, ask:

- **What is the main idea of "Good Job!"?** (People work hard at many different kinds of jobs.)
- **What details tell more about the jobs in the selection?** (Details could include: Some jobs are inside buildings; some jobs are outside; some people drive trucks; some people make cars.)
- **Why is it important to do a good job?** Record children's responses in a list on the board. (For example, it is important to do a good job to help others, to make something work well, to make things safe, to feel proud of your work, and so on.) Children will use the list for Activity 4.

Make connections.

To Do: Have children make connections across texts.

To Say: We also read "Soaring Skyscrapers." Find that. Why does it take teamwork to do a good job building a skyscraper? Add children's ideas to the list started above. (It takes many workers and many steps to build a skyscraper. Each step must be done just right.)

We also read "Three Small Frogs," about frogs that build houses out of different things. Did all the frogs do a good job building their houses? Why or why not? (The third frog did a good job because his brick home was strong. Snake couldn't blow it down.) Ask children to name any other thoughts they have about why it is important to do a good job. Add new suggestions to the list on the board.

What did all the selections we read this week show us about doing a good job? What is the big idea? (It is always important to do a good job.)

ACTIVITY 4 Write

Response to Literature Independent Writing

| To Do | To Say | *5–10 minutes* |

Assign expository writing.

Guide sentence correction.

To Do: Writing elements: conventions, organization, support

To Say: Today you will write about why it is important to do a good job. Think about jobs you do at home and write reasons it is important that you do a good job. Encourage children to use words you wrote on the board for Activity 3 as they write.

Have children check their writing by asking themselves these questions.

- Did I begin each sentence and proper noun with a capital letter?
- Did I use correct marks at the ends of sentences?
- Did I check that I spelled words correctly?
- Did I add details?

MORE PRACTICE

Have children share their sentences with the group. Write their sentences on the board and have children practice reading and writing each other's sentences.

Homework Practice Book, p. 101, Writing

Unit 5 Week 2 *Taking Care of Animals*

Why should we take care of animals?

Objectives *This week students will . . .*

Phonemic Awareness
- segment words into syllables and syllables into sounds

Phonics
- blend and read words with syllables: consonant + *le*
- apply knowledge of letter-sounds to decode unknown words when reading
- recognize high-frequency words *boy, either, hundred, several, you're*

Fluency
- practice fluency with oral rereading

Vocabulary
- build concepts and oral vocabulary: *concern, growth, litter, protection, veterinarian*

Text Comprehension
- read connected text
- identify sequence to improve comprehension
- write in response to literature

Word Work *This week's phonics focus is . . .*

Syllables Consonant + *le*

High-Frequency Words *Tested Vocabulary*

The first appearance of each word in the Student Reader is noted below.

boy	A **boy** is a male child. (p. 36)
either	Choose **either** of these two toys to give to the baby. (p. 42)
hundred	One **hundred** is the number after ninety-nine. (p. 38)
several	**Several** means more than two or three but not many. (p. 37)
you're	**You're** is a short way to write you are. (p. 40) **You're** very funny.

Amazing Words *Oral Vocabulary*

The week's vocabulary is related to the concept of taking care of animals.

concern	a feeling of worry about something or a special interest in something
growth	when something gets bigger in size, length, or amount
litter	a group of young animals born at the same time to one mother
protection	keeping something safe from being harmed or damaged
veterinarian	a doctor who treats animals

Student Reader Unit 5 *This week students will read the following selections.*

Daily Lesson Plan

	ACTIVITIES	MATERIALS
Day 1	**Word Work** Phonemic Awareness: Segment Words and Syllables Phonics: Blend Words with Syllables: Consonant + *le* High-Frequency Words *boy, either, hundred, several, you're* **Build Concepts** *concern, growth, protection* **Read a Passage** "Taking Care of Animals," pp. 36–45 Comprehension: Use Strategies Reread for Fluency	Student White Boards Tested Vocabulary Cards *Sing with Me Big Book* and Audio CD Student Reader: Unit 5 Routine Cards 1, 2, 3, 4, 6, 7 AudioText Practice Book, p. 102, Syllables: Consonant + *le*
Day 2	**Reread for Fluency** **Word Work** Phonemic Awareness: Segment Words and Syllables Phonics: Blend and Build Words with Syllables: Consonant + *le* High-Frequency Words *boy, either, hundred, several, you're* **Read a Passage** "Safe Places for Strays," pp. 46–53 Comprehension: Use Strategies **Write** Response to Literature: Shared Writing	Student Reader: Unit 5 Student White Boards Letter Tiles *a, b, e, g, g, g, i, j, l, n, t, u, w* Tested Vocabulary Cards Routine Cards 1, 2, 3, 4, 6, 7 AudioText
Day 3	**Reread for Fluency** **Word Work** Phonemic Awareness: Segment Words and Syllables Phonics: Fluent Word Reading High-Frequency Words *boy, either, hundred, several, you're* **Build Concepts** *litter, veterinarian* **Read a Passage** "Snuggles and Cuddles," pp. 54–65 Comprehension: Sequence	Student Reader: Unit 5 Student White Boards Tested Vocabulary Cards Routine Cards 1, 2, 3, 4, 6 AudioText Practice Book, p. 103, Sequence
Day 4	**Reread for Fluency** **Word Work** Phonics: Spiral Review Phonological and Phonemic Awareness Activities, pp. 280–283 **Read Together** "The Monster's Pet," p. 66 Comprehension: Listening **Build Concepts** *concern, growth, litter, protection, veterinarian* **Write** Response to Literature: Interactive Writing	Student Reader: Unit 5 Routine Cards 1, 4 AudioText Student White Boards Practice Book, p. 104, High-Frequency Words
Day 5	**Assessment Options** Fluency, Comprehension Sentence Reading; Passage Reading Phonological and Phonemic Awareness Activities, pp. 280–283 **Use Concepts** *concern, growth, litter, protection, veterinarian* **Read to Connect** "Taking Care of Animals," pp. 36–45 Comprehension: Sequence **Write** Response to Literature: Independent Writing	Reproducible p. 249 Sentence Reading Chart, p. 253 Student White Boards Fluency Progress Chart, p. 245 Student Reader: Unit 5 Routine Card 5 Practice Book, p. 105, Writing

See pp. xvi–xvii for how *My Sidewalks* integrates instructional practices for ELL.

Phonemic Awareness Segment Words into Syllables, Syllables into Sounds

| | To Do | To Say | *2 minutes* |

Scaffold instruction.

Distribute white boards.
Write *little.*

Model Listen to the sounds in *little.* I hear two syllables in *little.* Point to each syllable as you read *lit/tle.* Listen to the sounds in each syllable. Stretch the sounds /lllliiit/ /tlll/ as you write *lit, tle.* Repeat. This time have children write letters as you write.

Lead children in segmenting words and syllables.

Teach and Practice Have children say the sounds in each syllable as you point to the letters. **How many syllables are there?** (two) **What are they?** *(lit, tle)* **What word does *lit/tle* make?** *(little)* Continue with these words:

mid/dle   can/dle   ta/ble   puz/zle   ca/ble   cra/dle

Blending Strategy Syllables: Consonant + *le*

| | To Do | To Say | *5–10 minutes* |

Use the blending routine.

Write *rabbit, sandy,* and *robot.*

1 Connect You already can read words like these. What are these words? *(rabbit, sandy, robot)* How many syllables do these words have? (two) What do you know about reading these words? (We can divide them into syllables, read each syllable, and blend them together to read the word.) Today we'll learn more about reading two-syllable words.

Routine

Scaffold instruction.

Write *candle.*

2 Model When you read a word that ends in a consonant plus *le,* the consonant and *le* usually make up the word's last syllable. I'll divide this word before the *d* to keep *dle* together. Draw a line before the *d.*

First I read each syllable. Cover *dle.* This is how I blend this syllable: /k/ /a/ /n/, *can.* Cover *can.* This is how I blend this syllable: /d/ /l/, *dle.* Then I blend the syllables together to read the word: *can, dle, candle.*

Write *table.*

Repeat with *table.* Remind children when a syllable ends with a consonant, the vowel sound is usually short. When it ends with a vowel, the vowel sound is usually long.

c a n d l e   t a b l e

Write *turtle.*

3 Listen and Write Write *turtle.* Draw a line before the consonant that comes before the *le.* As you write, say each syllable to yourself: *tur, tle.* Now blend the two syllables and say the word aloud.

CORRECTIVE FEEDBACK

Write each practice word. Monitor student practice.

4 Group Practice Let's try reading these words. Give feedback, using the *if . . . then* statements on Routine Card 1.

giggle   cuddle   purple   title   simple*   beetle*

5 Individual Practice Write the words; have each child blend two of them.

riddle   gentle   bottle   fable*   maple   startle*   snuggle   eagle

Check understanding of practice words.

*Children need to make sense of words that they segment and blend. If needed, help children with meanings. *Simple* means "easy." A *beetle* is a small insect. A *fable* is a make-believe story that teaches a lesson. If you *startle* someone, you surprise or scare the person. (Demonstrate looking startled.)

MORE PRACTICE

Model building words with syllables consonant + *le.*

Build Words Write pairs of syllables that can be combined to make words. Have children write the word for each pair. Call on them read the words aloud.

wig + gle   bub + ble   gen + tle   sta + ple   crum + ble   nee + dle

High-Frequency Words *boy, either, hundred, several, you're*

To Do	To Say	

3 minutes

Teach high-frequency words.

Display *boy*.

1 Say, Spell, Write Use the Tested Vocabulary Cards. Display *boy*. Here are some words that we won't sound out. We'll spell them. This word is *boy*: b, o, y (point to each letter), *boy*. What is this word? What are the letters in the word? Now you write *boy*.

Point to the *b* in *boy*.

2 Identify Letter-Sounds Let's look at the sounds in *boy* that you do know. What is this letter? *(b)* What is the sound for this letter? *(/b/)*

3 Demonstrate Meaning Tell me a sentence using *boy*. Model a sentence if children need help.

Display *either, hundred, several,* and *you're*.

Repeat the Routine with *either, hundred, several,* and *you're*. Children can identify these letter-sounds and word parts: *either* (*th*/th/, *er*/ər/), *hundred* (hun, dred), *several* (*sev*, *l*/l/), and *you're* (*y*/y/, *r*/r/). Have children write the words in their word banks. Add the words to the Word Wall. Point out that the words they are learning are on p. 67.

ACTIVITY **2** ## Build Concepts

Oral Vocabulary *concern, growth, protection*

To Do	To Say	

5–10 minutes

Introduce oral vocabulary.

Display p. 22 of *Sing with Me Big Book.* Play audio CD.

This week you will learn about taking care of animals. Listen for the Amazing Words *concern, growth,* and *protection* as I sing this song. Play or sing the song. Then have children sing it with you.

1 Introduce, Demonstrate, and Apply

Scaffold instruction.

Follow the Routine to teach *concern, growth,* and *protection.*

concern The song mentions that we should show our *concern* for animals. When you have a reason to worry about something or have a special interest in something, you have *concern* about it. Have children say the word. People have *concern* about some animals becoming extinct, or no longer existing. How might you show *concern* for these animals?

growth The song says that when we protect and care for animals, we help their *growth.* When something gets bigger in size, length, or amount, it shows *growth.* Have children say the word. A puppy's *growth* during its first year is amazing. If you need a bigger bowl for a fish, what does this tell you about the fish's *growth?*

protection The song tells us we must give animals *protection.* If you keep something from being harmed or damaged, you give it *protection.* Have children say the word. A barn gives cows *protection* from bad weather. How can people give *protection* to a pet? to wild animals?

Display the words on the Amazing Words board.

2 Display the Words Have children say each word as they look at it. You can find sounds and word parts you know in big words. Read *pro/tec/tion* as you run your hand under the syllables. How do you say the first part of the first syllable? *(/pr/)* Continue with *tec*/tek/ and *n*/n/. For *con/cern,* children can identify (*c*/k/, *n*/n/, *cern*). They can decode *growth.*

Monitor understanding.

3 Use the Words Ask children to use each word in a sentence. Model a sentence if children need help.

MORE PRACTICE

Use oral vocabulary to discuss the song. Look at the pictures of the otters and the bird. How can you tell that the animals did not have *protection?* Why might the oil hurt the animals' *growth?* How are the people showing *concern?*

Read a Passage

Build Background "Taking Care of Animals," pp. 36–45

	To Do	To Say	
			10 minutes

Develop language and concepts.

See Routine Card 7. Read aloud p. 35 of the student book.

Preview the Week Use the photograph on p. 34 to introduce this week's concept of taking care of animals. Why is it important to take care of animals? Read aloud the titles and descriptions on p. 35. Ask children what they think each selection will be about.

Scaffold instruction.

See Routine Card 6. Display pp. 36–45.

Ask questions and elaborate on answers to develop language.

Key concepts: *exercise, healthy, concern, protection, growth, gerbils, cage*

Before Reading Read the title aloud. Do a structured picture walk with children.

pp. 36–37 How are these boys taking care of their dogs? Walking a dog gives it exercise. Dogs need exercise every day to stay healthy.

pp. 38–39 This dog is running with a ball. Dogs like to play. How are the kids showing concern for their dog? (They're giving it a bath.) This dog looks like it enjoys its bath. Some may not like baths, but they need to be kept clean. People take care of pets by keeping them clean and healthy.

pp. 40–41 What are these cats doing? (hiding in a paper bag; playing with a jingle ball) Cats like to explore and play. They also need food and water every day to grow strong and healthy. How could you tell if a kitten showed growth? (It would get bigger and become a cat.)

pp. 42–43 Where do we keep pet gerbils? A wire or glass cage gives these pets protection. How does the boy show concern for his pet? He feeds it every day. The gerbil also needs fresh water and a clean cage.

pp. 44–45 Pet birds live in cages too. Like other pets, they need fresh water and food every day. Which pet do you think you could care for? Let's read to find out more about taking care of animals.

Guide comprehension.

Monitor independent reading. Model strategic reading. Use Routine Cards 2 and 3.

During Reading Read the page in a whisper. Raise your hand if you need help with a word. Stop at the end of each page to model asking questions. For example, for p. 37: After I read, I ask myself: What am I learning about taking care of animals? What is the page mainly about? The author tells how pets need to be fed and kept clean. Some pets need you to walk them and play with them. This page is mainly about how taking care of pets can be hard work.

Summarize.

Use oral vocabulary to develop the concept.

After Reading Why do pets need *protection?* Do you think it's simple or difficult to give pets *protection?* Why? What can a person do to help a young pet's *growth?* How do the kids in the selection show *concern* for their pets?

Reread for Fluency "Taking Care of Animals," pp. 36–39

	To Do	To Say	
			5–10 minutes

CORRECTIVE FEEDBACK

Monitor oral reading.

Read pp. 36–39 aloud. Read them three or four times so your reading gets better each time. Give feedback on children's oral reading and use of the blending strategy. See Routine Cards 1 and 4.

MORE PRACTICE

Instead of rereading just pp. 36–39, have children reread the entire selection three or four times. You may want to have children read along with the AudioText.

Homework   Practice Book, p. 102, Phonics: Syllables: Consonant + *le*

ACTIVITY 1 Reread for Fluency

Paired Reading "Taking Care of Animals," pp. 40–43

5–10 minutes

	To Do	To Say
CORRECTIVE FEEDBACK	Pair children. Monitor paired reading.	Children read pp. 40–43 orally, switching readers at the end of the first page. Have partners reread; now the other partner begins. For optimal fluency, children should reread three or four times. Give feedback on children's oral reading and use of the blending strategy. See Routine Cards 1 and 4.
MORE PRACTICE		Instead of rereading just pp. 40–43, have children reread the entire selection three or four times. You may want to have children read along with the AudioText.

ACTIVITY 2 Word Work

Phonemic Awareness Segment Words into Syllables, Syllables into Sounds

2 minutes

	To Do	To Say
Scaffold instruction.	Distribute white boards. Write *simple*.	**Model** Listen to the sounds in *simple*. I hear two syllables in *simple*. Point to each syllable as you read *sim/ple*. Listen to the sounds in each syllable. Stretch the sounds /sssiiimmm/ /plll/ as you write *sim, ple*. Repeat. This time have children write the letters as you write.
	Lead children in segmenting words and syllables as they write.	**Teach and Practice** Have children say the sounds in each syllable as you point to the letters. **How many syllables are there?** (two) **What are they?** *(sim, ple)* **What word does** *sim/ple* **make?** *(simple)* **Continue the activity with these words:**
		rid/dle lit/tle snug/gle cra/dle scram/ble boo/tle

Blend and Build Words Syllables: Consonant + *le*

Review blending words with syllables C + *le*.

CORRECTIVE FEEDBACK

Write *middle*.

Remember, when you read a word that ends in a consonant plus *le*, the consonant and *le* usually make up the word's last syllable. Draw a line before the second *d*. I read each syllable and then blend them together to read the whole word: *mid, dle, middle.*

Write the practice words. Monitor student practice.

Write the words; have each child blend two of them. Give feedback, using the *if . . . then* statements on Routine Card 1.

puddle   handle   bugle*   circle   bottles   able*   stumbled*

Check understanding of practice words.

*Children need to make sense of words that they segment and blend. If needed, help children with meanings. **A *bugle* is a small horn similar to a trumpet.** Mimic blowing a bugle. **Being *able* means having the power or skill to do something.** Cats are *able* to see well in the dark. *Stumbled* means "tripped or slipped." Demonstrate.

Provide letter tiles *a, b, e, g, g, g, i, j, l, n, t, u, w.*

Build Words Write *wiggle*. Can you blend this word? *(wiggle)* Spell *wiggle* with letter tiles. Change the *w* in *wiggle* to *g*. What is the new word? *(giggle)*

- Change the *g* in *giggle* to *j*. What is the new word? *(jiggle)*
- Change the *i* in *jiggle* to *u*. What is the new word? *(juggle)*
- Change the first *g* in *juggle* to *n*. What is the new word? *(jungle)*
- Change the *ju* in *jungle* to *ta*. What is the new word? *(tangle)*
- Change the *ng* in *tangle* to *b*. What is the new word? *(table)*

MORE PRACTICE

Distribute white boards. Model sorting words with syllables C + *le*.

Sort Words Have children write these headings at the tops of their boards: *dle, ble, ple, gle.* Then list these words on the board: *apple, bubble, puddle, bugle, simple, eagle, table, candle, purple, scribble, wiggle, cradle.* Have children copy the words into the appropriate columns. Model sorting *apple.* Then call on children to read the sorted words.

dle	*ble*	*ple*	*gle*
puddle	bubble	apple	bugle
candle	table	simple	eagle
cradle	scribble	purple	wiggle

High-Frequency Words *boy, either, hundred, several, you're*

Teach high-frequency words.

Lead cumulative review.

Display *boy, either, hundred, several,* and *you're.*

Use the Tested Vocabulary Cards. Point to a word. Say and spell it. Have children say and spell the word. Ask children to identify familiar letter-sounds and word parts. Have them take turns reading the words.

Use the Tested Vocabulary Cards to review high-frequency words from previous weeks.

ACTIVITY 3 Read a Passage

Reading "Safe Places for Strays," pp. 46–53

	To Do	To Say	10–15 minutes

Develop language and concepts.

Scaffold instruction.

See Routine Cards 6 and 7. Display pp. 46–53.

Ask questions and elaborate on answers to develop language.

Key concepts: *animal shelter, protection, strays, stable, vet, concern, adopt, train*

Before Reading Have children recall what they learned about taking care of animals. Read the title. Do a structured picture walk with children.

pp. 46–47 Do you know what an animal shelter is? It is a place that gives protection to strays. Strays are pets that don't have homes.

pp. 48–49 Workers at the shelter take care of the animals and try to find safe, stable homes for them. A vet is an animal doctor. How can a vet help at the shelter? (A vet can help animals get healthy.)

pp. 50–51 This pet lost its home because of a bad storm. How does the worker show concern? Sometimes shelters take strays to shopping malls. They hope families will give the strays new homes.

pp. 52–53 Workers at shelters teach people how to train their dogs to sit, stay, or come. Let's read to find out more about animal shelters.

Guide comprehension.

Monitor independent reading.

Use Routine Cards 2 and 3.

During Reading Read the pages in a whisper. Raise your hand if you need help with a word. As you read, ask yourself: What am I learning about animal shelters? What is this mainly about?

pp. 46–49 What did you learn about animal shelters? (Animal shelters are places where animals without homes are cared for.) Who helps at these shelters? (workers and vets)

pp. 50–51 What did you learn about how shelter workers help after a bad storm? (If pets lose their homes after a storm, workers take them to shelters. Sometimes they take them to malls so families can adopt them.)

pp. 52–53 Why does the author say "check out a shelter for pets"? (Shelters are a good place to get a pet. Strays at shelters need homes.)

Model summarizing.

Think aloud.

After Reading What did you learn about animal shelters? What was the selection mainly about? Model how to summarize. The first part told how strays are cared for in animal shelters. The next part told how shelter workers find homes for strays and how they teach people how to train their new pets. This selection is mainly about the ways workers at animal shelters take care of strays.

MORE PRACTICE

Develop oral vocabulary.

How does an animal shelter give *protection* to strays? Why would a vet be *concerned* about a pet's *growth?* How might you show your *concern* about strays?

ACTIVITY 4 Write

Response to Literature Shared Writing

	To Do	To Say	5 minutes

Guide shared writing.

Write sentence frames. Read the questions.

What is an animal shelter? An animal shelter is _____.
How do shelter workers help strays? Shelter workers _____.

Invite children to suggest answers. Discuss and record answers to complete the sentence frames. While writing, model connecting sounds to letters and forming letters. (See pp. 257–259.) Have children read answers aloud as you track print.

ACTIVITY **1** Reread for Fluency

Oral Reading "Safe Places for Strays," pp. 46–49

	To Do	To Say	5–10 minutes
CORRECTIVE FEEDBACK	Monitor oral reading.	Read pp. 46–49 aloud. Read them three or four times so your reading gets better each time. Give feedback on children's oral reading and use of the blending strategy. See Routine Cards 1 and 4.	
MORE PRACTICE		Instead of rereading just pp. 46–49, have children reread the entire selection three or four times. You may want to have children read along with the AudioText.	

ACTIVITY **2** Word Work

Phonemic Awareness Segment Words into Syllables, Syllables into Sounds

	To Do	To Say	2 minutes
Scaffold instruction.	Distribute white boards. Write *cradles.*	**Model** Listen to the sounds in *cradles.* I hear two syllables in *cradles.* Point to each syllable as you read *cra/dles.* Listen to the sounds in each syllable. Stretch the sounds /krrrāāā/ /dlllzzz/ as you write *cra, dles.* Repeat. Have children write the letters as you write.	
	Lead children in segmenting words and syllables as they write.	**Teach and Practice** Have children say the sounds in each syllable as you point to the letters. How many syllables are there? (two) What are they? *(cra, dles)* What word does *cra/dles* make? *(cradles)* Continue the activity with these words:	
		able rattle struggle purple cuddles beagle	

Fluent Word Reading Syllables: Consonant + *le*

	To Do	To Say	5–10 minutes
Use the word-reading routine.	Write *handle.*	**1 Connect** You can read this word because you know how to read two-syllable words that end with a consonant plus *le.* Remember, first divide the word before the consonant that comes before the *le.* Then read each syllable. Finally, blend the syllables together. What are the syllables in this word? *(han, dle)* What is the word? *(handle)*	*Routine*
Scaffold instruction.	Write *nibble, table,* and *startle.*	**2 Model** When you come to a new word, look at all the letters in the word and think about its vowel sounds and its parts. Say the sounds and word parts to yourself, and then read the word. Model reading *nibble, table,* and *startle* in this way. When you come to a new word, what will you do?	
	Write each practice word.	**3 Group Practice** Let's read these words. Look at all the letters, think about the vowel sounds and word parts, and say the sounds to yourself. We will read words with two syllables that end with a consonant plus *le.* When I point to the word, let's read it together. Allow 2–3 seconds previewing time for each word.	
		paddle sample turtles stable wiggled bottles maple sparkle needle	
CORRECTIVE FEEDBACK	**MONITOR PROGRESS**	*If . . .* children have difficulty previewing and reading whole words, *then . . .* have them use sound-by-sound blending.	
		If . . . children can't read the words fluently at a rate of 1–2 seconds per word, *then . . .* continue practicing the list.	

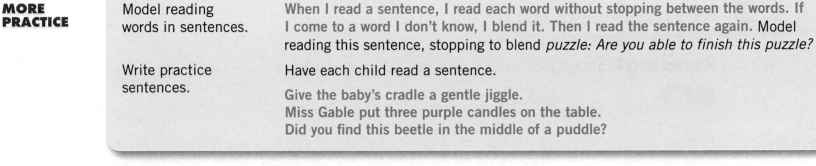

MORE
PRACTICE

	Model reading words in sentences.	When I read a sentence, I read each word without stopping between the words. If I come to a word I don't know, I blend it. Then I read the sentence again. Model reading this sentence, stopping to blend *puzzle: Are you able to finish this puzzle?*
	Write practice sentences.	Have each child read a sentence.

Give the baby's cradle a gentle jiggle.
Miss Gable put three purple candles on the table.
Did you find this beetle in the middle of a puddle?

High-Frequency Words *boy, either, hundred, several, you're*

To Do   **To Say**   *3 minutes*

Review high-frequency words. | Display *boy, either, hundred, several,* and *you're.* | Use the Tested Vocabulary Cards. Point to a word. Say and spell it. Have children say and spell the word. Ask children to identify familiar letter-sounds and word parts. Have them take turns reading the words.

ACTIVITY **3**   Build Concepts

Oral Vocabulary *litter, veterinarian*

To Do   **To Say**   *5–10 minutes*

Teach oral vocabulary. | Display p. 54 of the student book. | Today you will read a story about Snuggles and Cuddles Shelter for Animals. At shelters like these, *veterinarians* and other workers take care of animals until a new home can be found for them. Sometimes they may take care of a *litter* of puppies or kittens.

Routine

1 Introduce, Demonstrate, and Apply

Scaffold instruction. | Follow the Routine to teach *litter* and *veterinarian.* | **litter** It would be amazing to see a *litter* at Snuggles and Cuddles Shelter. A *litter* is a group of young animals born at the same time to one mother. Have children say the word. Pigs have *litters* of piglets. Have you ever seen a *litter* of kittens?

veterinarian *Veterinarians* help animals get healthy at the shelter. A *veterinarian* is a doctor who treats animals. The word *vet* is short for *veterinarian.* Have children say the word. A *veterinarian* might check a dog's heartbeat. Would you like to be a *veterinarian?* Why or why not?

| Display the words on the Amazing Words board. | **2 Display the Words** Have children say each word as they look at it. You can find sounds you know in big words. Read *lit/ter* as you run your hand under the syllables. What sounds do you hear in the first syllable of *litter?* (/lit/) in the last syllable? (/tər/) Read *vet/er/i/nar/i/an* as you run your hand under the syllables. Children can identify *vet, r/r/,* and *n/n/.*

| Monitor understanding. | **3 Use the Words** Ask children to use each word in a sentence. Model a sentence if children need help.

MORE
PRACTICE | | Use oral vocabulary to discuss taking care of animals. Describe what a mother dog's *litter* would look like. What kinds of things do you think a *veterinarian* needs to know? Why might you take a pet to see a *veterinarian?*

Read a Passage

Reading "Snuggles and Cuddles," pp. 54–65

To Do	To Say	10 minutes

Teach sequence.

Scaffold instruction.

Introduce the skill.

Model the skill. Display p. 50.

Today you will keep track of a story's sequence, the order in which things happen. As you read, think about what happens first, next, and last. For example, think about "Safe Places for Strays." Look at p. 50. First, we read that a bad storm leaves many animals without homes. Next, workers try to save the pets. Last, they bring hundreds of pets back to shelters.

Apply the skill. Display p. 51.

Look at p. 51. Tell what happens first, next, and last at the mall. (First, shelter workers bring strays to the mall. Next, they walk around with the cute pets. Last, they let family members hold the pets.)

Develop language and concepts.

See Routine Card 6. Display pp. 54–65.

Model using key words and concepts.

Key concepts: *TV reporter, cameraperson, news story, beagle, veterinarians, concerned, growth, protect, bundle*

Monitor children's use of vocabulary.

Before Reading Read the title. Do a structured picture walk.

pp. 54–57 The TV reporter and cameraperson are making a news story about the dogs and cats at Snuggles and Cuddles Shelter. Is Snuggles and Cuddles a good name for an animal shelter?

pp. 58–59 This dog is a beagle named Freckles. Veterinarians are concerned with Freckles's growth, so they feed him to help him get bigger and stronger. Later, a family takes Freckles home with them.

pp. 60–61 Point to the cat. Vets protect Spunky by placing him on a bundle of blankets. Later, a family adopts Spunky and takes him home.

pp. 62–63 Vets take care of this dog, Babe. What happens next? (A woman adopts her.) A sweet, older dog is a good pet for this lady.

pp. 64–65 At the end of his story, the reporter tells about the new homes that the pets got. Why? (so others will want to adopt pets too)

Now turn to your partner and talk about the pictures, using the same words I did.

Guide comprehension.

Monitor independent reading.

Use Routine Cards 2 and 3.

During Reading Read the pages in a whisper. Raise your hand if you need help with a word. As you read, ask yourself: what happens first, next, and last in this story?

pp. 54–57 What happens at the beginning of this story? (A reporter named Gimble Gomez starts telling a news story about the shelter.)

pp. 58–59 What happens first to Freckles? next? last? (First, someone gives him to the shelter. Next, vets feed him bottles of milk. Last, Caleb's family takes Freckles home.)

pp. 60–61 What happens after Spunky gets lost? (A man finds him and gives him to the shelter. Then vets feed him and he grows stronger. Last, Amber's family takes him home.)

pp. 62–63 What happens before the lady takes Babe home? (Someone dropped Babe off at the shelter and vets fed her.)

pp. 64–65 What might happen after people see Gimble Gomez's news story? (People might go to the shelter and adopt other pets.)

Guide retelling.

Prompt children as they retell the story.

After Reading Have one child retell the story while the others assist. What happens first? next? last? See Monitor Retelling, p. 246.

Homework

Practice Book, p. 103, Sequence

ACTIVITY 1 Reread for Fluency

Paired Reading "Snuggles and Cuddles," pp. 54–59

To Do	To Say	
		5–10 minutes

CORRECTIVE FEEDBACK

Pair children. Monitor paired reading.

Children read pp. 54–59 orally, switching readers at the end of the first page. Have partners reread; now the other partner begins. For optimal fluency, children should reread three or four times. Give feedback on children's oral reading and use of the blending strategy. See Routine Cards 1 and 4.

MORE PRACTICE

Instead of rereading just pp. 54–59, have children reread the entire selection three or four times. You may want to have children read along with the AudioText.

ACTIVITY 2 Word Work

Spiral Review Reading Longer Words (Syllables VCCV, VCV, C + *le*)

To Do	To Say	
		5–10 minutes

Review reading two-syllable words.

Scaffold instruction.

Write *kitten* and *chapter*.

If there are two consonants in the middle of a word, divide between them. Model with *kit/ten* and *chap/ter*. **Read each syllable. Then blend the syllables together. What are these words?** *(kitten, chapter)*

Write *tiger* and *camel*.

If a word has just one consonant in the middle, first try dividing before that consonant and making the first vowel sound long. Model with *ti/ger*. **If the word doesn't make sense when it is divided in this way, try dividing it after the consonant and using a short vowel sound.** Model *ca/mel* and then *cam/el*. **What are these words?** *(tiger, camel)*

Write *middle, turtle,* and *bugle*.

If a word ends with a consonant plus *le*, divide the word before the consonant that comes before the *le*. Model with *mid/dle, tur/tle,* and *bu/gle*. **What are these words?** *(middle, turtle, bugle)*

Remind children that if a syllable ends with a consonant, it usually has a short vowel sound. If a syllable ends with a vowel, it usually has a long vowel sound. If a vowel is followed by an *r*, its vowel sound is affected by the *r*.

Distribute white boards.

Sort Words Write and explain the headings. Then list the words below in a random order on the board. Have children copy and sort the words according to the vowel sound of the first syllable. Then have children read them.

Long Vowel	Short Vowel	Vowel with *r*
table	ribbon	corner
title	puppy	garden
music	pencil	purple
needle	candle	sparkle

CORRECTIVE FEEDBACK

MONITOR PROGRESS

If . . . children have difficulty reading the words,
then . . . review rules for the syllable patterns and have them blend each word sound-by-sound.

For more practice, see next page.

MORE PRACTICE	Model reading words in sentences.	When I read a sentence, I read each word without stopping between the words. If I come to a word I don't know, I blend it. Then I read the sentence again. Model reading this sentence, stopping to blend *purple: The baby's cradle and rattle are purple.*
	Write practice sentences.	Have each child read a sentence. **Martin put a saddle on the pony.** **Turtles and lizards are able to eat apple chunks.** **We made a simple robot out of bottle caps and seven boxes.**

Phonological and Phonemic Awareness	Optional practice activities, pp. 280–283

ACTIVITY 3 Read Together

Choral Reading "The Monster's Pet," p. 66

	To Do	**To Say**	*10 minutes*
Develop language and concepts.	Display p. 66.	**Before Reading** This is a monster. Monsters are make-believe creatures. Does this monster look silly or scary? (silly) Read the title of the poem. Ask children to predict what it is about. What do you think a monster's pet would act like? sound like? Allow children to share their ideas.	
Model fluent reading.	Model prosody.	Poems often have a rhythm, or a beat. Listen to my voice as I read this poem. Read the poem with rhythm and expression. Read it a second time, having children point to each word. Have children identify rhyming words and explain that a poem may include nonsense words such as *wuffle* or *bribble*, to make the poem fun or silly.	
	Build fluency through choral reading.	**Choral Reading** Now read the poem aloud with me. Try to make your voice sound like mine as we read. Reread the poem several times with children.	
Develop concepts.	Monitor listening comprehension.	**After Reading** What kinds of noises might the monster's pet make? How might it move? Tell me, using words from the poem. Then show me. What might the monster do to show *concern* for its pet? Which words rhyme in this poem? Which rhyming words are your favorites?	

ACTIVITY 4 Build Concepts

Oral Vocabulary *concern, growth, litter, protection, veterinarian*

	To Do	**To Say**	*5–10 minutes*
Review oral vocabulary.	Read the words on the Amazing Words board.	**Focus on Letter-Sounds** Remember, you can find sounds and word parts you know in big words. • What word has two *c*'s? What sound does each *c* make? • Which word has *grow* in it? has *lit*? has *vet*? • Which three words end with *n*?	

To Do	To Say
Encourage discussion.	**Provide Multiple Contexts** Review the meanings of the words. Then ask questions to place the words in diverse contexts. • What is something a good *veterinarian* might do? • Name a word that means about the same as "worry." (concern) • Firefighters give us *protection* when there is a fire. What other workers give people *protection?* • What are some ways you can measure your *growth?* • Where might you go to see a *litter* of piglets?

MORE PRACTICE

Apply oral vocabulary to new situations.	• If the things I say give us *protection* from bad weather, cover your head and say, "Protection." If not, do nothing. Raincoats (protection), umbrellas (protection), staples (not). • If the things I say can make up a *litter,* clap your hands and say, "Litter." If not, do nothing. Pups (litter), flowers (not), bunnies (litter), children (not). • If the things I say can show *growth,* stand up and say, "Growth." If not, do nothing. A plant (growth), a book (not), a baby (growth).

ACTIVITY **5** Write

Response to Literature Interactive Writing

5–10 minutes

	To Do	To Say
Generate ideas.	Review the story "Snuggles and Cuddles."	**What might happen after Caleb's family brings Freckles home?** Discuss what might happen first, next, and last as the family welcomes Freckles to his new home.
Share the pen.	Have children participate in writing a sequence of events that tells about welcoming a pet to its new home.	Write *First, _____. Next, _____. Last, _____.* Have children read the words you wrote. Then have them supply endings for each sentence. Invite individuals to write familiar letter-sounds, word parts, and high-frequency words. Have them find the spelling of high-frequency words on the Word Wall. Ask questions such as: • How do you divide *tumbles* into syllables? (Put a line before the *b.*) • How many syllables does *tumbles* have? (two) What are they? *(tum, bles)* • What word does *tum/bles* make? *(tumbles)*
	Writing elements: conventions	Frequently reread what has been written while tracking the print. Point out that each sentence starts with a capital letter and ends with a period. Point out the extra space between words. Read the completed sentences aloud, having children read with you. (For example, *First, Caleb runs and tumbles with Freckles in the yard. Next, Dad feeds Freckles and gives him fresh water. Last, Mom puts Freckles on a little dog bed.)*
MORE PRACTICE	Prompt independent writing.	**Journal Writing** Tell about a pet you have or would like to have.
	Homework	Practice Book, p. 104, High-Frequency Words

ACTIVITY 1 Assessment Options

Sentence Reading

	To Do	To Say	5 minutes

Assess sentence reading.

Use reproducible p. 249.

Have each child read the sentences. Record scores on the Sentence Reading Chart, p. 253. Work with one child as others complete Write Sentences below.

The boy can either eat an apple or drink a bottle of milk.
This puzzle has several hundred little parts.
You're going to startle the kitten if you jiggle that rattle.

CORRECTIVE FEEDBACK

MONITOR PROGRESS

If . . . children have trouble reading words that end with consonant + *le* syllables, ***then . . .*** reteach the blending strategy lesson on p. 100.

If . . . children cannot read a high-frequency word, ***then . . .*** mark the missed word or words on a high-frequency word list and send the list home for additional practice or have them practice with a fluent reader.

If . . . children misread a word in the sentence, ***then . . .*** correct the error and have them reread the word and then the sentence.

Practice sentence writing.

Provide white boards.

Write Sentences Have children copy the sentences from reproducible p. 249 on white boards. Have them confirm their spellings by comparing the words they wrote to the words in the sentences.

Phonological and Phonemic Awareness

Optional practice activities, pp. 280–283

Passage Reading

	To Do	To Say	5–10 minutes

Assess fluency and comprehension.

Determine which children to assess this week.

Chose from these options: monitoring fluency (see pp. 244–245) and/or monitoring retelling (see p. 246). Have children reread "Snuggles and Cuddles." Be sure each child is assessed every other week.

If you have time, assess every child.

ACTIVITY 2 Use Concepts

Oral Vocabulary *concern, growth, litter, protection, veterinarian*

	To Do	To Say	5 minutes

Check understanding of oral vocabulary.

Use the Amazing Words to wrap up the week's concept.

Monitor understanding of oral vocabulary, using Routine Card 5.

As time allows, ask questions such as these.
- Tell me about the pictures on pp. 36–45 using some of the week's Amazing Words.
- What do you call a group of newborn kittens? (litter)
- Clap to show how much *concern* you have (not at all, a little bit, a lot) for animals in an animal shelter. Why?
- How might workers provide *protection* for animals in a wildlife park?
- If you see a *veterinarian* at a farm, what might the *veterinarian* be doing?
- What changes might you notice that show a puppy's *growth?*

Preview next week's concept.

Next week you will read about family jobs.

ACTIVITY 3 Read to Connect

Reread "Taking Care of Animals," pp. 36–45

To Do	To Say	10 minutes

Monitor comprehension: sequence.

To Do: Have children reread "Taking Care of Animals" silently.

To Say: As you read, think about the order in which pets and their care are described. After rereading, ask:

- **Which pets are described first?** (dogs) **What are some ways to take care of dogs?** (walk them, throw balls to them, brush their fur, give them a bath)
- **Which pets are described next?** (cats) **What are some ways to take care of cats?** (hold them gently, watch them carefully, give them jingle toys)
- **Which pets are described after cats?** (gerbils) **What are some ways to take care of gerbils?** (give them water and food, keep their cages clean)
- **Which pets are described last?** (birds) **What are some ways to take care of birds?** (give them water and food, keep their cages clean)

Record children's ideas about ways to take care of animals in a list on the board. Children will use the list for Activity 4.

Make connections.

To Do: Have children make connections across texts.

To Say: We also read "Safe Places for Strays." Find that. How do the shelter workers and vets take care of stray dogs and cats? Add children's answers to the list of ways to take care of animals.

We also read "Snuggles and Cuddles" that told the stories of three stray animals who eventually go home with new families. How is Snuggles and Cuddles Shelter like the animal shelter in "Safe Places for Strays"? Record children's comparisons on the board.

What did all the selections we read this week show us about animals? What is the big idea? (People need to take care of animals.)

ACTIVITY 4 Write

Response to Literature Independent Writing

To Do	To Say	5–10 minutes

Assign descriptive writing.

To Say: Today you will describe ways that we can show our concern for animals. Write about things we can do to show animals that we care about them. Encourage children to use words you wrote on the board for Activity 3 as they write.

Guide sentence correction.

To Do: Writing elements: conventions, support

To Say: Have children check their writing by asking themselves these questions.

- **Did I begin each sentence with a capital letter?**
- **Did I use correct marks at the ends of sentences?**
- **Did I leave space between words and between sentences?**
- **Did I add details?**

MORE PRACTICE

Have children share their sentences with the group. Write their sentences on the board and have children practice reading and writing each other's sentences.

Homework Practice Book, p. 105, Writing

Unit 5 Week 3 *Family Jobs*

How can we be responsible family members?

Objectives *This week students will . . .*

Phonemic Awareness
- segment and blend sounds in words
- add phonemes

Phonics
- blend and read words with diphthongs *ou, ow*/ou/ and suffixes *-ly, -ful*
- apply knowledge of letter-sounds to decode unknown words when reading
- recognize high-frequency words *ago, break, certain, probably, since*

Fluency
- practice fluency with oral rereading

Vocabulary
- build concepts and oral vocabulary: *assign, behavior, cooperate, obedient, properly*

Text Comprehension
- read connected text
- draw conclusions to improve comprehension
- write in response to literature

Word Work *This week's phonics focus is . . .*

Diphthongs *ou, ow*/ou/   Suffixes *-ly, -ful*

High-Frequency Words *Tested Vocabulary*

The first appearance of each word in the Student Reader is noted below.

ago   If it happened long **ago,** it happened in the past. (p. 71)

break   When you **break** something, you make it fall to pieces or stop working. (p. 73)
                 A **break** is also a short period of rest.

certain   If you are **certain** about something, you are very sure. (p. 73)
                 Certain can also mean some but not all. Only **certain** trees grow here.

probably   You **probably** know my brother. (p. 76)

since   I have been up **since** 6:00. (p. 71)
                 Since you are hungry, we can eat.

Amazing Words *Oral Vocabulary*

The week's vocabulary is related to the concept of being responsible family members.

assign   to give someone a job to do

behavior   the way people and animals act or behave

cooperate   to work together

obedient   willing to do what you are told to do

properly   done in a correct way

Student Reader Unit 5 *This week students will read the following selections.*

70	**Let's Find Out: Family Jobs**	Narrative Nonfiction
80	**Tools for You and Me**	Expository Nonfiction
88	**Counting on Tess**	Realistic Fiction
100	**Make a Chores Calendar**	Instructions

Daily Lesson Plan

	ACTIVITIES	MATERIALS
Day 1	**Word Work** Phonemic Awareness: Segment and Blend Sounds Phonics: Blend Words with Diphthongs *ou, ow*/ou/ High-Frequency Words *ago, break, certain, probably, since* **Build Concepts** *behavior, cooperate, obedient* **Read a Passage** "Family Jobs," pp. 70–79 Comprehension: Use Strategies Reread for Fluency	Student White Boards Sound Spelling Card 27 Tested Vocabulary Cards *Sing with Me Big Book* and Audio CD Student Reader: Unit 5 Routine Cards 1, 2, 3, 4, 6, 7 AudioText Practice Book, p. 106, Diphthongs *ou, ow*/ou/
Day 2	**Reread for Fluency** **Word Work** Phonemic Awareness: Add Phonemes Phonics: Blend Words with Suffixes *-ly, -ful* High-Frequency Words *ago, break, certain, probably, since* **Read a Passage** "Tools for You and Me," pp. 80–87 Comprehension: Use Strategies **Write** Response to Literature: Shared Writing	Student Reader: Unit 5 Student White Boards Tested Vocabulary Cards Routine Cards 1, 2, 3, 4, 6, 7 AudioText Practice Book, p. 107, Suffixes *-ly, -ful*
Day 3	**Reread for Fluency** **Word Work** Segment and Blend Sounds Phonics: Fluent Word Reading High-Frequency Words *ago, break, certain, probably, since* **Build Concepts** *assign, properly* **Read a Passage** "Counting on Tess," pp. 88–99 Comprehension: Draw Conclusions	Student Reader: Unit 5 Student White Boards Tested Vocabulary Cards Routine Cards 1, 2, 3, 4, 6 AudioText Practice Book, p. 108, Draw Conclusions
Day 4	**Reread for Fluency** **Word Work** Phonics: Spiral Review Phonological and Phonemic Awareness Activities, pp. 280–283 **Read Together** "Make a Chores Calendar," pp. 100–101 Comprehension: Listening **Build Concepts** *assign, behavior, cooperate, obedient, properly* **Write** Response to Literature: Interactive Writing	Student Reader: Unit 5 Routine Cards 1, 4 AudioText Student White Boards Practice Book, p. 109, High-Frequency Words
Day 5	**Assessment Options** Fluency, Comprehension Sentence Reading; Mid-Unit Passage Reading Phonological and Phonemic Awareness Activities, pp. 280–283 **Use Concepts** *assign, behavior, cooperate, obedient, properly* **Read to Connect** "Family Jobs," pp. 70–79 Comprehension: Draw Conclusions **Write** Response to Literature: Independent Writing	Reproducible p. 249 Sentence Reading Chart, p. 253 Student White Boards Fluency Progress Chart, p. 245 Assessment Book, p. 83 Student Reader: Unit 5 Routine Card 5 Practice Book, p. 110, Writing

See pp. xvi–xvii for how *My Sidewalks* integrates instructional practices for ELL.

ACTIVITY **1** Word Work

Phonemic Awareness Segment and Blend Sounds

	To Do	To Say	2 minutes

Scaffold instruction.

Distribute white boards. Write *mouth*.

Write *now*. Lead children in segmenting and blending sounds as they write.

Model Listen to the sounds in *mouth*. Stretch the sounds /mmm/ /ououou/ /ththth/ as you write *m, ou, th*. Repeat. Have children write letters as you write.

Teach and Practice Have children say the sounds with you as you point to the letters (/m/ /ou/ /th/) and blend the sounds to say the word. *(mouth)* **Listen to the sounds in** *now*. Say /n/ /ou/ as you write *n, ow*. Have children say sounds as you point to letters and blend sounds to say the word. Continue with these words:

how   count   town   south   growls   shouts

Blending Strategy Diphthongs *ou, ow*/ou/

	To Do	To Say	5–10 minutes

Use the blending routine.

Scaffold instruction.

Write *snow*.

1 Connect You already can read this word. What vowel sound do you hear in this word? (the long *o* sound) What letters stand for the long *o* sound? *(ow)* Today we'll learn about another sound the letters *ow* can stand for.

Routine

Display Sound-Spelling Card 27.

2 Use Sound-Spelling Card This is an owl. What sound do you hear at the beginning of *owl*? (/ou/) Say it with me: /ou/. The letters *ow* can stand for the vowel sound /ou/.

3 Listen and Write Write the letters *ow* for /ou/. As you write, say the sound to yourself: /ou/. Now say the sound aloud.

Write *how*.

4 Model In this word, the letters *ow* stand for /ou/. This is how I blend this word: /h/ /ou/, *how*. Now you try it: /h/ /ou/, *how*.

Write *loud*.

Repeat steps 2 and 3 for *ou*/ou/, using *loud*. Then model blending *loud*: /l/ /ou/ /d/, *loud*. Point out the letters *ou* and *ow* can stand for the vowel sound /ou/.

h o w   l o u d

CORRECTIVE FEEDBACK

Write each practice word. Monitor student practice.

5 Group Practice Let's try the same thing with these words. Give feedback, using the *if . . . then* statements on Routine Card 1.

owl   proud   couch   chow*   sprout*   shower

6 Individual Practice Write the words; have each child blend two of them.

out   cow   sound   howls*   found   down   flower   powder

Check understanding of practice words.

*Children need to make sense of words that they segment and blend. If needed, help children with meanings. *Chow* is food, especially packaged food for pets. When something *sprouts*, it begins to grow. Seeds *sprout* outdoors in the spring. When an animal *howls*, it gives a loud, long cry. Dogs might *howl* at night.

MORE PRACTICE

Build words with *own* and *ound*.

Build Words Have children write *own* and *ound* at the tops of their boards. Have them build new words by adding the letters *d, t, g, br,* and *cl* to the front of *own* and *f, p, r, s,* and *gr* to the front of *ound*. Model blending with bigger chunks of words: *d, own, down*. Call on children to read each word and use it in a sentence or tell what it means.

High-Frequency Words *ago, break, certain, probably, since*

Teach high-frequency words.

To Do	To Say
Display *ago*.	**1 Say, Spell, Write** Use the Tested Vocabulary Cards. Display *ago*. Here are some words that we won't sound out. We'll spell them. This word is *ago*: *a, g, o* (point to each letter), *ago*. What is this word? What are the letters in the word? Now you write *ago*.
Point to *go* in *ago*.	**2 Identify Letter-Sounds** Let's look at the sounds and word parts in *ago* that you do know. Read *a/go* as you run your hand under each syllable. What letters make up the second syllable of *ago*? (*go*) How do you say this syllable? (/gō/)
	3 Demonstrate Meaning Tell me a sentence using *ago*. Model a sentence if children need help.
Display *break, certain, probably,* and *since*.	Repeat the Routine with *break, certain, probably,* and *since*. Children can identify these letter-sounds and word parts: *break* (*br*/br/, *k*/k/), *certain* (*cert, n*/n/), *probably* (*prob, bly*/blē/), and *since* (*sin, c*/s/). Have children write the words in their word banks. Add the words to the Word Wall. Point out that the words they are learning are on pp. 102–103.

ACTIVITY 2 Build Concepts

Oral Vocabulary *behavior, cooperate, obedient*

To Do	To Say
Introduce oral vocabulary. Display p. 23 of *Sing with Me Big Book*. Play audio CD.	This week you will learn about how we can be responsible family members. Listen for the Amazing Words *behavior, cooperate,* and *obedient* as I sing this song. Play or sing the song. Then have children sing it with you.
	1 Introduce, Demonstrate, and Apply
Scaffold instruction. Follow the Routine to teach *behavior, cooperate,* and *obedient*.	**behavior** In the song, the owner wants to change the puppy's *behavior*. The way people and animals act or behave is called their *behavior*. Have children say the word. How could the owner help improve the puppy's *behavior*? Give an example of good *behavior* that you show in class.
	cooperate The puppy in this song won't *cooperate* with its owner. When people or animals work together, they *cooperate* with each other. Have children say the word. How would a good puppy *cooperate* with its owner during a walk? What problems might come up if it won't *cooperate*?
	obedient The owner wants the puppy to be more *obedient*. When people or animals are willing to do what they are told to do, they are *obedient*. Have children say the word. An *obedient* puppy doesn't chew on shoes. What does an *obedient* puppy do? What is an *obedience* school for dogs?
Display the words on the Amazing Words board.	**2 Display the Words** Have children say each word as they look at it. You can find sounds and word parts you know in big words. Read *co/op/er/ate*. Children can identify *c*/k/, *ate*. For *behavior* and *obedient*, they can identify these letter-sounds and word parts: *behavior* (*b*/b/, *h*/h/, *v*/v/), *obedient* (*b*/b/, *d*/d/, *nt*/nt/).
Monitor understanding.	**3 Use the Words** Ask children to use each word in a sentence. Model a sentence if children need help.

MORE PRACTICE

Use oral vocabulary to discuss the song. Why does the owner want to change the puppy's *behavior*? Why do people want *obedient* pets? What ways can a puppy *cooperate* with its owner?

ACTIVITY 3 Read a Passage

Build Background "Family Jobs," pp. 70–79

	To Do	**To Say**	*10 minutes*

Develop language and concepts.

See Routine Card 7. Read aloud p. 69 of the student book.

Preview the Week Use the illustration on p. 68 to introduce this week's concept of how to be a responsible family member. **What family job is this boy doing? What responsibilities, or jobs, do you have at home?** Read aloud the titles and descriptions on p. 69. Ask children what they think each selection will be about.

Scaffold instruction.

See Routine Card 6. Display pp. 70–79.

Ask questions and elaborate on answers to develop language.

Key concepts: *townhouse, cooperate, responsibilities, vacuum* (v.,n.), *responsible, behavior*

Before Reading Read the title aloud. Do a structured picture walk with children.

pp. 70–71 Describe the family members in the picture. This family lives in a townhouse. A townhouse is one in a row of houses in a city or suburb. Family members cooperate to keep the house clean and neat.

pp. 72–73 What is Mom doing? (mopping) What is Dad doing? (fixing a pipe) They share the responsibilities of taking care of their home.

pp. 74–75 What is the boy doing? (vacuuming) A vacuum is a tool that sucks dirt and dust up into a bag. How does the girl help? (by dusting) They show responsible behavior by helping their parents.

pp. 76–77 What job is the little girl responsible for at home? (feeding the puppy) Even the puppy has a job. His job is to make the family smile!

pp. 78–79 The family rests after their jobs are done. Work gets done quickly when everyone helps out. How do you help out at home?

Teach story words.

Write *vacuum.*

You will read this word in the story. It is *vacuum.* Have children say the word and spell it. Review its meanings as a verb and a noun. **Let's read to find out more about family jobs.**

Guide comprehension.

Monitor independent reading. Model strategic reading. Use Routine Cards 2 and 3.

During Reading Read the pages in a whisper. Raise your hand if you need help with a word. Stop at the end of each page to model asking questions. For example, for p. 72: After I read, I ask myself: What did I learn about family jobs? The author writes, "Mom's job this day is to mop the kitchen tile." I think this page is mainly about how Mom does the job of mopping to help keep the family's home clean.

Summarize.

Use oral vocabulary to develop the concept.

After Reading How do the family members *cooperate* to keep the house clean and neat? Do the children show good *behavior?* Explain. Is Mister Howl *obedient?* How can you tell?

Reread for Fluency "Family Jobs," pp. 70–73

	To Do	**To Say**	*5–10 minutes*

CORRECTIVE FEEDBACK

Monitor oral reading.

Read pp. 70–73 aloud. Read them three or four times so your reading gets better each time. Give feedback on children's oral reading and use of the blending strategy. See Routine Cards 1 and 4.

MORE PRACTICE

Instead of rereading just pp. 70–73, have children reread the entire selection three or four times. You may want to have children read along with the AudioText.

Homework

Practice Book, p. 106, Phonics: Diphthongs *ou, ow*/ou/

ACTIVITY 1 Reread for Fluency

Paired Reading "Family Jobs," pp. 74–77

To Do	To Say	
		5–10 minutes

CORRECTIVE FEEDBACK

Pair children. Monitor paired reading.

Children read pp. 74–77 orally, switching readers at the end of the first page. Have partners reread; now the other partner begins. For optimal fluency, children should reread three or four times. Give feedback on children's oral reading and use of the blending strategy. See Routine Cards 1 and 4.

MORE PRACTICE

Instead of rereading just pp. 74–77, have children reread the entire selection three or four times. You may want to have children read along with the AudioText.

ACTIVITY 2 Word Work

Phonemic Awareness Add Phonemes

To Do	To Say	
		2 minutes

Scaffold instruction.

Distribute white boards. Write *neat.* Then add *-ly* to form *neatly.*

Lead children in adding *-ly* and *-ful* and blending new words as they write.

Model Listen to the sounds in *neat.* Stretch the sounds /nnn/ /ēēē/ /t/ as you write n, ea, t. Repeat. This time have children write the letters as you write. Add *-ly* to *neat.* Now listen as I add /lē/ to the end of *neat: neat, ly, neatly.* Repeat. Have children add *-ly* as you write.

Teach and Practice Have children say the sounds as you point to the letters (/n/ /ē/ /t/ /lē/) and blend the word with you. *(neat, ly, neatly)* What word do we make when we add *-ly* to *neat? (neatly)* What is the last syllable of *neatly? (ly)* Repeat the process, adding *-ful* to *help.* Then continue the activity by adding *-ly* and *-ful* to form these words:

gladly   playful   nicely   painful   safely   hopeful

Blending Strategy Suffixes -ly, -ful

	To Do	To Say	5–10 minutes

Use the blending routine.

Write *quicker* and *quickest*.

1 Connect You studied words like these already. What do you know about reading these words? (Read the base word, read the ending, and then blend the parts.) What are these words? *(quicker, quickest)* Both *-er* and *-est* are endings. Today we'll learn about other endings called suffixes.

Scaffold instruction.

Write *quickly* and *hopeful*.

2 Model These words both end with suffixes. The suffix *-ly* means "in a _____ way." *Quickly* means "in a quick way." This is how I blend this word: *quick, ly, quickly.* The suffix *-ful* means "full of." *Hopeful* means "full of hope." This is how I blend this word: *hope, ful, hopeful.*

Write *happily* with *happy* underneath.

The base word of this word is *happy.* When the base word has two syllables and ends in a *y,* the *y* changes to *i* before *-ly* is added. This is how I blend this word: *hap, pi, ly, happily.*

q u i c k l y   h o p e f u l   h a p p i l y

3 Listen and Write Write the word *quick.* Write *-ly* on the end of it. As you write, say each part to yourself: *quick, ly.* Now blend the parts together and say the word aloud. Have children do the same with *hopeful.*

CORRECTIVE FEEDBACK

Write each practice word. Monitor student practice.

4 Group Practice Let's try reading these words with suffixes. Give feedback, using the *if . . . then* statements on Routine Card 1.

sweetly   hurtful   easily   powerful*   correctly   mouthful

5 Individual Practice Write the words; have each child blend two of them.

bravely   frightful   useful   simply   perfectly*   peaceful*

Check understanding of practice words.

*Encourage children to use the meanings of the base words and the meanings of the suffixes to figure out the meanings of the practice words. If needed, help children with meanings. A *powerful* storm can be dangerous. If something is done *perfectly,* it is done without any mistakes. A quiet neighborhood is very *peaceful.*

MORE PRACTICE

Model building words with suffixes *-ly* and *-ful.*

Build Words Have children copy the suffixes *-ly* and *-ful* at the tops of their boards. Have them add *-ly* to these base words: *soft, tight, sad, happy.* Have them add *-ful* to these base words: *harm, thank, grace, play.* Model building and blending *soft, ly, softly.* When finished, call on children to read the new words and use them in sentences or explain their meanings.

-ly	-ful
softly	harmful
tightly	thankful
sadly	graceful
happily	playful

High-Frequency Words *ago, break, certain, probably, since*

	To Do	To Say	3 minutes

Teach high-frequency words.

Display *ago, break, certain, probably,* and *since.*

Use the Tested Vocabulary Cards. Point to a word. Say and spell it. Have children say and spell the word. Ask children to identify familiar letter-sounds and word parts. Have children take turns reading the words.

Lead cumulative review.

Use the Tested Vocabulary Cards to review high-frequency words from previous weeks.

ACTIVITY 3 Read a Passage

Reading "Tools for You and Me," pp. 80–87

10–15 minutes

To Do	To Say

Develop language and concepts.

Scaffold instruction.

See Routine Cards 6 and 7. Display pp. 80–87.

Ask questions and elaborate on answers to develop language.

Key concepts: *tools, useful, chores, vacuum*

Before Reading Have children recall the things the Brown family used to get jobs done. Read the title. Do a structured picture walk with children.

pp. 80–81 A tool helps you do work. Point to the tools that were useful long ago. How do you think people used these tools?

pp. 82–85 Which tools are useful for inside chores? Help children name the tools and their uses. Which tools for outside jobs? Help children name the tools and their uses.

pp. 86–87 Look at the pictures. Which tools have you used?

Teach story words.

Write *tools* and *vacuum.*

You will read these words in the selection: *tools, vacuum.* Have children say and spell each word. Review their meanings. Let's read to find out more about tools.

Guide comprehension.

Monitor independent reading.

During Reading Read the pages in a whisper. Raise your hand if you need help with a word. As you read, ask yourself: What am I learning about tools? What is this mainly about?

Use Routine Cards 2 and 3.

pp. 80–81 What did you learn about tools of long ago? (Tools were simple. They could break easily. They were useful.)

pp. 82–85 What are these four pages mainly about? (tools you use for inside and outside jobs) What did you learn about mops and vacuums? What did you learn about rakes and hoses?

pp. 86–87 What are these pages mainly about? (Tools help us with chores. It is important to use tools correctly and put them back.)

Model summarizing.

Think aloud.

After Reading What did you learn about tools? What was the selection mainly about? Model how to summarize. The first part was about tools used long ago. The next pages told about tools that are useful for inside and outside jobs. I pick the most important ideas. This selection is mainly about how tools are useful to get jobs done.

MORE PRACTICE

Develop oral vocabulary.

How can you *cooperate* with others to keep a tool shed neat? How can you show responsible *behavior* when you use tools? Why would a parent want a child to be *obedient* about using or not using tools?

ACTIVITY 4 Write

Response to Literature Shared Writing

5 minutes

To Do	To Say

Guide shared writing.

Write sentence frames. Read the questions.

What are tools you use inside? One tool is a _____.
How do you use this tool? You use a _____ to _____.

Invite children to suggest answers. Repeat questions for outside tools. Discuss and record answers to complete the sentence frames. While writing, model connecting sounds to letters and forming letters. (See pp. 257–259.) Have children read answers aloud as you track print.

Homework   Practice Book, p. 107, Phonics: Suffixes *-ly, -ful*

ACTIVITY 1 — Reread for Fluency

Oral Reading "Tools for You and Me," pp. 80–83

	To Do	To Say	
			5–10 minutes
CORRECTIVE FEEDBACK	Monitor oral reading.	Read pp. 80–83 aloud. Read them three or four times so your reading gets better each time. Give feedback on children's oral reading and use of the blending strategy. See Routine Cards 1 and 4.	
MORE PRACTICE		Instead of rereading just pp. 80–83, have children reread the entire selection three or four times. You may want to have children read along with the AudioText.	

ACTIVITY 2 — Word Work

Phonemic Awareness Segment and Blend Sounds

	To Do	To Say	
			2 minutes
Scaffold instruction.	Distribute white boards. Write *loud* and *loudly.*	**Model** Listen to the sounds in *loud.* Stretch the sounds /lll/ /ouououu/ /d/ as you write *l, ou, d.* Repeat. Have children write the letters as you write.	
	Lead children in segmenting and blending sounds.	**Teach and Practice** Have children say the sounds with you as you point to the letters (/l/ /ou/ /d/) and blend the sounds to say the word. *(loud)* Now listen to the sounds in *loudly.* Say *loud, ly* as you write *loud, ly.* Have children blend the base word and ending to say the word. Continue with these words:	
		proud proudly power powerful	

Fluent Word Reading Diphthongs *ou, ow*/ou/; Suffixes *-ly, -ful*

	To Do	To Say	
			5–10 minutes
Use the word-reading routine.	Write *cloud* and *clown.*	**1 Connect** You can read these words because you know that the letters *ou* and *ow* can stand for /ou/. What is the vowel sound in these words? (/ou/) What are the words? *(cloud, clown)*	
Scaffold instruction.	Write *house, plow, brightly,* and *useful.*	**2 Model** When you come to a new word, look at all the letters in the word and think about its vowel sounds and its parts. Say the sounds and word parts to yourself, and then read the word. Model reading *house, plow, brightly,* and *useful.* When you come to a new word, what will you do?	
	Write each practice word.	**3 Group Practice** Let's read these words. Look at all the letters, think about the vowel sounds, and say the sounds to yourself. We will read words with *ou, ow,* and suffixes *-ly* and *-ful.* When I point to the word, let's read it together. Allow 2–3 seconds previewing time for each word.	
		shout crowd shyly harmful sounds powder easily thankful nicely	
CORRECTIVE FEEDBACK	**MONITOR PROGRESS**	*If . . .* children have difficulty previewing and reading whole words, *then . . .* have them use sound-by-sound blending.	
		If . . . children can't read the words fluently at a rate of 1–2 seconds per word, *then . . .* continue practicing the list.	

MORE PRACTICE

Model reading words in sentences.	When I read a sentence, I read each word without stopping between the words. If I come to a word I don't know, I blend it. Then I read the sentence again. Model reading this sentence, stopping to blend *counted: Farmer Brown quickly counted his cows.*
Write practice sentences.	Have each child read a sentence. **Please don't shout so loudly down the hall.** **The skillful player did not kick the ball out of bounds.** **We are thankful that the rain showers fell softly on the house.**

High-Frequency Words *ago, break, certain, probably, since*

3 minutes

	To Do	**To Say**
Review high-frequency words.	Display *ago, break, certain, probably,* and *since.*	Use the Tested Vocabulary Cards. Point to a word. Say and spell it. Have children say and spell the word. Ask children to identify familiar letter-sounds and word parts. Have them take turns reading the words.

ACTIVITY 3 Build Concepts

Oral Vocabulary *assign, properly*

5–10 minutes

	To Do	**To Say**
Teach oral vocabulary.	Display p. 88 of the student book.	Today you will read a story about a girl who does not do her *assigned* job *properly.*
		1 Introduce, Demonstrate, and Apply
Scaffold instruction.	Follow the Routine to teach *assign* and *properly.*	***assign*** This story is about family members *assigned* to jobs before leaving on a camping trip. When you *assign* something, you give someone a job to do. Have children say the word. Teachers often *assign* homework. Who else *assigns* you jobs?
		properly In this story, Dad uses a hose *properly* to wash the van. When something is done *properly,* it is done in a correct way. Have children say the word. When workers build houses, they use drills and saws *properly.* What tools do you use *properly?* What happens if you don't do a job *properly?*
	Display the words on the Amazing Words board.	**2 Display the Words** Have children say each word as they look at it. Let's look at the sounds in *assign* that you do know. Children can identify these letter-sounds: *assign* (*ss*/s/ and *n*/n/). Then read *prop/er/ly* as you run your hand under the syllables. Children can decode *properly.*
	Monitor understanding.	**3 Use the Words** Ask children to use each word in a sentence. Model a sentence if children need help.

MORE PRACTICE

Use oral vocabulary to discuss family jobs. What kinds of jobs do your parents *assign* to you? How would you clean your bedroom *properly?*

Read a Passage

Reading "Counting on Tess," pp. 88–99

| To Do | To Say | 10 minutes |

Teach draw conclusions. Scaffold instruction.

To Do
Introduce the skill.

Display p. 86. Model the skill.

To Say
Today you are going to draw conclusions. To draw conclusions, we use what we know about real life and what we read to figure out things that are not written in the selection. For example, the author of "Tools for You and Me" says we must use tools correctly, but doesn't tell us why this is important. I read that tools help us with chores. I know if we don't use tools correctly, the tool might not do the job well or it might be unsafe. So I think the reason we must use tools correctly is to get the job done well and to be safe.

Apply the skill.

Why do you think we need to be careful to put tools back neatly? (so the tools last longer and can be found easily)

Develop language and concepts.

See Routine Card 6. Display pp. 88–99.

Model using key words and concepts.

Key concepts: *pins and needles, assignment, properly, cooperating, responsible, behavior*

Monitor children's use of vocabulary.

Before Reading Read the title. Do a structured picture walk.

pp. 88–91 Tess is on pins and needles. That means she can't wait for something to happen. She tells her mom that she'll pack for the camping trip. How can you tell that Tess doesn't complete the assignment properly? (She falls asleep. Nothing is packed.)

pp. 92–97 The other family members are cooperating to get ready for the trip. How do they show this? (They each do jobs to get ready for the trip.) Is Tess showing responsible behavior? Why not?

pp. 98–99 Mom shouts that it is time to go. It wakes Tess up. How do you think she feels? Why? (She's upset because she fell asleep before she finished packing.) What do you think Tess will do now?

Now turn to your partner and talk about the pictures, using the same words I did.

Guide comprehension.

Monitor independent reading.

Use Routine Cards 2 and 3.

During Reading Read the pages in a whisper. Raise your hand if you need help with a word. As you read, think about what the characters say and do. Think about your own life too. Ask yourself: What conclusions can I draw about the family?

pp. 88–91 What do you think Tess means when she says, "You can count on me"? (She plans on packing her bag.) When the job is hard, Tess falls asleep. What does this tell you about Tess? (Possible answers: She isn't used to hard work. She gives up easily. She isn't responsible.)

pp. 92–97 What are the other family members like? (hardworking, responsible) How do you know? (They do their assignments properly.)

pp. 98–99 How might the family feel when they find out Tess hasn't packed? Why? (Possible answers: disappointed because they counted on Tess; upset because they won't be able to leave for the camping trip on time) At the end, Tess says, "You can count on me—but next time!" Do you think the family will believe her? Why or why not? (Possible answers: Yes, she didn't mean to fall asleep, so they will give her another chance. No, Tess has not shown responsible behavior.)

Guide retelling.

Prompt children as they retell the story.

After Reading Have one child retell the story while the others assist. What happens at the beginning? in the middle? at the end? See Monitor Retelling, p. 246.

Homework

Practice Book, p. 108, Draw Conclusions

ACTIVITY 1 Reread for Fluency

Paired Reading "Counting on Tess," pp. 88–91

To Do	To Say	*5–10 minutes*

CORRECTIVE FEEDBACK

Pair children. Monitor paired reading.

Children read pp. 88–91 orally, switching readers at the end of the first page. Have partners reread; now the other partner begins. For optimal fluency, children should reread three or four times. Give feedback on children's oral reading and use of the blending strategy. See Routine Cards 1 and 4.

MORE PRACTICE

Instead of rereading just pp. 88–91, have children reread the entire selection three or four times. You may want to have children read along with the AudioText.

ACTIVITY 2 Word Work

Spiral Review Endings -s, -es, -ed, -ing, -er, -est and Suffixes -ly, -ful

To Do	To Say	*5–10 minutes*

Review base words with endings and suffixes.

Scaffold instruction.

Write *growls, likes, shouted, stopping, easier,* and *happiest.*

You can read these words because you know how to blend base words with endings. Remember, read the base word, read the ending, and then blend the parts together. Point to each word and have children read it aloud. Have them identify base word and ending and tell if the base word spelling changed before adding the ending.

Write *loudly, powerful, simply,* and *playful.*

You can read these words because you know how to blend base words with suffixes. Remember, read the base word, read the suffix, and then blend the parts together. Point to each word and have children read it aloud. Have them identify base word and suffix and tell if the base word spelling changed before adding the suffix.

Distribute white boards.

Build Words Use a chart to make new words. Write -s or -es, -ed, -ing, -er, -est, -ly, and -ful as headings of a seven-column chart. Write base words in each column. Have children copy the chart on their boards and add the ending or suffix to each base word. Then have children read the new words and use them in sentences. If needed, review when to use -s or -es. Remind children to use base words and endings or suffixes to help figure out the meanings of the new words.

-s or -es	-ed	-ing	-er	-est	-ly	-ful
fixes	shopped	playing	quicker	sharpest	gladly	harmful
gowns	frowned	raining	funnier	simplest	easily	skillful
houses	pounded	howling	louder	toastiest	proudly	hopeful

CORRECTIVE FEEDBACK

MONITOR PROGRESS

If . . . children have difficulty reading the words,
then . . . have them blend base words sound-by-sound before adding endings or suffixes. Have them read words again after adding endings or suffixes.

For more practice, see next page.

Continued Spiral Review

MORE PRACTICE

Model reading words in sentences.	When I read a sentence, I read each word without stopping between the words. If I come to a word I don't know, I blend it. Then I read the sentence again. Model reading this sentence, stopping to blend *fearful: The flying owl spied a fearful mouse.*
Write practice sentences.	Have each child read a sentence. **The hopeful clown wishes to tell the funniest joke.** **She dropped the hottest cup, but it landed safely on the rug.** **A helpful kid is placing peaches neatly in the smaller box.**

Phonological and Phonemic Awareness   Optional practice activities, pp. 280–283

ACTIVITY 3   Read Together

Choral Reading "Make a Chores Calendar," pp. 100–101

	To Do	**To Say** *10 minutes*
Develop language and concepts.	Display pp. 100–101.	**Before Reading** This is a calendar. What does a calendar show? (months of the year, days of the week) What kinds of notes are listed on your family's calendar? Allow time for children to give examples.
Model fluent reading.		Read the title of the article. Ask children to predict what it is about. The sentences by the dots tell you how to make a chores calendar, one step at a time. I read these sentences carefully and not too fast so I don't make mistakes. When I read how to make something, I read the steps in order. Read the text with accuracy and at the appropriate rate. Read it a second time, having children point to each word.
	Build fluency through choral reading.	**Choral Reading** Now read with me. Try to make your voice sound like mine as we read. Reread the instructions several times with children. Help children compare the chores shown with chores they might put on their own calendars.
Develop concepts.	Monitor listening comprehension.	**After Reading** Why do you need this month's calendar to make a chores calendar? In your family, how would chores be *assigned* for different days? Where might the chores calendar be displayed in your home?

ACTIVITY 4   Build Concepts

Oral Vocabulary *assign, behavior, cooperate, obedient, properly*

	To Do	**To Say** *5–10 minutes*

Review oral vocabulary.	Read the words on the Amazing Words board.	**Focus on Letter-Sounds** Remember, you can find sounds and word parts you know in big words.
		  • Which word begins with *a?* begins with *be?* ends with *rate?*
		  • Which word has /nt/ at the end? What letters stand for /nt/?
		  • Which word ends with a suffix? What is the suffix?

To Do	To Say
Encourage discussion.	**Provide Multiple Contexts** Review the meanings of the words. Then ask questions to place the words in diverse contexts. • How might you dress *properly* for a hot day at the beach? • Show me what good *behavior* during a school assembly looks like. • What kinds of jobs might an art teacher *assign*? • If people are *cooperating* at the park, what might be happening? • What would an *obedient* dog do if you said, "Stay"?
MORE PRACTICE Apply oral vocabulary to new situations.	• If you *cooperate* with someone, do you argue or work together? (work together) • If you study people's *behavior*, do you watch what they do or ask how they feel? (watch what they do) • If you *assign* a job, do you do it yourself or tell someone else to do it? (tell someone else to do it) • Does an *obedient* person make up rules or follow them? (follow them) • If someone cooks a meal *properly*, does it taste good or is it burnt? (tastes good)

ACTIVITY **5** Write

Response to Literature Interactive Writing

5–10 minutes

	To Do	To Say
Generate ideas.	Review the story "Counting on Tess."	Think about Tess's family. Do you think each person was a responsible member of the family? Why or why not? Discuss each family member's behavior as they got ready to go on the camping trip.
Share the pen.	Have children participate in writing a list that shows how family members can be responsible.	Write *Family members can _____.* Have children read the words you wrote. Then have them supply endings for the sentence. Invite individuals to write familiar letter-sounds, word parts, and high-frequency words. Have them find the spelling of high-frequency words on the Word Wall. Ask questions such as: • What are the first two sounds in *proud*? (/pr/) What letters stand for /pr/? *(pr)* • What is the vowel sound in *proud*? (/ou/) What letters can stand for /ou/? *(ou)* • What is the last sound in *proud*? (/d/) What is the letter for it? *(d)*
	Writing elements: conventions	Frequently reread what has been written while tracking the print. Point out that each sentence starts with a capital letter and ends with a period. Point out the extra space between words. Read the completed sentences aloud, having children read with you. (For example, *Family members can keep the house clean. Family members can make one another proud. Family members can treat one another nicely.*)
MORE PRACTICE	Prompt independent writing.	**Journal Writing** Tell about a time you took a trip and how you helped.
	Homework	Practice Book, p. 109, High-Frequency Words

ACTIVITY 1 | Assessment Options

Sentence Reading

To Do	To Say	5 minutes

Assess sentence Reading.

Use reproducible p. 249.

Have each child read the sentences. Record scores on the Sentence Reading Chart, p. 253. Work with one child as others complete Write Sentences below.

Long ago, towns were probably not as crowded as they are now.
If you suddenly drop that houseplant, the pot is certain to break.
Since the brown pup is so playful, I will crouch down and pet it gently.

CORRECTIVE FEEDBACK

MONITOR PROGRESS

If . . . children have trouble reading words with diphthongs *ou, ow*/ou/ or suffixes *-ly, -ful,*
then . . . reteach the blending strategy lessons on pp. 116 and 120.

If . . . children cannot read a high-frequency word,
then . . . mark the missed word or words on a high-frequency word list and send the list home for additional practice or have them practice with a fluent reader.

If . . . children misread a word in the sentence,
then . . . correct the error and have them reread the word and then the sentence.

Practice sentence reading.

Provide white boards.

Write Sentences Have children copy the sentences from reproducible p. 249 on white boards. Have them confirm spellings by comparing the words they wrote to the words in the sentences.

Phonological and Phonemic Awareness

Optional practice activities, pp. 280–283

Mid-Unit Passage Reading

To Do	To Say	5–10 minutes

Assess fluency and comprehension.

Determine which children to assess. Use Assessment Book, p. 83.

Choose from these options: monitoring fluency (see pp. 244–245) and/or monitoring retelling (see p. 246). Have children read the Unit 5 Mid-Unit Fluency Passage in the Assessment Book. Be sure each child is assessed every other week.

If you have time, assess every child.

ACTIVITY 2 | Use Concepts

Oral Vocabulary *assign, behavior, cooperate, obedient, properly*

To Do	To Say	5 minutes

Check understanding of oral vocabulary.

Use the Amazing Words to wrap up the week's concept.

Monitor understanding of oral vocabulary, using Routine Card 5.

Preview next week's concept.

As time allows, ask questions such as these.

- Tell me about the pictures on pp. 70–79 using some of the week's Amazing Words.

- Describe a time when you *cooperated* with a family member.

- If you studied a bird's *behavior*, what might you see?

- Why might parents want to *assign* a job to an *obedient* child rather than one who doesn't *behave properly*?

Next week you will read about what good friends and neighbors do.

ACTIVITY 3 Read to Connect

Reread "Family Jobs," pp. 70–79

To Do	To Say	

Monitor comprehension: draw conclusions.

Have children reread "Family Jobs" silently.

As you read, use what you already know and what the author says to draw conclusions about family jobs. After rereading, ask:

- **Do you think there are jobs that all family members can do, no matter how old or how young they are? Tell why you think this.**
- **Why is it important for families to cooperate to get family jobs done?**

Record children's conclusions on the board. Then make a list of different family jobs. (For example: mopping floors, fixing pipes, vacuuming, dusting, feeding pets, and so on.) Children will use the list for Activity 4.

Make connections.

Have children make connections across texts.

We also read "Tools for You and Me." Find that. **Which tools in the closet could the Brown family use to do their family jobs?** (mop, pail, vacuum, rag, cleaners) **For which jobs might the tools in the shed be helpful?** Add children's answers to the list of family jobs.

We also read "Counting on Tess," about a girl whose family counts on her to do a family job. **Compare Tess's job and behavior with Krissy's job and behavior in "Family Jobs." Which girl do you think is more responsible? Why?** Record children's conclusions on the board.

What did all the selections we read this week show us about family jobs? What is the big idea? (We can be responsible family members by doing family jobs.)

ACTIVITY 4 Write

Response to Literature Independent Writing

To Do	To Say	

Assign personal narrative.

Guide sentence correction.

Writing elements: conventions, support

Today you will write about a time when you behaved in a responsible way by doing a family job. Describe what you did. Encourage children to use words you wrote on the board for Activity 3 as they write.

Have children check their writing by asking themselves these questions.

- Did I use capital letters at the beginning of sentences and for proper nouns?
- Did I use correct marks at the ends of sentences?
- Did I use words with the suffix -ly to tell how I did something?
- Did I use describing words?

MORE PRACTICE

Have children share their sentences with the group. Write their sentences on the board and have children practice reading and writing each other's sentences.

Homework   Practice Book, p. 110, Writing

Unit 5 Week 4 *My Neighbors, My Friends*

What do good friends and neighbors do?

Objectives *This week students will . . .*

Phonemic Awareness
- segment and blend sounds in words; add phonemes

Phonics
- blend and read words with the sound of *oo* in *moon* and prefixes *un-*, *re-*
- apply knowledge of letter-sounds to decode unknown words when reading
- recognize high-frequency words *been, brother, course, special, whole*

Fluency
- practice fluency with oral rereading

Vocabulary
- build concepts and oral vocabulary: *acquaintance, appreciate, communicate, local, respect*

Text Comprehension
- read connected text
- draw conclusions to improve comprehension
- write in response to literature

Word Work *This week's phonics focus is . . .*

Sound of *oo* in *moon*   Prefixes *un-*, *re-*

High-Frequency Words *Tested Vocabulary*

The first appearance of each word in the Student Reader is noted below.

been	This boy has **been** here for hours. (p. 111)
brother	Your **brother** is a boy or man with the same parents as you. (p. 110)
course	Of **course,** we can go! (p. 107)
special	Your birthday is a **special** day. (p. 111)
whole	Something that is **whole** is in one piece. (p. 107)

Amazing Words *Oral Vocabulary*

The week's vocabulary is related to the concept of being good friends and neighbors.

acquaintance	someone known to you, but not a close friend
appreciate	to feel thankful for or like something
communicate	to talk to someone or keep in touch in other ways
local	someone or something near your house or not far away
respect	to honor or admire someone

Student Reader Unit 5 *This week students will read the following selections.*

Daily Lesson Plan

	ACTIVITIES	MATERIALS
Day 1	**Word Work** Phonemic Awareness: Segment and Blend Sounds Phonics: Blend Words with Sound of *oo* in *moon* High-Frequency Words *been, brother, course, special, whole* **Build Concepts** *appreciate, communicate, respect* **Read a Passage** "My Neighbors, My Friends," pp. 106–111 Comprehension: Use Strategies Reread for Fluency	Student White Boards Sound Spelling Card 37 Tested Vocabulary Cards *Sing with Me Big Book* and Audio CD Student Reader: Unit 5 Routine Cards 1, 2, 3, 4, 6, 7 AudioText Practice Book, p. 111, Sound of *oo* in *moon*
Day 2	**Reread for Fluency** **Word Work** Phonemic Awareness: Add Phonemes Phonics: Blend Words with Prefixes *un-, re-* High-Frequency Words *been, brother, course, special, whole* **Read a Passage** "What Makes a Nice Neighbor?" pp. 112–117 Comprehension: Use Strategies **Write** Response to Literature: Shared Writing	Student Reader: Unit 5 Student White Boards Tested Vocabulary Cards Routine Cards 1, 2, 3, 4, 6, 7 AudioText Practice Book, p. 112, Prefixes *un-, re-*
Day 3	**Reread for Fluency** **Word Work** Phonemic Awareness: Segment and Blend Sounds Phonics: Fluent Word Reading High-Frequency Words *been, brother, course, special, whole* **Build Concepts** *acquaintance, local* **Read a Passage** "The Twins Next Door," pp. 118–125 Comprehension: Draw Conclusions	Student Reader: Unit 5 Student White Boards Tested Vocabulary Cards Routine Cards 1, 2, 3, 4, 6 AudioText Practice Book, p. 113, Draw Conclusions
Day 4	**Reread for Fluency** **Word Work** Phonics: Spiral Review Phonological and Phonemic Awareness Activities, pp. 280–283 **Read Together** "How Does Jack Get to School?" p. 126 Comprehension: Listening **Build Concepts** *acquaintance, appreciate, communicate,* *local, respect* **Write** Response to Literature: Interactive Writing	Student Reader: Unit 5 Routine Cards 1, 4 AudioText Practice Book, p. 114, High-Frequency Words
Day 5	**Assessment Options** Fluency, Comprehension Sentence Reading; Passage Reading Phonological and Phonemic Awareness Activities, pp. 280–283 **Use Concepts** *acquaintance, appreciate, communicate,* *local, respect* **Read to Connect** "My Neighbors, My Friends," pp. 106–111 Comprehension: Draw Conclusions **Write** Response to Literature: Independent Writing	Reproducible p. 249 Sentence Reading Chart, p. 253 Student White Boards Fluency Progress Chart, pp. 245 Student Reader: Unit 5 Routine Card 5 Practice Book, p. 115, Writing

See pp. xvi–xvii for how *My Sidewalks* integrates instructional practices for ELL.

Phonemic Awareness Segment and Blend Sounds

To Do	To Say	2 minutes
Scaffold instruction. Distribute white boards. Write *room*.	**Model** Listen to the sounds in *room*. Stretch the sounds /rrr/ /üüü/ /mmm/ as you write *r, oo, m.* Repeat. Have children write letters as you write.	
Lead children in segmenting and blending sounds as they write.	**Teach and Practice** Have children say the sounds with you as you point to the letters (/r/ /ü/ /m/) and blend the sounds to say the word. *(room)* Continue with these words. zoo tool moon food spoons poodle	

Blending Strategy Sound of *oo* in *moon*

To Do	To Say	5–10 minutes
Use the blending routine. Write *hot* and *go*.	**1 Connect** You already can read words like these. What vowel sound does the first word have? (the short *o* sound) What vowel sound does the second word have? (the long *o* sound) What are the words? *(hot, go)* Today we'll learn the vowel sound of two *o*'s together.	Routine
Scaffold instruction. Display Sound-Spelling Card 37.	**2 Use Sound-Spelling Card** This is the moon. What vowel sound do you hear in *moon?* (/ü/) Say it with me: /ü/. The letters *oo* can stand for /ü/.	
	3 Listen and Write Write the letters *oo* for /ü/. As you write, say the sound to yourself: /ü/. Now say the sound aloud.	
Write *tool*.	**4 Model** The letters *oo* can stand for /ü/. This is how I blend this word: /t/ /ü/ /l/, *tool.* Now you try: /t/ /ü/ /l/, *tool.*	

$$\underset{\xrightarrow{\hspace{2cm}}}{t \xrightarrow{} o\ o \xrightarrow{} l}$$

CORRECTIVE FEEDBACK Write each practice word. Monitor student practice.	**5 Group Practice** Let's try the same thing with these words. Give feedback, using the *if . . . then* statements on Routine Card 1. too cool zoom pool smooth balloons bloom	
	6 Individual Practice Write the words; have each child blend two of them. boo noon loop* scoot* droop* boost* goofy raccoon	
Check understanding of practice words.	*Children need to make sense of words that they segment and blend. If needed, help children with meanings. A *loop* is a part of a curved string or ribbon that crosses itself. *Scoot* means "to go quickly." I saw a girl *scoot* by on skates. When something *droops,* it hangs down. A dog's long ears can *droop.* When you give someone a *boost,* you lift or push to help the person up to or over something. The toddler needed a *boost* to get onto his chair.	
MORE PRACTICE Model spelling *oo* words.	**Spell and Write** What sounds do you hear in *tool?* (/t/ /ü/ /l/) What is the letter for /t/? Let's all write *t.* What are the letters for /ü/ in this word? Write *oo.* What is the letter for /l/? Write *l.* Continue practice as time allows. Have children confirm their spellings by comparing them to what you've written. zoo boot fool hoop soon food broom tooth spooky	

High-Frequency Words *been, brother, course, special, whole*

To Do	To Say	
		3 minutes

Teach high-frequency words.

Display *been*.

1 Say, Spell, Write Use the Tested Vocabulary Cards. Display *been*. Here are some words that we won't sound out. We'll spell them. This word is *been*: *b, e, e, n* (point to each letter), *been*. What is this word? What are the letters in the word? Now you write *been*.

Point to the *b* and *n* in *been*.

2 Identify Letter-Sounds Let's look at the sounds in *been* that you do know. What is this letter? *(b)* What is the sound for this letter? *(/b/)* Continue with *n*/n/.

3 Demonstrate Meaning Tell me a sentence using *been*. Model a sentence if children need help.

Display *brother, course, special,* and *whole*.

Repeat the Routine with *brother, course, special* and *whole*. Children can identify these letter-sounds and word parts: *brother* (*br*/br/, the high-frequency word *other*), *course* (*c*/k/, *s*/s/), *special* (*spe*/spe/, */l*/l/), and *whole (hole)*. Have children write the words in their word banks. Add the words to the Word Wall. Point out that the words they are learning are on p. 127.

 ACTIVITY **2** Build Concepts

Oral Vocabulary *appreciate, communicate, respect*

To Do	To Say	
		5–10 minutes

Introduce oral vocabulary.

Display p. 24 of *Sing with Me Big Book*. Play audio CD.

This week you will learn about what good friends and neighbors do. Listen for the Amazing Words *appreciate, communicate,* and *respect* as I sing this song. Play or sing the song. Then have children sing it with you.

1 Introduce, Demonstrate, and Apply

Scaffold instruction.

Follow the Routine to teach *appreciate, communicate,* and *respect*.

appreciate The song talks about *appreciating* your friends. When you *appreciate* something, you feel thankful for it. You can also *appreciate*, or like, the things about people that make them special. Have children say the word. I *appreciate* how funny my best friend is. What do you *appreciate* about your friends?

communicate The song mentions that good friends *communicate*. If you *communicate* with a person, you talk to each other or keep in touch in other ways. Have children say the word. I often *communicate* by e-mail with friends who live far away. How do you *communicate* with your friends?

respect The song says to *respect* our friends. When you *respect* someone, you honor or admire that person. Have children say the word. We can show *respect* for others by paying attention when they speak. How do you show *respect* for your parents?

Display the words on the Amazing Words board.

2 Display the Words Have children say each word as they look at it. You can find sounds and word parts you know in big words. Read *ap/pre/ci/ate*. How do you say the second syllable? *(/prē/)* the last syllable? *(/āt/)* Children can also identify these letter-sounds and word parts: *respect* (*r*/r/, *spect*), *communicate* (*c*/k/, *m*/m/, *n*/n/, *cate*).

Monitor understanding.

3 Use the Words Ask children to use each word in a sentence. Model a sentence if children need help.

MORE PRACTICE

Use oral vocabulary to discuss the song. Why is it important to tell your friends that you *appreciate* them? If you *respect* a friend, how might you *communicate* this to him or to her?

ACTIVITY 3 Read a Passage

Build Background "My Neighbors, My Friends," pp. 106–111

| To Do | To Say | *10 minutes* |

Develop language and concepts.

See Routine Card 7. Read aloud p. 105 of the student book.

Preview the Week Use the photograph on p. 104 to introduce this week's concept of being good neighbors and friends. These kids live near each other. They are neighbors. I think they are also good friends because they're having fun together. How would you describe a good friend? a good neighbor? Read aloud the titles and descriptions on p. 105. Ask children what they think each selection will be about.

Scaffold instruction.

See Routine Card 6. Display pp. 106–111.

Ask questions and elaborate on answers to develop language.

Key concepts: *neighborhood, neighbors, communicating, project, playground*

Before Reading Read the title aloud. Do a structured picture walk with children.

pp. 106–107 This group of people lives near each other. They live in the same neighborhood. The neighbors are communicating with each other at a meeting. Point to the empty lot. What project, or plan, might the neighbors suggest for this empty lot?

pp. 108–109 What are the neighbors building on the empty lot? (a playground) How might a playground make the neighborhood better?

pp. 110–111 Look at the big neighborhood picnic. How do the neighbors feel? How can you tell? Would you like to have neighbors like these? Why or why not?

Teach story words.

Write *neighborhood*.

You will read this word in the selection. It is *neighborhood*. Have children say the word and spell it. Review its meaning. Let's read to find out what happens in a neighborhood when neighbors work together.

Guide comprehension.

Monitor independent reading. Model strategic reading. Use Routine Cards 2 and 3.

During Reading Read the pages in a whisper. Raise your hand if you need help with a word. Stop at the end of each page to model asking questions. For example, for p. 107: After I read, I ask myself: What am I learning about neighbors? What is this page mainly about? The author tells how neighbors meet to talk about a playground that their neighborhood needs. I read that the whole neighborhood will help on the project. This page is mainly about how neighbors will work together to build the playground.

Summarize.

Use oral vocabulary to develop the concept.

After Reading Why did the neighbors have to *communicate* before building the playground? What might have happened if some neighbors didn't *respect* each other's ideas for the playground? Is a picnic a good way for the neighbors to show how much they *appreciate* each other? Why or why not?

Reread for Fluency "My Neighbors, My Friends," pp. 106–109

| To Do | To Say | *5–10 minutes* |

CORRECTIVE FEEDBACK

Monitor oral reading.

Read pp. 106–109 aloud. Read them three or four times so your reading gets better each time. Give feedback on children's oral reading and use of the blending strategy. See Routine Cards 1 and 4.

MORE PRACTICE

Instead of rereading just pp. 106–109, have children reread the entire selection three or four times. You may want to have children read along with the AudioText.

Homework

Practice Book, p. 111, Phonics: Sound of *oo* in *moon*

ACTIVITY 1 Reread for Fluency

Paired Reading "My Neighbors, My Friends," pp. 108–111

5–10 minutes

	To Do	To Say
CORRECTIVE FEEDBACK	Pair children. Monitor paired reading.	Children read pp. 108–111 orally, switching readers at the end of the first page. Have partners reread; now the other partner begins. For optimal fluency, children should reread three or four times. Give feedback on children's oral reading and use of the blending strategy. See Routine Cards 1 and 4.
MORE PRACTICE		Instead of rereading just pp. 108–111, have children reread the entire selection three or four times. You may want to have children read along with the AudioText.

ACTIVITY 2 Word Work

Phonemic Awareness Add Phonemes

2 minutes

	To Do	To Say
Scaffold instruction.	Distribute white boards. Write *lock.* Then add *un-* to form *unlock.* Lead children in adding *un*/un/ and *re*/rē/ as they write.	**Model** Listen to the sounds in *lock.* Stretch the sounds /lll/ /ooo/ /k/ as you write *l, o, ck.* Repeat. This time have children write the letters as you write. Add *un-* to *lock.* Now listen as I add /un/ to the beginning of *lock: un, lock, unlock.* Repeat. Have children add *un-* as you write. **Teach and Practice** Have children say the sounds as you point to the parts *(un, lock)* and blend the parts to say the word. *(unlock)* What word do we make when we add *un-* to the beginning of *lock? (unlock)* Repeat the process, adding *re-* to *fill.* Then continue the activity by adding *un-* and *re-* to form these words: repaint unpack resend unload retell unhappy

Blending Strategy Prefixes *un-*, *re-*

To Do	To Say	

5–10 minutes

Routine

Use the blending routine.

Write *quickly* and *hopeful*.

1 Connect You studied words like these already. What do you see on the end of both words? (a suffix) What do you know about reading these words? (Read the base word, read the suffix, then blend the parts.) Today we'll learn about another kind of word part called a prefix. A prefix comes at the beginning of a word.

Scaffold instruction.

Write *unpack* and *repack*.

2 Model These words both start with prefixes. The prefix *un-* means "not" or "the opposite of." *Unpack* means "the opposite of *pack*." The prefix *re-* means "again." *Repack* means "to pack again." This is how I blend these words. First, I figure out the base word by covering up the prefix. The base word is *pack*. I read the prefix, then I read the base word, and then I blend the parts together: *un, pack, unpack; re, pack, repack*.

u n p a c k   r e p a c k

3 Listen and Write Write the word *pack*. Write *un-* at the beginning of it. As you write, say each part to yourself: *un, pack*. Now blend the parts together and say the word aloud. Have children do the same with *repack*.

CORRECTIVE FEEDBACK

Write each practice word. Monitor student practice.

4 Group Practice Let's try reading these words with prefixes. Give feedback, using the *if . . . then* statements on Routine Card 1.

rethink   unwell   revisit   unable*   replace*   unlucky

5 Individual Practice Write the words; have each child blend two of them.

unzip   remake   replay   unlike*   replant   unclean   unspoken

Check understanding of practice words.

*Encourage children to use the meanings of the prefixes and the base words to figure out the meanings of the practice words. If needed, help children with meanings. A newborn baby is *unable* to walk or talk. I will *replace* the books on the shelf. *Unlike* means "not like." *Unlike* my sister, I love cats!

MORE PRACTICE

Model building words with prefixes *un-* and *re-*.

Build Words Have children write the prefixes *un-* and *re-* at the tops of their boards. Then have them add *un-* to these base words: *safe, tie, common, button, tangle*. Have them add *re-* to these base words: *use, read, heat, start, check*. Model building and blending *un-, safe, unsafe*. Call on children to read the new words and use them in a sentence or explain their meanings.

un-	*re-*
unsafe	reuse
untie	reread
uncommon	reheat
unbutton	restart
untangle	recheck

High-Frequency Words *been, brother, course, special, whole*

To Do	To Say	

3 minutes

Teach high-frequency words.

Lead cumulative review.

Display *been, brother, course, special,* and *whole*.

Use the Tested Vocabulary Cards. Point to a word. Say and spell it. Have children say and spell the word. Ask children to identify familiar letter-sounds and word parts. Have children take turns reading the words.

Use the Tested Vocabulary Cards to review high-frequency words from previous weeks.

ACTIVITY 3 Read a Passage

Reading "What Makes a Nice Neighbor?" pp. 112–117

To Do   **To Say**   *10–15 minutes*

Develop language and concepts. **Scaffold instruction.**	See Routine Cards 6 and 7. Display pp. 112–117. Ask questions and elaborate on answers to develop language. Key concepts: *neighbors, helpful, friendly, repainting, unloading, appreciates*	**Before Reading** Have children recall what they learned about neighbors working together. Read the title. Do a structured picture walk. **pp. 112–113** What do you see in these photos? (the country and a city) How might the woman standing by the van be helpful? What might she be doing? (giving the kids a ride) **pp. 114–115** These young neighbors look friendly. These neighbors help out on a farm by unloading hay and repainting the barn. **pp. 116–117** What are these neighbors doing? (blowing bubbles, walking a dog) The girl appreciates having a neighbor who is a friend. This helpful boy is taking his neighbor's dog on a walk. Let's read to find out more about what makes a nice neighbor.
Guide comprehension.	Monitor independent reading. Use Routine Cards 2 and 3.	**During Reading** Read the pages in a whisper. Raise your hand if you need help with a word. As you read, ask yourself: What am I learning about neighbors? What is this mainly about? **pp. 112–115** What did you learn about these children's neighbors? What makes them nice? (Kim's neighbors step in when Mom can't. Cooper's neighbors are friendly. Abby's neighbors help out on her farm.) **pp. 116–117** What did you learn about Kelly's neighbor David? (He is Kelly's special pal. He is like her brother.) Were you surprised when you read about Lucky? Why or why not? (I was surprised because Lucky is a dog. He thinks a nice neighbor takes long walks.)
Model summarizing.	Think aloud.	**After Reading** What did you learn about neighbors? What was the selection mainly about? Model how to summarize. The first few pages told how friendly neighbors step in when Mom can't do something. The next pages told how nice neighbors help each other and are like family. I put that all together and pick the most important ideas. This selection is mainly about what makes a neighbor nice.
MORE PRACTICE	Develop oral vocabulary.	Why do people *appreciate* having nice neighbors? Do you think the people we read about *respect* their neighbors? How can you tell? What are some ways neighbors *communicate* with one another?

ACTIVITY 4 Write

Response to Literature Shared Writing

To Do   **To Say**   *5 minutes*

Guide shared writing.	Write sentence frames. Read the questions.	Where do neighbors live? Neighbors live _____. What makes a nice neighbor? A nice neighbor _____. Invite children to suggest answers. Discuss and record answers to complete the sentence frames. While writing, model connecting sounds to letters and forming letters. (See pp. 241–243.) Have children read answers aloud as you track print.
Homework		Practice Book, p. 112, Phonics: Prefixes *un-, re-*

ACTIVITY **1** Reread for Fluency

Oral Reading "What Makes a Nice Neighbor?" pp. 112–115

	To Do	To Say	5–10 minutes
CORRECTIVE FEEDBACK	Monitor oral reading.	**Read pp. 112–115 aloud. Read them three or four times so your reading gets better each time.** Give feedback on children's oral reading and use of the blending strategy. See Routine Cards 1 and 4.	
MORE PRACTICE		Instead of rereading just pp. 112–115, have children reread the entire selection three or four times. You may want to have children read along with the AudioText.	

ACTIVITY **2** Word Work

Phonemic Awareness Segment and Blend Sounds

	To Do	To Say	2 minutes
Scaffold instruction.	Distribute white boards. Write *lit* and *unlit.*	**Model** Listen to the sounds in *lit.* Stretch the sounds /lll/ /iii/ /t/ as you write *l, i, t.* Repeat. Have children write letters as you write.	
	Lead children in segmenting and blending sounds as they write.	**Teach and Practice** Have children say the sounds with you as you point to the letters (/l/ /i/ /t/) and blend the sounds to say the word. *(lit)* **Listen to the sounds in** *lit.* Say *un, lit* as you write *un, lit.* Have children blend the prefix and the base word to say the word. Continue with these words:	

broom   unzip   repay   stool   unlucky   spooky

Fluent Word Reading Sound of *oo* in *moon*; Prefixes *un-, re-*

	To Do	To Say	5–10 minutes
Use the word-reading routine.	Write *booth.*	**1 Connect** You can read this word because you know that the letters *oo* can stand for /ü/. What sound does *oo* stand for in this word? (/ü/) What is the word? *(booth)*	*Routine*
Scaffold instruction.	Write *room, unpack,* and *retell.*	**2 Model** When you come to a new word, look at all the letters in the word and think about its vowel sounds and its parts. Say the sounds and word parts to yourself, and then read the word. Model reading *room, unpack,* and *retell* in this way. When you come to a new word, what will you do?	
	Write each practice word.	**3 Group Practice** Let's read these words. Look at all the letters, think about the vowel sounds, and say the sounds to yourself. We will read words with *oo* and the prefixes *un-* and *re-*. When I point to the word, let's read it together. Allow 2–3 seconds previewing time for each word.	

zoo   fool   scoop   unhappy   rethink   unable   smoothly   restart   gloomy

CORRECTIVE FEEDBACK	**MONITOR PROGRESS**	*If . . .* children have difficulty previewing and reading whole words, *then . . .* have them use sound-by-sound blending.
		If . . . children can't read the words fluently at a rate of 1–2 seconds per word, *then . . .* continue practicing the list.

MORE PRACTICE	Model reading words in sentences.	When I read a sentence, I read each word without stopping between the words. If I come to a word I don't know, I blend it. Then I read the sentence again. Model reading this sentence, stopping to blend *scoop: Refill the gloomy poodle's dish with one more scoop of food.*
	Write practice sentences.	Have each child read a sentence.
		Is it unsafe to restart this power tool? Dad is unhappy because he must repaint the huge bedroom. When the moon shines brightly, the raccoon snoops.

High-Frequency Words *been, brother, course, special, whole*

	To Do	To Say	3 minutes
Review high-frequency words.	Display *been, brother, course, special,* and *whole.*	Use the Tested Vocabulary Cards. Point to a word. Say and spell it. Have children say and spell the word. Ask children to identify familiar letter-sounds and word parts. Have them take turns reading the words.

ACTIVITY **3** Build Concepts

Oral Vocabulary *acquaintance, local*

	To Do	To Say	5–10 minutes
Teach oral vocabulary.	Display pp. 118–119 of the student book.	Today you will read a story that may remind you of your *local* neighborhood. Neighbors in this place are more than just *acquaintances.*	Routine
		1 Introduce, Demonstrate, and Apply	
Scaffold instruction.	Follow the Routine to teach *acquaintance* and *local.*	**acquaintance** In this story, a neighbor thinks of the twins next door as special friends rather than just *acquaintances.* An *acquaintance* is someone known to you, but not a close friend. Have children say the word. You probably have *acquaintances* at school—you know someone's name but don't know the person very well. Name some other places where you have *acquaintances.*	
		local In this story, the twins help a *local* woman in their neighborhood. When someone or something is near your house or not far away, it is *local.* I go to a *local* doctor rather than one in another town. Do you think it is easier to shop at *local* stores? Explain.	
	Display the words on the Amazing Words board.	**2 Display the Words** Have children say each word as they look at it. You can find sounds and word parts you know in big words. Read *ac/quaint/ance* as you run your hand under the syllables. Children can identify *quaint, n/n/, c/s/.* Children can decode *local.*	
	Monitor understanding.	**3 Use the Words** Ask children to use each word in a sentence. Model a sentence if children need help.	
MORE PRACTICE		Use oral vocabulary to discuss being a good neighbor and friend. How might a person change from being a neighbor's *acquaintance* to being the neighbor's good friend? If a *local* park had problems with people littering, how might a group of good neighbors solve the problem?	

ACTIVITY 4 Read a Passage

Reading "The Twins Next Door," pp. 118–125

| To Do | To Say | *10 minutes* |

Teach draw conclusions.

Introduce the skill.

Authors don't tell us everything, so we have to draw conclusions to figure things out for ourselves. When we draw conclusions, we think about what we read and what we know about life to figure out more about the people and events in a selection. For example, in the previous selection, we read that Lindy and James helped Abby and her dad unload hay. Sam and Brent helped repaint the barn. I know that nice neighbors help each other. I put this together and draw the conclusion that Lindy, James, Sam, and Brent are nice neighbors.

Scaffold instruction.

Model the skill. Display p. 115.

Apply the skill. Display p. 117.

Do you think Travis is a nice neighbor? Why do you think that? (Yes, because he walks Lucky when Ellen can't)

Develop language and concepts.

See Routine Card 6. Display pp. 118–125.

Model using key words and concepts.

Key concepts: *twins, appreciates, neighbors, chores, tricks, snooping raccoon, spooky*

Before Reading Read the title. Do a structured picture walk.

pp. 118–119 Miss Boon waits for the twins who live next door to visit her. She appreciates that her neighbors help her with chores.

pp. 120–121 The twins like to play tricks. One boy scratches on the wall to try to fool Miss Boon into thinking she hears a mouse or snooping raccoon. They yell "Boo!" to be spooky. Do the tricks upset Miss Boon? How can you tell? (No, she smiles at the tricks.)

pp. 122–123 The twins will unpack the messy boxes, refill the jars with rice, and unload Miss Boon's car. What do these actions tell you about the twins? (They're nice neighbors. They're helpful.)

pp. 124–125 What happens after the chores are done? (They play a game.) Do you think the twins enjoy visiting Miss Boon? How do you know? (Yes, they play games with her. They all laugh at the tricks.)

Monitor children's use of vocabulary.

Now turn to your partner and talk about the pictures, using the same words I did.

Guide compre-hension.

Monitor independent reading.

During Reading Read the pages in a whisper. Raise your hand if you need help with a word. As you read, ask yourself: What conclusions can I draw about the three neighbors?

Use Routine Cards 2 and 3.

pp. 118–119 How can you tell that Miss Boon looks forward to the twins' visits? (She looks at the clock and hopes they arrive soon.)

pp. 120–121 Do you think Miss Boon really thinks there is a mouse or a raccoon in her house? (No, she wants to join in on the twins' trick.)

pp. 122–123 Why do you think Miss Boon plans to play a game with the twins? (to show her appreciation for their help, to have fun with them)

pp. 124–125 How do the twins feel about Miss Boon? Why do you think that? (They like her. They help her with chores every weekend; they play tricks on her and games with her.) How does Miss Boon feel about the twins? Explain. (She likes them too. She makes popcorn for them, plays games with them, and plays along with their tricks.)

Guide retelling.

Prompt children as they retell the story.

After Reading Have one child retell the story while the others assist. Who are the characters? What happens at the beginning? in the middle? at the end? See Monitor Retelling, p. 246.

Homework Practice Book, p. 113, Draw Conclusions

ACTIVITY **1** Reread for Fluency

Paired Reading "The Twins Next Door," pp. 118–121

To Do	To Say	*5–10 minutes*

CORRECTIVE FEEDBACK

Pair children. Monitor paired reading.

Children read pp. 118–121 orally, switching readers at the end of the first page. Have partners reread; now the other partner begins. For optimal fluency, children should reread three or four times. Give feedback on children's oral reading and use of the blending strategy. See Routine Cards 1 and 4.

MORE PRACTICE

Instead of rereading just pp. 118–121, have children reread the entire selection three or four times. You may want to have children read along with the AudioText.

ACTIVITY **2** Word Work

Spiral Review Reading Longer Words with Affixes

To Do	To Say	*5–10 minutes*

Review reading words with affixes.

Scaffold instruction.

Write *peaceful.*

You can read this word because you know how to read words with suffixes. Remember, read the base word, read the suffix, and then blend the parts together. What is the word? *(peaceful)*

Write *peacefully.*

This longer word shows a base word and two suffixes. Read each part and then blend all the parts together. What is the word? *(peacefully)*

Write *unbutton.*

You can read this word because you can read words with prefixes. Remember, read the prefix, read the base word, and then blend the parts together. What is the word? *(unbutton)*

Write *unbuttoned.*

This longer word shows a prefix, a base word, and an ending. Read each part and then blend all the parts together. What is the word? *(unbuttoned)*

Make a class chart.

Build Words List prefixes, base words, suffixes, and endings in the first three columns as shown below. Have children write the longer words in the last column and read them aloud. Review the meanings of the affixes and discuss the meanings of the longer words.

Prefix	Base Word	Suffixes/Endings	Longer Word
un–	load	-ing	unloading
re–	start	-ed	restarted
	hope	-ful, -ly	hopefully
re–	print	-ing	reprinting
	thank	-ful, -ly	thankfully
un–	finish	-ed	unfinished

CORRECTIVE FEEDBACK

MONITOR PROGRESS

If . . . children have difficulty reading the words,
then . . . have them blend base words sound-by-sound before adding prefixes or suffixes. Have them read words again after adding affixes.

For more practice, see next page.

Continued Spiral Review

MORE PRACTICE

Model reading words in sentences.	When I read a sentence, I read each word without stopping between the words. If I come to a word I don't know, I blend it. Then I read the sentence again. Model reading this sentence, stopping to blend *replanted: We carefully replanted the tree to help it grow.*	
Write practice sentences.	Have each child read a sentence.	
	Hopefully, all the unfinished chores will be done by noon. The baby was sleeping peacefully until we restarted the car. Our pooch, Snoopy, faithfully waits for us to come home.	

Phonological and Phonemic Awareness Optional practice activities, pp. 280–283

ACTIVITY 3 Read Together

Choral Reading "How Does Jack Get to School?" p. 126

	To Do	To Say	*10 minutes*

Develop language and concepts.

Model fluent reading.

Display p. 126.

Before Reading This is a map. What do you know about maps? Allow children to share what they know. Labels on the map tell you the names of places and streets. You can use a map to find the shortest way to get from one place to another.

Read the title and have children predict what the map will show. This map shows Jack's neighborhood. When I read maps, I look at the pictures and read the labels carefully. Point to labels as you read them carefully. Repeat, having children point to each label as you read it. Then read the text under the map. Show me a way to get from Jack's house to the school. Is this the shortest way? Help children determine the shortest path.

Build fluency through choral reading.

Choral Reading I'll point to a place on the map and then we'll read the label together. Remember to read labels carefully.

Develop concepts.

Monitor listening comprehension.

After Reading Why do people like to find the shortest route between two places? Where can you get food in Jack's neighborhood? Which streets are near Pat's home?

ACTIVITY 4 Build Concepts

Oral Vocabulary *acquaintance, appreciate, communicate, local, respect*

	To Do	To Say	*5–10 minutes*

Review oral vocabulary.

Read the words on the Amazing Words board.

Focus on Letter-Sounds Remember, you can find sounds and word parts you know in big words.

- Which word begins and ends with /l/? Which word has /kwānt/ in it?
- Which word begins with /rē/? What letters stand for /rē/?
- Which words end with /āt/? What letters stand for /āt/?

To Do	To Say
Encourage discussion.	**Ask for Reasons and Examples** Review the meanings of the words. Then ask questions that require children to provide reasons and examples. • Is your best friend an *acquaintance?* Why or why not? • What are some things you do to show friends you *appreciate* them? • Name ways that you can *communicate* with people. • Name some *local* shops. Are they near your home or far away? • What are some ways you show *respect* for a teacher?
MORE PRACTICE Apply oral vocabulary to new situations.	• If you write a thank you note, are you showing someone that you *appreciate* or *acquaintance* them? • If a dog wags its tail, what might it be trying to *communicate?* • If your name is in the *local* newspaper, what might have happened? • If a coach wanted the *respect* of all team members, what should he or she do?

ACTIVITY 5 Write

Response to Literature Interactive Writing

5–10 minutes

	To Do	To Say
Generate ideas.	Review the story "The Twins Next Door."	**Why do you think the twins help Miss Boon?** Discuss what children read in the story and what they know from real life about helping neighbors, then have them draw conclusions.
Share the pen.	Have children participate in writing a list of reasons neighbors help.	Write *Neighbors help because* _____. Have children read the words you wrote. Then have them supply endings for the sentence. Invite individuals to write familiar letter-sounds, word parts, and high-frequency words. Have them find the spelling of high-frequency words on the Word Wall. Ask questions such as: • What is the first sound in *mood?* (/m/) What is the letter for /m/? *(m)* • What is the vowel sound in *mood?* (/ü/) What letters stand for /ü/? *(oo)* • What is the last sound in *mood?* (/d/) What letter stands for /d/? *(d)*
	Writing elements: conventions	Frequently reread what has been written while tracking the print. Point out that each sentence starts with a capital letter and ends with a period. Point out the extra space between words. Read the completed sentences aloud, having children read with you. (For example, *Neighbors help because helping puts them in a happy mood. Neighbors help because others may have helped them. Neighbors help because they want to make the neighborhood better.*)
MORE PRACTICE	Prompt independent writing.	**Journal Writing** Tell how you have helped someone.
	Homework	Practice Book, p. 114, High-Frequency Words

ACTIVITY 1 Assessment Options

Sentence Reading

To Do	To Say	5 minutes

Assess sentence reading.

Use reproducible p. 249.

Have each child read the sentences. Record scores on the Sentence Reading Chart, p. 253. Work with one child as others complete Write Sentences below.

This has been a special afternoon, but I'm unable to stay all night.
The unlucky boy had to reheat a whole plate of cool food.
Of course, my brother will replace the balloons he popped!

CORRECTIVE FEEDBACK

MONITOR PROGRESS

If . . . children have trouble reading words with the sound of *oo* in *moon* or the prefixes *un-* and *re-*,
then . . . reteach the blending strategy lessons on pp. 132 and 136.

If . . . children cannot read a high-frequency word,
then . . . mark the missed word or words on a high-frequency word list and send the list home for additional practice or have them practice with a fluent reader.

If . . . children misread a word in the sentence,
then . . . correct the error and have them reread the word and then the sentence.

Practice sentence writing.

Provide white boards.

Write Sentences Have children copy the sentences from reproducible p. 249 on white boards. Have them confirm spellings by comparing the words they wrote to the words in the sentences.

Phonological and Phonemic Awareness

Optional practice activities, pp. 280–283

Passage Reading

To Do	To Say	5–10 minutes

Assess fluency and comprehension.

Determine which children to assess this week.

Chose from these options: monitoring fluency (see pp. 244–245) and/or monitoring retelling (see p. 246). Have children reread "The Twins Next Door." Be sure each child is assessed every other week.

If you have time, assess every child.

ACTIVITY 2 Use Concepts

Oral Vocabulary *acquaintance, appreciate, communicate, local, respect*

To Do	To Say	5 minutes

Check understanding of oral vocabulary.

Use the Amazing Words to wrap up the week's concept.

Monitor understanding of oral vocabulary, using Routine Card 5.

As time allows, ask questions such as these.

- Describe the pictures on pp. 106–111 using some of the week's Amazing Words.
- If the mayor made your neighborhood a better place to live, would you *respect* the mayor or replace the mayor? Why?
- Why do neighbors *appreciate* their *local* police and firefighters?
- If you have trouble *communicating* with a friend, what would you do?
- When you first meet new neighbors, are they good friends or *acquaintances?* Why?

Preview next week's concept.

Next week you will read about doing the right thing.

ACTIVITY 3 Read to Connect

Reread "My Neighbors, My Friends," pp. 106–111

To Do | **To Say** | *10 minutes*

Monitor comprehension: draw conclusions.

To Do: Have children reread "My Neighbors, My Friends" silently.

To Say: As you read, use what you already know and what the author says to draw conclusions about neighbors and friends. After rereading, ask:

- **How do you think the neighbors make decisions about the playground project?** (The neighbors communicate. They respect each other. They work out problems. They work together.)

- **Why do you think the neighbors plan a picnic?** (The neighbors appreciate the work each person has done to build the playground. They want to celebrate together. They want to have fun together.)

For each question, record children's conclusions in a list on the board of what good friends and neighbors do. Children will use the list for Activity 4.

Make connections.

To Do: Have children make connections across texts.

To Say: In "What Makes a Nice Neighbor?" we read about different things neighbors do. How do the neighbors in this selection show they are good neighbors and friends? Add children's responses to the list of what good friends and neighbors do.

We also read "The Twins Next Door." Find that. How are Miss Boon, Devin, and Cole like the neighbors you read about in the other selections? Record children's comparisons on the board.

What did all the selections we read this week show us about friends and neighbors? What is the big idea? (We can all be good friends and neighbors.)

ACTIVITY 4 Write

Response to Literature Independent Writing

To Do | **To Say** | *5–10 minutes*

Assign descriptive writing.

To Say: Today you will write about how you can show your friends and neighbors that you appreciate them. You can get ideas from the things that friends and neighbors did for each other in this week's selections. Use details to describe what you would do. Encourage children to use words you wrote on the board for Activity 3 as they write.

Guide sentence correction.

To Do: Writing elements: conventions, focus, support

To Say: Have children check their writing by asking themselves these questions.

- Did I use a capital letter to begin sentences and proper nouns?

- Did I use correct marks at the ends of sentences?

- Did I use words with prefixes correctly?

- Did I use my own experiences?

MORE PRACTICE

Have children share their sentences with the group. Write their sentences on the board and have children practice reading and writing each other's sentences.

Homework Practice Book, p. 115, Writing

Unit 5 Week 5 *Doing the Right Thing*

What happens when we do the wrong thing?

Objectives *This week students will . . .*

Phonemic Awareness
- segment, blend, and count sounds in words

Phonics
- blend and read words with diphthongs *oi, oy*/oi/ and silent consonants *kn*/n/, *wr*/r/, *mb*/m/
- apply knowledge of letter-sounds to decode unknown words when reading
- recognize high-frequency words *hour, leave, minute, sorry, watch*

Fluency
- practice fluency with oral rereading

Vocabulary
- build concepts and oral vocabulary: *apologize, citizen, judgment, law, scold*

Text Comprehension
- read connected text
- compare and contrast to improve comprehension
- write in response to literature

Word Work *This week's phonics focus is . . .*

Diphthongs *oi, oy*   Silent Consonants *kn*/n/, *wr*/r/, *mb*/m/

High-Frequency Words *Tested Vocabulary*

The first appearance of each word in the Student Reader is noted below.

hour	An **hour** is a unit of time. (p. 137) There are 60 minutes in one **hour.**
leave	When you **leave,** you go away. (p. 130)
minute	A **minute** is one of the 60 equal parts of an hour. (p. 135) A **minute** is 60 seconds.
sorry	Someone who is **sorry** feels sad about something. (p. 133)
watch	When you **watch** something, you look at it for a while. (p. 130)

Amazing Words *Oral Vocabulary*

The week's vocabulary is related to the concept of consequences for doing the wrong thing.

apologize	to say you are sorry for something you did
citizen	a person who lives in a city or town
judgment	a decision you make
law	a rule made for all people
scold	to speak harshly, telling someone what they did wrong

Student Reader Unit 5 *This week students will read the following selections.*

Daily Lesson Plan

	ACTIVITIES	MATERIALS
Day 1	**Word Work** Phonemic Awareness: Segment and Blend Sounds Phonics: Blend Words with Diphthongs *oi, oy*/oi/ High-Frequency Words *hour, leave, minute, sorry, watch* **Build Concepts** *apologize, citizen, judgment* **Read a Passage** "Doing the Right Thing," pp. 130–137 Comprehension: Use Strategies Reread for Fluency	Student White Boards Sound-Spelling Card 26 Tested Vocabulary Cards *Sing with Me Big Book* and Audio CD Student Reader: Unit 5 Routine Cards 1, 2, 3, 4, 6, 7 AudioText Practice Book, p. 116, Diphthongs *oi, oy*/oi/

Day 2	**Reread for Fluency**
	Word Work Phonemic Awareness: Segment and Count Sounds
	Phonics: Blend Words with Silent Consonants *kn*/n/, *wr*/r/, *mb*/m/
	High-Frequency Words *hour, leave, minute, sorry, watch*
	Read a Passage "Who Teaches Us Rules?" pp. 138–145
	Comprehension: Use Strategies
	Write Response to Literature: Shared Writing
		Student Reader: Unit 5
		Student White Boards
		Sound-Spelling Cards 19, 20, 30
		Tested Vocabulary Cards
		Routine Cards 1, 2, 3, 4, 6, 7
		  AudioText
		Practice Book, p. 117, Silent Consonants
		  kn/n/, *wr*/r/, *mb*/m/

Day 3	**Reread for Fluency** **Word Work** Phonemic Awareness: Segment and Blend Sounds Phonics: Fluent Word Reading High-Frequency Words *hour, leave, minute, sorry, watch* **Build Concepts** *law, scold* **Read a Passage** "No Rules Day," pp. 146–157 Comprehension: Compare/Contrast	Student Reader: Unit 5 Student White Boards Tested Vocabulary Cards Routine Cards 1, 2, 3, 4, 6 AudioText Practice Book, p. 118, Compare and Contrast
Day 4	**Reread for Fluency** **Word Work** Phonics: Spiral Review Phonological and Phonemic Awareness Activities, pp. 280–283 **Read Together** "Funny Laws," p. 158 Comprehension: Listening **Build Concepts** *apologize, citizen, judgment, law, scold* **Write** Response to Literature: Interactive Writing	Student Reader: Unit 5 Routine Cards 1, 4 AudioText Student White Boards Practice Book, p. 119, High-Frequency Words
Day 5	**Assessment Options** Fluency, Comprehension Sentence Reading; End-of-Unit Test Phonological and Phonemic Awareness Activities, pp. 280–283 **Use Concepts** *apologize, citizen, judgment, law, scold* **Read to Connect** "Doing the Right Thing," pp. 130–137 Comprehension: Compare/Contrast **Write** Response to Literature: Independent Writing	Reproducible p. 250 Sentence Reading Chart, p. 253 Student White Boards Assessment Book, p. 60 Student Reader: Unit 5 Routine Card 5 Practice Book, p. 120, Writing

See pp. xvi–xvii for how *My Sidewalks* integrates instructional practices for ELL.

ACTIVITY **1** | Word Work

Phonemic Awareness Segment and Blend Sounds

| | To Do | To Say | *2 minutes* |

Scaffold instruction.

Distribute white boards. Write *join*.

Write *boy*. Lead children in segmenting and blending sounds as they write.

Model Listen to the sounds in *join*. Stretch the sounds /j/ /oioioi/ /nnn/ as you write *j, oi, n*. Repeat. Have children write letters as you write.

Teach and Practice Have children say the sounds with you as you point to the letters (/j/ /oi/ /n/) and blend sounds to say the word. *(join)* **Now listen to the sounds in *boy*.** Say /b/ /oi/ as you write *b, oy*. Have children say sounds as you point to letters and blend sounds to say the word. Continue with these words:

toy   boil   joy   coins   enjoy   noisy

Blending Strategy Diphthongs *oi, oy*/oi/

| | To Do | To Say | *5–10 minutes* |

Routine

Use the blending routine.

Write *loud* and *cow*.

1 Connect You already can read these words. What are the words? *(loud, cow)* What vowel sound do you hear in these words? (/ou/) What letters stand for /ou/ in *loud*? *(ou)* in *cow*? *(ow)* Today we will learn about the vowel pairs *oi* and *oy*.

Display Sound-Spelling Card 26.

2 Use Sound-Spelling Card This is *oil*. What vowel sound do you hear at the beginning of *oil*? (/oi/) Say the sound with me: /oi/. The letters *oi* can stand for the vowel sound /oi/.

Scaffold instruction.

3 Listen and Write Write the letters *oi* for /oi/. As you write, say the sound to yourself: /oi/. Now say the sound aloud.

Write *boil*.

4 Model The two letters *oi* stand for /oi/ in this word. This is how I blend this word: /b/ /oi/ /l/, *boil*. Now you try: /b/ /oi/ /l/, *boil*.

Write *toy*.

Repeat steps 2 and 3 for *oy*/oi/. Then model blending *toy*: /t/ /oi/, *toy*. Point out that vowel pairs *oi* and *oy* can stand for /oi/.

b o i l   t o y

CORRECTIVE FEEDBACK

Write each practice word. Monitor student practice.

5 Group Practice Let's try the same thing with these words. Give feedback, using the *if . . . then* statements on Routine Card 1.

toys   oink*   joyful   joint*   foil*   voices

6 Individual Practice Write the words; have each child blend two of them.

soil*   cowboy   choices   soybean*   pointing   enjoys

Check understanding of practice words.

*Children need to make sense of words that they segment and blend. If needed, help children with meanings. *Oink* is the sound a pig makes. A *joint* is the place in your body where two bones meet. Point to elbow and knee joints. *Foil* is a very thin sheet of metal we use to wrap food to keep it fresh. *Soil* is dirt. You plant *soybeans* in *soil*. *Soy* sauce is a salty brown sauce made from *soybeans*.

MORE PRACTICE

Model sorting words with *oi, oy*/oi/.

Sort Words Have children write the headings *oi* and *oy* on their boards. List these words: *Roy, spoil, noise, joystick, poison, oyster.* Have children sort the words by their spellings for /oi/. Call on children to read the sorted words and use them in sentences or tell their meanings.

oi: spoil, noise, poison   *oy:* Roy, joystick, oyster

High-Frequency Words *hour, leave, minute, sorry, watch*

	To Do	To Say
Teach high-frequency words.	Display *hour*.	**1 Say, Spell, Write** Use the Tested Vocabulary Cards. Display *hour*. Here are some words that we won't sound out. We'll spell them. This word is *hour*: *h, o, u, r* (point to each letter), *hour*. What is this word? What are the letters in the word? Now you write *hour*.
	Point to *our* in *hour*.	**2 Identify Letter-Sounds** Let's look at the sounds and word parts in *hour* that you do know. What is a smaller word that you know that appears in *hour*? (*our*)
		3 Demonstrate Meaning Tell me a sentence using *hour*. Model a sentence if children need help.
	Display *leave, minute, sorry,* and *watch*.	Repeat the Routine with *leave, minute, sorry,* and *watch*. Children can decode *leave*. They can identify these letter-sounds and word parts in the other words: *minute* (*min, t*/t/), *sorry* (*s*/s/, *ry*/rē/), *watch* (*w*/w/, *tch*/ch/). Have children write the words in their word banks. Add the words to the Word Wall. Point out that the words they are learning are on p. 159.

ACTIVITY 2 ## Build Concepts

Oral Vocabulary *apologize, citizen, judgment*

	To Do	To Say
Introduce oral vocabulary.	Display p. 25 of *Sing with Me Big Book*. Play audio CD.	This week you will learn about doing the right thing. Listen for the Amazing Words *apologize, citizen,* and *judgment* as I sing this song. Play or sing the song. Then have children sing it with you.
		1 Introduce, Demonstrate, and Apply
Scaffold instruction.	Follow the Routine to teach *apologize, citizen,* and *judgment*.	**apologize** The song says people should *apologize* when they make mistakes. When you *apologize*, you say you are sorry for what you did. Have children say the word. Sometimes it can be hard to *apologize*. Why? How do you feel after you've *apologized* for a mistake you made?
		citizen The song says every *citizen* tries to be good. You are a *citizen* of a city or town if you live there. Have children say the word. Good *citizens* vote and obey laws. What else do good *citizens* do?
		judgment The song says we all try to use our best *judgment*. A *judgment* is a decision you make. Using your best *judgment* means trying to make good decisions. Have children say the word. When you tell the truth, are you using good *judgment*? Why or why not?
	Display the words on the Amazing Words board.	**2 Display the Words** Have children say each word as they look at it. You can find sounds and parts you know in big words. Read *judg/ment* as you run your hand under the syllables. What sound does *j* stand for in *judgment*? (/j/) Continue with *u*/u/, *m*/m/, and *nt*/nt/. For *citizen* and *apologize*, children can identify these letter-sounds and word parts: *citizen* (*cit, z*/z/, *n*/n/), *apologize* (*pol, gize*).
	Monitor understanding.	**3 Use the Words** Ask children to use each word in a sentence. Model a sentence if children need help.
MORE PRACTICE		Use oral vocabulary to discuss the song. Should the boy *apologize* to the owners of the house? Why? Will he be using good *judgment* if he *apologizes*? How would his *apology* show that he is a good *citizen*?

ACTIVITY 3 Read a Passage

Build Background "Doing the Right Thing," pp. 130–137

	To Do	**To Say**	*10 minutes*

Develop language and concepts.

See Routine Card 7. Read aloud p. 129 of the student book.

Preview the Week Use the photo on p. 128 to introduce this week's concept of doing the right thing. **Is it easy to do the right thing? What happens when we do something wrong?** Read aloud the titles and descriptions on p. 129. Ask children what they think each selection will be about.

Scaffold instruction.

See Routine Card 6. Display pp. 130–137.

Ask questions and elaborate on answers to develop language.

Key concepts: *judgment, choices, decisions, hard*

Before Reading Read the title aloud. Do a structured picture walk with children.

pp. 130–131 Are you showing good judgment if you watch and wait before crossing the street? if you pick up your toys? Every day you have to make decisions about doing the right thing.

pp. 132–133 Mom is planning a surprise birthday party for Dad. Keeping the surprise a secret is hard! These pictures show two choices the girl can make. What are they? (tell Dad about the party or not tell him) Which choice shows good judgment? Why? (don't tell so Dad can be surprised)

pp. 134–135 The boy is excited to find money, but the bag doesn't belong to him. These pictures show two choices he can make. What are they? (pretend he doesn't have the bag or give it to the girl) Which choice shows good judgment? Why? (give the bag to the girl because it is hers)

pp. 136–137 The kids are having fun, but it's getting late and the neighbors don't like the noise. Which choices do the kids have? (keep playing or leave) Which choice shows good judgment? Why? (leave because it will make the neighbors happy)

Let's read to find out more about doing the right thing.

Guide comprehension.

Monitor independent reading. Model strategic reading. Use Routine Cards 2 and 3.

During Reading Read the pages in a whisper. Raise your hand if you need help with a word. Stop at the end of each page to model asking questions. For example, for p. 133: After I read, I ask myself: What did I learn? What is this page mainly about? The author writes, "Joy must think long and hard." The page shows two choices Joy can make. This page is mainly about whether Joy will tell Dad about his surprise. I learned that sometimes you have to think hard about deciding the right thing to do.

Summarize.

Use oral vocabulary to develop the concept.

After Reading Why is it sometimes hard to use good *judgment?* Why might you need to *apologize* if you used bad *judgment?* If Troy gives the money back to the girl, is he being a good *citizen?* Why is it important for *citizens* to obey laws about not making too much noise?

Reread for Fluency "Doing the Right Thing," pp. 130–133

	To Do	**To Say**	*5–10 minutes*

CORRECTIVE FEEDBACK

Monitor oral reading.

Read pp. 130–133 aloud. Read them three or four times so your reading gets better each time. Give feedback on children's oral reading and use of the blending strategy. See Routine Cards 1 and 4.

MORE PRACTICE

Instead of rereading just pp. 130–133, have children reread the entire selection three or four times. You may want to have children read along with the AudioText.

Homework Practice Book, p. 116, Phonics: Diphthongs *oi, oy*/oi/

ACTIVITY 1 Reread for Fluency

Paired Reading "Doing the Right Thing," pp. 134–137

	To Do	**To Say**	*5–10 minutes*
CORRECTIVE FEEDBACK	Pair children. Monitor paired reading.	Children read pp. 134–137 orally, switching readers at the end of the first page. Have partners reread; now the other partner begins. For optimal fluency, children should reread three or four times. Give feedback on children's oral reading and use of the blending strategy. See Routine Cards 1 and 4.	
MORE PRACTICE		Instead of rereading just pp. 134–137 have children reread the entire selection three or four times. You may want to have children read along with the AudioText.	

ACTIVITY 2 Word Work

Phonemic Awareness Segment and Count Sounds

	To Do	**To Say**	*2 minutes*
Scaffold instruction.	Distribute white boards. Write *knee*.	**Model** Listen to the sounds in *knee.* Stretch the sounds /nnn/ /ēēē/ as you write *kn, ee.* Repeat. Have children write letters as you write. Now let's count the sounds in *knee.* I will say the word slowly and hold up a finger for each sound: /n/ /ē/. There are two sounds in *knee.*	
	Lead children in segmenting and counting sounds as they write.	**Teach and Practice** Have children say the sounds with you as you point to the letters (/n/ /ē/). Hold up a finger for each sound. How many sounds in *knee?* (2) How many letters in *knee?* (4) Continue counting sounds with these words:	

know (2)   wrist (4)   thumb (3)   knock (3)   wreck (3)   crumbs (5)

Blending Strategy Silent Consonants kn/n/, wr/r/, mb/m/

Routine

To Do	To Say	5–10 minutes

Use the blending routine.

Write *not*, *rap*, and *them*.

1 Connect You already can read these words. What are the words? *(not, rap, them)* What sound do you hear at the beginning of *not?* (/n/) at the beginning of *rap?* (/r/) at the end of *them?* (/m/) Today we will learn about other letters that stand for /n/, /r/, and /m/.

Scaffold instruction.

Display Sound-Spelling Card 20.

2 Use Sound-Spelling Card This is a nurse. What sound do you hear at the beginning of *nurse?* (/n/) Say the sound with me: /n/. The letters *kn* can stand for /n/. When you see *kn* together, the *k* is usually silent.

3 Listen and Write Write the letters *kn* for /n/. As you write, say the sound to yourself: /n/. Now say the sound aloud.

Write *knot*.

4 Model The two letters *kn* stand for /n/ in this word. The *k* is silent. This is how I blend this word: /n/ /o/ /t/, *knot*. Now you try: /n/ /o/ /t/, *knot*. Have children compare the intial consonant sounds in *not* and *knot*.

Display Sound-Spelling Card 30. Write *wrap*.

Repeat steps 2 and 3 for *wr*/wr/. Then model blending *wrap*: /r/ /a/ /p/, *wrap*. Explain that when the letters *wr* are together, they stand for /r/ and the *w* is silent. Have children compare the initial consonant sounds of *rap* and *wrap*.

Display Sound-Spelling Card 19. Write *thumb*.

Repeat steps 2 and 3 for *mb*/m/. Then model blending *thumb*: /th/ /u/ /m/, *thumb*. Explain that when the letters *mb* are together, they stand for /m/ and the *b* is silent. Have children compare the final consonant sounds of *them* and *thumb*.

k n o t   w r a p   t h u m b

CORRECTIVE FEEDBACK

Write each practice word. Monitor student practice.

5 Group Practice Let's try reading these words. Give feedback, using the *if . . . then* statements on Routine Card 1.

knob   wrong   lamb   knuckle*   wriggle   plumber*

6 Individual Practice Write the words; have each child blend two of them.

knife   write   crumbs   knights   wreath*   limb*

Check understanding of practice words.

*Children need to make sense of the words they segment and blend. If needed, help children with meanings. A *knuckle* is a joint in your finger. Point to a knuckle. A *plumber* fixes pipes, sinks, and other things that use water in a building. A *wreath* is a ring of flowers or branches. We might hang a *wreath* on our front door. A *limb* is a large tree branch. Our arms and legs are also called *limbs*.

MORE PRACTICE

Model sorting words with *kn*/n/, *wr*/r/, *mb*/m/.

Sort Words Have children write the headings *kn*, *wr*, and *mb* on their boards. List these words: *knit, crumb, wreck, writing, thumb, kneel, lamb, wrist, knapsack*. Have children copy the words into appropriate columns, read the sorted words, and use them in sentences or tell their meanings.

kn	wr	mb
knit	wreck	crumb
kneel	writing	thumb
knapsack	wrist	lamb

High-Frequency Words *hour, leave, minute, sorry, watch*

To Do	To Say	3 minutes

Teach high-frequency words.

Lead cumulative review.

Display *hour, leave, minute, sorry,* and *watch*.

Use the Tested Vocabulary Cards. Point to a word. Say and spell it. Have children say and spell the word. Ask children to identify familiar letter-sounds and word parts. Have them take turns reading the words.

Use the Tested Vocabulary Cards to review high-frequency words from previous weeks.

ACTIVITY 3 Read a Passage

Reading "Who Teaches Us Rules?" pp. 138–145

	To Do	To Say	10–15 minutes

Develop language and concepts.

Scaffold instruction.

See Routine Cards 6 and 7. Display pp. 138–145.

Ask questions and elaborate on answers to develop language.

Key concepts: *rules, bus driver, teachers, playground, nurse, firefighter, police officer, laws, citizens*

Before Reading Have children recall what they learned about doing the right thing. Read the title. Do a structured picture walk with children.

pp. 138–139 What jobs do these people do? Point to each worker, read each label, and have children tell what they know about each job. **All these people teach us rules and make sure we follow them. What rules might a bus driver teach?**

pp. 140–141 What rules do teachers have? Why are these rules important?

pp. 142–143 Playground rules keep kids from getting hurt. But sometimes kids get hurt or sick even if they follow the rules. Then a school nurse can help them feel better and call their parents.

pp. 144–145 Firefighters teach rules that can prevent fires from starting. What else can firefighters teach us? (how to stay safe if a fire starts) Police officers explain laws, which are rules that all citizens must follow.

Let's read to learn more about people who teach us rules.

Guide comprehension.

Monitor independent reading.

Use Routine Cards 2 and 3.

During Reading Read the pages in a whisper. Raise your hand if you need help with a word. As we read, ask yourself: What am I learning about rules? What is this mainly about?

pp. 138–143 What are these pages mainly about? (the rules that bus drivers, teachers, and school nurses teach) These rules help us stay safe.

pp. 144–145 What did you learn about firefighters' rules? police officers' rules? (Firefighters' rules can help prevent fires and help us be safe if a fire starts. Police officers' rules keep our city safe.)

Model summarizing.

Think aloud.

After Reading What did you learn about rules? What was the selection mainly about? Model how to summarize. The first part told about rules that bus drivers, teachers, and nurses teach us to help us stay safe. The next pages told about rules firefighters and police officers teach us. I pick out the most important ideas. This selection is mainly about the rules people teach us to help us stay safe.

MORE PRACTICE

Develop oral vocabulary.

Do you show good *judgment* when you follow rules? Should you *apologize* if you break a rule? How do laws keep *citizens* safe?

ACTIVITY 4 Write

Response to Literature Shared Writing

	To Do	To Say	5 minutes

Guide shared writing.

Write sentence frames. Read the questions.

Who teaches us rules? We learn rules from _____.
What rules should we follow to be safe? We should _____.

Invite children to suggest answers. Discuss and record answers to complete the sentence frames. While writing, model connecting sounds to letters and forming letters. (See pp. 257–259.) Have children read answers aloud as you track print.

Homework Practice Book, p. 117, Phonics: Silent Consonants *kn*/n/, *wr*/r/, *mb*/m/

ACTIVITY **1** Reread for Fluency

Oral Reading "Who Teaches Us Rules?" pp. 138–141

5–10 minutes

	To Do	To Say
CORRECTIVE FEEDBACK	Monitor oral reading.	**Read pp. 138–141 aloud. Read them three or four times so your reading gets better each time.** Give feedback on children's oral reading and use of the blending strategy. See Routine Cards 1 and 4.
MORE PRACTICE		Instead of rereading just pp. 138–141, have children reread the entire selection three or four times. You may want to have children read along with the AudioText.

ACTIVITY **2** Word Work

Phonemic Awareness Segment and Blend Sounds

2 minutes

	To Do	To Say
Scaffold instruction.	Distribute white boards. Write *toys.* Write *kneel.* Lead children in segmenting and blending sounds as they write.	**Model** Listen to the sounds in *toys.* Stretch the sounds /t/ /oioioi/ /zzz/ as you write *t, oy, s.* Repeat. This time have children write the letters as you write. **Teach and Practice** Have children say the sounds with you as you point to the letters (/t/ /oi/ /z/) and blend sounds to say the word. *(toys)* **Now listen to the sounds in** *kneel.* Say /n/ /ē/ /l/ as your write *kn, ee, l.* Have children say sounds as you point to letters and blend sounds to say the word. Continue with these words: **spoil royal knuckle wrench limbs noises**

Fluent Word Reading Diphthongs *oi, oy*/oi/; Silent *kn*/n/, *wr*/r/, *mb*/m/

5–10 minutes

	To Do	To Say
Use the word-reading routine. **Scaffold instruction.**	Write *Roy* and *point.* Write *voice, enjoy, knitting, wrong,* and *crumbs.* Write each practice word.	**1 Connect** You can read these words because you know that *oy* and *oi* can stand for /oi/. What are the words? *(Roy, point)* **2 Model** When you come to a new word, look at all the letters in the word and think about its vowel sounds and its parts. Say the sounds and word parts to yourself, and then read the word. Model reading *voice, enjoy, knitting, wrong,* and *crumbs* in this way. When you come to a new word, what are you going to do? **3 Group Practice** Let's read these words. Look at all the letters, think about the vowel sounds and parts, and say the sounds to yourself. We will read words with *oi, oy,* and silent letters. When I point to a word, let's read it together. Allow 2–3 seconds previewing time for each word. **boys coin wrote knocked limbs boiling joy knuckles wrist**
CORRECTIVE FEEDBACK	**MONITOR PROGRESS**	*If . . .* children have difficulty previewing and reading whole words, *then . . .* have them use sound-by-sound blending. *If . . .* children can't read the words fluently at a rate of 1–2 seconds per word, *then . . .* continue practicing the list.

MORE PRACTICE	Model reading words in sentences.	When I read a sentence, I read each word without stopping between the words. If I come to a word I don't know, I blend it. Then I read the sentence again. Model reading this sentence, stopping to blend *knows: Troy knows that ants enjoy eating crumbs.*
	Write practice sentences.	Have each child read a sentence.
		Bend your knee joints and wriggle your thumbs. I'm writing about a noisy knight who is loyal. That spoiled boy has too many toys in his knapsack.

High-Frequency Words *hour, leave, minute, sorry, watch*

	To Do	**To Say**	*3 minutes*
Review high-frequency words.	Display *hour, leave, minute, sorry,* and *watch.*	Use the Tested Vocabulary Cards. Point to a word. Say and spell it. Have children say and spell the word. Ask children to identify familiar letter-sounds and word parts. Have them take turns reading the words.	

ACTIVITY **3** Build Concepts

Oral Vocabulary *law, scold*

	To Do	**To Say**	*5–10 minutes*
Teach oral vocabulary.	Display p. 146 of the student book.	Today you will read a story about a boy who suddenly decides not to follow any rules. The King of Rules *scolds* the boy and shows him what the world would be like without any *laws.*	*Routine*
		1 Introduce, Demonstrate, and Apply	
Scaffold instruction.	Follow the Routine to teach *law* and *scold.*	***law*** In the story, the boy sees what happens when drivers don't follow traffic *laws.* A *law* is a rule made for all people. Have children say the word. It is a *law* that cars must stop at red traffic lights. What might happen if someone broke this traffic *law?* Who makes sure people follow *laws?*	
		scold The boy in the story doesn't care if grown-ups *scold* him for not following rules. When you *scold* people, you speak harshly, telling them what they did wrong. Have children say the word. Mom and Dad may *scold* you for not cleaning your room. How does it feel to be *scolded?*	
	Display the words on the Amazing Words board.	**2 Display the Words** Have children say each word as they look at it. You can find sounds and parts you know in unfamiliar words. Read *law.* What letter is at the beginning of *law?* (l) What sound does that letter stand for? (/l/) Read *scold.* Children can identify *sc*/sk/ and the high-frequency word *old.*	
	Monitor understanding.	**3 Use the Words** Ask children to use each word in a sentence. Model a sentence if children need help.	
MORE PRACTICE		Use oral vocabulary to discuss rules and laws. Are *laws* important to have? Why or why not? Do you get *scolded* for breaking a rule? Do you get *scolded* for breaking a *law?* What can happen if people break *laws?*	

Read a Passage

Reading "No Rules Day," pp. 146–157

To Do	To Say	*10 minutes*

Teach compare/ contrast.

Scaffold instruction.

Introduce the skill.

Model the skill. Display pp. 139–141.

Apply the skill.

Today you will compare and contrast as you read. Remember, when you compare and contrast, you tell how two or more things are alike and different. For example, we can compare bus drivers and teachers. One way they are alike is that both teach kids rules. One way they are different is that bus drivers tell kids how to behave on the bus, and teachers tell kids how to behave in class.

Listen to this story. Cate and Carol are twins. Both girls like to listen to music. Cate likes to sing and dance. Carol likes to dance, but she doesn't like to sing. How are the girls alike and different? (Both like to listen to music and dance. Cate likes to sing, but Carol doesn't.)

Develop language and concepts.

See Routine Card 6. Display pp. 146–157.

Model using key words and concepts.

Key concepts: *usually, follows rules, neat, messy*

Before Reading Read the title. Do a structured picture walk.

pp. 146–147 What is Roy doing in this picture? (walking his dog with a pal) Roy usually does his chores. He follows his parents' rules. Roy decides to have a No Rules Day.

pp. 148–149 What rules is Roy thinking about not following? Right, Roy is thinking about not behaving in class and making a mess in the lunchroom!

pp. 150–151 Usually, Roy keeps his room neat, but on No Rules Day he plans on leaving it messy.

pp. 152–153 As Roy gets ready for school, the King of Rules comes in. The king doesn't knock because it's No Rules Day.

pp. 154–157 The king shows Roy what might happen without rules. Then he asks Roy if he thinks it is wrong to have rules. What do you think Roy said? Roy starts picking up his clothes, so I think he's decided rules are important. Do you agree? Why or why not?

Monitor children's use of vocabulary.

Now turn to your partner and talk about the pictures, using the same words I did.

Guide compre-hension.

Monitor independent reading.

Use Routine Cards 2 and 3.

During Reading Read the pages in a whisper. Raise your hand if you need help with a word. As you read, compare and contrast how Roy usually acts with how he plans on acting on No Rules Day.

pp. 146–149 On No Rules Day, will Roy act the same way he usually does or will he act differently? Explain. (differently; Roy usually follows rules, but on No Rules Day he won't follow any rules.)

pp. 150–151 On No Rules Day, will Roy's room look the same as it does at the beginning of the story? Explain. (No, usually he keeps his room neat. On No Rules Day, he plans on leaving his room messy.)

pp. 152–157 Compare how Roy plans to act at the end of the story with how he acts at the beginning of the story. (After meeting the king, Roy plans to follow rules like he does at the beginning of the story.)

Guide retelling.

Prompt children as they retell the story.

After Reading Have one child retell the story while the others assist. Who are the characters? What happens at the beginning of the story? in the middle? at the end? See Monitor Retelling, p. 246.

Homework Practice Book, p. 118, Compare and Contrast

ACTIVITY 1 Reread for Fluency

Paired Reading "No Rules Day," pp. 146–149

5–10 minutes

	To Do	To Say
CORRECTIVE FEEDBACK	Pair children. Monitor paired reading.	Children read pp. 146–149 orally, switching readers at the end of the first page. Have partners reread; now the other partner begins. For optimal fluency, children should reread three or four times. Give feedback on children's oral reading and use of the blending strategy. See Routine Cards 1 and 4.
MORE PRACTICE		Instead of rereading just pp. 146–149, have children reread the entire selection three or four times. You may want to have children read along with the AudioText.

ACTIVITY 2 Word Work

Spiral Review Diphthongs *ou, ow/ou/; oi, oy/oi/*

5–10 minutes

	To Do	To Say
Review the diphthongs *ou, ow/ou/* and *oi, oy/oi/*. **Scaffold instruction.**	Write *house* and *brown*.	**You can read these words because you know how to blend words with *ou* and *ow*. Remember, the letters *ou* and *ow* can stand for /ou/. What vowel sound do these words have?** (/ou/) **What are the words?** *(house, brown)*
	Write *join* and *boys*.	**You can read these words because you know how to blend words with *oi* and *oy*. Remember, the letters *oi* and *oy* can stand for /oi/. What vowel sound do these words have?** (/oi/) **What are the words?** *(join, boys)*
	Distribute white boards.	**Sort Words** Use a two-column T-chart to sort words according to their vowel sounds. Write *brown house* as the first heading and *join boys* as the second heading. Then list these words on the board: *point, gown, shout, toy, cloudy, flower, moist, noisy, proudly, enjoy*. Have children copy the words into appropriate columns. **How are the words in the first column alike?** (They all have the vowel sound /ou/. They all have the letters *ow* or *ou*.) **How are the words in the second column alike?** (They all have the vowel sound /oi/. They all have the letters *oi* or *oy*.) Call on volunteers to read the words aloud and use them in sentences or tell their meanings.

brown house	join boys
gown	point
shout	toy
cloudy	moist
flower	noisy
proudly	enjoy

CORRECTIVE FEEDBACK	**MONITOR PROGRESS**	***If . . .*** children have difficulty reading the words. ***then . . .*** have them use sound-by-sound blending.

For more practice, see next page

Continued Spiral Review

Model reading words in sentences.	When I read a sentence, I read without stopping between the words. If I come to a word I don't know, I blend it. Then I read the sentence again. Model reading this sentence, stopping to blend *cowboys: Noisy cowboys shout in the bunkhouse.*
Write practice sentences.	Have each child read a sentence. Troy proudly points out the loud owl on the tree limb. The royal mouse enjoys using a wreath of flowers for his crown. Kneel down on the ground and plant the soybeans in the moist soil.
Phonological and Phonemic Awareness	Optional practice activities, pp. 280–283

ACTIVITY 3 Read Together

Choral Reading "Funny Laws," p. 158

	To Do	**To Say**	*10 minutes*
Develop language and concepts.	Display p. 158.	**Before Reading** This page has a list of laws that were made a long time ago. Do you think people still have to obey laws if they were written long ago? Allow children to share their ideas. You have to obey all laws, even if they were written long ago. Sometimes, governments will change old laws or get rid of them, but some laws never get changed.	
Model fluent reading.		Read the title and ask children to predict what some of the laws might be about. When I read bits of information, I make sure I read carefully and not too fast. I'll read the state name first and then its law. I'll pause to think about each law before I read the next one. Read the laws at an appropriate rate, pausing after each state name and each law.	
	Build fluency through choral reading.	**Choral Reading** Now read the laws aloud with me. Try to make your voice sound like mine as we read. Reread the laws several times with children.	
Develop concepts.	Monitor listening comprehension.	**After Reading** Which law did you think was the funniest? Do you think some people may have really tied elephants to parking meters in Florida long ago? Explain. Should the states spend time and money to get rid of these laws?	

ACTIVITY 4 Build Concepts

Oral Vocabulary *apologize, citizen, judgment, law, scold*

	To Do	**To Say**	*5–10 minutes*
Review oral vocabulary.	Read the words on the Amazing Words board.	**Focus on Letter-Sounds** Remember, you can find sounds and word parts you know in big words. • Which words have /z/? What letter stands for /z/ in these words? • Which words have /l/? Which word has *old* in it? • Which words have *c?* Does *c* make the same sound in both words? • Which words have /j/? What letters make /j/ in these words?	

To Do	To Say
Encourage discussion.	**Provide One Context for All the Words** Review the meanings of the words. Then ask questions to place all the words in one context. • Do you think a good *citizen* always uses good *judgment?* • Do good *citizens* ever break *laws?* Should *citizens apologize* for breaking *laws?* • Do police officers *scold* citizens who break *laws?* What else might they do?

MORE PRACTICE

Apply oral vocabulary to new situations.	• If a person speaks angrily to you, is that person *scolding* you or *apologizing* to you? Explain. (scolding) • If a driver drives too fast, is the driver breaking a *citizen* or a *law?* (law) • If you run in the halls at school, are you using good *judgment* or poor *judgment?* (poor judgment)

ACTIVITY **5** ## Write

Response to Literature Interactive Writing

5–10 minutes

Generate ideas.

To Do	To Say
Review the story "No Rules Day."	**What lesson does Roy learn about following rules?** Have children compare and contrast how Roy usually acts and his plans for No Rules Day. Discuss how Roy's plans change after he meets the King of Rules.

Share the pen.

Have children participate in writing a list of reasons to follow rules.	Write *I follow rules because* _____. Have children read the words you wrote. Then have them supply endings for the sentence. Invite individuals to write familiar letter-sounds, word parts, and high-frequency words. Have them find the spelling of high-frequency words on the Word Wall. Ask questions such as: • **What consonant sound do you hear at the beginning of *know?* (/n/) What two letters stand for this sound in *know?* (kn)** • **What vowel sound do you hear in *know?* (long *o* sound) What two letters stand for this sound in *know?* (ow)**
Writing elements: conventions	Frequently reread what has been written while tracking the print. Point out that each sentence starts with a capital letter and ends with a period. Point out the extra space between words. Read the completed list aloud, having children read with you. (For example, *I follow rules because I know it is the right thing to do. I follow rules because it makes Mom and Dad happy. I follow rules because I like my room to be neat. I follow rules because I don't want my teacher to scold me.*)

MORE PRACTICE

Prompt independent writing.	**Journal Writing** Tell about some rules you follow every day.

Homework Practice Book, p. 119, High-Frequency Words

ACTIVITY 1 — Assessment Options

Sentence Reading

To Do	To Say	
		5 minutes

Assess sentence reading.

Use reproducible p. 250.

Have each child read the sentences. Record scores on the Sentence Reading Chart, p. 253. Work with one child as others complete Write Sentences below.

I'm sorry that boy hurt his wrist, thumb, and knee.
We have a choice of writing or playing for an hour.
When you watch noisy lambs, you can't leave them even for a minute!

CORRECTIVE FEEDBACK

MONITOR PROGRESS

If . . . children have trouble reading words with diphthongs *oi*, *oy*/oi/ or silent consonants *kn*/n/, *wr*/r/, *mb*/m/,
then . . . reteach the blending strategy lessons on pp. 148 and 152.

If . . . children cannot read a high-frequency word,
then . . . mark the missed word or words on a high-frequency word list and send the list home for additional practice or have them practice with a fluent reader.

If . . . children misread a word in the sentence,
then . . . correct the error and have them reread the word and then the sentence.

Practice sentence writing.

Provide white boards.

Write Sentences Have children copy the sentences from reproducible p. 250 on white boards. Have them confirm spellings by comparing the words they wrote to the words in the sentences.

Phonological and Phonemic Awareness

Optional practice activities, pp. 280–283

End-of-Unit Test

To Do	To Say	
		10 minutes

Assess fluency and comprehension.

Use Assessment Book, p. 60.

Options for end-of-unit assessment are available in the Assessment Book.

ACTIVITY 2 — Use Concepts

Oral Vocabulary *apologize, citizen, judgment, law, scold*

To Do	To Say	
		5 minutes

Check understanding of oral vocabulary.

Use the Amazing Words to wrap up the week's concept.

Monitor understanding of oral vocabulary, using Routine Card 5.

As time allows, ask questions such as these.

• Describe the pictures on pp. 130–137 using some of the week's Amazing Words.

• Do you usually *apologize* after being *scolded* by a teacher or parent? Explain.

• Do you think a *law* that says you can't walk with an ice-cream cone in your pocket is a good *law?*

• If all *citizens* used good *judgment* all of the time, do you think we would still need *laws?* Why or why not?

Preview next week's concept.

Next week you will read about why sports are important in our country.

ACTIVITY **3** Read to Connect

Reread *"Doing the Right Thing,"* pp. 130–137

To Do	To Say	5 minutes

Monitor comprehension: compare and contrast.

To Do: Have children reread "Doing the Right Thing" silently.

To Say: As you read, compare and contrast the choices the children in the selection must make. After rereading, ask:

- **In what way are the children's choices alike?** (All the children must decide what is the right thing to do.)

- **In what way are the children's choices different?** (Each situation is different. Joy must decide whether to keep a secret; Troy must decide whether to return money; Jing and her pals must decide whether they should stop playing.)

List each situation on the board and record children's ideas about what is the right thing to do in each case and why. Add to the list as you discuss the other selections below. Children will use the list for Activity 4.

Make connections.

To Do: Have children make connections across texts.

To Say: We also read "Who Teaches Us Rules?" about workers who teach us rules. If a kid asks you to move to a different seat while the bus is moving, what is the right thing to do? Why?

We also read "No Rules Day." Find that. If you make a mess at the lunchroom table, what is the right thing to do? Why?

How did all the selections we read this week show us about doing the right thing? What is the big idea? (Doing the right thing helps keep us safe, healthy, and happy.)

ACTIVITY **4** Write

Response to Literature Independent Writing

To Do	To Say	5–10 minutes

Assign personal narrative.

To Say: Today you will write about doing the right thing. Think of a time when you had to decide what was the right thing to do. Describe the choice you made and your reasons for it. Encourage children to use words you wrote on the board for Activity 3 as they write.

Guide sentence correction.

To Do: Writing elements: conventions, organization, support

To Say: Have children check their writing by asking themselves these questions.

- **Did I use a capital letter to begin each sentence and for proper nouns?**
- **Did I use the correct mark at the end of each sentence?**
- **Did I check the spelling of words, such as those with silent consonants?**
- **Are all the sentences about my choice?**
- **Did I add details?**

MORE PRACTICE

Have children share their sentences with the group. Write their sentences on the board and have children practice reading and writing each other's sentences.

Homework   Practice Book, p. 120, Writing

Unit 6 Week 1 *Sports*

Why are sports important in our country?

Objectives *This week students will . . .*

Phonemic Awareness
- segment and blend sounds in words
- add phonemes to make new words

Phonics
- blend and read words with the sound of *oo* in *book* and suffixes *-er, -or*
- apply knowledge of letter-sounds to decode unknown words when reading
- recognize high-frequency words *bought, buy, clothes, won, worst*

Fluency
- practice fluency with oral rereading

Vocabulary
- build concepts and oral vocabulary: *athlete, challenge, champion, effort, rival*

Text Comprehension
- read connected text
- compare and contrast to improve comprehension
- write in response to literature

Word Work *This week's phonics focus is . . .*

Sound of *oo* in *book*   Suffixes *-er, -or*

High-Frequency Words *Tested Vocabulary*

The first appearance of each word in the Student Reader is noted below.

bought   She **bought** a new coat. (p. 8)

buy   When you **buy** something, you get it by paying money for it. (p. 10)

clothes   **Clothes** are things you wear on your body. (p. 8)

won   Their team **won** the game. (p. 9)

worst   Something that is the **worst** is as bad as it can be. (p. 11)

Amazing Words *Oral Vocabulary*

The week's vocabulary is related to the concept of the importance of sports in our country.

athlete   somebody who competes in games and sports

challenge   a hard task or a test of someone's abilities

champion   the winner of a game or competition

effort   what you use to do something or to achieve a goal

rival   someone who wants and tries to get the same thing as you do

Student Reader Unit 6 *This week students will read the following selections.*

6	**Let's Find Out: Sports**	Expository Nonfiction
14	**Play Ball!**	Expository Nonfiction
22	**THAT'S a Football?**	Realistic Fiction
34	**Get Ready to Play Ice Hockey!**	Diagram

Daily Lesson Plan

	ACTIVITIES	MATERIALS
Day 1	**Word Work** Phonemic Awareness: Segment and Blend Sounds Phonics: Blend Words with Sound of *oo* in *book* High-Frequency Words *bought, buy, clothes, won, worst* **Build Concepts** *athlete, challenge, effort* **Read a Passage** "Sports," pp. 6–13 Comprehension: Use Strategies Reread for Fluency	Student White Boards Sound Spelling Card 38 Tested Vocabulary Cards *Sing with Me Big Book* and Audio CD Student Reader: Unit 6 Routine Cards 1, 2, 3, 4, 6, 7 AudioText Practice Book, p. 121, Sound of *oo* in *book*
Day 2	**Reread for Fluency** **Word Work** Phonemic Awareness: Add Phonemes Phonics: Blend Words with Suffixes *-er, -or* High-Frequency Words *bought, buy, clothes, won, worst* **Read a Passage** "Play Ball!" pp. 14–21 Comprehension: Use Strategies **Write** Response to Literature: Shared Writing	Student Reader: Unit 6 Student White Boards Tested Vocabulary Cards Routine Cards 1, 2, 3, 4, 6, 7 AudioText Practice Book, p. 122, Suffixes *-er, -or*
Day 3	**Reread for Fluency** **Word Work** Phonemic Awareness: Segment and Blend Sounds Phonics: Fluent Word Reading High-Frequency Words *bought, buy, clothes, won, worst* **Build Concepts** *champion, rival* **Read a Passage** "THAT'S a Football?" pp. 22–33 Comprehension: Compare/Contrast	Student Reader: Unit 6 Student White Boards Tested Vocabulary Cards Routine Cards 1, 2, 3, 4, 6 AudioText Practice Book, p. 123, Compare and Contrast
Day 4	**Reread for Fluency** **Word Work** Phonics: Spiral Review Phonological and Phonemic Awareness Activities, pp. 280–283 **Read Together** "Get Ready to Play Ice Hockey!" p. 34 Comprehension: Listening **Build Concepts** *athlete, challenge, champion, effort, rival* **Write** Response to Literature: Interactive Writing	Student Reader: Unit 6 Routine Cards 1, 4 AudioText Student White Boards Practice Book, p. 124, High-Frequency Words
Day 5	**Assessment Options** Fluency, Comprehension Sentence Reading; Passage Reading Phonological and Phonemic Awareness Activities, pp. 280–283 **Use Concepts** *athlete, challenge, champion, effort, rival* **Read to Connect** "Sports," pp. 6–13 Comprehension: Compare/Contrast **Write** Response to Literature: Independent Writing	Reproducible p. 250 Sentence Reading Chart, p. 254 Student White Boards Fluency Progress Chart, pp. 245 Student Reader: Unit 6 Routine Card 5 Practice Book, p. 125, Writing

See pp. xvi–xvii for how *My Sidewalks* integrates instructional practices for ELL.

Word Work

Phonemic Awareness Segment and Blend Sounds

To Do	To Say	2 minutes

Scaffold instruction.

Distribute white boards. Write *look.*

Model Listen to the sounds in *look.* Stretch the sounds /lll/ /u̇u̇u̇/ /k/ as you write *l, oo, k.* Repeat. Have children write letters as you write.

Lead children in segmenting and blending sounds as they write.

Teach and Practice Have children say the sounds with you as you point to the letters (/l/ /u̇/ /k/) and blend sounds to say the word. *(look)* Continue with these words:

wood   foot   good   hooks   shook   stood

Blending Strategy Sound of *oo* in *book*

To Do	To Say	5–10 minutes

Use the blending routine.

Write *moon.*

1 Connect You already can read this word. What is the word? *(moon)* What vowel sound do your hear in *moon?* (/ü/) Today we will learn about another sound the vowels *oo* can stand for. *Routine*

Display Sound-Spelling Card 38.

2 Use Sound-Spelling Card This is a book. What vowel sound do you hear in *book?* (/u̇/) Say it with me: /u̇/. The vowels *oo* can stand for /u̇/ when they are together.

Scaffold instruction.

3 Listen and Write Write the letters *oo* for /u̇/. As you write, say the sound to yourself: /u̇/. Now say the sound aloud.

Write *good.*

4 Model The letters *oo* stand for /u̇/ in this word. This is how I blend it: /g/ /u̇/ /d/, *good.* Now you try: /g/ /u̇/ /d/, *good.*

Have children compare the vowel sounds in *moon* and *good.* Point out that the vowels *oo* can stand for either /ü/ as in *moon* or /u̇/ as in *book.* Children may need to try out both sounds to figure out the word.

$$\underrightarrow{g} \quad \underrightarrow{o \quad o} \quad \underrightarrow{d}$$

CORRECTIVE FEEDBACK

Write each practice word. Monitor student practice.

5 Group Practice Let's try the same thing with these words. Give feedback, using the *if . . . then* statements on Routine Card 1.

wood   soot*   wool*   looks   woof*   stood

6 Individual Practice Write the words; have each child blend two of them.

foot   cook   took   hood   crook*   brook*   shook

Check understanding of practice words.

*Children need to make sense of words that they segment and blend. If needed, help children with meanings. *Soot* is what makes smoke dark. *Wool* is the soft curly fur that covers a sheep's body. *Woof* is the sound a dog makes. Demonstrate. A *crook* is a thief. A *brook* is a small stream.

MORE PRACTICE

Model spelling words with sound of *oo* in *book.*

Spell and Write What sounds do you hear in *hood?* (/h/ /u̇/ /d/) What is the letter for /h/? Let's all write *h.* What letters stand for /u̇/? Write *oo.* What is the letter for /d/ at the end of *hood?* Write *d.* Continue practice as time allows. Have children compare their spellings to what you've written.

wood   foot   wool   hooks   shook   cooking

High-Frequency Words *bought, buy, clothes, won, worst*

To Do	To Say	
		3 minutes

Teach high-frequency words.

Display *bought*.

1 Say, Spell, Write Use the Tested Vocabulary Cards. Display *bought*. Here are some words that we won't sound out. We'll spell them. This word is *bought*: *b, o, u, g, h, t* (point to each letter), *bought*. What is this word? What are the letters in the word? Now you write *bought*.

Point to *b* and *t* in *bought*.

2 Identify Letter-Sounds Let's look at the sounds in *bought* that you do know. What is this letter? *(b)* What is the sound for this letter? *(/b/)* Continue with *t*/t/.

3 Demonstrate Meaning Tell me a sentence using *bought*. Model a sentence if children need help.

Display *buy, clothes, won,* and *worst*.

Repeat the Routine with *buy, clothes, won,* and *worst*. Children can identify these letter-sounds: *buy* (*b*/b/), *clothes* (*cl*/kl/), *won* (*w*/w/, *n*/n/), *worst* (*w*/w/, *st*/st/). Have children write the words in their word banks. Add the words to the Word Wall. Point out that the words they are learning are on p. 35.

 ACTIVITY **2** ## Build Concepts

Oral Vocabulary *athlete, challenge, effort*

To Do	To Say	
		5–10 minutes

Introduce oral vocabulary.

Display p. 26 of *Sing with Me Big Book.* Play audio CD.

This week you will learn about sports. Listen for the Amazing Words *athlete, challenge,* and *effort* as I sing this song. Play or sing the song. Then have children sing it with you.

1 Introduce, Demonstrate, and Apply

Scaffold Instruction.

Follow the Routine to teach *athlete, challenge,* and *effort.*

athlete The song is about being an *athlete* on a team. An *athlete* is somebody who competes in games and sports. Have children say the word. An *athlete* on a basketball team is skilled at shooting baskets and dribbling the ball. What kind of *athlete* wears a bathing suit and races others in a pool?

challenge The song says that each game is a *challenge* for an athlete. A *challenge* is a hard task or a test of someone's abilities. Have children say the word. It may be a *challenge* to write a report. What is something you do at home that is a *challenge* for you?

effort The song says that athletes make their best *effort* when they play a sport. *Effort* is what you use to do something or to achieve a goal. Have children say the word. I may have to use a lot of *effort* to pick up a heavy box. What is something you do at school that takes a lot of *effort*?

Display the words on the Amazing Words board.

2 Display the Words Have children say each word as they look at it. You can find sounds and word parts you know in big words. Read *ath/lete* as you run your hand under the syllables. How do you say the first syllable of *athlete*? (/ath/) the second syllable of *athlete*? (/lēt/) For *challenge* and *effort*, children can identify these letter-sounds and word parts: *challenge* (*ch*/ch/, *n*/n/, *g*/j/), *effort* (*eff*, *t*/t/).

Monitor understanding.

3 Use the Words Ask children to use each word in a sentence. Model a sentence if children need help.

MORE PRACTICE

Use oral vocabulary to discuss the song. What *challenges* might an *athlete* face? How might the *athlete* use *effort* to face these *challenges*?

ACTIVITY **3** Read a Passage

Build Background "Sports," pp. 6–13

To Do	To Say	

10 minutes

Develop language and concepts.

See Routine Card 7. Read aloud pp. 1–5 of the student book.

Preview the Book Read aloud the title on p. 1. The selections in this book are about traditions. A tradition is a custom or belief handed down from one person to another, especially from a parent to a child. Use pp. 2–3 to preview the weeks in this unit and p. 5 to preview the selections in this week. Ask children what they think each selection will be about.

Scaffold instruction.

See Routine Card 6. Display pp. 6–13.

Ask questions and elaborate on answers to develop language.

Key concepts: *sports, baseball, football, track, bowling, teams, uniforms, pads, helmets, touchdown, track meet, pins*

Before Reading Read the title aloud. Do a structured picture walk.

pp. 6–7 Which sports are these kids involved in? (baseball, football, track, bowling) When you play baseball and football, two teams play against each other. You don't need teams for track or bowling.

pp. 8–9 These boys are playing football. What do you know about football? Players wear uniforms with pads and helmets to stay safe. One team throws and runs with the football while the other team tries to stop them. The team in black just scored a touchdown! They won the game!

pp. 10–11 This kid is competing in a track meet. Track is a sport with contests in running, jumping, and throwing. How do you win these contests? (run the fastest; jump or throw the farthest)

p. 12 These kids are bowling. What do you know about bowling? Point to the pins. These are bowling pins. The boy will roll the bowling ball and try to knock down as many pins as he can. He'll get points when pins fall.

p. 13 Do you always need a team to play a sport? No, some sports you can play by yourself. Which sports do you like best? Let's read to find out more about sports.

Guide comprehension.

Monitor independent reading. Model strategic reading. Use Routine Cards 2 and 3.

During Reading Read the pages in a whisper. Raise your hand if you need help with a word. Stop at the end of each page to model asking questions. For example, for p. 10: After I read, I ask myself: What did I learn about sports? What is this page mainly about? The author says, "At track meets, some kids run. Other kids jump." I learned what happens at track meets. This page is mainly about the sport of track.

Summarize.

Use oral vocabulary to develop the concept.

After Reading Is it a *challenge* for an *athlete* to throw or catch a football during a game? Why? Which sport do you think takes the most *effort:* football, track, or bowling? Why do you think that?

Reread for Fluency "Sports," pp. 6–9

To Do	To Say

5–10 minutes

CORRECTIVE FEEDBACK

Monitor oral reading.

Read pp. 6–9 aloud. Read them three or four times so your reading gets better each time. Give feedback on children's oral reading and use of the blending strategy. See Routine Cards 1 and 4.

MORE PRACTICE

Instead of rereading just pp. 6–9, have children reread the entire selection three or four times. You may want to have children read along with the AudioText.

Homework

Practice Book, p. 121, Phonics: Sound of *oo* in *book*

ACTIVITY **1** # Reread for Fluency

Paired Reading "Sports," pp. 10–13

To Do	To Say
	5–10 minutes

CORRECTIVE FEEDBACK

Pair children. Monitor paired reading.

Children read pp. 10–13 orally, switching readers at the end of the first page. Have partners reread; now the other partner begins. For optimal fluency, children should reread three or four times. Give feedback on children's oral reading and use of the blending strategy. See Routine Cards 1 and 4.

MORE PRACTICE

Instead of rereading just pp. 10–13, have children reread the entire selection three or four times. You may want to have children read along with the AudioText.

ACTIVITY **2** # Word Work

Phonemic Awareness Add Phonemes

To Do	To Say
	2 minutes

Scaffold instruction.

Distribute white boards. Write *play.* Then add *-er* to form *player.*

Lead children in adding *-er* and *-or* as they write.

Model Listen to the sounds in *play.* Stretch the sounds /p/ /lll/ /āāā/ as you write *p, l, ay.* Repeat. This time have children write the letters as you write. Add *-er* to *play.* Now listen as I add /ər/ to the end of *play: play, er, player.* Repeat. Have children add *-er* as you write.

Teach and Practice Have children say the base word and suffix as you point to each part *(play, er)* and blend the parts to say the word. *(player)* **What word do we make when we add *-er* to the end of *play?*** *(player)* **What sound do you hear at the end of *player?*** *(/ər/)* Repeat with *act* and *actor.* Continue adding *-er/ər/* and *-or/ər/* to form these words:

farmer   sailor   teacher   visitor   pitcher   inventor

Blending Strategy Suffixes -er, -or

5–10 minutes

To Do	To Say
Use the blending routine. Write *safely* and *hopeful*.	**1 Connect** You studied words like these already. They each have a base word and a suffix. What are the words? (*safely, hopeful*) What are the base words? (*safe, hope*) What are the suffixes? (*-ly, -ful*) Today we will learn about two more suffixes.
Scaffold instruction. Write *buzzer* and *sailor*.	**2 Model** These words end with the suffixes *-er* and *-or*. The suffixes *-er* and *-or* mean "a person or thing that ____s." *Buzzer* means "a thing that buzzes." *Sailor* means "a person who sails."
	To read these words, cover the suffix, read the base word, then read the suffix, and then blend the parts together. This is how I blend these words: *buzz, er, buzzer; sail, or, sailor.*
Write *runner* beneath *run* and *writer* beneath *write.*	Sometimes the spelling of the base word must change when we add the suffixes *-er* or *-or*. Review doubling final consonants and dropping final *e*. When we add *-er* to *run*, we double the last consonant, *n*. When we add *-er* to *write*, we drop the final *e* before adding *-er*.
Write *inventor.*	Longer words may have base words with more than one syllable. To read these words, break the base word into parts. Then blend the parts with the suffix. This is how I blend this word: *in, vent, or, inventor.*

b u z z e r   s a i l o r   r u n n e r

w r i t e r   i n v e n t o r

	3 Listen and Write Write the word *sail.* Write the ending *-or* next to it. As you write, say each part to yourself: *sail, or.* Now say the word aloud. Repeat with *buzzer, runner, writer,* and *inventor.* Instruct children to add or erase letters for *runner* and *writer.*
CORRECTIVE FEEDBACK Write each practice word. Monitor student practice.	**4 Group Practice** Let's try reading these words. Give feedback, using the *if . . . then* statements on Routine Card 1.
	kicker visitor toaster speaker batter collector
	5 Individual Practice Write the words; have each child blend two of them.
	player singer editor winner baker conductor
MORE PRACTICE Model building words with suffixes *-er* and *-or*.	**Build Words** Write the headings and base words shown below. Have children complete the second and fourth columns by adding *-er* or *-or* to each base word. Call on children to read the new words and explain their meanings. Have them identify which base word had spelling changes.

Base Word	+ er	Base Word	+ or
help	helper	act	actor
swim	swimmer	edit	editor
drive	driver	visit	visitor
report	reporter	direct	director

High-Frequency Words *bought, buy, clothes, won, worst*

3 minutes

To Do	To Say
Teach high-frequency words. Display *bought, buy, clothes, won,* and *worst.*	Use the Tested Vocabulary Cards. Point to a word. Say and spell it. Have children say and spell the word. Ask children to identify familiar letter-sounds. Have them take turns reading the words.
Lead cumulative review.	Use the Tested Vocabulary Cards to review high-frequency words from previous weeks.

ACTIVITY 3 Read a Passage

Reading "Play Ball!" pp. 14–21

	To Do	**To Say**	
			10–15 minutes
Develop language and concepts.	See Routine Cards 6 and 7. Display pp. 14–21.	**Before Reading** Have children recall what they learned about sports. Read the title. Do a structured picture walk with children.	
Scaffold instruction.	Ask questions and elaborate on answers to develop language.	**pp. 14–15** This boy collects balls from different sports. What kinds of balls do you see? Have children point to and name types of balls.	
	Key concepts: *baseball, inspector, perfect, soccer ball, panels, stitched, football*	**pp. 16–17** Point to a baseball. What is it like? (round, white) This inspector makes sure each baseball is the perfect shape, size, and color. An inspector's job is to check something very carefully.	
		pp. 18–19 Point to a soccer ball. What is it like? (round, sometimes black and white, sometimes colorful) Soccer balls are made of little parts called panels that are stitched, or sewn, together. Point to a panel.	
		pp. 20–21 Point to a football. Does a football have a round shape like the other balls? No, a football has a long and pointed shape. Let's read to find out more about balls from different sports.	
Guide comprehension.	Monitor independent reading.	**During Reading** Read the pages in a whisper. Raise your hand if you need help with a word. As you read, ask yourself: What am I learning about balls? What is this mainly about?	
	Use Routine Cards 2 and 3.	**pp. 14–15** What did you learn about balls used in sports? (Players may hit, kick, throw, spin, or catch balls.)	
		pp. 16–19 What did you learn about baseballs? What did you learn about soccer balls?	
		pp. 20–21 What did you learn about footballs? (Now they have a long and pointed shape. Long ago, they looked like watermelons.)	
Model summarizing.	Think aloud.	**After Reading** What did you learn about balls? What was the selection mainly about? Model how to summarize. The first part told how balls are used in different sports. The next part described baseballs, soccer balls, and footballs. I pick the most important ideas. The selection is mainly about balls used for different sports.	
MORE PRACTICE	Develop oral vocabulary.	Would it be a *challenge* for an *athlete* to hit a baseball that isn't perfect? Does it take a lot of *effort* to make a soccer ball by hand?	

ACTIVITY 4 Write

Response to Literature Shared Writing

	To Do	**To Say**	
			5 minutes
Guide shared writing.	Write a sentence frame. Read the question.	What does a baseball look like? A baseball _____.	
		Invite children to suggest answers. Discuss and record answers to complete the sentence frame. Repeat for soccer balls and footballs. While writing, model connecting sounds to letters and forming letters. (See pp. 257–259.) Have children read answers aloud as you track print.	
Homework		Practice Book, p. 122, Phonics: Suffixes *-er, -or*	

ACTIVITY 1 Reread for Fluency

Oral Reading "Play Ball!" pp. 14–17

To Do	To Say	5–10 minutes

	To Do	To Say
CORRECTIVE FEEDBACK	Monitor oral reading.	Read pp. 14–17 aloud. Read them three or four times so your reading gets better each time. Give feedback on children's oral reading and use of the blending strategy. See Routine Cards 1 and 4.
MORE PRACTICE		Instead of rereading just pp. 14–17, have children reread the entire selection three or four times. You may want to have children read along with the AudioText.

ACTIVITY 2 Word Work

Phonemic Awareness Segment and Blend Sounds

To Do	To Say	2 minutes

	To Do	To Say
Scaffold instruction.	Distribute white boards. Write *woof*.	**Model** Listen to the sounds in *woof*. Stretch the sounds /www/ /u̇u̇u̇/ /fff/ as you write *w, oo, f*. Repeat. This time have children write the letters as you write.
	Write *sailor*. Lead children in segmenting and blending sounds.	**Teach and Practice** Have children say the sounds with you as you point to the letters (/w/ /u̇/ /f/) and blend sounds to say the word. *(woof)* Repeat with *sailor: sail, or, sailor.* Then continue with these words:

hood	actor	books	looking	reader	collector

Fluent Word Reading Sound of *oo* in *book;* Suffixes *-er, -or*

To Do	To Say	5–10 minutes

	To Do	To Say
Use the word-reading routine.	Write *hook*.	**1 Connect** You can read this word because you know that *oo* can stand for /u̇/. What sound does *oo* stand for in this word? (/u̇/) What is the word? *(hook)*
	Write *books, leader,* and *inspector.*	**2 Model** When you come to a new word, look at all the letters in the word and think about its vowel sounds and its parts. Say the sounds and word parts to yourself, and then read the word. Model reading *books, leader,* and *inspector* in this way. When you come to a new word, what will you do?
Scaffold instruction.	Write each practice word.	**3 Group Practice** Let's read these words. Look at all the letters, think about the vowel sounds and parts, and say the sounds and parts to yourself. We will read words with *oo* and the suffixes *-er* and *-or*. When I point to the word, let's read it together. Allow 2–3 seconds previewing time per word.

Routine

wool	reader	printer	brooks	batter
cooking	gardener	racer	director	

CORRECTIVE FEEDBACK	**MONITOR PROGRESS**	*If . . .* children have difficulty previewing and reading whole words, *then . . .* have them use sound-by-sound blending.
		If . . . children can't read the words fluently at a rate of 1–2 seconds per word, *then . . .* continue practicing the list.

	Model reading words in sentences.	When I read a sentence, I read each word without stopping between the words. If I come to a word I don't know, I blend it. Then I read the sentence again. Model reading this sentence, stopping to blend *player: Look at that football player run!*
	Write practice sentences.	Have each child read a sentence.
		The baker and his helper cooked good snacks for us. The actors stood next to the director on the wooden stage. The shopper looks for books written by good writers.

High-Frequency Words *bought, buy, clothes, won, worst*

	To Do	**To Say**	3 minutes
Review high-frequency words.	Display *bought, buy, clothes, won,* and *worst.*	Use the Tested Vocabulary Cards. Point to a word. Say and spell it. Have children say and spell the word. Ask children to identify familiar letter-sounds. Have them take turns reading the words.	

ACTIVITY **3** Build Concepts

Oral Vocabulary *champion, rival*

	To Do	**To Say**	5–10 minutes
Teach oral vocabulary.	Display pp. 22–23 of the student book.	Today you will read a story where kids teach a visitor from another country how to play American football. The kids form football teams that are *rivals*. The players of the team that wins are the *champions* of the game.	*Routine*
		1 Introduce, Demonstrate, and Apply	
Scaffold instruction.	Follow the Routine to teach *champion* and *rival*.	**champion** In this story, the kids on the winning football team are the *champions*. A *champion* is the winner of a game or competition. Have children say the word. *Champ* is a short way of saying *champion*. A school's *champion* math team wins lots of math contests. Have you ever been on a *champion* team? What kind of team was it?	
		rival In this story, the kids on the two football teams are *rivals*. A *rival* is someone who wants and tries to get the same thing as you do. Have children say the word. Have you ever been another person's *rival*? What were you competing for?	
	Display the words on the Amazing Words board.	**2 Display the Words** Have children say each word as they look at it. You can find sounds and word parts you know in big words. Read *cham/pi/on* as you run your hand under the syllables. What smaller word do you see at the beginning of *champion*? (champ) Children can also identify */n/*. Read *ri/val*. Children can decode *rival* using V/CV syllable pattern.	
	Monitor understanding.	**3 Use the Words** Ask children to use each word in a sentence. Model a sentence if children need help.	

		Use oral vocabulary to discuss sports. Name sports where two *rival* teams play against each other. Would a *champion* usually win or lose a lot of games in a season? Explain.

ACTIVITY **4** # Read a Passage

Reading "THAT'S a Football?" pp. 22–33

	To Do	**To Say**	*10 minutes*

Teach compare/ contrast. | Introduce the skill. | Today you are going to compare and contrast as you read. Remember, when you compare and contrast, you tell how two or more things are alike and different. Look for clue words such as *both* and *like* that tell how things are alike. Look for words such as *but, unlike,* and *not like* that tell how things are different. For example, I can compare and contrast these books. Display two books. They are alike because they both have titles, pages, and words. But they are different because they are different sizes and are about different subjects.

Scaffold instruction. | Model the skill. Hold up two books.

Apply the skill. Display pp. 16–19. | How are a baseball and a soccer ball alike? How are they different? (Alike: Both can be used for sports. Both are round and have stitches. Different: A baseball is small, but a soccer ball is big. You hit a baseball, but you kick a soccer ball.) Record answers on a Venn diagram.

Develop language and concepts. | See Routine Card 6. Display pp. 22–33.

Model using key words and concepts.

Key concepts: *football, player, teams, visitor, country, soccer ball, score, touchdown, champion*

Monitor children's use of vocabulary as they talk.

Introduce proper nouns before reading. | **Before Reading** Read the title. Do a structured picture walk.

pp. 22–23 These kids want to play football. They need another player. They ask Ismail to play. He's a visitor from another country.

pp. 24–25 Ismail has a soccer ball. How are the soccer ball and football alike? (Both balls can be used for sports.) How are the balls different? (A soccer ball is round, but a football is pointed.) In Ismail's country, soccer balls are called footballs and the game of soccer is called football. He has never played American football.

pp. 26–29 The kids are showing Ismail how to play American football. Ismail will try to play football. How do you think he feels?

pp. 30–31 Ismail is running with the football. He will score a touchdown and his team will win! Ismail is a champion!

pp. 32–33 Now the kids play Ismail's football game. What do we call that game in the United States? (soccer)

Now turn to your partner and talk about the pictures, using the same words I did.

You'll see this name in the story. It is Ismail *(ish/mail).*

Guide comprehension. | Monitor independent reading.

Use Routine Cards 2 and 3. | **During Reading** Read the pages in a whisper. Raise your hand if you need help with a word. As you read, ask yourself: How are football and soccer alike? How are they different?

pp. 22–26 What did Ken buy? (a football) Why did Brook say they needed one more player? (so the teams would be even) How do you think Ismail felt when the others invited him to play?

pp. 27–33 How is a football game like a soccer game? (In both games, players use a ball and run down a field.) How is football different from soccer? (Players can touch the ball with their hands during a football game, but they can't in a soccer game, except for the goalie.) On p. 29, why do you think Ismail says, "I will be the worst player"? Is he right?

Guide retelling. | Prompt children as they retell the story. | **After Reading** Have one child retell the story while the others assist. Who are the characters? What happens at the beginning? in the middle? at the end? See Monitoring Retelling, p. 246.

| *Homework* | Practice Book, p. 123, Compare and Contrast |

ACTIVITY **1** Reread for Fluency

Paired Reading "THAT'S a Football?" pp. 22–25

	To Do	To Say	*5–10 minutes*
CORRECTIVE FEEDBACK	Pair children. Monitor paired reading.	Children read pp. 22–25 orally, switching readers at the end of the first page. Have partners reread; now the other partner begins. For optimal fluency, children should reread three or four times. Give feedback on children's oral reading and use of the blending strategy. See Routine Cards 1 and 4.	
MORE PRACTICE		Instead of rereading just pp. 22–25 orally, have children reread the entire selection three or four times. You may want to have children read along with the AudioText.	

ACTIVITY **2** Word Work

Spiral Review Compound Words

	To Do	To Say	*5–10 minutes*
Review compound words.	Write *bookstore.*	This is a compound word. It is made up of two shorter words. How do you blend a compound word? (Read each shorter word and then blend them into one word.) What is the first shorter word? *(book)* What is the second shorter word? *(store)* What is the compound word? *(bookstore)*	
Scaffold instruction.	Distribute white boards.	**Build Words** List pairs of shorter words that form compound words in two columns on the board. Have children join the pairs together and write the compound words. You could also challenge children by writing each list of words in a random order and having them figure out how to pair them to create compound words.	

Call on children to read the compound words and tell their meanings. Remind them that the meaning of a compound word is often made up of the meanings of the other two shorter words. Then have children use the compound words in sentences.

First Word	Second Word	Compound Word
zoo	keeper	zookeeper
book	mark	bookmark
farm	yard	farmyard
cook	book	cookbook
fire	place	fireplace
grass	hoppers	grasshoppers

CORRECTIVE FEEDBACK	**MONITOR PROGRESS**	**If . . .** children have difficulty reading the words **then . . .** have them blend each shorter word sound-by-sound first.
MORE PRACTICE	Model reading words in sentences. Write practice sentences.	When I read a sentence, I read without stopping between the words. If I come to a word I don't know, I blend it. Then I read the sentence again. Model reading this sentence, stopping to blend *beekeeper: The beekeeper started her work at sunrise.* Have each child read a sentence. It felt good to walk barefoot in the backyard. Look at the woodpecker and bluebird in that treetop! She took a textbook and her homework from her backpack.
	Phonological and Phonemic Awareness	Optional practice activities, pp. 280–283

Read Together

Choral Reading "Get Ready to Play Ice Hockey!" p. 34

	To Do	To Say	*10 minutes*
Develop language and concepts.	Display p. 34.	**Before Reading** This is a diagram. What do you know about diagrams? Allow children to share what they know. **A diagram is a picture with labels. The labels tell the names of the parts of the picture. A diagram can be a good way to show how things go together or how something works.**	
Model fluent reading.		Read the title and ask children to predict what the page is about. **This page shows a diagram of a hockey player's uniform. When I read a diagram, I read each label carefully. I pause after reading each label and use the picture to help me understand what the label means.** Read each label once as you point to the related uniform part. Pause after each label. Repeat, having children point to each label as you read. Then read the questions and have children answer them.	
	Build fluency through choral reading.	**Choral Reading** Now read and point to the labels with me. We'll pause after each label. Reread the diagram several times with children.	
Develop concepts.	Monitor listening comprehension.	**After Reading** What part of the body does the helmet cover? Why does a hockey player need a face mask? Repeat for other uniform parts. How does a diagram help you understand the parts of a hockey player's uniform?	

Build Concepts

Oral Vocabulary *athlete, challenge, champion, effort, rival*

	To Do	To Say	*5–10 minutes*
Review oral vocabulary.	Read the words on the Amazing Words board.	**Focus on Letter-Sounds** Remember, you can find letter-sounds and word parts you know in big words.	
		• What word begins with /r/? Which words begin with /ch/?	
		• What word has a *th?* What sound does *th* stand for?	
		• Which word has a *g?* What sound does the *g* stand for?	
		• Which word has /lēt/ in it? Which word has *champ* in it?	
	Encourage discussion.	**Provide One Context for All the Words** Review the meanings of the words. Then ask questions to place all the words in one context.	
		• Who is your favorite *athlete?* What sport does this *athlete* play?	
		• Do you think your favorite *athlete* is a *champion* player? Explain.	
		• Does your favorite *athlete* have a *rival?* Who is it? Does the *athlete* use a lot of *effort* when he or she plays against a *rival?*	
		• What has been your favorite *athlete's* biggest *challenge?*	
MORE PRACTICE	Apply oral vocabulary to new situations.	• If a book is a *challenge* to read, is it easy or difficult to read? (difficult)	
		• If a student is the *champion* of the spelling bee, is he or she the best or the worst at spelling words? (the best)	
		• If two *athletes* are *rivals* in a game, do they play with each other or against each other? (against each other)	
		• If a task doesn't take much *effort,* is it easy or difficult to complete? (easy)	

ACTIVITY 5 | Write

Response to Literature Interactive Writing

| | | 5–10 minutes |

	To Do	**To Say**
Generate ideas.	Review the story "THAT'S a Football?"	**How is football different from soccer?** Compare and contrast the two sports, including the types of ball each sport uses. Encourage children to use information from the story and their own experiences.
Share the pen.	Have children make a chart comparing and contrasting football and soccer.	Write these questions as headings in a two-column T-chart: *How is football like soccer? How is football different from soccer?* Under the left heading, write *Both sports _____.* Under the right heading, write *Football _____, but soccer _____.* Have children read the words you wrote. Then have them supply ideas for each sentence frame. Invite individuals to write familiar letter-sounds, word parts, and high-frequency words. Have them find the spelling of high-frequency words on the Word Wall. Ask questions such as:
		• **What is the first sound in teams?** (/t/) **What is the letter for /t/?** *(t)*
		• **What is the vowel sound in teams?** (long *e*) **What two letters stand for the long *e* sound in teams?** *(ea)*
		• **What consonant sound do you hear right after the long *e* sound?** (/m/) **What is the letter for /m/?** *(m)*
		• **What ending do you add to make the word mean "more than one team"?** *(-s)*
	Writing elements: conventions	Frequently reread what has been written while tracking the print. Point out that each sentence starts with a capital letter and ends with a period. Point out the extra space between words.
		Read the completed chart aloud, having children read with you. (For example, *Both sports have teams. Both sports use balls. Both sports have running and kicking. Both sports are fun. Football has a pointy ball, but soccer has a round ball. Football players use their hands, but soccer players use their feet.*)
MORE PRACTICE	Prompt independent writing.	**Journal Writing** Tell about a sport you enjoy playing with your friends.
Homework		Practice Book, p. 124, High-Frequency Words

ACTIVITY 1 — Assessment Options

Sentence Reading

| To Do | To Say | *5 minutes* |

Assess sentence reading.

Use reproducible p. 250.

Have each child read the sentences. Record scores on the Sentence Reading Chart, p. 254. Work with one child as others complete Write Sentences below.

The visitor will buy a good book at the gift shop.
After we won the game, our coach bought each player ice cream.
The worst rainstorm in March got my clothes all wet.

CORRECTIVE FEEDBACK

MONITOR PROGRESS

If . . . children have trouble reading words with vowels in *book* or suffixes *-er, -or,*
then . . . reteach the blending strategy lessons on pp. 164 and 168.

If . . . children cannot read a high-frequency word,
then . . . mark the missed word or words on a high-frequency word list and send the list home for additional practice or have them practice with a fluent reader.

If . . . children misread a word in the sentence,
then . . . correct the error and have them reread the word and then the sentence.

Practice sentence writing.

Provide white boards.

Write Sentences Have children copy the sentences from reproducible p. 250 on white boards. Have them confirm spellings by comparing the words they wrote to the words in the sentences.

Phonological and Phonemic Awareness

Optional practice activities, pp. 280–283

Passage Reading

| To Do | To Say | *5–10 minutes* |

Assess fluency and comprehension.

Determine which children to assess this week.

Choose from these options: monitoring fluency (see pp. 244–245) and/or monitoring retelling (see p. 246). Have children reread "THAT'S a Football?" Be sure each child is assessed every other week.

If you have time, assess every child.

ACTIVITY 2 — Use Concepts

Oral Vocabulary *athlete, challenge, champion, effort, rival*

| To Do | To Say | *5 minutes* |

Check understanding of oral vocabulary.

Use the Amazing Words to wrap up the week's concept.

Monitor understanding of oral vocabulary, using Routine Card 5.

As time allows, ask questions such as these.

- **Describe the pictures on pp. 6–13 using some of the week's Amazing Words.**
- **Are you an *athlete?* Which sport do you like to play?**
- **What subject is a *challenge* for you at school?**
- **What is something you do at school or home that takes a lot of *effort?***
- **Name a sport or other contest where two *rivals* compete to win. What will it take for one of the *rivals* to become the *champion?***

Preview next week's concept.

Next week you will read about the American flag and what it means.

ACTIVITY 3 Read to Connect

Reread "Sports," pp. 6–13

To Do	To Say	10 minutes

Monitor comprehension: compare/contrast.

To Do: Have children reread "Sports" silently.

To Say: **As you read, think about how different types of sports are alike and different. After rereading, ask:**

- **How are baseball and football alike? How are they different?** (Both are team sports. Both sports have throwing, catching, and running. Players on both teams wear special clothes. Baseball uses a round ball, but football uses a pointy ball. Football players kick the ball, but baseball players don't kick.)

- **How are track and bowling alike? How are they different?** (Both can be played without a team. Kids run and jump at a track meet, but they don't when they bowl. A ball is used in bowling, but not in track.)

Have children give details about each sport and record this information in lists on the board. Then have them use the lists to compare and contrast sports. Children will use these lists for Activity 4.

Make connections.

To Do: Have children make connections across texts.

To Say: **We also read "Play Ball!" Find that. Which type of balls do you like to play with the most: baseballs, soccer balls, or footballs? Why?** Add new information to the lists above about the sports that use these balls.

We also read "THAT'S a Football?" about kids teaching a visitor from another country how to play American football. Is Ismail's football the same as American football? Explain. (The sport Ismail calls *football* is called *soccer* in the United States.) Add any new information about football and soccer to the lists above.

What did all the selections we read this week show us about sports? What is the big idea? (There are different kinds of sports, and all can be fun to play.)

ACTIVITY 4 Write

Response to Literature Independent Writing

To Do	To Say	5–10 minutes

Assign descriptive writing.

Guide sentence correction.

To Do: Writing elements: conventions, support

To Say: **Today you will compare and contrast two sports. Choose two sports we read about this week and write to explain how these sports are alike and different.** Encourage children to use words you wrote on the board for Activity 3 as they write.

Have children check their writing by asking themselves these questions.

- **Did I begin sentences and proper nouns with capital letters?**
- **Did I use correct marks at the end of sentences?**
- **Did I use *both* or *like* to tell how things are alike? Did I use *but, unlike,* or *not like* to tell how things are different?**
- **Did I add details to explain the differences?**

MORE PRACTICE

Have children share their sentences with the group. Write their sentences on the board and have children practice reading and writing each other's sentences.

Homework Practice Book, p. 125, Writing

Unit 6 Week 2 *The American Flag*

What does our flag mean?

Objectives *This week students will . . .*

Phonemic Awareness
- segment and blend sounds in words
- add phonemes to make new words

Phonics
- blend and read words with vowel patterns *ew, ue* and prefixes *pre-, dis-*
- apply knowledge of letter-sounds to decode unknown words when reading
- recognize high-frequency words *air, America, beautiful, Earth, world*

Fluency
- practice fluency with oral rereading

Vocabulary
- build concepts and oral vocabulary: *anthem, history, independence, patriotic, symbol*

Text Comprehension
- read connected text
- identify sequence to improve comprehension
- write in response to literature

Word Work *This week's phonics focus is . . .*

Vowel Patterns *ew, ue*   Prefixes *pre-, dis-*

High-Frequency Words *Tested Vocabulary*

The first appearance of each word in the Student Reader is noted below.

air	The **air** is what we breathe. (p. 38)
America	**America** means the United States. (p. 39)
beautiful	If something is **beautiful,** it is very pretty to see or hear. (p. 44)
Earth	**Earth** is the planet we live on. (p. 44) The **earth** is also the ground.
world	The **world** is the Earth and everything on it. (p. 39)

Amazing Words *Oral Vocabulary*

The week's vocabulary is related to the concept of the meaning of the American flag.

anthem	a song that praises or declares loyalty to something
history	all that has happened in the life of a people or a country
independence	the freedom to make your own decisions
patriotic	having or showing love and loyal support for your country
symbol	something that stands for something else

Student Reader Unit 6 *This week students will read the following selections.*

38	**Let's Find Out: The American Flag**	Expository Nonfiction
46	**Taking Care of Our Flag**	Expository Nonfiction
54	**Broad Stripes and Bright Stars**	Realistic Fiction
64	**Old Glory**	Song

Daily Lesson Plan

	ACTIVITIES	MATERIALS
Day 1	**Word Work** Phonemic Awareness: Segment and Blend Sounds Phonics: Blend Words with Vowel Patterns *ew, ue* High-Frequency Words *air, America, beautiful, Earth, world* **Build Concepts** *history, independence, symbol* **Read a Passage** "The American Flag," pp. 38–45 Comprehension: Use Strategies Reread for Fluency	Student White Boards Sound-Spelling Card 37 Tested Vocabulary Cards *Sing with Me Big Book* and Audio CD Student Reader: Unit 6 Routine Cards 1, 2, 3, 4, 6, 7 AudioText Practice Book, p. 126, Vowel Patterns *ew, ue*
Day 2	**Reread for Fluency** **Word Work** Phonemic Awareness: Add Phonemes Phonics: Blend Words with Prefixes *pre-, dis-* High-Frequency Words *air, America, beautiful, Earth, world* **Read a Passage** "Taking Care of Our Flag," pp. 46–53 Comprehension: Use Strategies **Write** Response to Literature: Shared Writing	Student Reader: Unit 6 Student White Boards Tested Vocabulary Cards Routine Cards 1, 2, 3, 4, 6, 7 AudioText Practice Book, p. 127, Prefixes *pre-, dis-*
Day 3	**Reread for Fluency** **Word Work** Phonemic Awareness: Segment and Blend Sounds Phonics: Fluent Word Reading High-Frequency Words *air, America, beautiful, Earth, world* **Build Concepts** *anthem, patriotic* **Read a Passage** "Broad Stripes and Bright Stars," pp. 54–63 Comprehension: Sequence	Student Reader: Unit 6 Student White Boards Tested Vocabulary Cards Routine Cards 1, 2, 3, 4, 6 AudioText Practice Book, p. 128, Sequence
Day 4	**Reread for Fluency** **Word Work** Phonics: Spiral Review Phonological and Phonemic Awareness Activities, pp. 280–283 **Read Together** "Old Glory," p. 64 Comprehension: Listening **Build Concepts** *anthem, history, independence, patriotic, symbol* **Write** Response to Literature: Interactive Writing	Student Reader: Unit 6 Routine Cards 1, 4 AudioText Letter Tiles *b, c, d, e, g, l, m, o, o, r, t, u, w, z* Practice Book, p. 129, High-Frequency Words
Day 5	**Assessment Options** Fluency, Comprehension Sentence Reading; Passage Reading Phonological and Phonemic Awareness Activities, pp. 280–283 **Use Concepts** *anthem, history, independence, patriotic, symbol* **Read to Connect** "The American Flag," pp. 38–45 Comprehension: Sequence **Write** Response to Literature: Independent Writing	Reproducible p. 250 Sentence Reading Chart, p. 254 Student White Boards Fluency Progress Chart, p. 245 Student Reader: Unit 6 Routine Card 5 Practice Book, p. 130, Writing

See pp. xvi–xvii for how *My Sidewalks* integrates instructional practices for ELL.

Word Work

Phonemic Awareness Segment and Blend Sounds

2 minutes

	To Do	To Say
Scaffold instruction.	Distribute white boards. Write *new.*	**Model** Listen to the sounds in *new.* Stretch the sounds /nnn/ /üüü/ as you write *n, ew.* Repeat. This time have children write the letters as you write.
	Write *blue.* Lead children in segmenting and blending sounds as they write.	**Teach and Practice** Have children say the sounds with you as you point to the letters (/n/ /ü/) and blend sounds to say the word. *(new)* **Now listen to the sounds in *blue.*** Say /b/ /l/ /ü/ as you write *b, l, ue.* Have children say sounds as you point to letters and blend sounds to say the word. Continue with these words:

| flew | glue | grew | true | chew | clues |

Blending Strategy Vowel Patterns *ew, ue*

5–10 minutes

	To Do	To Say
Use the blending routine.	See Routine Card 1. Write *boot.*	**1 Connect** You already can read this word. What is the word? *(boot)* What vowel sound do your hear in *boot?* (/ü/) What two letters stand for /ü/ in *boot?* (oo) Today we will learn about other pairs of letters that can stand for /ü/.
	Display Sound-Spelling Card 37.	**2 Use Sound-Spelling Cards** This shows the moon. What vowel sound do you hear in *moon?* (/ü/) Say it with me: /ü/. The two letters *ew* can stand for the sound /ü/ when they are together.
Scaffold instruction.		**3 Listen and Write** Write the letters *ew* for /ü/. As you write, say the sound to yourself: /ü/. Now say the sound aloud.
	Write *grew.*	**4 Model** The letters *ew* stand for /ü/ in this word. This is how I blend it: /g/ /r/ /ü/, *grew.* Now you blend it: /g/ /r/ /ü/, *grew.*
	Write *true.*	Repeat steps 2 and 3 for *ue*/ü/. Then model blending *true:* /t/ /r/ /ü/, *true.* Point out that the letters *ew* and *ue* can stand for the vowel sound /ü/.

g r e w   t r u e

	To Do	To Say
CORRECTIVE FEEDBACK	Write each practice word. Monitor student practice.	**5 Group Practice** Let's try the same thing with these words. Give feedback, using the *if . . . then* statements on Routine Card 1.
		flew due news glue threw newt*
		6 Individual Practice Write the words; have each child blend two of them.
		crew* threw knew true chew bluebird screw Sue
	Check understanding of practice words.	*Children need to make sense of words that they segment and blend. If needed, help children with meanings. **A *newt* is a small salamander.** *Newts* look like lizards. **A *crew* is a group of people that work together.** Point out homophones such as *due, do,* and *dew,* or *knew* and *new,* and remind children to pay attention to spelling and context to figure out meanings.
MORE PRACTICE	Model building words with *ew* and *ue.*	**Build Words** Have children build words by adding *dr, fl, st, bl, ch* to the front of *ew,* and *cl, bl, gl, tr* to the front of *ue.* Model blending the sounds before the vowel together and then saying the vowel sound: *dr, ew, drew.* Call on children to read the words and use them in sentences or tell their meanings.

High-Frequency Words *air, America, beautiful, Earth, world*

To Do	To Say	
		3 minutes

Teach high-frequency words.

Display *air*.

1 Say, Spell, Write Use the Tested Vocabulary Cards. Display *air*. Here are some words that we won't sound out. We'll spell them. This word is *air: a, i, r* (point to each letter), *air*. What is this word? What are the letters in the word? Now you write *air*.

Point to *r* in *air*.

2 Identify Letter-Sounds Let's look at the sound in *air* that you do know. What is this letter? *(r)* What is the sound for this letter? *(/r/)*

3 Demonstrate Meaning Tell me a sentence using *air*. Model a sentence if children need help.

Display *America, beautiful, Earth,* and *world*.

Repeat the Routine with *America, beautiful, Earth,* and *world*. Children can identify these letter-sounds and word parts: *America* (*m*/m/, *c*/k/), *beautiful* (*b*/b/, *t*/t/, *-ful*), *Earth* (*th*/th/), *world* (*w*/w/, *ld*/ld/). Have children write the words in their word banks. Add the words to the Word Wall. Point out that the words they are learning are on p. 65.

ACTIVITY 2 Build Concepts

Oral Vocabulary *history, independence, symbol*

To Do	To Say	
		5–10 minutes

Introduce oral vocabulary.

Display p. 27 of *Sing with Me Big Book*. Play audio CD.

This week you will learn about the American flag. Listen for the Amazing Words *history, independence,* and *symbol* as I sing this song. Play or sing the song. Then have children sing it with you.

1 Introduce, Demonstrate, and Apply

Scaffold instruction.

Follow the Routine to teach *history, independence,* and *symbol*.

history According to the song, all of us share the *history* of the flag. *History* is all that has happened in the life of a people or a country. Have children say the word. The war against England was an important event in the *history* of the United States. What is an important event in your family's *history*?

independence The song says the flag is also a *symbol* of *independence*. *Independence* means freedom to make your own decisions. Have children say the word. Many years ago, the colonies fought a war to win *independence* from England. Why would a person or country want *independence*?

symbol The song says our flag is a *symbol* of our country. A *symbol* is something that stands for something else. Have children say the word. The plus sign is a *symbol* for addition. What *symbol* stands for snow on a weather forecast?

Display the words on the Amazing Words board.

2 Display the Words Have children say each word as they look at it. You can find sounds and word parts you know in big words. Read *sym/bol* as you run your hand under the syllables. What sound do you hear at the beginning of *symbol*? (/s/) What letter stands for /s/ in *symbol*? (s) Continue for *m*/m/, *b*/b/, and *l*/l/. For *independence* and *history*, children can identify these letter-sounds and word parts: *independence* (*in, d*/d/, *pen, n*/n/, *c*/s/), *history* (*his*/his/, *tor*/tər/, *y*/ē/).

Monitor understanding.

3 Use the Words Ask children to use each word in a sentence. Model a sentence if children need help.

MORE PRACTICE

Use oral vocabulary to discuss the song. Is the American flag an important *symbol*? Explain. What do you know about the flag's *history*? Why do people think of *independence* when they look at the flag?

ACTIVITY **3** Read a Passage

Build Background "The American Flag," pp. 38–45

	To Do	To Say	*10 minutes*

Develop language and concepts.

See Routine Card 7. Read aloud p. 37 of the student book.

Preview the Week Use the photo on p. 36 to introduce this week's concept of the American flag. **This is the American flag. What do you already know about it?** Read aloud the titles and descriptions on p. 37. Ask children what they think each selection will be about.

Scaffold instruction.

See Routine Card 6. Display pp. 38–45.

Ask questions and elaborate on answers to develop language.

Key concepts: *country, flag, symbol, American, homeland, pride, free, stripes, stars, states, beautiful*

Before Reading Read the title aloud. Do a structured picture walk with children.

pp. 38–39 What do these pictures show? (flags) **A country's flag is a symbol that tells about the country. People fly flags to show their pride in their homeland, the place where they were born or call home. Point to the American flag. The selection says the flag shows that people in America are free. When you are free, you can think and speak your own ideas.**

pp. 40–41 How are these flags alike? (Both have stripes and stars.) **How are they different?** (Today's flag has more stars.) **Both flags have 7 red and 6 white stripes because the United States started with 13 colonies. Colonies were the communities that grew before America was a country. The first flag (point to it) had 13 stars for the first 13 colonies. Why does today's flag have 50 stars?** (The United States now has 50 states.)

pp. 42–45 How are these pictures alike? (All show the American flag.) **We can see the American flag in many places, even on the moon! Where have you seen the flag? Some people think the flag is beautiful. Do you agree?**

Teach story words.

Write *colonies.*

You will read this word in the selection. It is *colonies.* **Have children review the word and spell it. Review its meaning. Let's read to find out more about the American flag.**

Guide comprehension.

Monitor independent reading. Model strategic reading. Use Routine Cards 2 and 3.

During Reading Read the pages in a whisper. Raise your hand if you need help with a word. Stop at the end of each page to model asking questions. For example, for p. 43: **After I read, I ask myself: What does this page mainly tell us about the flag? The author writes, "You will see it in lots of other places too." The page is mainly about the different places you can see the American flag.**

Summarize.

Use oral vocabulary to develop the concept.

After Reading The American flag is a *symbol* that stands for the country's *independence,* or freedom. Why do people think of *independence* when they look at the American flag? The stars and stripes on the flag are also *symbols.* What do the stars and stripes stand for? What do they tell us about the *history* of the United States?

Reread for Fluency "The American Flag," pp. 39–41

	To Do	To Say	*5–10 minutes*

CORRECTIVE FEEDBACK

Monitor oral reading.

Read pp. 39–41 aloud. Read them three or four times so your reading gets better each time. Give feedback on children's oral reading and use of the blending strategy. See Routine Cards 1 and 4.

MORE PRACTICE

Instead of rereading just pp. 39–41, have children reread the entire selection three or four times. You may want to have children read along with the AudioText.

Homework   Practice Book, p. 126, Phonics: Vowel Patterns *ew, ue*

ACTIVITY 1 Reread for Fluency

Paired Reading "The American Flag," pp. 42–45

To Do	To Say	
		5–10 minutes

CORRECTIVE FEEDBACK

Pair children. Monitor paired reading.

Children read pp. 42–45 orally, switching readers at the end of the first page. Have partners reread; now the other partner begins. For optimal fluency, children should reread three or four times. Give feedback on children's oral reading and use of the blending strategy. See Routine Cards 1 and 4.

MORE PRACTICE

Instead of rereading just pp. 42–45, have children reread the entire selection three or four times. You may want to have children read along with the Audiotext.

ACTIVITY 2 Word Work

Phonemic Awareness Add Phonemes

To Do	To Say	
		2 minutes

Scaffold instruction.

Distribute white boards. Write *heat*. Then add *pre-* to form *preheat*.

Lead children in adding *pre*/prē/ and *dis*/dis/ as they write.

Model Listen to the sounds in *heat*. Stretch the sounds /h/ /ēēē/ /t/ as you write *h, ea, t*. Repeat. This time have children write the letters as you write. Add *pre-* to *heat*. Now listen as I add /prē/ to *heat: pre, heat, preheat*. You preheat the oven before you cook something in it.

Teach and Practice Have children say the sounds as you point to the parts *(pre, heat)* and blend the parts to say the word. *(preheat)* What word do we make when we add *pre-* to the beginning of *heat*? *(preheat)* Repeat the process, adding *dis-* to *like*. Then continue the activity by adding *pre-* and *dis-* to form these words:

pregame	distrust	prepay	disloyal	preschool	disrespect

Blending Strategy Prefixes *pre-*, *dis-*

To Do	To Say	

Routine

Use the blending routine.

Write *unsafe* and *reread*.

1 Connect You studied words like these already. They both have a base word and a prefix. What are the words? *(unsafe, reread)* What are the base words? *(safe, read)* What are the prefixes? *(un-, re-)* Today we will learn about two more prefixes: *pre-* and *dis-*.

Scaffold instruction.

Write *pregame* and *distrust*.

2 Model These words both start with prefixes. The prefix *pre-* means "before." *Pregame* means "before the game." The prefix *dis-* means "the opposite of" or "not." *Distrust* means "not trust." To read these words, cover the prefix, read the base word, and then blend the prefix and the base word. Model blending *pregame* and *distrust*: *pre, game, pregame; dis, trust, distrust.*

Write *disloyal*.

Longer words may have base words with more than one syllable. To read these words, break the base word into parts and blend the parts together to figure out the base word. Then blend the prefix and the base word. Cover up *dis-*. The base word is /loi/ /əl/, *loyal.* Now blend the prefix and base word: *dis, loyal, disloyal. Disloyal* means "not loyal."

p r e g a m e   d i s t r u s t   d i s l o y a l

3 Listen and Write Write the word *game.* Write *pre-* at the beginning of it. As you write, say each part to yourself: *pre, game.* Now blend the parts together and say the word aloud. Have children do the same for *distrust.*

CORRECTIVE FEEDBACK

Write each practice word. Monitor student practice.

4 Group Practice Let's try reading these words. Give feedback, using the *if . . . then* statements on Routine Card 1.

precut   dislike*   preteen*   disgrace*   preheat   distaste*

5 Individual Practice Write the words; have each child blend two of them.

prepay   displease   precook   disconnect   preflight   disrespect*

Check understanding of practice words.

*Encourage children to use the meanings of the prefixes and the base words to help them figure out the meanings of the words. If needed, help children with meanings. A *preteen* is a child who is not yet a teenager, usually between 10 and 12 years old. *Disgrace* and *disrespect* mean to show no respect. Dragging the American flag on the ground shows *disrespect.* It is a *disgrace. Distaste* and *dislike* are feelings of not liking something. He *disliked* onions. His *distaste* for them showed on his face. Grimace.

MORE PRACTICE

Model building words with prefixes *pre-* and *dis-*.

Build Words Have children add *pre-* to these base words: *heat, cut, school, cooked.* Have them add *dis-* to these base words: *like, please, infect, loyal.* Model building and blending *pre-, heat, preheat.* Call on children to read the new words and use them in sentences or explain their meanings.

pre-	dis-
preheat	dislike
precut	displease
preschool	disinfect
precooked	disloyal

High-Frequency Words *air, America, beautiful, Earth, world*

To Do	To Say	

Teach high-frequency words.

Display *air, America, beautiful, Earth,* and *world.*

Use the Tested Vocabulary Cards. Point to a word. Say and spell it. Have children say and spell the word. Ask children to identify familiar letter-sounds and word parts. Have them take turns reading the words.

Lead cumulative review.

Use the Tested Vocabulary Cards to review high-frequency words from previous weeks.

ACTIVITY 3 Read a Passage

Reading "Taking Care of Our Flag," pp. 46–53

			10–15 minutes

To Do / **To Say**

Develop language and concepts.

Scaffold instruction.

See Routine Cards 6 and 7. Display pp. 46–53.

Ask questions and elaborate on answers to develop language.

Key concepts: *flag, pride, respect, disrespect, rules, proper, patches, disrespectful, national anthem*

Before Reading Have children recall what they learned about the American flag. Read the title. Do a structured picture walk with children.

pp. 46–47 Flying the flag is a way to show pride and respect for the United States. People take good care of these flags. They do not want to show disrespect.

pp. 48–51 If the flag flies at night, it must be lit up. When you hang a flag, the blue part is always at the top. The proper way to get rid of an old flag is to burn it.

p. 52 Point to the flag patches on these clothes. Wearing pins or patches of the flag is fine, but many people dislike it if the flag is used to make shirts or other clothes. They think that is disrespectful.

p. 53 These people are singing the national anthem, "The Star-Spangled Banner," a special song about the flag. Sing a few bars. When this song is played, it is respectful to stand, face the flag, and place your hand over your heart.

Guide comprehension.

Monitor independent reading.

Use Routine Cards 2 and 3.

During Reading Read the pages in a whisper. Raise your hand if you need help with a word. As we read, ask yourself: What am I learning about taking care of the flag? What is this mainly about?

pp. 46–49 What did you learn about flying the flag and hanging it? (take it down at night or light it up; blue part on top) Why do people follow these rules?

pp. 50–52 What did you learn about keeping the flag clean? (Don't let the flag touch the ground; clean it if it does. Burn old flags.) What did you learn about wearing the flag? (Wear patches or pins only.)

p. 53 What is this page mainly about? (the national anthem)

Model summarizing.

Think aloud.

After Reading What did you learn about the flag? What was the selection mainly about? Model how to summarize. The first two pages explain why we should respect the flag. The next pages tell rules for taking care of the flag. I pick the most important ideas. This selection is mainly about how to take care of the flag.

MORE PRACTICE

Develop oral vocabulary.

How can you tell that the flag is an important *symbol?* Many people fly the flag on *Independence* Day, July 4. Why? Do you think you would see the American flag in a *history* book about the United States?

ACTIVITY 4 Write

Response to Literature Shared Writing

		5 minutes

To Do / **To Say**

Guide shared writing.

Write a sentence frame. Read the question.

How can you take care of the flag? I can take care of the flag by _____.

Invite children to suggest answers. Discuss and record answers to complete the sentence frame. While writing, model connecting sounds to letters and forming letters. (See pp. 257–259.) Have children read answers aloud as you track print.

Homework   Practice Book, p. 127, Phonics: Prefixes *pre-, dis-*

ACTIVITY 1　Reread for Fluency

Oral Reading "Taking Care of Our Flag," pp. 46–49

	To Do	To Say	
			5–10 minutes
CORRECTIVE FEEDBACK	Monitor oral reading.	**Read pp. 46–49 aloud. Read them three or four times so your reading gets better each time. Give feedback on children's oral reading and use of the blending strategy.** See Routine Cards 1 and 4.	
MORE PRACTICE		Instead of rereading just pp. 46–49, have children reread the entire selection three or four times. You may want to have children read along with the AudioText.	

ACTIVITY 2　Word Work

Phonemic Awareness Segment and Blend Sounds

	To Do	To Say	
			2 minutes
Scaffold instruction.	Distribute white boards. Write *glue.*

Write *displease.* Lead children in segmenting and blending sounds. | **Model** Listen to the sounds in *glue.* Stretch the sounds /g/ /lll/ /üüü/ as you write g, l, ue. Repeat. This time have children write the letters as you write.

Teach and Practice Have children say the sounds with you as you point to the letters (/g/ /l/ /ü/) and blend sounds to say the word. (*glue*) Repeat with *displease: dis, please, displease.* Continue with these words:

blew　　true　　dislike　　prepaid　　due　　disconnect　　crew | |

Fluent Word Reading Vowel Patterns *ew, ue*; Prefixes *pre-, dis-*

	To Do	To Say	
			5–10 minutes
Use the word-reading routine.

Scaffold instruction. | Write *new* and *blue.*

Write *chew, Sue, prepays,* and *disorder.*

Write each practice word. | **1 Connect** You can read these words because you know that *ew* and *ue* can stand for /ü/. What vowel sound do you hear in both words? (/ü/) What are the words? *(new, blue)*

2 Model When you come to a new word, look at all the letters and think about its vowel sounds and its parts. Say the sounds and word parts to yourself, and then read the word. Model reading *chew, Sue, prepays,* and *disorder* in this way. **When you come to a new word, what will you do?**

3 Group Practice Let's read these words. Look at all the letters, think about the vowel sounds and parts, and say the sounds and parts to yourself. We will read words with *ew, ue,* and the prefixes *pre- and dis-.* When I point to the word, let's read it together. Allow 2–3 seconds previewing time for each word.

knew　　clues　　pretest　　disgrace　　grew　　glue　　preheat　　disrespect | *Routine* |
| **CORRECTIVE FEEDBACK** | **MONITOR PROGRESS** | *If . . .* children have difficulty previewing and reading whole words, *then . . .* have them use sound-by-sound blending.

If . . . children can't read the words fluently at a rate of 1–2 seconds per word, *then . . .* continue practicing the list. | |

MORE PRACTICE	Model reading words in sentences.	When I read a sentence, I read each word without stopping between the words. If I come to a word I don't know, I blend it. Then I read the sentence again. Model reading this sentence, stopping to blend *preflight: The crew did a preflight check of the plane.*
	Write practice sentences.	Have each child read a sentence.
		Disconnect the lamp before you unscrew the light bulb.
		Drew precooked the meat before he added it to the stew.
		The preschool teacher was displeased when a few kids threw some glue.

High-Frequency Words *air, America, beautiful, Earth, world*

	To Do	**To Say**	*3 minutes*
Review high-frequency words.	Display *air, America, beautiful, Earth,* and *world.*	Use the Tested Vocabulary Cards. Point to a word. Say and spell it. Have children say and spell the word. Ask children to identify familiar letter-sounds and word parts. Have them take turns reading the words.	

ACTIVITY 3 | ## Build Concepts

Oral Vocabulary *anthem, patriotic*

	To Do	**To Say**	*5–10 minutes*
Teach oral vocabulary.	Display pp. 54–55 of the student book.	Today you will read a story in which a *patriotic* family goes to Washington, D.C., on Flag Day and sings the national *anthem.*	*Routine*
		1 Introduce, Demonstrate, and Apply	
Scaffold instruction.	Follow the Routine to teach *anthem* and *patriotic.*	**anthem** The boys in this story know America's national *anthem* because they sing it at ballgames. An *anthem* is a song that praises or declares loyalty to something. Have children say the word. America's national *anthem* is like a cheer for the flag. Have you ever sung this *anthem?* When?	
		patriotic In this story, the boys show they are *patriotic* by wearing red, white, and blue and by singing the national *anthem.* When you show your love for and loyal support of your country, you are being *patriotic.* Have children say the word. *Patriotic* citizens often fly the flag of their country. What are some other ways you can show you are *patriotic?*	
	Display the words on the Amazing Words board.	**2 Display the Words** Have children say each word as they look at it. You can find sounds and word parts you know in big words. Read *an/them* as you run your hand under the syllables. What two letters make up the first syllable of *anthem? (an)* How do you say the first syllable of *anthem?* (/an/) Continue with *th*/th/ and *m*/m/. For *patriotic,* children can identify *pa*/pā/, *tr*/tr/, *ot*/ot/, *ic*/ik/.	
	Monitor understanding.	**3 Use the Words** Ask children to use each word in a sentence. Model a sentence if children need help.	
MORE PRACTICE		Use oral vocabulary to discuss the American flag. Is America's national *anthem* a *patriotic* song? Why or why not? Why do *patriotic* people celebrate on the Fourth of July? Is it *patriotic* to follow the rules for taking care of the American flag? Explain.	

ACTIVITY **4** Read a Passage

Reading "Broad Stripes and Bright Stars," pp. 54–63

| To Do | To Say | 10 minutes |

Teach sequence.

Scaffold instruction.

Introduce the skill.

Model the skill. Display p. 22.

Apply the skill.

Today you will practice keeping track of a story's sequence. Sequence is the order in which things happen in a story. For example, we read "THAT's a Football?" last week. First, the kids ask Ismail to play football. Next, they show him how to play. Then they play together and Ismail's team wins. Last, they play soccer.

Listen to this story: Matt's family had a special Fourth of July. First, they went to the parade. Next, they had a picnic in the park. Then they played tag. Finally, when it got dark, they watched the fireworks. What was the first thing the family did? (went to a parade)

Develop language and concepts.

See Routine Card 6. Display pp. 54–63.

Model using key words and concepts.

Key concepts: *Washington, D.C., capital, landmarks, Flag Day, Francis Scott Key, patriotic, anthem, respect, tattered, discolored*

Before Reading Read the title. Do a structured picture walk.

pp. 54–55 This family is in Washington, D.C. This city is the capital of the United States. It has many famous landmarks, such as the White House, the Lincoln Memorial, and the Washington Monument.

pp. 56–59 The family goes to a Flag Day party. Flag Day is when we celebrate the anniversary of the U.S. flag officially becoming the country's flag. At the party, actors are dressed like people from America's past. This actor is pretending to be Francis Scott Key. Francis Scott Key wrote a patriotic song about the flag. This song became America's national anthem.

pp. 60–61 Look at the family singing America's national anthem. Why do they have their hands over their hearts? Yes, they are showing their respect and love for the flag and the United States.

Monitor children's use of vocabulary.

Introduce proper nouns.

pp. 62–63 The family is looking at a very special flag. It is the one Francis Scott Key described in the song he wrote. The old flag is tattered and discolored. It looks ragged and its colors have faded.

Now turn to your partner and talk about the pictures, using the same words I did.

You'll see these names in the story: Washington, D.C., and Francis Scott Key. What did you just learn about this place and this person?

Guide comprehension.

Monitor independent reading.

Use Routine Cards 2 and 3.

During Reading Read the pages in a whisper. Raise your hand if you need help with a word. As you read, ask yourself: What is the order that things happen in this story?

pp. 54–56 Where does the family go first? (to a Flag Day party)

pp. 57–61 What happens first at the Flag Day party? (Actors greet them.) What do the boys do next? (make flags) What happens after that? (An actor playing Francis Scott Key tells about the song he wrote and invites people to sing it.)

pp. 62–63 What does the family do last? (They see the flag that Francis Scott Key wrote about.)

Guide retelling.

Prompt children as they retell the story.

After Reading Have one child retell the story while the others assist. What happened at the beginning of the story? in the middle? at the end? See Monitor Retelling, p. 246.

Homework

Practice Book, p. 128, Sequence

ACTIVITY 1 Reread for Fluency

Paired Reading "Broad Stripes and Bright Stars," pp. 54–57

To Do	To Say	*5–10 minutes*

CORRECTIVE FEEDBACK

Pair children. Monitor paired reading.

Children read pp. 54–57 orally, switching readers at the end of the first page. Have partners reread; now the other partner begins. For optimal fluency, children should reread three or four times. Give feedback on children's oral reading and use of the blending strategy. See Routine Cards 1 and 4.

MORE PRACTICE

Instead of rereading just pp. 54–57, have children reread the entire selection three or four times. You may want to have children read along with the AudioText.

ACTIVITY 2 Word Work

Spiral Review Vowel Patterns *ew, ue;* Sound of *oo* in *moon*

To Do	To Say	*5–10 minutes*

Review vowel patterns *ew, ue;* sound of *oo* in *moon.*

Scaffold instruction.

Write *threw, glue,* and *moon.*

You can read these words because you know how to blend words with *ew, ue,* and *oo*. Remember, the letters *ew, ue,* and *oo* can stand for the vowel sound /ü/. What are these words? *(threw, glue, moon)*

Provide letter tiles *b, c, d, e, g, l, m, o, o, r, t, u, w, z.*

Build Words Write *due.* Can you blend this word? *(due)* Spell *due* with letter titles. Now replace the *d* in *due* with *tr.* What is the new word? *(true)*

- Change the *tr* in *true* to *cl.* What is the new word? *(clue)*
- Change the *c* in *clue* to *b.* What is the new word? *(blue)*
- Change the *b* in *blue* to *g.* What is the new word? *(glue)*
- Change the *lue* in *glue* to *rew.* What is the new word? *(grew)*
- Change the *ew* in *grew* to *oom.* What is the new word? *(groom)*
- Change the *gr* in *groom* to *z.* What is the new word? *(zoom)*
- Remove the *m* from the end of *zoom.* What is the new word? *(zoo)*

CORRECTIVE FEEDBACK

MONITOR PROGRESS

If . . . children have difficulty reading the words,
then . . . have them blend the words sound-by-sound.

MORE PRACTICE

Model reading words in sentences.

When I read a sentence, I read each word without stopping between the words. If I come to a word I don't know, I blend it. Then I read the sentence again. Model reading this sentence, stopping to blend *loose: The zookeeper was displeased when the blue goose got loose and flew away.*

Write practice sentences.

Have each child read a sentence.

We had no clue that Sue knew Drew.
I dislike eating stew if it gets too cool or tastes like glue.
Is it true that Lew prepaid those tickets?

Phonological and Phonemic Awareness

Optional practice activities, pp. 280–283

ACTIVITY 3 Read Together

Choral Reading "Old Glory," p. 64

	To Do	**To Say**	10 minutes
Develop language and concepts.	Display p. 64.	**Before Reading** Read the title. Ask children to predict what the song will be about. This song tells about how the speaker feels about Old Glory. Old Glory is a nickname for the American flag. Glory is something that makes you feel great pride and joy. Do you think Old Glory is a good nickname for the flag? Why or why not? Allow children to share their ideas.	
Model fluent reading.	Model prosody.	A song is like a poem. It has rhythm, or a beat. Sometimes it has words that rhyme. Listen to my voice as I sing the song. Sing the song with rhythm and expression. Sing it a second time, having children point to each word. Have children identify rhyming words. *(by, sky; free, me)*	
	Build fluency through choral reading.	**Choral Reading** Now sing the song aloud with me. Try to use the same rhythm as I do and make your voice sound like mine as we sing. Sing the song several times with children.	
Develop concepts.	Monitor listening comprehension.	**After Reading** What is Old Glory? How does the speaker feel about Old Glory? Do you think this is a *patriotic* song? How is this song like America's national *anthem?*	

ACTIVITY 4 Build Concepts

Oral Vocabulary *anthem, history, independence, patriotic, symbol*

	To Do	**To Say**	5–10 minutes
Review oral vocabulary.	Read the words on the Amazing Words board.	**Focus on Letter-Sounds** Remember, you can find sounds and word parts you know in big words. • Which word begins with the sound /an/? Which word begins with /in/? • Which words have /s/? What letter stands for /s/ in each word? • Which word ends with /ē/? Which word ends with /k/?	
	Encourage discussion.	**Place Words in a Personal Context** Review the meanings of the words. Then ask children to use the words in a personal context. • Tell about a time you sang or heard America's national *anthem.* Did you feel *patriotic* when you sang or heard it? Why or why not? • How do you learn about your family's *history?* What do you know about family members who lived long ago? • In the past, families had *symbols* that told something about them. For example, the *symbol* of a lion showed that a family was brave. What *symbols* would you use to tell about your family? Why? • When you grow up, will you have more *independence?* Explain.	
MORE PRACTICE	Apply oral vocabulary to new situations.	• If the things I say are *patriotic,* put your right hand over your heart and say, "Patriotic." If not, do nothing. Flying your country's flag (patriotic), watching a movie (not), standing for the national anthem (patriotic), marching in a Fourth of July parade (patriotic), eating spaghetti (not). • If the things I say are from America's past, smile and say, "History." If not, do nothing. A flag with 13 stars (history), computers that can talk (not), homes on the moon (not), Francis Scott Key (history).	

ACTIVITY 5 | Write

Response to Literature Interactive Writing

To Do   **To Say**   *5–10 minutes*

Generate ideas.

Review the story "Broad Stripes and Bright Stars."

What did the boys learn about Francis Scott Key? What did Francis Scott Key do to celebrate the American flag? Discuss how Key came to write "The Star-Spangled Banner," America's national anthem.

Share the pen.

Have children participate in writing a list of ways to be patriotic.

Write *I can be patriotic by _____.* Have children read the words you wrote. Then have them supply endings for the sentence. Invite individuals to write familiar letter-sounds, word parts, and high-frequency words. Have them find the spelling of high-frequency words on the Word Wall. Ask questions such as:

- **What are the first two sounds you hear in** *blue?* (/bl/) **What letters stand for /bl/?** *(bl)*

- **What is the vowel sound in** *blue?* (/ü/) **What two letters stand for /ü/ that will make the word mean the color** *blue? (ue)*

Writing elements: conventions

Frequently reread what has been written while tracking the print. Point out that each sentence starts with a capital letter and ends with a period. Point out the extra space between words.

Read the completed list aloud, having children read with you. (For example, *I can be patriotic by dressing in red, white, and blue. I can be patriotic by flying the flag. I can be patriotic by taking care of the flag. I can be patriotic by singing America's national anthem.*)

MORE PRACTICE

Prompt independent writing.

Journal Writing Tell about a time when you sang the national anthem.

Homework   Practice Book, p. 129, High-Frequency Words

ACTIVITY 1   Assessment Options

Sentence Reading

5 minutes

	To Do	**To Say**
Assess sentence reading.	Use reproducible p. 250.	Have each child read the sentences. Record scores on the Sentence Reading Chart, p. 254. Work with one child as others complete Write Sentences below.
		Our new fan blew cool air until you disconnected it. I think America is the most beautiful place in the world. The space crew is due to return to Earth after their preflight check.
CORRECTIVE FEEDBACK	**MONITOR PROGRESS**	**If . . .** children have trouble reading words that have the vowel patterns *ew, ue* or the prefixes *pre-* and *dis-,* **then . . .** reteach the blending strategy lessons on pp. 180 and 184.
		If . . . children cannot read a high-frequency word, **then . . .** mark the missed word or words on a high-frequency word list and send the list home for additional practice or have them practice with a fluent reader.
		If . . . children misread a word in the sentence, **then . . .** correct the error and have them reread the word and then the sentence.
Practice sentence writing.	Provide white boards.	**Write Sentences** Have children copy the sentences from reproducible p. 250 on white boards. Have them confirm spellings by comparing the words they wrote to the words in the sentences.
Phonological and Phonemic Awareness		Optional practice activities, pp. 280–283

Passage Reading

5–10 minutes

	To Do	**To Say**
Assess fluency and comprehension.	Determine which children to assess this week.	Choose from these options: monitoring fluency (see pp. 244–245) and/or monitoring retelling (see p. 246). Have children reread "Broad Stripes and Bright Stars." Be sure each child is assessed every other week.
		If you have time, assess every child.

ACTIVITY 2   Use Concepts

Oral Vocabulary *anthem, history, independence, patriotic, symbol*

5 minutes

	To Do	**To Say**
Check understanding of oral vocabulary.	Use the Amazing Words to wrap up the week's concept. Monitor understanding of oral vocabulary, using Routine Card 5.	As time allows, ask questions such as these. • Tell me about the pictures on pp. 38–45 using some of the week's Amazing Words. • Do children have a lot of *independence?* Explain. • What kinds of things might be described in a country's national *anthem?* • Name an important person in America's *history.* What did this person do? • What kinds of *symbols* might you see on a map of a zoo? • What is a good way to tell if someone is *patriotic?*
Preview next week's concept.		Next week you will read about family celebrations.

Read to Connect

Reread "The American Flag," pp. 38-45

To Do	To Say

10 minutes

Monitor comprehension: sequence.

Have children reread "The American Flag" silently.

As you read, think about the sequence, or order in which things happen. After rereading, ask:

Did the flag with 50 stars come before or after the flag with 13 stars? How do you know? (The flag with 50 stars came after the flag with 13 stars. The selection said the flag with 13 stars was the first flag. It said that as the country grew, more stars were added to the flag.) Record children's responses in a *Past/Now* chart on the board.

Make connections.

Have children make connections across texts.

We also read "Taking Care of Our Flag." Find that. What are some of the rules you learned for taking care of the American flag? Why do people follow these rules? Record children's responses on a two-column T-chart, listing rules for taking care of the flag on the left and reasons these rules are important on the right. (For example, Rule: Keep the flag looking like new. Reason: To show respect for the flag.) Children will use the chart for Activity 4.

We also read "Broad Stripes and Bright Stars," about a family that celebrates Flag Day. What special flag does the family see at the end of the story? How are people taking care of that special flag? Record children's details about the special flag on a word web. Add any new information about taking care of special flags to the chart above.

What did all the selections we read this week show us about the American flag? What is the big idea? (The American flag is an important symbol, so people should treat it with respect.)

Write

5–10 minutes

Response to Literature Independent Writing

To Do	To Say

Assign personal narrative.

Guide sentence correction.

Writing elements: conventions, support

Today you will write about what the American flag means to you. Write about how you feel when you see the flag and how you show that you care about it. Encourage children to use words you wrote on the board for Activity 3 as they write.

Have children check their writing by asking themselves these questions.

- **Did I use a capital letter to begin each sentence and proper noun?**
- **Did I use the correct mark at the end of each sentence?**
- **Did I use good words to describe my feelings?**

MORE PRACTICE

Have children share their sentences with the group. Write their sentences on the board and have children practice reading and writing each other's sentences.

Homework   Practice Book, p. 130, Writing

Unit 6 Week 3 *Family Celebrations*

Why are family celebrations special?

Objectives *This week students will . . .*

Phonemic Awareness
- delete phonemes to make new words
- segment and count sounds in words

Phonics
- blend and read contractions *'re, 've, 'd,* and words with *ph*/f/ and *dge*/j/
- apply knowledge of letter-sounds to decode unknown words when reading
- recognize high-frequency words *believe, company, everybody, money, young*

Fluency
- practice fluency with oral rereading

Vocabulary
- build concepts and oral vocabulary: *celebration, custom, occasion, sibling, tradition*

Text Comprehension
- read connected text
- draw conclusions to improve comprehension
- write in response to literature

Word Work *This week's phonics focus is . . .*

Contractions *'re, 've, 'd* *ph*/f/, *dge*/j/

High-Frequency Words *Tested Vocabulary*

The first appearance of each word in the Student Reader is noted below.

believe	If you **believe** something, you think that it is true. (p. 70)
company	When you have **company,** you have guests. (p. 76)
everybody	**Everybody** likes the new teacher. (p. 69)
money	**Money** is the coins and paper used for buying and selling things. (p. 70)
young	When something is **young,** it is in the early part of its life. (p. 70)

Amazing Words *Oral Vocabulary*

The week's vocabulary is related to the concept of how family celebrations can be special.

celebration	a party or other joyful gathering to mark a big event
custom	something that people always do or have done for a long time
occasion	a special or important event
sibling	a brother or a sister
tradition	a way of handing down beliefs, customs, and ideas from one person to another, especially from parents to children

Student Reader Unit 6 *This week students will read the following selections.*

Daily Lesson Plan

	ACTIVITIES	MATERIALS
Day 1	**Word Work** Phonemic Awareness: Delete Phonemes Phonics: Blend Contractions *'re, 've, 'd* High-Frequency Words *believe, company, everybody, money, young* **Build Concepts** *celebration, custom, tradition* **Read a Passage** "Family Celebrations," pp. 68–77 Comprehension: Use Strategies Reread for Fluency	Student White Boards Tested Vocabulary Cards *Sing with Me Big Book* and Audio CD Student Reader: Unit 6 Routine Cards 1, 2, 3, 4, 6, 7 AudioText Practice Book, p. 131, Contractions *'re, 've, 'd*
Day 2	**Reread for Fluency** **Word Work** Phonemic Awareness: Segment and Count Sounds Phonics: Blend Words with *ph*/f/, *dge*/j/ High-Frequency Words *believe, company, everybody, money, young* **Read a Passage** "Angel Food Bakery," pp. 78–87 Comprehension: Use Strategies **Write** Response to Literature: Shared Writing	Student Reader: Unit 6 Student White Boards Sound-Spelling Cards 12, 17 Tested Vocabulary Cards Routine Cards 1, 2, 3, 4, 6, 7 AudioText Practice Book, p. 132, *ph*/f/, *dge*/j/
Day 3	**Reread for Fluency** **Word Work** Phonemic Awareness: Delete Phonemes Phonics: Fluent Word Reading High-Frequency Words *believe, company, everybody, money, young* **Build Concepts** *occasion, sibling* **Read a Passage** "Twice as Nice," pp. 88–95 Comprehension: Draw Conclusions	Student Reader: Unit 6 Student White Boards Tested Vocabulary Cards Routine Cards 1, 2, 3, 4, 6 AudioText Practice Book, p. 133, Draw Conclusions
Day 4	**Reread for Fluency** **Word Work** Phonics: Spiral Review Phonological and Phonemic Awareness Activities, pp. 280–283 **Read Together** "Watch Where You Sit!" p. 96 Comprehension: Listening **Build Concepts** *celebration, custom, occasion, sibling, tradition* **Write** Response to Literature: Interactive Writing	Student Reader: Unit 6 Routine Cards 1, 4 AudioText Student White Boards Practice Book, p. 134, High-Frequency Words
Day 5	**Assessment Options** Fluency, Comprehension Sentence Reading; Mid-Unit Passage Reading Phonological and Phonemic Awareness Activities, pp. 280–283 **Use Concepts** *celebration, custom, occasion, sibling, tradition* **Read to Connect** "Family Celebrations," pp. 68–77 Comprehension: Draw Conclusions **Write** Response to Literature: Independent Writing	Reproducible p. 251 Sentence Reading Chart, p. 254 Student White Boards Fluency Progress Chart, p. 245 Assessment Book, p. 84 Routine Card 5 Practice Book, p. 135, Writing

See pp. xvi–xvii for how *My Sidewalks* integrates instructional practices for ELL.

ACTIVITY 1 Word Work

Phonemic Awareness Delete Phonemes

To Do	To Say	*2 minutes*

Scaffold instruction.

Distribute white boards.
Write *we've.*

Erase *'ve* at the end of *we've.*

Lead children in deleting final /v/, /r/, or /d/ as they write.

Model We've had a busy morning. Listen to the sounds in *we've.* Stretch the sounds /www/ /ēēē/ /vvv/ as you write *we've.* Repeat. Have children write letters as you write.

Teach and Practice Have children say the sounds with you as you point to the letters (/w/ /ē/ /v/) and blend the sounds to say the word. *(we've)* Now listen as I take off the sound /v/ at the end of *we've*: /w/ /ē/, *we.* Have children say the sounds with you. What new word did we make? *(we)* Continue the activity with these words:

we're—we   she'd—she   they've—they   you're—you   he'd—he

Blending Strategy Contractions *'re, 've, 'd*

To Do	To Say	*5–10 minutes*

Routine

Use the blending routine.

Write *aren't.*

1 Connect You studied words like this already. What do you know about reading this word? (*Aren't* is a contraction of the words *are* and *not.* An apostrophe takes the place of the letter *o* in *not.*) Today we'll learn about contractions made from other words.

Scaffold instruction.

Write *we're.*

Write *we are* beneath *we're.*

2 Model This word is a contraction, a short way of saying and writing two words as one. An apostrophe takes the place of the letter *a* in contractions with *are.* What two words make the contraction *we're? (we, are)* To read contractions, I first read the word before the apostrophe and then blend it with what comes after the apostrophe. This is how I blend this word: /wē/, /r/, *we're.*

$$w \quad e \quad 're$$

Write *you have* beneath *you've.*

Write *he had* and *he would* beneath *he'd.*

The contraction *you've* is made from the words *you* and *have.* An apostrophe takes the place of the letters *ha* in contractions with *have.*

The contraction *he'd* is sometimes made of the words *he* and *had.* The contraction *he'd* can also be made of the words *he* and *would.*

3 Listen and Write Write the word *we.* Write *are* next to it. Now erase the *a* in *are* and put in an apostrophe. As you write, say the contraction to yourself: *we're.* Now say the word aloud.

CORRECTIVE FEEDBACK

Write each practice word. Monitor student practice.

4 Group Practice Let's try reading these contractions and saying the two words that form each one. Give feedback, using the *if . . . then* statements on Routine Card 1.

you're (you are)   I've (I have)   she'd (she had/she would)
they're (they are)   you've (you have)   they'd (they had/they would)

5 Individual Practice Write the words; have each child blend two of them.

we've   I'd   they've   we're   you'd

MORE PRACTICE

Model building contractions *'re, 've, 'd.*

Build Words Write the pairs of words below. Have children copy the pairs on their white boards. With the first pair, model erasing letters and adding an apostrophe. Then have children continue the activity. Have them read the contractions and use them in sentences.

they would (they'd)   I have (I've)   you are (you're)   we had (we'd)

High-Frequency Words *believe, company, everybody, money, young*

To Do	To Say	

3 minutes

Teach high-frequency words.

Display *believe.*

1 Say, Spell, Write Use the Tested Vocabulary Cards. Display *believe.* Here are some words that we won't sound out. We'll spell them. This word is *believe: b, e, l, i, e, v, e* (point to each letter), *believe.* **What is this word? What are the letters in the word? Now you write** *believe.*

Point to the *b, l,* and *v* in *believe.*

2 Identify Letter-Sounds Let's look at the sounds in *believe* that you do know. **What is this letter?** *(b)* **What is the sound for this letter?** *(/b/)* Continue with /l/l/ and /v/v/.

3 Demonstrate Meaning Tell me a sentence using *believe.* Model a sentence if children need help.

Display *company, everybody, money,* and *young.*

Repeat the Routine with *company, everybody, money,* and *young.* Children can identify these letter-sounds and word parts: *company* (*c*/k/, *m*/m/, *p*/p/, *n*/n/, *y*/ē/), *everybody,* (high-frequency word *every, b*/b/, *d*/d/, *y*/ē/), *money* (*m*/m/, *n*/n/), and *young* (*y*/y/, *ng*/ng/). Have children write the words in their word banks. Add the words to the Word Wall. Point out that the words they are learning are on p. 97.

ACTIVITY **2** ## Build Concepts

Oral Vocabulary *celebration, custom, tradition*

To Do	To Say	

5–10 minutes

Introduce oral vocabulary.

Display p. 28 of *Sing with Me Big Book.* Play audio CD.

This week you will learn about family celebrations. Listen for the Amazing Words *celebration, custom,* and *tradition* as I sing this song. Play or sing the song. Then have children sing it with you.

1 Introduce, Demonstrate, and Apply

Scaffold instruction.

Follow the Routine to teach *celebration, custom,* and *tradition.*

celebration The song mentions group *celebrations.* A *celebration* is a party or other joyful gathering to mark a big event. Have children say the word. Weddings and graduations are times when families have *celebrations.* **Why do you think people enjoy family** *celebrations?*

custom The song says every family *custom* unites us. A *custom* is something that people always do or have done for a long time. Have children say the word. The *custom* of some families is to eat pancakes every Saturday morning. **What is a weekend** *custom* **your family has?**

tradition The song says *tradition* is important. *Tradition* is a way of handing down beliefs, customs, and ideas from one person to another, especially from parents to children. Have children say the word. I learned the *tradition* of making quilts from my mother. **What is one of your family's holiday** *traditions?*

Display the words on the Amazing Words board.

2 Display the Words Have children say each word as they look at it. **You can find sounds and word parts you know in big words.** Read *tra/di/tion* as you run your hand under the syllables. **What sounds do** *tr* **stand for?** *(/tr/)* Continue with /d/d/ and /n/n/. For *celebration,* children can identify *cel*/sel/ and /n/n/. They can decode *custom.*

Monitor understanding.

3 Use the Words Ask children to use each word in a sentence. Model a sentence if children need help.

MORE PRACTICE

Use oral vocabulary to discuss the song. **How can you tell the family shown is having a** *celebration?* **Can grandparents teach** *traditions* **to their grandchildren? Can bringing food to a** *celebration* **be a family** *custom?*

ACTIVITY **3** Read a Passage

Build Background "Family Celebrations," pp. 68–77

	To Do	To Say	10 minutes

Develop language and concepts.

See Routine Card 7. Read aloud p. 67 of the student book.

Preview the Week Use the illustration on p. 66 to introduce this week's concept of family celebrations. **What kind of celebration is shown? Do you think family celebrations are fun? Why or why not?** Read aloud the titles and descriptions on p. 67. Ask children what they think each selection will be about.

Scaffold instruction.

See Routine Card 6. Display pp. 68–77.

Ask questions and elaborate on answers to develop language.

Key concepts: *celebration, special, customs, tradition, bride, gown, wedding, fuss, company, crowd*

Before Reading Read the title aloud. Do a structured picture walk with children.

pp. 68–69 This girl tells about her family's celebrations. **What are her family members doing at this celebration?** (eating a meal, playing a game) The family is having fun sharing a special day together.

pp. 70–71 The girl's family has some birthday customs. **What customs are shown?** (sharing a birthday cake, giving gifts)

pp. 72–73 **What kind of celebration is the girl describing now?** (a wedding) In some families, it is a tradition for the bride to wear a white dress, or gown, on her wedding day.

pp. 74–75 **Why do you think the children are bringing cards and gifts to Mom and Dad? What might they be celebrating?** (Mother's Day, Father's Day) Mom and Dad seem to like all the fuss, or attention, they get on these special days.

pp. 76–77 The girl tells about times her family invites company, or guests, to parties. **Why might a big crowd make a celebration more fun? Let's read to find out more about family celebrations.**

Guide comprehension.

Monitor independent reading. Model strategic reading. Use Routine Cards 2 and 3.

During Reading Read the pages in a whisper. Raise your hand if you need help with a word. Stop at the end of each page to model asking questions. For example, for p. 71: **After I read, I ask myself: What am I learning about family celebrations? What is this page mainly about?** The girl tells how her mom bakes birthday cakes for family birthday celebrations. I read that her family sings the birthday song loudly. This page is mainly about a family birthday celebration.

Summarize.

Use oral vocabulary to develop the concept.

After Reading **Can baking birthday cakes be a family *tradition*? Do all families have the same wedding *customs*? What *customs* do you have for Mother's Day and Father's Day? If you could be a guest at one of this family's *celebrations*, which would you choose? Why?**

Reread for Fluency "Family Celebrations," pp. 68–71

	To Do	To Say	5–10 minutes

CORRECTIVE FEEDBACK

Monitor oral reading.

Read pp. 68–71 aloud. Read them three or four times so your reading gets better each time. Give feedback on children's oral reading and use of the blending strategy. See Routine Cards 1 and 4.

MORE PRACTICE

Instead of rereading just pp. 68–71, have children reread the entire selection three or four times. You may want to have children read along with the AudioText.

Homework

Practice Book, p. 131, Phonics: Contractions: *'re, 've, 'd*

ACTIVITY 1 Reread for Fluency

Paired Reading "Family Celebrations," pp. 72–77

To Do	To Say	5–10 minutes

CORRECTIVE FEEDBACK

Pair children. Monitor paired reading.

Children read pp. 72–77 orally, switching readers at the end of the first page. Have partners reread; now the other partner begins. For optimal fluency, children should reread three or four times. Give feedback on children's oral reading and use of the blending strategy. See Routine Cards 1 and 4.

MORE PRACTICE

Instead of rereading just pp. 72–77, have children reread the entire selection three or four times. You may want to have children read along with the AudioText.

ACTIVITY 2 Word Work

Phonemic Awareness Segment and Count Sounds

To Do	To Say	2 minutes

Scaffold instruction.

Distribute white boards.
Write *phone*.

Model Listen to the sounds in *phone*. Stretch the sounds /fff/ /ōōō/ /nnn/ as you write ph, o, n, e. Repeat. This time have children write the letters as you write. **Now let's count the sounds in** *phone*. **I will say the word slowly and hold up a finger for each sound: /f/ /ō/ /n/. There are three sounds in** *phone*.

Lead children in segmenting and counting sounds as they write.

Teach and Practice Have children say the sounds as you point to the letters. (/f/ /ō/ /n/) **Hold up a finger for each sound. How many sounds in** *phone?* (3) **How many letters in** *phone*? (5) Continue segmenting and counting sounds with these words:

fudge (3)　　**Steph** (4)　　**bridge** (4)　　**graph** (4)

Blending Strategy Words with *ph*/f/, *dge*/j/

To Do	To Say	*5–10 minutes*

Use the blending routine.

Write *fish* and *jam*.

1 Connect You already can read words like these. What are the words? What sounds do they start with? (/f/, /j/) What letter stands for the sound /f/ at the beginning of *fish*? (*f*) What letter stands for the sound /j/ at the beginning of *jam*? (*j*) Today we will learn about other letters that stand for the sounds /f/ and /j/.

Scaffold instruction.

Display Sound-Spelling Card 12.

2 Use Sound-Spelling Card This is a firefighter. What sound do you hear at the beginning of *firefighter*? (/f/) Say it with me: /f/. The letter *f* stands for /f/ at the beginning of *firefighter*. The letters *ph* can also stand for /f/.

3 Listen and Write Write the letters *ph* for /f/. As you write, say the sound to yourself: /f/. Now say the sound aloud.

Write *phone*.

4 Model In this word, the letters *ph* stand for /f/. This is how I blend this word: /f/ /ō/ n/, *phone*. Now you try it: /f/, /ō/, /n/, *phone*.

Write *graph* and *nephew*.

Repeat with *graph* and *nephew*. Point out that *ph* can come at the beginning, middle, or end of a word. Explain that when *ph* is in the middle of a longer word, children should divide the word either before or after *ph*: *neph, ew, nephew*.

Display Sound-Spelling Card 17. Write *bridge*.

Repeat steps 2 and 3 for the sound /j/. Use Sound-Spelling Card 17, depicting a jet. Explain that *jet* begins with /j/, but the letters *dge* can also stand for /j/. Then model blending *bridge*: /b/ /r/ /i/ /j/, *bridge*.

p h o n e g r a p h n e p h e w b r i d g e

CORRECTIVE FEEDBACK

Write each practice word. Monitor student practice.

5 Group Practice Let's try the same thing with these words. Give feedback, using the *if . . . then* statements on Routine Card 1.

phase* badge graph pledge* dolphin smudge

6 Individual Practice Write the words; have each child blend two of them.

phone judge phrase* hedge* gopher* ledge orphan* porridge*

Check understanding of practice words.

*Children need to make sense of words as they segment and blend. If needed, help children with meanings. A *phase* is a stage in a person or animal's life. A puppy goes through a *phase* when it chews everything. A *pledge* is a serious promise. A *phrase* is a group of words that go together. A *hedge* is a thick row of bushes. A *gopher* is a small animal that digs long tunnels. An *orphan* is a child whose parents aren't living. *Porridge* is a breakfast food that looks like thick oatmeal.

MORE PRACTICE

Model spelling words with *ph* and *dge*.

Spell Words What sounds do you hear in *bridge*? (/b/ /r/ /i/ /j/) What two letters stand for /br/? Let's all write *br*. What is the letter for /i/? Write *i*. What three letters stand for /j/ in *bridge*? Write *dge*. Continue practice as time allows. Have children confirm their spellings by comparing them to what you've written.

phone badge graph ridge phrase budge nephew

High-Frequency Words *believe, company, everybody, money, young*

To Do	To Say	*3 minutes*

Teach high-frequency words.

Display *believe, company, everybody, money,* and *young*.

Use the Tested Vocabulary Cards. Point to a word. Say and spell it. Have children say and spell the word. Ask them to identify familiar letter-sounds and word parts. Have children take turns reading the words.

Lead cumulative review.

Use the Tested Vocabulary Cards to review high-frequency words from previous weeks.

ACTIVITY 3 Read a Passage

Reading "Angel Food Bakery," pp. 78–87

	To Do	To Say	
			10–15 minutes

Develop language and concepts.

Scaffold instruction.

To Do: See Routine Cards 6 and 7. Display pp. 78–87.

Ask questions and elaborate on answers to develop language.

Key concepts: *baker, ledge, celebrations, order, frosting, toppings, decorations*

To Say: **Before Reading** Have children recall the cake that Mom made for the birthday celebration. Read the title. Do a structured picture walk.

pp. 78–79 A baker named Steph made the beautiful cakes on this ledge. A ledge is a shelf. For what celebrations might you buy a cake?

pp. 80–81 People call and order special cakes. What does Steph need to make a cake? Have children name the tools and ingredients.

pp. 82–85 What does Steph do before she puts the pans in the oven? (fills them) She fills the cake pans with batter. She sets a timer so she knows when the cakes will be done. When the cakes are cool, she puts layers of frosting on them and adds toppings, or decorations. Have you ever seen these kinds of toppings?

pp. 86–87 Steph takes photos of her cakes and puts them in a book. This woman likes Steph's cake! Let's read to find out more.

Guide comprehension.

To Do: Monitor independent reading.

Use Routine Cards 2 and 3.

To Say: **During Reading** Read the pages in a whisper. Raise your hand if you need help with a word. As you read, ask yourself: What am I learning about Steph's cakes? What is this mainly about?

pp. 78–79 What did you learn about the kinds of cakes Steph makes?

pp. 80–85 What did you learn about how Steph makes a cake? Have children tell Steph's cake-making steps in order.

pp. 86–87 What are these pages mainly about? (When the cake is done, Steph takes a photo of it, then gives the cake to the lady who ordered it.)

Model summarizing.

To Do: Think aloud.

To Say: **After Reading** What did you learn about Steph's cakes? What was the selection mainly about? Model how to summarize. The first part told about the special cakes Steph makes. The next part told the steps Steph follows to make a cake. I pick the most important ideas. This selection is mainly about how Steph makes special cakes.

MORE PRACTICE

To Do: Develop oral vocabulary.

To Say: For what kinds of *celebrations* does Steph make cakes? Do you think the boy's mom will make it a *custom* to get birthday cakes from Steph? If Steph wanted baking to be a family *tradition,* what could she do?

ACTIVITY 4 Write

Response to Literature Shared Writing

5 minutes

	To Do	To Say

Guide shared writing.

To Do: Write sentence frames. Read the questions.

To Say: What kinds of cakes can Steph make? Steph can make _____.
What does Steph need to make a cake? Steph needs _____.

Invite children to suggest answers. Discuss and record answers to complete the sentence frames. While writing, model connecting sounds to letters and forming letters. (See pp. 257–259.) Have children read answers aloud as you track print.

Homework   Practice Book, p. 132, Phonics: *ph*/f/, *dge*/j/

ACTIVITY **1** Reread for Fluency

Oral Reading "Angel Food Bakery," pp. 78–82

5–10 minutes

	To Do	To Say
CORRECTIVE FEEDBACK	Monitor oral reading.	Read pp. 78–82 aloud. Read them three or four times so your reading gets better each time. Give feedback on children's oral reading and use of the blending strategy. See Routine Cards 1 and 4.
MORE PRACTICE		Instead of rereading just pp. 78–82, have children reread the entire selection three or four times. You may want to have children read along with the AudioText.

ACTIVITY **2** Word Work

Phonemic Awareness Delete Phonemes

2 minutes

	To Do	To Say
Scaffold instruction.	Distribute white boards. Write *I've*. Erase *'ve* at the end of *I've*. Lead children in deleting final /v/, /r/, or /d/.	**Model** Listen to the sounds in *I've*. Stretch the sounds /īīī/ /vvv/ as you write *I, 've*. Repeat. Have children write letters as you write. **Teach and Practice** Have children say the sounds with you as you point to the letters (/ī/ /v/) and blend the sounds to say the word. *(I've)* Now listen as I take off the sound /v/ at the end of *I've*: /ī/, *I*. Have children say the sounds with you. What new word did we make? *(I)* Continue the activity with these words:

they're–they   phoned–phone   we've–we   pledged–pledge   she'd—she

Fluent Word Reading Contractions *'re, 've, 'd; ph/f/, dge/j/*

5–10 minutes

	To Do	To Say
Use the word-reading routine.	Write *we've*.	**1 Connect** You can read this word because you know how to read contractions. Remember, read the word before the apostrophe and then blend it with what comes after the apostrophe. What word comes before the apostrophe? *(we)* What is the contraction? *(we've)*
Scaffold instruction.	Write *you're, I'd, graph,* and *ridge*.	**2 Model** When you come to a new word, look at all the letters in the word and think about its vowel sounds and its parts. Say the sounds and word parts to yourself, and then read the word. Model reading *you're, I'd, graph,* and *ridge* in this way. When you come to a new word, what will you do?
	Write each practice word.	**3 Group Practice** Let's read these words. Look at all the letters, think about the vowel sounds and parts, and say the sounds to yourself. We will read contractions and words with *ph* and *dge*. When I point to the word, let's read it together. Allow 2–3 seconds previewing time for each word.

they're   phrase   fridge   you've   trophy   judge   we'd   dolphin   lodge

CORRECTIVE FEEDBACK	**MONITOR PROGRESS**	*If . . .* children have difficulty previewing and reading whole words, *then . . .* have them use sound-by-sound blending.
		If . . . children can't read the words fluently at a rate of 1–2 seconds per word, *then . . .* continue practicing the list.

MORE PRACTICE	Model reading words in sentences.	When I read a sentence, I read each word without stopping between the words. If I come to a word I don't know, I blend it. Then I read the sentence again. Model reading this sentence, stopping to blend *bridge: Tell Joseph we're waiting for him under the bridge.*
	Write practice sentences.	Have each child read a sentence.
		Phil phoned the shop and said he'd like a wedge of cheese. They've seen badgers, hedgehogs, and gophers at the zoo. Steph made a bar graph showing all the trophies she'd won.

High-Frequency Words *believe, company, everybody, money, young*

	To Do	To Say	3 minutes
Review high-frequency words.	Display *believe, company, everybody, money,* and *young*.	Use the Tested Vocabulary Cards. Point to a word. Say and spell it. Have children say and spell the word. Ask children to identify familiar letter-sounds and word parts. Have them take turns reading the words.	

ACTIVITY **3** **Build Concepts**

Oral Vocabulary *occasion, sibling*

	To Do	To Say	5–10 minutes
Teach oral vocabulary.	Display p. 88 of the student book.	Today you will read a story about two *siblings* who celebrate a special *occasion*.	*Routine*
		1 Introduce, Demonstrate, and Apply	
Scaffold instruction.	Follow the Routine to teach *occasion* and *sibling*.	**occasion** In this story, twins plan what to do on an *occasion* that happens once a year—their birthday. An *occasion* is a special or important event. Have children say the word. A wedding is a happy *occasion*. Tell about a happy *occasion* you've experienced.	
		sibling In this story, the main characters are *siblings*. A *sibling* is a brother or a sister. Have children say the word. Some people do not have *siblings*. Others have one or more *siblings*. Describe a *sibling* you have or know. Is this *sibling* a brother or a sister? Is this *sibling* younger or older than you?	
	Display the words on the Amazing Words board.	**2 Display the Words** Have children say each word as they look at it. You can find sounds and word parts you know in big words. Read *oc/ca/sion* as you run your hand under the syllables. What sound do the *c*'s make in *occasion*? (/k/) What vowel sound do you hear at the end of the second syllable of *occasion*? (long *a*) What sound is at the end of *occasion*? (/n/) What letter stands for this sound? *(n)* Children can decode *sibling*.	
	Monitor understanding.	**3 Use the Words** Ask children to use each word in a sentence. Model a sentence if children need help.	
MORE PRACTICE		Use oral vocabulary to discuss family celebrations. On which *occasions* do you and your family members wear special clothes? Explain. Would you like to have the same birthday as your *sibling?* Why or why not?	

ACTIVITY **4** Read a Passage

Reading "Twice as Nice," pp. 88–95

To Do	To Say	*10 minutes*

Teach draw conclusions.

Scaffold instruction.

Introduce the skill.

Model the skill.
Display pp. 86–87.

Today you will draw conclusions. Remember, when we draw conclusions, we think about what we read and what we know about real life to figure out more about the people and events in a selection. For example, in "Angel Food Bakery," I read that Steph takes pictures of all her cakes. I know that before people order cakes, they often like to see cakes a baker has made. I put that all together and draw the conclusion that Steph has a book of cake photos so people can get ideas for the kinds of cakes they might want to order.

Apply the skill.

Do you think the boy will like the birthday cake Steph made for him? How can you tell? (Possible answer: Yes, because we read that his mom believes he will, and people usually like special cakes.)

Develop language and concepts.

See Routine Card 6.
Display pp. 88–95.

Model using key words and concepts.

Key concepts:
sibling, sister, twins, brother, celebration, occasion, gifts, ledge, custom, guests, tradition

Monitor children's use of vocabulary.

Before Reading Read the title. Do a structured picture walk.

pp. 88–89 Point to the girl. Midge is Phil's sister. She is his sibling. Point to the boy. Phil is Midge's brother. He is her sibling. They are twins. They were born on the same day, so they have the same birthday.

pp. 90–92 The family plans the twins' ninth birthday celebration. They want it to be a special occasion. What games will they play? The twins like different games, so they will play both games at the party.

pp. 93–95 Point to the gifts on the ledge. It is often a custom for guests to bring gifts to a birthday party. I wonder how the tradition of singing "Happy Birthday" and blowing out candles started.

Now turn to your partner and talk about the pictures, using the same words I did.

Guide comprehension.

Monitor independent reading.

Use Routine Cards 2 and 3.

During Reading Read the pages in a whisper. Raise your hand if you need help with a word. As you read, ask yourself: What conclusions can I draw about the twins and about story events?

pp. 88–89 How can you tell that Phil and Midge want to have the same big party but not in the same way? (They both smile and grin about the party, but then say they will invite their own pals to the party.)

pp. 90–91 The twins will have company at the party. What does this tell you about the twins? (They have good friends to share their special day with. They have fun parties.) **Why do you think Mom agrees to make two cakes?** (She knows the twins like different kinds of cakes. Having your own cake on your birthday is special.)

pp. 92–93 What do you learn about Phil and Midge when they plan the party games? (They both like to play games, but they like different games. Midge likes tag and Phil likes hide-and-seek.)

pp. 94–95 When it is time to eat the cake, what do Midge and Phil finally decide to do? Why? (have a piece of both kinds of cakes; Both look good, and they like to share.)

Guide retelling.

Prompt children as they retell the story.

After Reading Have one child retell the story while the others assist. **What happens at the beginning of the story? in the middle? at the end?** See Monitor Retelling, p. 246.

Homework

Practice Book, p. 133, Draw Conclusions

ACTIVITY 1 Reread for Fluency

Paired Reading "Twice as Nice," pp. 88–92

5–10 minutes

	To Do	To Say
CORRECTIVE FEEDBACK	Pair children. Monitor paired reading.	Children read pp. 88–92 orally, switching readers at the end of the first page. Have partners reread; now the other partner begins. For optimal fluency, children should reread three or four times. Give feedback on children's oral reading and use of the blending strategy. See Routine Cards 1 and 4.
MORE PRACTICE		Instead of rereading just pp. 88–92, have children reread the entire selection three or four times. You may want to have children read along with the AudioText.

ACTIVITY 2 Word Work

Spiral Review Silent Consonants; *ph*/f/, *dge*/j/

5–10 minutes

	To Do	To Say
Review silent consonants and *ph*/f/, *dge*/j/. **Scaffold instruction.**	Write *knit, wrench,* and *limb.*	You can read these words because you know that some words have silent consonants. What sound do you hear at the beginning of this first word? (/n/) Which consonant is silent in this word? (k) What is the word? (knit) Repeat for *wrench* and *limb*. Point out that *kn* can stand for /n/, *wr* can stand for /r/, and *mb* can stand for /m/.
	Write *trophy.*	You can read this word because you know that *ph* can stand for the sound /f/. What is the word? (trophy) Remind children that *ph* can come at the beginning, middle, or end of a word. When *ph* is in the middle of a longer word, they should divide the word before or after the *ph*.
	Write *ledge.*	You can read this word because you know that *dge* stands for /j/. What is the word? (ledge)
	Distribute white boards.	**Build Words** Write these headings on a five-column chart: *kn, wr, mb, ph, dge*. Below each heading, write several words with those letters omitted. For example, for *know,* write _ow. Have children copy the headings and add the missing letters to make each word. Model adding *kn* to *ow* to form *know*. Call on children to read the words and use them in sentences or tell their meanings.

kn	wr	mb	ph	dge
_ow	_ist	cru_	_one	e_
_ife	_ong	la_	gra_	Mi_
_ee	_eath	thu_	Ste_	ju_

CORRECTIVE FEEDBACK	**MONITOR PROGRESS**	*If . . .* children have difficulty reading the words, *then . . .* review silent consonants and have them blend words sound-by-sound.

For more practice, see next page.

Continued Spiral Review

Model reading words in sentences.	When I read a sentence, I read each word without stopping between the words. If I come to a word I don't know, I blend it. Then I read the sentence again. Model reading this sentence, stopping to blend *crumbs: Ralph knows it is wrong to brush crumbs off the edge of the table onto the floor.*
Write practice sentences.	Have each child read a sentence.
	Do you know what phrase was written on the badges? **Madge knew she'd made the smudge with her thumb.** **His nephew stood by the hedge and wrapped the lamb's knee.**

Phonological and Phonemic Awareness   Optional practice activities, pp. 280–283

ACTIVITY **3** Read Together

Choral Reading "Watch Where You Sit!" p. 96

	To Do	To Say	
			10 minutes
Develop language and concepts.	Display p. 96.	**Before Reading** This is a comic strip about a new puppy at a birthday party. **What do you know about new puppies?** Allow children to share what they know. New puppies like to play. They often get into things. You can train a puppy to do tricks.	
Model fluent reading.	Model prosody.	Read the title on the comic. Ask children to predict what it is about. Point to a speech balloon. **These sentences tell what the characters are saying. When I read words the characters say, I speak like I am talking to my friends. When I read comics, I read each box in order.** Point to show the order. Read the comic, using a conversational tone. Read it a second time, having children point to each word.	
	Build fluency through choral reading.	**Choral Reading** Now read the comic strip aloud with me. **Try to make your voice sound like mine as we read.** Reread the comic several times with children.	
Develop concepts.	Monitor listening comprehension.	**After Reading** Why do you think the girl wants Pudge to sit instead of run around at her birthday *celebration?* What happens when Pudge finally sits? Do you think the girl is upset when Pudge sits? Explain.	

ACTIVITY **4** Build Concepts

Oral Vocabulary *celebration, custom, occasion, sibling, tradition*

	To Do	To Say	
			5–10 minutes
Review oral vocabulary.	Read the words on the Amazing Words board.	**Focus on Letter-Sounds** Remember, you can find sounds and word parts you know in big words. • **Which words have /k/? What letter or letters stand for /k/ in each of the words?** • **Which words begin with /s/? What letter stands for /s/ in each of these words?** • **Which word begins with /tr/? Which word ends with /ling/?**	

To Do	To Say
Encourage discussion.	**Ask for Reasons and Examples** Review the meanings of the words. Then ask children to give reasons or examples using these words. • Name a family *celebration.* Tell what happens at this *celebration.* • Tell about a morning *custom* you have. What makes it a *custom?* • What are some special *occasions* that take place at school? • If a family has just one child, does that child have *siblings?* Explain. • Is eating turkey on Thanksgiving an American *tradition?* Why or why not?

MORE PRACTICE

Apply oral vocabulary to new situations.	• If I name two people who are each other's *siblings,* nod your head and say, "Sibling." If not, do nothing. Mom and Dad (not), brother and sister (sibling), twins (sibling), Mom and daughter (not), brothers (sibling). • If I name a special *occasion,* clap your hands and say, "Occasion." If not, do nothing. Grass (not), birthday (occasion), Field Day (occasion), trucks (not), graduation (occasion).

ACTIVITY 5 Write

Response to Literature Interactive Writing

5–10 minutes

	To Do	To Say
Generate ideas.	Review the story "Twice as Nice."	**What do you think the twins will always remember about their ninth birthday party?** Discuss what children read in the story and what they know from real life about birthday parties to draw conclusions.
Share the pen.	Have children participate in writing a list of reasons a birthday party is a special celebration.	Write *A birthday party is special because* _____. Have children read the words you wrote. Then have them supply endings for the sentence. Invite individuals to write familiar letter-sounds, word parts, and high-frequency words. Have them find the spelling of high-frequency words on the Word Wall. Ask questions such as: • **What is the first sound in** *fudge?* (/f/) **What letter stands for /f/ in** *fudge? (f)* • **What is the vowel sound in** *fudge* (/u/) **What letter stands for /u/ in** *fudge? (u)* • **What is the last sound in** *fudge?* (/j/) **What three letters stand for /j/ in** *fudge? (dge)*
	Writing elements: conventions	Frequently reread what has been written while tracking the print. Point out that each sentence starts with a capital letter and ends with a period. Point out the extra space between words. Read the completed sentences aloud, having children read with you. (For example, *A birthday party is special because Mom makes my favorite fudge cake. A birthday party is special because lots of pals come. A birthday party is special because we play lots of games. A birthday party is special because you get gifts and cards.*)

MORE PRACTICE

Prompt independent writing.	**Journal Writing** Tell about a favorite party you went to.

Homework   Practice Book, p. 134, High-Frequency Words

ACTIVITY 1 Assessment Options

Sentence Reading

To Do	To Say	5 minutes

Assess sentence reading.

Use reproducible p. 251.

Have each child read the sentences. Record scores on the Sentence Reading Chart, p. 254. Work with one child as others complete Write Sentences below.

Steph said she'd play dodgeball with everybody.
I believe they're having lots of company at Ralph's party.
We've saved enough money to buy a fudge cake for the young boy.

CORRECTIVE FEEDBACK

MONITOR PROGRESS

If . . . children have trouble reading contractions *'re, 've, 'd* or *ph*/f/ and *dge*/j/ words,
then . . . reteach the blending strategy lessons on pp. 196 and 200.

If . . . children cannot read a high-frequency word,
then . . . mark the missed word or words on a high-frequency word list and send the list home for additional practice or have them practice with a fluent reader.

If . . . children misread a word in the sentence,
then . . . correct the error and have them reread the word and then the sentence.

Practice sentence writing.

Provide white boards.

Write Sentences Have children copy the sentences from reproducible p. 251 on white boards. Have them confirm spellings by comparing the words they wrote to the words in the sentences.

Phonological and Phonemic Awareness

Optional practice activities, pp. 280–283

Mid-Unit Passage Reading

To Do	To Say	5–10 minutes

Assess fluency and comprehension.

Determine which children to assess. Use Assessment Book, p. 84.

Choose from these options: monitoring fluency (see pp. 244–245) and/or monitoring retelling (see p. 246). Have children read the Unit 6 Mid-Unit Fluency Passage in the Assessment Book. Be sure each child is assessed every other week.

If you have time, assess every child.

ACTIVITY 2 Use Concepts

Oral Vocabulary *celebration, custom, occasion, sibling, tradition*

To Do	To Say	5 minutes

Check understanding of oral vocabulary.

Use the Amazing Words to wrap up the week's concept.

Monitor understanding of oral vocabulary, using Routine Card 5.

Preview next week's concept.

As time allows, ask questions such as these.

- Tell me about the pictures on pp. 68–77 using some of the week's Amazing Words.
- If a family member comes home after being away for a long time, what kind of *celebration* might you have?
- What is something a *sibling* might do for your birthday?
- How might a family *tradition* of making quilts get handed down?
- Is a *custom* something you never do or always do? Explain.
- How does a special *occasion* make a day different from other days?

Next week you will read about a cowboy's life.

ACTIVITY 3 Read to Connect

Reread "Family Celebrations," pp. 68–77

	To Do	**To Say**
Monitor comprehension: draw conclusions.	Have children reread "Family Celebrations" silently.	As you read, use what you already know and what the author says to draw conclusions about family celebrations. After rereading, ask: • How does the girl feel about family celebrations? How do you know? • What makes a family celebration special? Make a list of different things the family does to celebrate and what children know about family celebrations. Then record children's conclusions on the board. (For example: *The girl thinks family celebrations are important because the family shares happy times together. Homemade cakes and gifts make birthdays special.*) Children will use the list for Activity 4.
Make connections.	Have children make connections across texts.	We also read "Angel Food Bakery." Find that. Do you think the family you read about in "Family Celebrations" would buy a birthday cake from Steph? Why or why not? (Possible answer: Probably not, because the girl says her mom makes the best birthday cakes and making something for a family member is special.) Record children's conclusions on the board. We also read "Twice as Nice," about the twins who like the same things but not in the same ways. Suppose Midge and Phil wanted to order a cake from Steph for their next birthday. What questions might Steph ask them? How do you think the twins would answer? List children's ideas for questions and answers on a T-chart. What did all the selections we read this week show us about family celebrations? What is the big idea? (Family celebrations are special because they are fun times with people we love.)

ACTIVITY 4 Write

Response to Literature Independent Writing

	To Do	**To Say**
Assign narrative writing. **Guide sentence correction.**	Writing elements: conventions, organization, support	Today you will write a story about a family celebration. Tell a story about what the family did as they celebrated. Encourage children to use words you wrote on the board for Activity 3 as they write. Have children check their writing by asking themselves these questions. • Did I use capital letters at the beginning of sentences and proper nouns? • Did I use correct marks at the ends of sentences? • Did I form contractions correctly? • Did I use words to tell the order of what happens? • Did I add details?
MORE PRACTICE		Have children share their sentences with the group. Write their sentences on the board and have children practice reading and writing each other's sentences.
Homework		Practice Book, p. 135, Writing

Unit 6 Week 4 *A Cowboy's Life*

Why should we learn about cowboys?

Objectives *This week students will . . .*

Phonemic Awareness
- segment and blend sounds in words
- add phonemes to make new words

Phonics
- blend and read words with short *e: ea,* and base words and affixes
- apply knowledge of letter-sounds to decode unknown words when reading
- recognize high-frequency words *alone, between, notice, question, woman*

Fluency
- practice fluency with oral rereading

Vocabulary
- build concepts and oral vocabulary: *climate, herd, livestock, occupation, rodeo*

Text Comprehension
- read connected text
- compare and contrast to improve comprehension
- write in response to literature

Word Work *This week's phonics focus is . . .*

Short *e: ea*   Base Words and Affixes

High-Frequency Words *Tested Vocabulary*

The first appearance of each word in the Student Reader is noted below.

alone	If you are **alone,** you don't have anyone with you. (p. 106)
between	There is a rock **between** the two trees. (p. 100)
notice	If you **notice** something, you see it. (p. 102)
question	A **question** is what you ask in order to find out something. (p. 107)
woman	A **woman** is a grown-up female person. (p. 101)

Amazing Words *Oral Vocabulary*

The week's vocabulary is related to the concept of learning about the life of cowboys.

climate	the kind of weather a place has
herd	a group of large animals moving together
livestock	farm animals
occupation	the work that a person does to earn a living; a job
rodeo	a contest or show where cowboys and cowgirls show their skills

Student Reader Unit 6 *This week students will read the following selections.*

Daily Lesson Plan

	ACTIVITIES	MATERIALS
Day 1	**Word Work** Phonemic Awareness: Segment and Blend Sounds Phonics: Blend Words with Short *e: ea* High-Frequency Words *alone, between, notice, question, woman* **Build Concepts** *climate, livestock, occupation* **Read a Passage** "A Cowboy's Life," pp. 100–107 Comprehension: Use Strategies Reread for Fluency	Student White Boards Sound Spelling Card 9 Tested Vocabulary Cards *Sing with Me Big Book* and Audio CD Student Reader: Unit 6 Routine Cards 1, 2, 3, 4, 6, 7 AudioText Practice Book, p. 136, Short *e: ea*
Day 2	**Reread for Fluency** **Word Work** Phonemic Awareness: Add Phonemes Phonics: Blend Base Words and Affixes High-Frequency Words *alone, between, notice, question, woman* **Read a Passage** "Nat Love: A Great Cowboy," pp. 108–115 Comprehension: Use Strategies **Write** Response to Literature: Shared Writing	Student Reader: Unit 6 Student White Boards Tested Vocabulary Cards Routine Cards 1, 2, 3, 4, 6, 7 AudioText Practice Book, p. 137, Base Words and Affixes
Day 3	**Reread for Fluency** **Word Work** Phonemic Awareness: Add Phonemes Phonics: Fluent Word Reading High-Frequency Words *alone, between, notice, question, woman* **Build Concepts** *herd, rodeo* **Read a Passage** "Heather at the Rodeo," pp. 116–125 Comprehension: Compare/Contrast	Student Reader: Unit 6 Student White Boards Tested Vocabulary Cards Routine Cards 1, 2, 3, 4, 6 AudioText Practice Book, p. 138, Compare and Contrast
Day 4	**Reread for Fluency** **Word Work** Phonics: Spiral Review Phonological and Phonemic Awareness Activities, pp. 280–283 **Read Together** "Did You Know?" p. 126 Comprehension: Listening **Build Concepts** *climate, herd, livestock, occupation, rodeo* **Write** Response to Literature: Interactive Writing	Student Reader: Unit 6 Routine Cards 1, 4 AudioText Practice Book, p. 139, High-Frequency Words
Day 5	**Assessment Options** Fluency, Comprehension Sentence Reading; Passage Reading Phonological and Phonemic Awareness Activities, pp. 280–283 **Use Concepts** *climate, herd, livestock, occupation, rodeo* **Read to Connect** "A Cowboy's Life," pp. 100–107 Comprehension: Compare/Contrast **Write** Response to Literature: Independent Writing	Reproducible p. 251 Sentence Reading Chart, p. 254 Student White Boards Fluency Progress Chart, p. 245 Student Reader: Unit 6 Routine Card 5 Practice Book, p. 140, Writing

See pp. xvi–xvii for how *My Sidewalks* integrates instructional practices for ELL.

ACTIVITY **1** Word Work

Phonemic Awareness Segment and Blend Sounds

To Do	To Say	2 minutes

Scaffold instruction.

Distribute white boards.
Write *bread.*

Model Listen to the sounds in *bread.* Stretch the sounds /b/ /rrr/ /eee/ /d/ as you write *b, r, ea, d.* Repeat. Have children write letters as you write.

Lead children in segmenting and blending sounds as they write.

Teach and Practice Have children say the sounds with you as you point to the letters (/b/ /r/ /e/ /d/) and blend the sounds to say the word. *(bread)* Continue the activity with these words:

head   thread   health   spread   breath   sweater

Blending Strategy Short *e: ea*

To Do	To Say	5–10 minutes

Routine

Use the blending routine.

Write *treat* and *dream.*

1 Connect You already can read words like these. What vowel sound do you hear in these words? (/ē/) What letters stand for the sound /ē/ in these words? *(ea)* Today we'll learn about another sound the vowels *ea* can stand for.

Display Sound-Spelling Card 9.

2 Use Sound-Spelling Card This is an elephant. What sound do you hear at the beginning of *elephant?* (/e/) Say it with me: /e/. The letters *ea* can stand for /e/.

Scaffold instruction.

3 Listen and Write Write the letters *ea* for /e/. As you write, say the sound to yourself: /e/. Now say the sound aloud.

Write *head.*

4 Model The letters *ea* can stand for /e/. This is how I blend this word: /h/ /e/ /d/, *head.* Now you blend it: /h/ /e /d/, *head.*

$$\underset{\longrightarrow}{h} \quad \underset{\underset{\longrightarrow}{\longrightarrow}}{e\ a} \quad \underset{\longrightarrow}{d}$$

Write *read.*

When you come to a new word with *ea,* you may have to try the sounds /e/ and /ē/ and read the words around it to figure out the word. Point out that the word *read* can be pronounced /rēd/ or /red/, depending on its use in a sentence.

CORRECTIVE FEEDBACK

Write each practice word. Monitor student practice.

5 Group Practice Let's try the same thing with these words. Give feedback, using the *if . . . then* statements on Routine Card 1.

deaf   breath   dread*   heavy   steady*   weather

6 Individual Practice Write the words; have each child blend two of them.

dead   tread*   health   sweat   head   ready   leather   instead

Check understanding of practice words.

*Children need to make sense of words that they segment and blend. If needed, help children with meanings. **When you** *dread* **something, you fear what will happen. Something that is** *steady* **is not shaking. When you** *tread,* **you walk. (Model.)**

MORE PRACTICE

Model spelling *ea* words.

Spell and Write What sounds do you hear in *head?* (/h/ /e/ /d/) What is the letter for /h/? Let's all write *h.* What two letters stand for /e/ in *head?* Write *ea.* What is the letter for /d/? Write *d.* Continue practice as time allows. Have children confirm their spellings by comparing them to what you've written.

dead   bread   thread   health   meant   ready   heavy   feather

High-Frequency Words *alone, between, notice, question, woman*

	To Do	To Say
Teach high-frequency words.	Display *alone*.	**1 Say, Spell, Write** Use the Tested Vocabulary Cards. Display *alone*. Here are some words that we won't sound out. We'll spell them. This word is *alone*: *a, l, o, n, e* (point to each letter), *alone*. What is this word? What are the letters in the word? Now you write *alone*.
	Point to *lone* in *alone*.	**2 Identify Letter-Sounds** Let's look at the sounds and word parts in *alone* that you do know. What is this word part? *(lone)*
		3 Demonstrate Meaning Tell me a sentence using *alone*. Model a sentence if children need help.
	Display *between, notice, question,* and *woman*.	Repeat the Routine with *between, notice, question,* and *woman*. Children can identify these letter-sounds and word parts: *between* (*b*/b/, *tween*), *notice* (*no, t*/t/) *question* (*ques, n*/n/), and *woman* (*w*/w/, *m*/m/, *n*/n/). Have children write the words in their word banks. Add the words to the Word Wall. Point out that the words they are learning are on p. 127.

ACTIVITY **2** Build Concepts

Oral Vocabulary *climate, livestock, occupation*

	To Do	To Say
Introduce oral vocabulary.	Display p. 29 of *Sing with Me Big Book*. Play audio CD.	This week you will learn about a cowboy's life. Listen for the Amazing Words *climate, livestock,* and *occupation* as I sing this song. Play or sing the song. Then have children sing it with you.
		1 Introduce, Demonstrate, and Apply
Scaffold instruction.	Follow the Routine to teach *climate, livestock,* and *occupation*.	**climate** The song mentions that the *climate* made things risky, or dangerous, for the cowboy. *Climate* is the kind of weather a place has. Have children say the word. A desert has a dry *climate*. A rainforest has a wet *climate*. How would you describe the climate where we live?
		livestock The song tells us that cowboys drove frisky *livestock* down the trail. Farm animals are *livestock*. Have children say the word. Cattle and sheep are *livestock*. What are some other kinds of *livestock*?
		occupation The song says that a cowboy's *occupation* was tough. A person's *occupation*, or job, is the work that person does to earn a living. Have children say the word. Cowboy is one kind of *occupation*. What are some other *occupations*?
	Display the words on the Amazing Words board.	**2 Display the Words** Have children say each word as they look at it. You can find sounds and word parts you know in big words. Read *oc/cu/pa/tion* as you run your hand under the syllables. What letters are in the first syllable of *occupation*? *(oc)* What sounds do you hear in this syllable? (/ok/) Continue with *p*/p/ and *n*/n/. Children can decode the compound word *livestock*. They can identify these letter-sounds and word parts in *climate: cli, m*/m/, *t*/t/.
	Monitor understanding.	**3 Use the Words** Ask children to use each word in a sentence. Model a sentence if children need help.
MORE PRACTICE		Use oral vocabulary to discuss the song. Would you enjoy having a cowboy's *occupation*? Why or why not? In the song, what kind of *livestock* does the cowboy handle? What does he do with this *livestock*? Describe the *climate* the cowboy is in as he works outdoors.

ACTIVITY **3** | ## Read a Passage

Build Background "A Cowboy's Life," pp. 100–107

To Do	To Say	*10 minutes*

Develop language and concepts.

See Routine Card 7. Read aloud p. 99 of the student book.

Preview the Week Use the photograph on p. 98 to introduce this week's concept of a cowboy's life. **What does this picture show about a cowboy's life?** Read aloud the titles and descriptions on p. 99. Ask children what they think each selection will be about.

Scaffold instruction.

See Routine Card 6. Display pp. 100–107.

Ask questions and elaborate on answers to develop language.

Key concepts: *cowboy, cowgirl, Old West, herded, ranches, chaps, spurs, prod, livestock, saddle, stirrups, reins, occupation*

Before Reading Read the title aloud. Do a structured picture walk with children.

pp. 100–101 These pictures show a cowboy and a cowgirl from the Old West long ago. Cowboys rounded up and herded, or moved, cattle long distances. Cowgirls sometimes herded cattle too, but they usually helped run the ranches.

pp. 102–103 Point to the cowboy's hat and boots. Point to chaps. **These are chaps. Chaps are leather pants cowboys wore over other pants. Point to spurs. Cowboys used spurs to gently prod, or poke, a horse to go faster.**

pp. 104–105 What livestock are these cowboys riding? (horses) **Cowboys used horses to help them work. Point to the saddle, stirrups, and reins. They sat in leather saddles with their boots in stirrups. These leather straps are called reins. Cowboys used reins to steer their horses. How did cowboys use ropes in their occupation?** (to catch cows, to drag wood)

pp. 106–107 Is this cowboy working alone or with other cowboys? (alone) **Yes, cowboys spent a lot of time by themselves. There are still cowboys working today. How are the cowboys on p. 107 like cowboys from the past? How are they different?**

Let's read to find out more about a cowboy's life.

Guide comprehension.

Monitor independent reading. Model strategic reading. Use Routine Cards 2 and 3.

During Reading Read the pages in a whisper. Raise your hand if you need help with a word. Stop at the end of each page to model asking questions. For example, for p. 103: **After I read, I ask myself: What am I learning about a cowboy's life? What is this page mainly about? The author tells how cowboys wore leather chaps to keep their legs safe. I read that they wore leather boots with spurs on the heels. This page is mainly about the type of clothing cowboys wore.**

Summarize.

Use oral vocabulary to develop the concept.

After Reading How did cowboys work with *livestock* in the Old West? How did the cowboy's hat help him deal with the *climate?* Is being a cowboy or cowgirl an *occupation* a person can still have today? Explain.

Reread for Fluency "A Cowboy's Life," pp. 100–104

To Do	To Say	*5–10 minutes*

CORRECTIVE FEEDBACK

Monitor oral reading.

Read pp. 100–104 aloud. Read them three or four times so your reading gets better each time. Give feedback on children's oral reading and use of the blending strategy. See Routine Cards 1 and 4.

MORE PRACTICE

Instead of rereading just pp. 100–104, have children reread the entire selection three or four times. You may want to have children read along with the AudioText.

Homework

Practice Book, p. 136, Phonics: Short *e: ea*

ACTIVITY 1 Reread for Fluency

Paired Reading "A Cowboy's Life," pp. 105–107

5–10 minutes

	To Do	To Say
CORRECTIVE FEEDBACK	Pair children. Monitor paired reading.	Children read pp. 105–107 orally, switching readers at the end of the first page. Have partners reread; now the other partner begins. For optimal fluency, children should reread three or four times. Give feedback on children's oral reading and use of the blending strategy. See Routine Cards 1 and 4.
MORE PRACTICE		Instead of rereading just pp. 105–107, have children reread the entire selection three or four times. You may want to have children read along with the AudioText.

ACTIVITY 2 Word Work

Phonemic Awareness Add Phonemes

2 minutes

	To Do	To Say
Scaffold instruction.	Distribute white boards. Write *like*. Add *dis-* to form *dislike*. Erase *e* and add *-ed* to form *disliked*. Lead children in adding affixes as they write.	**Model** Listen to the sounds in *like*. Stretch the sounds /lll/ /īīī/ /k/ as you write *l, i, k, e*. Repeat. This time have children write the letters as you write. **Now listen as I add /dis/ to the beginning of *like*: dis, like, dislike. Repeat. Have children add** *dis-* as you write. **Teach and Practice** Have children say the sounds as you point to the parts *(dis, like)* and blend the parts to say the word. *(dislike)* **What new word do we make when we add *dis-* to the beginning of *like*? (dislike) Now listen as I add /t/ to the end of *dislike*: dislike, /t/, disliked.** Repeat. Have children add *-ed* as you write, say the parts, and blend the parts to say the word. Continue adding affixes to base words to form these words: distrustful reused unhappily preheated unluckiest rewrapping

Blending Strategy Base Words and Affixes

To Do	To Say	

5–10 minutes

Use the blending routine.

Write *dislike, hopeful, quickest,* and *passed.*

1 Connect You studied words like these already. What do you know about reading these words? (Figure out the base word, read each part, and then blend the parts to say the word.) Tell me the base word when I point to the longer word. Now read the whole word. Which word has a prefix? What is it? *(dislike, dis-)* Today we'll learn more about reading longer words.

Scaffold instruction.

Write *preheated.*

2 Model This word has a prefix, a base word, and an ending. When I read a longer word like this, I first figure out the base word. Cover up the prefix and ending. The base word is *heat.* Then I read each part and blend all the parts together. This is how I blend this word: *pre, heat, ed, preheated.*

Write *unkindly, repacking, distrustful,* and *premixes.*

Model blending *unkindly, repacking, distrustful,* and *premixes.* As needed, review the prefixes *un-, re-, dis-, pre-;* the suffixes *-ful, -ly;* and the endings *-ed, -ing, -s* or *-es, -er, -est.* Remind children to use the meanings of the base words and these affixes to help them figure out the meanings of the words.

Write *rewrapping, displeased,* and *unhappily.*

Sometimes the spelling of the base word changes before an ending or suffix is added. What spelling changes do you see? Review doubling the final consonant, dropping the final *e,* and changing *y* to *i.* Tell me the base word when I point to the longer word. Now read the whole word.

r e w r a p p i n g   d i s p l e a s e d   u n h a p p i l y

3 Listen and Write Write the word *wrap.* Write *re-* at the beginning of it. To add the ending *-ing,* double the final consonant, *p,* and then write *-ing* at the end. As you write, say each part to yourself: *re, wrap, ping.* Now blend the parts together and say the word aloud. Continue with *displeased* and *unhappily.*

CORRECTIVE FEEDBACK

Write each practice word. Monitor student practice.

4 Group Practice Let's try reading these longer words. Give feedback, using the *if . . . then* statements on Routine Card 1.

dislikes   unhelpful   prejudging   unzipping   unhappier   replaced

5 Individual Practice Write the words; have each child blend two of them.

replaying   precooked   uneasily   disregarded   remodeled   unluckiest

MORE PRACTICE

Model building words with affixes.

Build Words Make a class chart with the headings below. Fill in the first three columns. Model building and blending *unluckiest.* Have children write the longer words on their white boards. Call on them to read the longer words and identify any spelling changes. When finished, add the remaining longer words to the chart.

Prefix	Base Word	Suffixes/Endings	Longer Word
un-	lucky	-est	unluckiest
re-	wrap	-ed	rewrapped
pre-	judge	-ing	prejudging
dis-	taste	-ful	distasteful

High-Frequency Words *alone, between, notice, question, woman*

To Do	To Say	

3 minutes

Teach high-frequency words.

Display *alone, between, notice, question,* and *woman.*

Use the Tested Vocabulary Cards. Point to a word. Say and spell it. Have children say and spell the word. Ask children to identify familiar letter-sounds and word parts. Have children take turns reading the words.

Lead cumulative review.

Use the Tested Vocabulary Cards to review high-frequency words from previous weeks.

ACTIVITY 3 Read a Passage

Reading "Nat Love: A Great Cowboy," pp. 108–115

10–15 minutes

	To Do	**To Say**
Develop language and concepts. **Scaffold instruction.**	See Routine Cards 6 and 7. Display pp. 108–115. Ask questions and elaborate on answers to develop language. Key concepts: *slave, untamed, cowboy, skills, occupation, contests, ranchers, railroad*	**Before Reading** Have children recall what a cowboy's life was like in the past. Read the title. Do a structured picture walk with children. **pp. 108–109** This is Nat Love. Do you think Nat lived long ago or today? Nat was born a slave long ago. Slaves were not allowed to be free. When Nat was still a child, slavery in America ended. **pp. 110–111** When Nat was fifteen, he showed he could ride untamed, or wild, horses. Do you think the cowboys were surprised by Nat's skills? After showing good riding skills, Nat's occupation was a cowboy. **pp. 112–113** Nat entered contests to show his skills with horses and cattle. Do you think he won many contests? How do you know? **pp. 114–115** Nat worked as a cowboy until ranchers no longer needed lots of cowboys. What was Nat's next occupation? (He worked for a railroad.) Yes, he worked for the railroad. Then Nat wrote a book about his life. Now let's read to find out more about Nat Love.
Guide comprehension.	Monitor independent reading. Use Routine Cards 2 and 3.	**During Reading** Read the pages in a whisper. Raise your hand if you need help with a word. As you read, ask yourself: What am I learning about Nat Love? What is this mainly about? **pp. 108–113** What did you learn about Nat's life as a cowboy? (Nat tamed wild horses, herded cattle, and won contests for his cowboy skills.) **pp. 114–115** What did you learn about Nat's life after he was a cowboy? (He worked for a railroad, got married, and wrote a book about his life.)
Model summarizing.	Think aloud.	**After Reading** What did you learn about Nat Love? What was the selection mainly about? Model how to summarize. The first part told what Nat Love did when he was a cowboy. The last pages told about things Nat did when he was no longer a cowboy. This selection is mainly about Nat Love's life.
MORE PRACTICE	Develop oral vocabulary.	How did the contests show Nat's skills with *livestock?* What did the selection's pictures show you about the *climate* in the West? What do you think was Nat's favorite *occupation?* Why?

ACTIVITY 4 Write

Response to Literature Shared Writing

5 minutes

	To Do	**To Say**
Guide shared writing.	Write sentence frames. Read the questions.	What did Nat do as a cowboy? When he was a cowboy, Nat _____. What did Nat do after he was a cowboy? Later, Nat _____. Invite children to suggest answers. Discuss and record answers to complete the sentence frames. While writing, model connecting sounds to letters and forming letters. (See pp. 257–259.) Have children read answers aloud as you track print.
Homework		Practice Book, p. 137 Phonics: Base Words and Affixes

ACTIVITY 1 — Reread for Fluency

Oral Reading "Nat Love: A Great Cowboy," pp. 108–111

5–10 minutes

	To Do	To Say
CORRECTIVE FEEDBACK	Monitor oral reading.	Read pp. 108–111 aloud. Read them three or four times so your reading gets better each time. Give feedback on children's oral reading and use of the blending strategy. See Routine Cards 1 and 4.
MORE PRACTICE		Instead of rereading just pp. 108–111, have children reread the entire selection three or four times. You may want to have children read along with the AudioText.

ACTIVITY 2 — Word Work

Phonemic Awareness Add Phonemes

2 minutes

Scaffold instruction.

To Do

Distribute white boards. Write *steady*. Add *un-* to form *unsteady*.

Add *-ly* to form *unsteadily*. Lead children in adding affixes as they write.

To Say

Model Listen to the sounds in *steady*. Stretch the sounds /sss/ /t/ /eee/ /d/ /ēēē/ as you write *s, t, ea, d, y*. Repeat. Have children write letters as you write. **Now listen as I add /un/ to the beginning of *steady*: un, steady, unsteady.** Repeat. Have children add *un-* as you write.

Teach and Practice Have children say the parts *(un, steady)* and blend the parts to say the word. *(unsteady)* Then model changing *y* to *i*, adding *-ly*, and blending *unsteadily*. Have children add *-ly* as you write, say the parts, and blend the parts to say the word. Continue the activity, forming these words:

heavier	dreadfully	rewriting	prewrapped	unhealthiest	displeased

Fluent Word Reading Short e: *ea*; Base Words with Affixes

5–10 minutes

Use the word-reading routine.

Scaffold instruction.

To Do

Write *thread*.

Write *retraced*, *discovered*, and *unhealthiest*.

Write each practice word.

To Say

1 Connect You can read this word because you know *ea* can stand for /ē/ or /e/. What sound does *ea* stand for in this word? (/e/) What is the word? *(thread)*

Routine

2 Model When you come to new word, look at all the letters and think about its vowel sounds and parts. Say the letter-sounds and word parts to yourself, and then read the word. Model reading *retraced*, *discovered*, and *unhealthiest* in this way. When you see a new word, what will you do?

3 Group Practice Let's read these words. Look at all the letters, think about the vowel sounds and word parts, and say the parts to yourself. We will read words with *ea* and longer words. When I point to the word, let's read it together. Allow 2–3 seconds previewing time for each word.

head	meadow	retied	wealthier	prewrapped	unsaddled	unsteadily	disliking

CORRECTIVE FEEDBACK	**MONITOR PROGRESS**	*If . . .* children have difficulty previewing and reading whole words, *then . . .* have them use sound-by-sound blending.
		If . . . children can't read the words fluently at a rate of 1–2 seconds per word, *then . . .* continue practicing the list.

MORE PRACTICE	Model reading words in sentences.	When I read a sentence, I read each word without stopping between the words. If I come to a word I don't know, I blend it. Then I read the sentence again. Model reading this sentence, stopping to blend *resaddled: Luckily, Jed resaddled the horse for me and rechecked the leather straps.*
	Write practice sentences.	Have each child read a sentence.
		Heather was displeased with the blue thread, so she replaced it with red.
		With careful preplanning, our homemade bread will be ready by lunch.
		To stay healthy, she puts on her heaviest sweater in freezing weather.

High-Frequency Words *alone, between, notice, question, woman*

	To Do	To Say	3 minutes
Review high-frequency words.	Display *alone, between, notice, question,* and *woman.*	Use the Tested Vocabulary Cards. Point to a word. Say and spell it. Have children say and spell the word. Ask children to identify familiar letter-sounds and word parts. Have them take turns reading the words.	

ACTIVITY 3 Build Concepts

Oral Vocabulary *herd, rodeo*

	To Do	To Say	5–10 minutes
Teach oral vocabulary.	Display p. 108 and p. 116 of the student book.	Yesterday we read about Nat Love, a cowboy who was great at moving *herds* of cattle and winning *rodeo* contests. Today you will read about a girl who goes to a *rodeo* to watch today's cowboys and cowgirls show their roping and riding skills, the same skills Nat used long ago.	*Routine*
		1 Introduce, Demonstrate, and Apply	
Scaffold instruction.	Follow the Routine to teach *herd* (n., v.) and *rodeo.*	**herd** Nat used ropes to keep a *herd* of cattle together. A *herd* is a group of large animals moving together. When you *herd* animals, you drive or guide them in a specific direction. Have children say the word. In the past, cowboys *herded herds* of cattle between ranches and train stops. Why might it be difficult to keep a *herd* of cattle together?	
		rodeo Nat won roping and riding contests at a *rodeo.* Today's story also tells about a *rodeo.* A *rodeo* is a contest or show where cowboys and cowgirls show their skills. Have children say the word. At a *rodeo,* cowboys and cowgirls ride bulls and horses, have races, and rope cattle. Would you like to go to a *rodeo?* Why or why not?	
	Display the words on the Amazing Words board.	**2 Display the Words** Have children say each word as they look at it. You can find letter-sounds and word parts you know in big words. Read *ro/de/o* as you run your hand under the syllables. Children can identify *r*/r/ and *d*/d/. They can decode *herd.*	
	Monitor understanding.	**3 Use the Words** Ask children to use each word in a sentence. Model a sentence if children need help.	
MORE PRACTICE		Use oral vocabulary to discuss a cowboy's life. In the past, how might a cowboy have felt after *herding* cattle on a long trip? How might today's cowboy feel after riding a bucking horse at a *rodeo?*	

ACTIVITY 4 Read a Passage

Reading "Heather at the Rodeo," pp. 116–125

	To Do	To Say	*10 minutes*

Teach compare/ contrast.

Scaffold instruction.

Introduce the skill.

Model the skill. Display p. 110.

Apply the skill.

Today you will compare and contrast. When you compare and contrast, you tell how things are alike and different. For example, we can use a diagram to compare and contrast Nat Love with the cowboys he met in Dodge City. Draw a Venn diagram with the headings *Nat, Both,* and *Cowboys.* List *lived long ago* under *Both, teenager* under *Nat,* and *adults* under *Cowboys.*

What other ways was Nat like the cowboys? What other ways was Nat different from them? Record responses in the diagram above. (*Both:* wore hats, chaps, and spurs; *Nat:* was not yet a cowboy, did not know how to rope cattle; *Cowboys:* had jobs as cowboys, could rope and herd)

Develop language and concepts.

See Routine Card 6. Display pp. 116–125.

Model using key words and concepts.

Key concepts: *cowboy, bull, rodeo, contest, cowgirls, horses, barrels, roping, bareback, bucking, saddle, counts*

Monitor children's use of vocabulary.

Before Reading Read the title. Do a structured picture walk.

pp. 116–117 Where are Heather and her family? (at a rodeo) **This cowboy is riding a bull, or male cow, in a rodeo contest.**

pp. 118–119 At the rodeo, cowgirls race horses around containers with curved sides called barrels. Who will race the fastest?

pp. 120–122 Now the family is watching cowboys roping cows.

pp. 123–124 This cowboy is in a bareback riding contest—he tries to stay on a bucking horse without a saddle for eight counts, or seconds.

p. 125 Why do you think Heather is wearing Dad's cowboy hat? After watching the rodeo, she wants to be a cowgirl. Giddap!

Now turn to your partner and talk about the pictures, using the same words I did.

Teach story words.

Write *barrel* and *bull.*

You will read these words in the story: *barrel* and *bull.* Point to each word. Have children say and spell each word. Review their meanings. **Now let's read to find out more about Heather's visit to a rodeo.**

Guide comprehension.

Monitor independent reading.

Use Routine Cards 2 and 3.

During Reading Read the pages in a whisper. Raise your hand if you need help with a word. As you read, compare and contrast events at the rodeo. Also compare and contrast the cowboys and cowgirls of now with those of long ago.

pp. 116–119 How is the barrel race different from the other rodeo events? How is it the same? (It's different because only cowgirls are in this contest. It's the same because it's a contest to see who is the best.)

pp. 120–122 Compare and contrast why cowboys use ropes at the rodeo with why cowboys use ropes during their jobs? (Both use rope to catch cows. Cowboys on the job rope cows to keep cattle together. Cowboys at a rodeo rope young cows to win a contest.)

pp. 123–125 If Heather lived long ago, would she still want to be a cowgirl? How might her life be different? How might it be the same? (She might have had to help at a ranch. She would still ride horses.)

Guide retelling.

Prompt children as they retell the story.

After Reading Have one child retell the story while the others assist. When and where does this story take place? What happens at the beginning? in the middle? at the end? See Monitor Retelling, p. 246.

Homework Practice Book, p. 138, Compare and Contrast

Reread for Fluency

Paired Reading "Heather at the Rodeo," pp. 116–119

To Do	To Say	
		5–10 minutes

CORRECTIVE FEEDBACK | Pair children. Monitor paired reading. | Children read pp. 116–119 orally, switching readers at the end of the first page. Have partners reread; now the other partner begins. For optimal fluency, children should reread three or four times. Give feedback on children's oral reading and use of the blending strategy. See Routine Cards 1 and 4.

MORE PRACTICE | | Instead of rereading just pp. 116–119, have children reread the entire selection three or four times. You may want to have children read along with the AudioText.

ACTIVITY **2** # Word Work

Spiral Review Read Longer Words: Base Words and Affixes

5–10 minutes

Review reading base words and affixes with and without spelling changes.

Write *precooked* and *disconnecting.*

You can read these words because you know how to blend longer words. Remember, first figure out the base word, read each part, and then blend the parts together. Have children identify each base word and then read the longer word. For *disconnecting,* review breaking two-syllable base words into smaller parts. **Did the spelling of the base words change?** (no)

Write *replanning, explorer,* and *unhappily.*

Sometimes the spelling of a base word must change. Review the spelling changes: doubling the final consonant, dropping the final *e,* changing *y* to *i.* Then have children identify the base word and read the longer word.

Scaffold instruction. | Make a class chart.

Build Words Fill in the first three columns of the class chart below. Have children write the longer words in the last column, read them, and identify spelling changes. Discuss the meanings of the longer words, using the affixes.

Prefix	Base Word	Suffixes/Endings	Longer Word
	invent	-or	inventor
	garden	-er	gardener
	heavy	-er	heavier
	power	-ful, -ly	powerfully
un-	healthy	-est	unhealthiest
un-	steady	-ly	unsteadily
re-	place	-ing	replacing
dis-	cover	-ed	discovered
dis-	respect	-ful	disrespectful
pre-	order	-ed	preordered

CORRECTIVE FEEDBACK | **MONITOR PROGRESS** | *If . . .* children have difficulty reading the words, *then . . .* have them blend base words sound-by-sound before adding affixes.

For more practice, see next page.

MORE PRACTICE

Continued **Spiral Review**

Model reading words in sentences.	When I read a sentence, I read without stopping between the words. If I come to a word I don't know, I blend it. Then I read the sentence again. Model reading this sentence, stopping to blend *pretreated: She pretreated the stains on her sweater.*
	Have each child read a sentence.
Write practice sentences.	The gardener unhappily began retrimming the hedges.
	Thankfully, Heather liked the prefaded jeans we gave her.
	The unluckiest cowboy dismounted his horse after the riding contest.

Phonological and Phonemic Awareness — Optional practice activities, pp. 280–283

ACTIVITY 3 Read Together

Choral Reading "Did You Know?" p. 126

	To Do	**To Say**	*10 minutes*

Develop language and concepts.

To Do: Display p. 126. Display a world map.

To Say: **Before Reading** What facts have you learned about cowboys? Allow children to share what they know. You've learned that cowboys wear hats to protect their heads. In the Old West, cowboys also used their hats for another reason. Can you guess what it is? Often, cowboys brand, or burn marks on, cattle to show who owns the livestock. Branding began long, long ago in ancient Egypt. Point to Egypt.

Model fluent reading.

To Say: Read the title and ask children to predict what the text will be about. When I read facts, I read slowly and carefully. I pause after each fact to make sure I understand it before I read the next one. Read each fact at the appropriate rate, pausing between facts. Read them a second time, having children point to each word.

To Do: Build fluency through choral reading.

To Say: **Choral Reading** Read the facts aloud with me. Try to make your voice sound like mine as we read. Reread the facts several times with children.

Develop concepts.

To Do: Monitor listening comprehension.

To Say: **After Reading** How does a cowboy's hat help him in a sunny *climate*? Why do you think that cowboys long ago used their hats as water bowls? Would you see stirrups on boots or saddles? Explain. Why would ranchers brand their *livestock*?

ACTIVITY 4 Build Concepts

Oral Vocabulary *climate, herd, livestock, occupation, rodeo*

	To Do	**To Say**	*5–10 minutes*

Review oral vocabulary.

To Do: Read the words on the Amazing Words board.

To Say: **Focus on Letter-Sounds** Remember, you can find letter-sounds and word parts you know in big words.

- Which word has *live* and *stock* in it? Which word has two long *o*'s?
- Which word has the sound /èr/? What letters stand for /èr/? Which words have the sound /k/? What letter or letters stand for /k/ in each of these words?

To Do	To Say
Encourage discussion.	**Provide Multiple Contexts** Review the meanings of the words. Then ask questions to place the words in diverse contexts. • Describe the *climate* of the North Pole. • If a group of people are *herded* through a museum, are they finding their own way or are they following a guide? Explain. • What responsibilities would you have if you took care of *livestock?* • Who has a dangerous *occupation?* Why is this job dangerous? • Is a *rodeo* more like a track meet or a parade? Why?

MORE PRACTICE

Apply oral vocabulary to new situations.	• Would sunscreen protect you from the *climate* or a *herd?* Explain. • Do you think anyone has an *occupation* as a *rodeo* cowboy? • Would you find *livestock* on a farm or at the beach? Why?

ACTIVITY 5 Write

Response to Literature Interactive Writing

5–10 minutes

To Do	To Say
Generate ideas. Review the story "Heather at the Rodeo."	What do you think was the most amazing contest Heather watched at the rodeo? Discuss the various rodeo events.
Share the pen. Have children participate in listing the events cowboys and cowgirls participate in at a rodeo.	Write *At a rodeo, _____.* Have children read the words you wrote. Then have them supply endings for the sentence. Invite individuals to write familiar letter-sounds, word parts, and high-frequency words. Have them find the spelling of high-frequency words on the Word Wall. Ask questions such as: • What is the base word in *unsaddled?* (saddle) • What prefix is at the beginning of *unsaddled?* (un-) • What is the ending on *unsaddled?* (-ed) Does the spelling of the base word *saddle* need to change before we add *-ed?* (yes) What change is needed? (Drop the final *e* from *saddle.)*
Writing elements: conventions	Frequently reread what has been written while tracking the print. Point out that each sentence starts with a capital letter and ends with a period. Point out the extra space between words. Read the completed sentences aloud, having children read with you. (For example, *At a rodeo, cowboys ride unsaddled horses. At a rodeo, cowboys ride heavy bulls. At a rodeo, cowgirls race horses around barrels.)*

MORE PRACTICE

Prompt independent writing.	**Journal Writing** Tell what you would do if you were in a rodeo.

Homework	Practice Book, p. 139, High-Frequency Words

Assessment Options

Sentence Reading

To Do	To Say	
		5 minutes

Assess sentence reading.

Use reproducible p. 251.

Have each child read the sentences. Record scores on the Sentence Reading Chart, p. 254. Work with one child as others complete Write Sentences below.

The baker had a question about reusing the bread pan.
Did you notice that the woman untied her boots?
Instead of sitting alone, Jo sat between her pals on the leather couch.

CORRECTIVE FEEDBACK

MONITOR PROGRESS

If . . . children have trouble reading words with short *e*: *ea* or base words and affixes,
then . . . reteach the blending strategy lessons on pp. 212 and 216.

If . . . children cannot read a high-frequency word,
then . . . mark the missed word or words on a high-frequency word list and send the list home for additional practice or have them practice with a fluent reader.

If . . . children misread a word in the sentence,
then . . . correct the error and have them reread the word and then the sentence.

Practice sentence writing.

Provide white boards.

Write Sentences Have children copy the sentences from reproducible p. 251 on white boards. Have them confirm their spellings by comparing the words they wrote to the words in the sentences.

Phonological and Phonemic Awareness

Optional practice activities, pp. 280–283

Passage Reading

To Do	To Say	
		5–10 minutes

Assess fluency and comprehension.

Determine which children to assess this week.

Choose from these options: monitoring fluency (see pp. 244–245) and/or monitoring retelling (see p. 246). Have children reread "Heather at the Rodeo." Be sure each child is assessed every other week.

If you have time, assess every child.

Use Concepts

Oral Vocabulary *climate, herd, livestock, occupation, rodeo*

To Do	To Say	
		5 minutes

Check understanding of oral vocabulary.

Use the Amazing Words to wrap up the week's concept.

Monitor understanding of oral vocabulary, using Routine Card 5.

As time allows, ask questions such as these.

- **Describe the pictures on pp. 100–107 using some of the week's Amazing Words.**
- **When cowboys *herd* cattle, do they guide them or let them roam free?**
- **What types of *livestock* might you see at a *rodeo*?**
- **What do you think is the best thing about a cowboy's *occupation*?**

Preview next week's concept.

- **Tell about something a cowboy or cowgirl might do at a *rodeo*. Use the word *rodeo* when you tell about it.**

Next week you will read about ways that different people celebrate.

ACTIVITY 3 | Read to Connect

Reread "A Cowboy's Life," pp. 100–107

To Do	To Say	*10 minutes*

Monitor comprehension: compare/contrast.

To Do: Have children reread "A Cowboy's Life" silently.

To Say: **As you read, compare and contrast a cowboy's life long ago to a cowboy's life today. Think about what you already know as you compare and contrast. After rereading, ask:**

- **How is a cowboy's life today still like a cowboy's life long ago?**
- **How is a cowboy's life today different from a cowboy's life long ago?**

Draw a Venn diagram on the board with the headings: *Cowboys Long Ago, Both, Cowboys Today.* Record children's comparisons in appropriate parts of the diagram. (For example: *Both:* work with livestock on ranches; wear hats, chaps, and boots; ride horses; use ropes; have rodeo contests; *Cowboys Long Ago:* herded cattle on long trips, used rope to drag wood, spent lots of time riding; *Cowboys Today:* herd cattle, but not as far as in the past; not as many cowboys needed; now have machines they can use for dragging wood or for riding across the land) Children will use the diagram for Activity 4.

Make connections.

To Do: Have children make connections across texts.

To Say: **We also read "Nat Love: A Great Cowboy." Find that. What did you learn about a cowboy's life long ago from reading about Nat Love?** Add children's responses to the diagram above.

We also read "Heather at the Rodeo," a story about a visit to a rodeo that happens now. What did you learn about a cowboy's life today from this story? Add children's responses to the diagram above.

What did our selections this week tell us about a cowboy's life? What is the big idea? (Cowboys long ago and today have interesting lives with many challenges.)

ACTIVITY 4 | Write

Response to Literature Independent Writing

To Do	To Say	*5–10 minutes*

Assign descriptive writing.

Guide sentence correction.

To Do: Writing elements: focus, support, conventions

To Say: **Today you will compare and contrast cowboys from long ago with cowboys today. Encourage children to use words you wrote on the board for Activity 3 as they write.**

Have children check their writing by asking themselves these questions.

- **Did I use capital letters to begin sentences and proper nouns?**
- **Did I use correct marks at the ends of sentences?**
- **Did I use words such as *both* and *like* to show how things are alike? Did I use words such as *but* and *unlike* to show how things are different?**
- **Did I use describing words?**
- **Did I stick to the topic of cowboys today and long ago?**

MORE PRACTICE

Have children share their sentences with the group. Write their sentences on the board and have children practice reading and writing each other's sentences.

Homework   Practice Book, p. 140, Writing

Unit 6 Week 5 *Celebrations for Everyone*

How do different people celebrate?

Objectives *This week students will . . .*

Phonemic Awareness
- segment and blend sounds in words
- add phonemes to make new words

Phonics
- blend and read words with vowel patterns *aw, au, au(gh)*; base words and affixes
- apply knowledge of letter-sounds to decode unknown words when reading
- recognize high-frequency words *cold, finally, half, tomorrow, word*

Fluency
- practice fluency with oral rereading

Vocabulary
- build concepts and oral vocabulary: *ceremony, culture, festival, international, regional*

Text Comprehension
- read connected text
- identify main idea to improve comprehension
- write in response to literature

Word Work *This week's phonics focus is . . .*

Vowel Patterns *aw, au, au(gh)*   Base Words and Affixes

High-Frequency Words *Tested Vocabulary*

The first appearance of each word in the Student Reader is noted below.

cold   Something **cold** is not hot. (p. 132)
              I can't come to school because I have a **cold.**

finally   I **finally** figured it out. (p. 132)

half   A **half** is one of two equal parts. (p. 134)

tomorrow   **Tomorrow** is the day after today. (p. 135)

word   We speak **words** when we talk. (p. 130)

Amazing Words *Oral Vocabulary*

The week's vocabulary is related to the concept of celebrations for everyone.

ceremony   something people do to celebrate a special occasion

culture   the beliefs, customs, and behavior of groups of people at a certain time

festival   a time when people celebrate together, often to remember an important event

international between or among two or more countries

regional   happening in a specific place or area

Student Reader Unit 6 *This week students will read the following selections.*

Daily Lesson Plan

	ACTIVITIES	MATERIALS
Day 1	**Word Work** Phonemic Awareness: Segment and Blend Sounds Phonics: Blend Words with Vowel Patterns *aw, au, au(gh)* High-Frequency Words *cold, finally, half, tomorrow, word* **Build Concepts** *ceremony, culture, festival* **Read a Passage** "Celebrations for Everyone," pp. 130–137 Comprehension: Use Strategies Reread for Fluency	Student White Boards Sound Spelling Card 4 Tested Vocabulary Cards *Sing with Me Big Book* and Audio CD Student Reader: Unit 6 Routine Cards 1, 2, 3, 4, 6, 7 AudioText Practice Book, p. 141, Vowel Patterns *aw, au, augh*
Day 2	**Reread for Fluency** **Word Work** Phonemic Awareness: Add Phonemes Phonics: Blend Base Words and Affixes High-Frequency Words *cold, finally, half, tomorrow, word* **Read a Passage** "The Sweet Stink of Success," pp. 138–145 Comprehension: Use Strategies **Write** Response to Literature: Shared Writing	Student Reader: Unit 6 Student White Boards Tested Vocabulary Cards Routine Cards 1, 2, 3, 4, 6, 7 AudioText Practice Book, p. 142, Base Words and Affixes
Day 3	**Reread for Fluency** **Word Work** Phonemic Awareness: Add Phonemes Phonics: Fluent Word Reading High-Frequency Words *cold, finally, half, tomorrow, word* **Build Concepts** *international, regional* **Read a Passage** "Austin P. Crawler's Naughty Pig," pp. 146–157 Comprehension: Main Idea	Student Reader: Unit 6 Student White Boards Tested Vocabulary Cards Routine Cards 1, 2, 3, 4, 6 AudioText Practice Book, p. 143, Main Idea and Supporting Details
Day 4	**Reread for Fluency** **Word Work** Phonics: Spiral Review Phonological and Phonemic Awareness Activities, pp. 280–283 **Read Together** "Piñata Game," p. 158 Comprehension: Listening **Build Concepts** *ceremony, culture, festival, international, regional* **Write** Response to Literature: Interactive Writing	Student Reader: Unit 6 Routine Cards 1, 4 AudioText Student White Boards Practice Book, p. 144, High-Frequency Words
Day 5	**Assessment Options** Fluency, Comprehension Sentence Reading; End-of-Unit Test Phonological and Phonemic Awareness Activities, pp. 280–283 **Use Concepts** *ceremony, culture, festival, international, regional* **Read to Connect** "Celebrations for Everyone," pp. 130–137 Comprehension: Main Idea **Write** Response to Literature: Independent Writing	Reproducible p. 251 Sentence Reading Chart, p. 254 Student White Boards Assessment Book, p. 69 Student Reader: Unit 6 Routine Card 5 Practice Book, p. 145, Writing

See pp. xvi–xvii for how *My Sidewalks* integrates instructional practices for ELL.

ACTIVITY **1** Word Work

Phonemic Awareness Segment and Blend Sounds

2 minutes

	To Do	**To Say**
Scaffold instruction.	Distribute white boards. Write *saw*.	**Model** Listen to the sounds in *saw*. Stretch the sounds /sss/ /o͝oo͝o/ as you write *s, aw*. Repeat. Have children write letters as you write.
	Write *sauce* and *caught*. Lead children in segmenting and blending sounds.	**Teach and Practice** Have children say the sounds with you as you point to the letters (/s/ /o͝o/) and blend the sounds to say the word. *(saw)* Repeat the process with *sauce* (/s/ /o͝o/ /s/; *s, au, c, e*) and *caught* (/k/ /o͝o/ /t/; *c, augh, t*). Then continue with these words:
		lawn haul taught awful August naughty

Blending Strategy Vowel Patterns *aw, au, au(gh)*

5–10 minutes

Routine

	To Do	**To Say**
Use the blending routine.	Write *walk* and *ball*.	**1 Connect** You already can read words like these because you know that when the letter *a* is followed by *l* or *ll*, the vowel sound is usually /o͝o/. What vowel sound do you hear in these words? (/o͝o/) What are the words? *(walk, ball)* Today we'll learn about other letters that can stand for the sound /o͝o/.
Scaffold instruction.	Display Sound-Spelling Card 4.	**2 Use Sound-Spelling Card** This is an audience. What sound do you hear at the beginning of *audience*? (/o͝o/) Say it with me: /o͝o/. The letters *au* can stand for the vowel sound /o͝o/.
		3 Listen and Write Write the letters *au* for /o͝o/. As you write, say the sound to yourself: /o͝o/. Now say the sound aloud.
	Write *lawn*.	**4 Model** The letters *aw* stand for /o͝o/ in this word. This is how I blend it: /l/ /o͝o/ /n/, *lawn*. Now you blend it: /l/ /o͝o/ /n/, *lawn*.
	Write *haul* and *naughty*.	Repeat steps 2 and 3 for *au*. Then model blending *haul*: /h/ /o͝o/ /l/, *haul*. Repeat for *augh* and blend *naughty* using bigger word parts: /no͝o/ /te̅/. Tell children to keep *augh* together when dividing longer words. Point out that the letters *aw, au,* and *augh* can stand for /o͝o/.

l a w n   h a u l   n a u g h t y

CORRECTIVE FEEDBACK	Write each practice word. Monitor student practice.	**5 Group Practice** Let's try the same thing with these words. Give feedback, using the *if . . . then* statements on Routine Card 1.
		straw pause caught thawed* August daughter
		6 Individual Practice Write the words; have each child blend two of them.
		dawn* fault taught awful author naughty scrawny* because
	Check understanding of practice words.	*Children need to make sense of words that they segment and blend. If needed, help children with meanings. *Thawed* means something melted or became less cold. *Dawn* is the beginning of the day, or sunrise. If something is *scrawny*, it's very thin. Turkeys have *scrawny* necks.
MORE PRACTICE	Model building words with *awn, ause,* and *aught*.	**Build Words** Have children write *awn, ause,* and *aught* at the tops of their boards. Have them add *l, y, d, p,* and *dr* in front of *awn*; *c* and *p* in front of *ause*; and *c* and *t* in front of *aught*. Model blending using bigger word chunks: *l, awn, lawn*. Call on children to read each word and use it in a sentence.

High-Frequency Words *cold, finally, half, tomorrow, word*

3 minutes

	To Do	To Say
Teach high-frequency words.	Display *cold*.	**1 Say, Spell, Write** Use the Tested Vocabulary Cards. Display *cold*. Here are some words that we won't sound out. We'll spell them. This word is *cold*: *c, o, l, d* (point to each letter), *cold*. What is this word? What are the letters in the word? Now you write *cold*.
	Point to *c* and *ld* in *cold*.	**2 Identify Letter-Sounds** Let's look at the sounds in *cold* that you do know. What is this letter? *(c)* What is the sound for this letter? *(/k/)* Continue with *ld*/ld/.
		3 Demonstrate Meaning Tell me a sentence using *cold*. Model a sentence if children need help.
	Display *finally, half, tomorrow,* and *word*.	Repeat the Routine with *finally, half, tomorrow,* and *word*. Children can decode *finally*. They can also identify these letter-sounds and word parts: *half* (*h*/h/, *f*/f/), *tomorrow* (*t*/t/, *mor*/mor/, *ow*/ō/). Point out that in *finally* and *half*, *al* doesn't stand for /ò/. Have children write the words in their word banks. Add the words to the Word Wall. Point out that the words they are learning are on p. 159.

 ACTIVITY **2** Build Concepts

Oral Vocabulary *ceremony, culture, festival*

5–10 minutes

	To Do	To Say
Introduce oral vocabulary.	Display p. 30 of *Sing with Me Big Book*. Play audio CD.	This week you will learn about how different people celebrate. Listen for the Amazing Words *ceremony, culture,* and *festival* as I sing this song. Play or sing the song. Then have children sing it with you.
		1 Introduce, Demonstrate, and Apply
Scaffold instruction.	Follow the Routine to teach *ceremony, culture,* and *festival*.	***ceremony*** The singer asks us to come along to a *ceremony*. A *ceremony* is something people do to celebrate a special occasion. Have children say the word. When people get married, there is often a wedding *ceremony*. What are some *ceremonies* you have heard about or have gone to?
		culture The song says that we can learn about a *culture*. We call the beliefs, customs, and behavior of groups of people at a certain time their *culture*. Have children say the word. There are many different *cultures* in this country. What things are important to your *culture*?
		festival The title of this song is "Festival Time." A *festival* is a time when people celebrate together, often to remember an important event. Have children say the word. At our neighborhood's Fourth of July *festival*, you can find special foods, costumes, music, and activities. Tell about a *festival* you have been to or seen.
	Display the words on the Amazing Words board.	**2 Display the Words** Have children say each word as they look at it. You can find sounds and word parts you know in big words. Read *fes/ti/val*. What letters are in the first syllable of *festival?* *(fes)* What sounds do you hear in this syllable? *(/fes/)* Continue with *t*/t/, *v*/v/, and *l*/l/. For *ceremony* and *culture*, children can identify these letter-sounds and word parts: *ceremony* (*c*/s/, *r*/r/, *mo*/mō/, *ny*/nē/), *culture* (*cul*/kul/).
	Monitor understanding.	**3 Use the Words** Ask children to use each word in a sentence. Model a sentence if children need help.
MORE PRACTICE		Use oral vocabulary to discuss the song. Look at the picture. Do you think people of all *cultures* would think these *festivals* are fun? Why? How can going to a *ceremony* or a *festival* help you learn about a *culture?*

ACTIVITY 3 Read a Passage

Build Background "Celebrations for Everyone," pp. 130–137

10 minutes

	To Do	**To Say**
Develop language and concepts.	See Routine Card 7. Read aloud p. 129 of the student book.	**Preview the Week** Use the photograph on p. 128 to introduce this week's concept of celebrations for everyone. **What kind of celebration is shown? What are people doing?** Read aloud the titles and descriptions on p. 129. Ask children what they think each selection will be about.
Scaffold instruction.	See Routine Card 6. Display pp. 130–137 and a world map. Ask questions and elaborate on answers to develop language. Key concepts: *holiday, celebrate, culture, lanterns, Maypole, ceremony, carnivals, festival, crops*	**Before Reading** Read the title aloud. Do a structured picture walk. Read labels as you discuss the pictures. Use a world map to locate countries. **pp. 130–131** Look at the fireworks. What holiday is this? (Fourth of July or Independence Day) People in China celebrate, or do something special, for the new year. What can you learn about Chinese culture from this photo? Yes, we learn that people of this culture celebrate a new year by wearing red, lifting lanterns, and walking in a line under a big dragon. **pp. 132–133** In England, May Day is a special day celebrating the start of spring. What are these kids doing? (dancing around a pole) Dancing around a Maypole is a fun ceremony in this culture. **pp. 134–135** In Brazil, people have street parties for Carnival. How does this culture celebrate? Yes, they wear masks and costumes. They ride on floats. Do you know other cultures that have carnivals? **pp. 136–137** At the Homowo (/hō/ /mō/ /wō/) Festival, people in Ghana celebrate their crops, the foods they grew. How does this culture celebrate? (by dancing and playing drums)
Teach story words.	Write *celebrate*. Review proper nouns.	You will read this word in the selection. It is *celebrate.* Have children say the word and spell it. Review its meaning. You will also see the names of places and holidays. Review proper nouns in picture labels. Now let's read to find out more about how different cultures celebrate.
Guide comprehension.	Monitor independent reading. Model strategic reading. Use Routine Cards 2 and 3.	**During Reading** Read the pages in a whisper. Raise your hand if you need help with a word. Stop at the end of each page to model asking questions. For example, for p. 131: After I read, I ask myself: What am I learning about how different people celebrate? The author tells how Chinese people celebrate the new year for fifteen days. I read that they dress in red and carry lanterns. They also walk in a long line under a huge dragon. This page is mainly about how Chinese people celebrate the new year.
Summarize.	Use oral vocabulary to develop the concept.	**After Reading** What *culture* celebrates the new year with a dragon? What *ceremony* takes place on May Day in England? Is a carnival a type of *festival?* Explain. What do people celebrate at the Homowo *Festival* in Ghana?

Reread for Fluency "Celebrations for Everyone," pp. 130–133

5–10 minutes

	To Do	**To Say**
CORRECTIVE FEEDBACK	Monitor oral reading.	Read pp. 130–133 aloud. Read them three or four times so your reading gets better each time. Give feedback on children's oral reading and use of the blending strategy. See Routine Cards 1 and 4.
MORE PRACTICE		Instead of rereading just pp. 130–133, have children reread the entire selection three or four times. You may want to have children read along with the AudioText.
Homework		Practice Book, p. 141, Phonics: Vowel Patterns *aw, au, augh*

ACTIVITY **1** Reread for Fluency

Paired Reading "Celebrations for Everyone," pp. 134–137

5–10 minutes

	To Do	To Say
CORRECTIVE FEEDBACK	Pair children. Monitor paired reading.	Children read pp. 134–137 orally, switching readers at the end of the first page. Have partners reread; now the other partner begins. For optimal fluency, children should reread three or four times. Give feedback on children's oral reading and use of the blending strategy. See Routine Cards 1 and 4.
MORE PRACTICE		Instead of rereading just pp. 134–137, have children reread the entire selection three or four times. You may want to have children read along with the AudioText.

ACTIVITY **2** Word Work

Phonemic Awareness Add Phonemes

2 minutes

	To Do	To Say
Scaffold instruction.	Distribute white boards. Write *wrap*. Add *re-* to *wrap* to form *rewrap*. Double final *p* and add *-ing* to form *rewrapping*. Lead children in adding affixes as they write.	**Model** Listen to the sounds in *wrap*. Stretch the sounds /rrr/ /aaa/ /p/ as you write *wr, a, p*. Repeat. This time have children write the letters as you write. **Now listen as I add /rē/ to the beginning of *wrap: re, wrap, rewrap*.** Repeat. Have children add *re-* as you write. **Teach and Practice** Have children say the sounds with you as you point to the parts *(re, wrap)* and blend the parts to say the word. *(rewrap)* **What new word do we make when we add *re-* to *wrap*? (rewrap) Now listen as I add /ing/ to the end of *rewrap: rewrap, ping, rewrapping*.** Repeat. Have children add *-ing* as you write, say the parts, and blend the parts to say the word. Continue adding affixes to base words to form these words: **smelliest winning discovered unhappily replay expected**

Blending Strategy Base Words and Affixes

To Do	To Say

5–10 minutes

Use the blending routine.

Write *precooked*, *unhelpful*, and *rethinking*.

1 Connect You studied words like these already. What do you know about reading longer words like these? (Figure out the base word, read each part, and then blend the parts.) Read each word as I point to it and tell me its base word. Do these base words have spelling changes? (no) Today we'll review spelling changes that may be needed when suffixes and endings are added to base words.

Routine

Scaffold instruction.

Write *remaking*.

2 Model This word has a prefix, a base word, and an ending. First, I'll try to figure out the base word. When I cover the prefix and ending, I can tell the spelling of the base word has changed. The base word is *make*. The final *e* was dropped before *-ing* was added. Now I'll blend all the parts together: *re, mak, ing, remaking*.

Write *smelliest*.

This word has a longer base word with a spelling change. Cover up *-est*. The base word is *smelly*. The *y* was changed to *i* before *-est* was added. When I read words like this, I break up the base word into smaller parts. This is how I blend this word: *smel, li, est, smelliest*. Repeat for *undecided*. Identify the base word *(decide)* and point out the spelling change (final *e* dropped). Then model blending the word: *un, de, cid, ed, undecided*.

Write *undecided*.

r e m a k i n g   s m e l l i e s t   u n d e c i d e d

3 Listen and Write Write the word *make*. Write *re-* at the beginning of it. To add the ending *-ing*, drop the final *e*, and then write *ing* at the end. As you write, say each part to yourself: *re, mak, ing*. Now blend the parts together and say the word aloud. Continue with *smelliest* and *undecided*.

CORRECTIVE FEEDBACK

Write each practice word. Monitor student practice.

4 Group Practice Let's try reading these longer words. Give feedback, using the *if . . . then* statements on Routine Card 1.

sleepier   unplugging   replaced   preplan   luckily   unexpected

5 Individual Practice Write the words; have each child blend two of them.

dirtiest   thankfully   displease   preset   unhappily   unsaddled

MORE PRACTICE

Model building words with affixes.

Build Words Fill in the first three columns of the class chart below. Model building and blending *funniest*. Then have children write the longer words on their white boards. Call on them to read the longer words and identify spelling changes. When finished, add the remaining longer words to the class chart.

Prefix	Base Word	Suffixes/Endings	Longer Word
	funny	-est	funniest
dis-	like	-ing	disliking
re-	try	-ed	retried
un-	steady	-ly	unsteadily

High-Frequency Words *cold, finally, half, tomorrow, word*

To Do	To Say

3 minutes

Teach high-frequency words.

Lead cumulative review.

Display *cold, finally, half, tomorrow*, and *word*.

Use the Tested Vocabulary Cards. Point to a word. Say and spell it. Have children say and spell the word. Ask children to identify familiar letter-sounds and word parts. Have children take turns reading the words.

Use the Tested Vocabulary Cards to review high-frequency words from previous weeks.

ACTIVITY 3　Read a Passage

Reading "The Sweet Stink of Success," pp. 138–145

10–15 minutes

	To Do	To Say
Develop language and concepts. **Scaffold instruction.**	See Routine Cards 6 and 7. Display pp. 138–145. Ask questions and elaborate on answers to develop language. Key concepts: *sneakers, awful, stink, contest, worn out, judges, whiffs, winner, fumes*	**Before Reading** Have children recall what they learned about having fun at celebrations. Read the title. Do a structured picture walk with children. **pp. 138–139** How can you tell the boy's sneakers smell awful? (Parents hold their noses.) This boy might want to enter his stinky sneakers in the Rotten Sneaker Contest, a real contest where being a stinker makes you a winner! **pp. 140–141** What are these sneakers like? (dirty, smelly) They're worn out. How do you think the judges check the sneakers? (smell them) They take long whiffs. Inhale. They look at the sneaker parts. Which sneakers will win? (the ones with the worst smell and in the worst shape) **pp. 142–143** Here is the contest winner. The winner's sneakers go to the "Hall of Fumes." Fumes are strong odors, or smells. **pp. 144–145** To enter the contest, how can you get your sneakers to stink? (Don't wear socks. Sleep in them.) Let's read to find out more.
Guide comprehension.	Monitor independent reading. Use Routine Cards 2 and 3.	**During Reading** Read the pages in a whisper. Raise your hand if you need help with a word. As you read, ask yourself: What am I learning about the contest? What is this mainly about? **pp. 138–141** What did you learn about the Rotten Sneaker Contest? (At this contest in March, kids enter their smelliest, most worn-out sneakers. Judges pick the winners based on both looks and smell.) **pp. 142–145** What did you learn about winning the Rotten Sneaker Contest? (Winners get nice prizes. Winning stinky sneakers end up in the "Hall of Fumes." Winners say winning is hard but have some helpful tips.)
Model summarizing.	Think aloud.	**After Reading** What did you learn about the contest? What was the selection mainly about? Model how to summarize. The first part described the Rotten Sneaker Contest. The last part told about winning the contest. I pick the most important ideas. This selection is mainly about what happens at the Rotten Sneaker Contest.
MORE PRACTICE	Develop oral vocabulary.	Is wearing sneakers part of American *culture?* Explain. How could the Rotten Sneaker Contest become more like a *festival?* What do you think happens at the *ceremony* for the contest winner?

ACTIVITY 4　Write

Response to Literature Shared Writing

5 minutes

	To Do	To Say
Guide shared writing.	Write sentence frames. Read the questions.	What happens at the Rotten Sneaker Contest? At this contest, _____. How can you win the Rotten Sneaker Contest? You can win if _____. Invite children to suggest answers. Discuss and record answers to complete the sentence frames. While writing, model connecting sounds to letters and forming letters. (See pp. 257–259.) Have children read answers aloud as you track print.
Homework		Practice Book, p. 142, Phonics: Base Words and Affixes

Reread for Fluency

Oral Reading "The Sweet Stink of Success," pp. 138–142

To Do	To Say	
		5–10 minutes

CORRECTIVE FEEDBACK

Monitor oral reading.

Read pp. 138–142 aloud. Read them three or four times so your reading gets better each time. Give feedback on children's oral reading and use of the blending strategy. See Routine Cards 1 and 4.

MORE PRACTICE

Instead of rereading just pp. 138–142, have children reread the entire selection three or four times. You may want to have children read along with the AudioText.

Word Work

Phonemic Awareness Add Phonemes

To Do	To Say	
		2 minutes

Scaffold instruction.

Distribute white boards. Write *pause.* Add *-ed* to form *paused.*

Lead children in adding affixes as they write.

Model Listen to the sounds in *pause.* Stretch the sounds /p/ /ȯȯ/ /zzz/ as you write *p, au, s, e.* Repeat. Have children write letters as you write. Now listen as I add /d/ to the end of *pause: pause, /d/, paused.* Repeat. Have children erase the final *e* and add *-ed* as you write.

Teach and Practice Have children say the parts as you point to them *(pause, /d/)* and blend the parts to say the word. *(paused)* Continue adding affixes to base words to form these words:

hauling   predawn   scrawnier   retaught   naughtiest   redrawing

Fluent Word Reading Vowel Patterns *aw, au, au(gh);* Base Words with Affixes

To Do	To Say	
		5–10 minutes

Use the word-reading routine.

Scaffold instruction.

Write *saw, fault,* and *taught.*

1 Connect You can read these words because you know that the letters *aw, au,* and *augh* can stand for /ȯ/. What vowel sound do you hear in these words? (/ȯ/) What are these words? *(saw, fault, taught)*

Routine

Write *author, thawed,* and *unhappily.*

2 Model When you come to a new word, look at all the letters in the word and think about its vowel sounds and its parts. Say the letter-sounds and word parts to yourself, and then read the word. Model reading *author, thawed,* and *unhappily* in this way. When you see a new word, what will you do?

Write each practice word.

3 Group Practice Let's read these words. Look at all the letters, think about the vowel sounds and parts, and say the parts to yourself. We will read words with *aw, au,* and *augh,* and longer words. When I point to the word, let's read it together. Allow 2–3 seconds previewing time for each word.

straw   caught   sausage   daughters   pausing   unplanned   surprising

CORRECTIVE FEEDBACK

MONITOR PROGRESS

If . . . children have difficulty previewing and reading whole words, *then . . .* have them use sound-by-sound blending.

If . . . children can't read the words fluently at a rate of 1–2 seconds per word, *then . . .* continue practicing the list.

| MORE PRACTICE | Model reading words in sentences. | When I read a sentence, I read each word without stopping between the words. If I come to a word I don't know, I blend it. Then I read the sentence again. Model reading this sentence, stopping to blend *cutest: Last August, I spotted the cutest fawn running happily on my lawn.* |
| | Write practice sentences. | Have each child read a sentence.

We replaced the cows' straw after that awful storm.
The noisiest hawk gave a big squawk as it caught a fish.
"Are your sneakers smellier than mine?" my daughter asks jokingly. |

High-Frequency Words *cold, finally, half, tomorrow, word*

	To Do	**To Say**	3 minutes
Review high-frequency words.	Display *cold, finally, half, tomorrow,* and *word.*	Use the Tested Vocabulary Cards. Point to a word. Say and spell it. Have children say and spell the word. Ask children to identify familiar letter-sounds and word parts. Have them take turns reading the words.	

ACTIVITY 3 Build Concepts

Oral Vocabulary *international, regional*

	To Do	**To Say**	5–10 minutes
Teach oral vocabulary.	Display p. 146 of the student book.	Today you will read a story about a boy who enters his pig in a *regional* contest. Someday his pig might be ready for an *international* contest too!	*Routine*
		1 Introduce, Demonstrate, and Apply	
Scaffold instruction.	Follow the Routine to teach *international* and *regional.*	***international*** This story tells about an unusual contest. It is a *regional* contest, not an *international* contest. When something is *international*, it is between or among two or more countries. Have children say the word. An *international* airport has flights going to and from different countries. Have you or someone you know ever taken an *international* trip?	
		regional A part of this story happens at a county fair. A county fair is a *regional* event. When something is *regional*, it happens in a specific place. Have children say the word. People listen to a local radio station to get the *regional* news about their area. Why might people listen to the *regional* weather forecast?	
	Display the words on the Amazing Words board. Monitor understanding.	**2 Display the Words** Have children say each word as they look at it. You can find letter-sounds and word parts you know in big words. Read *in/ter/na/tion/al* as you run your hand under the syllables. What smaller word makes up the first syllable of *international*? (in) Children can also identify *t*/t/, *r*/r/, *n*/n/, and *l*/l/. For *regional*, children can identify *re*/rē/, *g*/j/, *n*/n/, and *l*/l/.	
		3 Use the Words Ask children to use each word in a sentence. Model a sentence if children need help.	
MORE PRACTICE		Use oral vocabulary to discuss celebrations. Where might you find information about your *regional* Fourth of July celebration? What kinds of foods might you find at an *international* festival?	

ACTIVITY 4 Read a Passage

Reading "Austin P. Crawler's Naughty Pig," pp. 146–157

	To Do	To Say	10 minutes

Teach main idea and supporting details.

Scaffold instruction.

Introduce the skill.

Model the skill. Display pp. 116–125.

Apply the skill. Display pp. 88–95.

Today as you read, you will ask yourself: What is this story all about? Look for details, little pieces of the story, that support your answer. For example, last week we read "Heather at the Rodeo." I read details about cowboys riding bulls and using ropes, and cowgirls racing horses around barrels. I put that all together. I think this story is all about what happens at a rodeo.

Let's revisit the story "Twice as Nice." What is this story all about: two birthday cakes, twins who like the same things in different ways, or inviting pals to a birthday party? (twins) What are some details that support your answer? Discuss supporting details.

Develop language and concepts.

See Routine Card 6. Display pp. 146–157.

Model using key words and concepts.

Key concepts: *naughty, scrawnier, gobbles, regional, hauling, huge, trailer, gigantic*

Before Reading Read the title. Do a structured picture walk.

pp. 146–147 This is Austin and his pig. This big pig likes to eat!

pp. 148–149 Austin's naughty pig eats the other animals' food, so the chickens and horses get scrawnier, or thinner, and the pig gets bigger. What else does he eat? Have children name the items shown.

pp. 150–151 The naughty pig even gobbles up a windmill! Is Austin upset with his naughty pig? No, he isn't yelling or frowning.

pp. 152–153 Austin is thinking about his pig winning the Big Pig Contest at a regional fair, the Sauk County Fair.

pp. 154–155 What is Austin's pig eating now? (a ladder) Why does Austin let his pig eat so much? (to win the contest) I wonder what the little girl is hauling in the huge trailer.

pp. 156–157 Who won the Big Pig Contest? (the girl's huge pig) Austin's pig isn't the biggest. Is he still a naughty pig? Yes, he eats all the shiny new ribbons.

Now turn to your partner and talk about the pictures, using the same words I did.

Guide compre-hension.

Monitor children's use of vocabulary.

Monitor independent reading.

Use Routine Cards 2 and 3.

During Reading Read the pages in a whisper. Raise your hand if you need help with a word. As you read this story, ask yourself: What is this story all about?

pp. 146–151 What are these pages all about? (Austin's naughty pig eats everything he sees.) What are some details? Children can name different things the pig eats.

pp. 152–155 What are these pages all about? (Austin gets his pig ready for the Big Pig Contest.) What are some details? (Austin thinks about the contest. He feeds his pig before the contest.)

pp. 156–157 What is the whole story all about? (a naughty pig who eats everything)

Guide retelling.

Prompt children as they retell the story.

After Reading Have one child retell the story while the others assist. What happens at the beginning of the story? in the middle? at the end? See Monitor Retelling, p. 246.

Homework

Practice Book, p. 143, Main Ideas and Supporting Details

ACTIVITY 1 Reread for Fluency

Paired Reading "Austin P. Crawler's Naughty Pig," pp. 146–150

5–10 minutes

	To Do	To Say
CORRECTIVE FEEDBACK	Pair children. Monitor paired reading.	Children read pp. 146–150 orally, switching readers at the end of the first page. Have partners reread; now the other partner begins. For optimal fluency, children should reread three or four times. Give feedback on children's oral reading and use of the blending strategy. See Routine Cards 1 and 4.
MORE PRACTICE		Instead of rereading just pp. 146–150, have children reread the entire selection three or four times. You may want to have children read along with the AudioText.

ACTIVITY 2 Word Work

Spiral Review Read Longer Words: Syllable Patterns

5–10 minutes

	To Do	To Say
Review syllable patterns in longer words.	Write *hamburger.* Model using VCCV pattern.	Look for smaller parts you know in big words. What smaller word is at the beginning of this word? *(ham)* How can you divide the rest of the word? (between *r* and *g*) Remember, when you see two consonants between two vowels, divide between the consonants. What are the parts? *(ham, bur, ger)* Blend the parts together. What is the word? *(hamburger)*
Scaffold instruction.	Write *crocodile.* Model using VCV pattern.	Point to *dile.* I know this last part is /dīl/. Now I'll figure out the other parts. Point to the second *c.* I see one *c* between two *o*'s. I need to decide if it make sense to divide before or after the *c.* If I divide after the *c,* I get three parts: *croc, o, dile.* I blend the parts: *croc, o, dile, crocodile.*
	Write *bumblebee.* Model using C + *le* pattern.	Point to *bee.* I see the word *bee.* Now I'll figure out the other parts. Point to *ble.* I see the letters *ble.* When a consonant is followed by *le,* I know I should keep that consonant with *le.* If I divide after the *m,* I get three parts: *bum, ble, bee.* I blend the parts: *bum, ble, bee, bumblebee.*
	Write *caterpillar.* Model using both VCV and VCCV patterns.	This word has more than three parts. Model breaking *cat/er/pil/lar* into four parts and blending them: *cat, er, pil, lar, caterpillar.*
	Distribute white boards.	**Sort Words** Write the headings below and list the words in random order. Have children copy the headings and write the words in the appropriate column. Have them read each word aloud and tell how they divided it.

Three Parts: ladybug, candlestick, gingerbread
Four Parts: kindergarten, helicopter, alligator |
| **CORRECTIVE FEEDBACK** | **MONITOR PROGRESS** | *If . . .* children have difficulty reading the words,
then . . . review the appropriate syllable patterns and have them use sound-by-sound blending. |

For more practice, see next page.

Continued Spiral Review

MORE PRACTICE

Model reading words in sentences.	When I read a sentence, I read each word without stopping between the words. If I come to a word I don't know, I blend it. Then I read the sentence again. Model reading this sentence, stopping to blend *turtleneck: This turtleneck sweater is a terrific present!*
Write practice sentences.	Have each child read a sentence. **The zookeeper fed the kangaroo.** **Let's play basketball on Saturday.** **The kindergarten class illustrated these books.**

Phonological and Phonemic Awareness   Optional practice activities, pp. 280–283

ACTIVITY 3 · Read Together

Choral Reading "Piñata Game," p. 158

To Do	**To Say**	*10 minutes*

Develop language and concepts.

Display p. 158.

Before Reading Point to the piñata. **This is a piñata. What do you know about piñatas?** Allow children to share what they know. **Piñatas are part of Mexican culture. This girl has a blindfold covering her eyes. What will happen if the girl hits the piñata with her stick?** (It will break open.) **When a piñata cracks open, fun things spill out and kids enjoy grabbing them.**

Model fluent reading.

Read the title of the selection, and ask children to predict what it is about. **The sentences by the dots are steps that tell how to play the piñata game. When I read directions for a game, I read each step carefully and not too fast. I read the steps in order.** Point out the order. Read the introduction and directions with an appropriate rate. Read the text a second time, having children point to each word.

Build fluency through choral reading.

Choral Reading **Now read the directions aloud with me. Try to make your voice sound like mine as we read.** Reread the text several times with children.

Develop concepts.

Monitor listening comprehension.

After Reading **What *culture* celebrates Cinco de Mayo? How is it like a *festival?* What are the steps do in the piñata game? Does this game look fun to play? Why?**

ACTIVITY 4 · Build Concepts

Oral Vocabulary *ceremony, culture, festival, international, regional*

To Do	**To Say**	*5–10 minutes*

Review oral vocabulary.

Read the words on the Amazing Words board.

Focus on Letter-Sounds **Remember, you can find sounds and word parts you know in big words.**

- **Which words end with /l/?**
- **Which word begins with *re?* Which word begins with *in?***
- **Which words begin with *c?* What sound does *c* stand for in each word?**

To Do	To Say
Encourage discussion.	**Ask for Reasons and Examples** Review the meanings of the words. Then ask children to give examples using these words. • **What happens at a wedding** *ceremony?* • **Tell about your** *culture* **or a** *culture* **you know. How are special days celebrated?** • **What might you see at an apple** *festival?* • **How would a** *regional* **ballgame be different from an** *international* **ballgame?**
MORE PRACTICE Apply oral vocabulary to new situations.	• **Does a** *culture* **tell about a group of animals or people?** (people) • **Is a street party more like a** *festival* **or a** *ceremony?* (festival) • **Would a world news program describe** *international* **or** *regional* **events?** (international)

ACTIVITY **5** Write

Response to Literature Interactive Writing

5–10 minutes

	To Do	To Say
Generate ideas.	Review the story "Austin P. Crawler's Naughty Pig."	**Do you think Austin's pig would win a Naughtiest Pig Contest?** Discuss reasons Austin's pig might win this type of contest.
Share the pen.	Have children participate in writing silly sentences about animals they would enter in contests.	Write *I'll enter my _____ in the _____ Contest.* Have children read the words you wrote. Then have them supply words to complete the sentence. Invite individuals to write familiar letter-sounds, word parts, and high-frequency words. Have them find the spelling of high-frequency words on the Word Wall. Ask questions such as: • **What is the first sound in** *jaws?* (/j/) **What is the letter for /j/ in** *jaws?* (j) • **What is the vowel sound in** *jaws?* (/ò/) **What letters stand for /ò/ in** *jaws?* (aw) • **What is the last sound in** *jaws?* (/z/) **What is the letter for /z/ in** *jaws?* (s)
	Writing elements: conventions	Frequently reread what has been written while tracking the print. Point out that each sentence starts with a capital letter and ends with a period. Remind children to capitalize the name of the contest. Point out the extra space between words. Read the completed sentences aloud, having children read with you. (For example, *I'll enter my alligator in the Snapping Jaws Contest. I'll enter my jackrabbit in the Fuzziest Paws Contest. I'll enter my creepy crawler in the Awful Bug Contest.*)
MORE PRACTICE Prompt independent writing.	**Journal Writing** Tell about a contest you would like to enter and what you would like to win.

Homework   Practice Book, p. 144, High-Frequency Words

ACTIVITY **1** | Assessment Options

Sentence Reading

5 minutes

	To Do	**To Say**
Assess sentence reading.	Use reproducible p. 251.	Have each child read the sentences. Record scores on the Sentence Reading Chart, p. 254. Work with one child as others complete Write Sentences below.

Miss Paul finally taught us the new spelling words.
The cold weather was displeasing because the ice wouldn't thaw.
Luckily, Dawn saved half of the sausages to cook for lunch tomorrow.

CORRECTIVE FEEDBACK	**MONITOR PROGRESS**	**If . . .** children have trouble reading words with vowels: *aw, au, au(gh)* or base words and affixes, **then . . .** reteach the blending strategy lessons on pp. 228 and 232.
		If . . . children cannot read a high-frequency word, **then . . .** mark the missed word or words on a high-frequency word list and send the list home for additional practice or have them practice with a fluent reader.
		If . . . children misread a word in the sentence, **then . . .** correct the error and have them reread the word and then the sentence.
Practice sentence writing.	Provide white boards.	**Write Sentences** Have children copy the sentences from reproducible p. 251 on white boards. Have them confirm spellings by comparing the words they wrote to the words in the sentences.

Phonological and Phonemic Awareness — Optional practice activities, pp. 280–283

End-of-Unit Test

10 minutes

	To Do	**To Say**
Assess fluency and comprehension.	Use Assessment Book, p, 69.	Options for end-of-unit assessment are available in the Assessment Book.

ACTIVITY **2** | Use Concepts

Oral Vocabulary *ceremony, culture, festival, international, regional*

5 minutes

	To Do	**To Say**
Check understanding of oral vocabulary.	Use the Amazing Words to wrap up the week's concept. Monitor understanding of oral vocabulary, using Routine Card 5.	As time allows, ask questions such as these.

- Describe the pictures on pp. 130–137 using some of the week's Amazing Words.
- Do all *cultures* celebrate holidays the same way? Give some examples to explain why or why not.
- You might see foods that are grown in your area at a *regional festival*. What else might you see at a *regional festival?*
- On September 21, world leaders are asked to celebrate the International Day of Peace. Suppose your school held an *international* peace *ceremony* that day. What might the *ceremony* be like? Use the words *international* and *ceremony* when you tell about it.

Read to Connect

Reread "Celebrations for Everyone," pp. 130–137

To Do	To Say	5 minutes

Monitor comprehension: main idea and supporting details.

Have children reread "Celebrations for Everyone" silently.

As you read, think about what is the most important idea in the selection. Look for details, smaller pieces of information, that tell more about the main idea. After rereading, ask:

- **What is the main idea of this selection?**
- **What are some details that tell more about the main idea?**

Make connections.

Have children make connections across texts.

Record children's answers in a graphic organizer on the board. List the main idea at the top. List supporting details describing different celebrations in boxes under the main idea. (For example, *Main Idea:* People all over the world celebrate special days. *Details:* Chinese New Year, dragon; May Day, dance around a Maypole; and so on.) Add to the list as you discuss the selections below. Children will use this organizer for Activity 4.

We also read about two contests—one in "The Sweet Stink of Success" and one in "Austin P. Crawler's Naughty Pig." Why do you think people like unusual contests like these? What do these contests celebrate?

What did all the selections we read this week show us about celebrations? What is the big idea? (Different people celebrate and have fun in different ways.)

Write

Response to Literature Independent Writing

To Do	To Say	5–10 minutes

Assign personal narrative.

Guide sentence correction.

Writing elements: conventions, organization

Today you will write about a celebration that you shared with family and friends. Tell what happened. Describe your feelings during the celebration. Encourage children to use words you wrote on the board for Activity 3 as they write.

Have children check their writing by asking themselves these questions.

- **Did I use capital letters to begin sentences and proper nouns?**
- **Did I use correct marks at the ends of sentences?**
- **Did I use words with prefixes, suffixes, and endings correctly?**
- **Did I use words to tell the order of what happened?**

MORE PRACTICE

Have children share their sentences with the group. Write their sentences on the board and have children practice reading and writing each other's sentences.

Homework   Practice Book, p. 145, Writing

Resources

Contents

Monitoring Fluency

Ongoing assessment of student reading fluency is one of the most valuable measures we have of children's reading skills. One of the most effective ways to assess fluency is taking timed samples of children's oral reading and measuring the number of words correct per minute (WCPM).

Fluency Goals

Level B End-of-Year Goal = 70–90 WCPM

Target Goals by Unit:

Unit 1 30 to 50 WCPM

Unit 2 38 to 58 WCPM

Unit 3 46 to 66 WCPM

Unit 4 54 to 74 WCPM

Unit 5 62 to 82 WCPM

Unit 6 70 to 90 WCPM

How to Measure Words Correct Per Minute—WCPM

Timed Reading of the Text

Make a copy of the text for yourself and have one for the child. Tell the child: **As you read this aloud, I want you to do your best reading. Read as quickly as you can without making mistakes. That doesn't mean it's a race. Just do your best reading. When I say** *begin,* **start reading.**

As the child reads, follow along in your copy. Mark words that are read incorrectly. Definitions and examples of these reading errors are given on p. 263.

Incorrect	Correct
• omissions	• self-corrections within 3 seconds
• substitutions	• repeated words
• mispronunciations	
• insertions	

After One Minute

At the end of one minute, draw a line after the last word that was read. Have the student finish reading but don't count any words beyond one minute. Arrive at the words correct per minute—WCPM—by counting the total number of words that the student read correctly in one minute.

Fluency Progress Chart

Copy the chart on the next page. Use it to record each child's progress across the year. Assist children in recording their scores on the chart and setting goals for the future.

Interpreting Results

Fluency goals are estimates, and children will vary considerably in their progress based on many factors. Also, student progress will depend greatly on where they start with respect to WCPM. Level B End-of-Year goals are the same as for children without reading difficulties at the end of Grade 2.

Fluency Progress Chart, Level B

Child's Name _____

	Unit 1					Unit 2					Unit 3					Unit 4					Unit 5					Unit 6				
100																														
95																														
90																														
85																														
80																														
75																														
70																														
65																														
60																														
55																														
50																														
45																														
40																														
35																														
30																														
25																														
20																														
15																														
10																														
5																														
	1	2	3*	4	5*	1	2	3*	4	5*	1	2	3*	4	5*	1	2	3*	4	5*	1	2	3*	4	5*	1	2	3*	4	5*

* = Fluency Assessment Using Unfamiliar Text

Monitoring Retelling

Retelling is a way to monitor and assess comprehension. Through retelling, children show whether they understand story grammar and can follow sequence, grasp main ideas, and draw conclusions about what they read. Help children learn how to retell by giving them many opportunities to retell stories and nonfiction selections. Scaffold their retellings by prompting them to tell more.

How to Do a Retelling

Have the child read quietly. If the child has difficulty with the passage, you may read it aloud.

Tell the child: **Read the story quietly to yourself. When you finish reading, I will ask you to tell me about what you read.**

When the child has finished, or when you have finished reading aloud, ask:

- (For fiction) **What happened in the story?**
- (For nonfiction) **What was the selection mostly about?**

Prompts for Retelling

If a retelling is incomplete, use prompts to encourage the child to tell more.

Narrative Prompts

- **Who is in the story?**
- **Where and when does the story take place?**
- **What happens first?**
- **Then what happens?**
- **What happens at the end?**

Expository Prompts

- **What did you learn about _____?**
- **What are the most important ideas?**

Looking Back

Encourage children to look back in the text to find answers or to confirm their answers.

- **Let's check the book to make sure.**
- **Show me where the book tells you that.**
- **Where can we look in the book to find the answer?**

See Assessment Handbook, pp. 12–13, for scoring rubrics for retelling. Use the rubrics to help children move toward a fluent retelling.

Unit 4, Week 1

My granddad has gone walking with a group of neighbors.
There is a sandbox for small kids inside the mall.
When classmates move, I promise to call and talk to them.

Unit 4, Week 2

We often wait for a sunny day to plant bean seeds.
Straight above the tree, a kite with a long tail sails by.
If it rains, almost all of these seeds may change to green plants.

Unit 4, Week 3

Will vets cover this sick animal with a warm blanket?
The biggest goat roams in the field with yellow roses.
I feel happier when I go for a slow walk in the country.

Unit 4, Week 4

It is important to tie the rope tight.
The children ate pie that was full of peaches.
High on the hill, one child spies a lake below him.

Unit 4, Week 5

Never pet a tiger on its large head!
Take the poor camel to the river and wash the mud off it.
The clever robot cannot talk, even though it looks human.

Unit 5, Week 1

Listen to the bluebirds sing from the treetops at sunrise!
I heard you ate a big piece of birthday cake.
My backpack can hold a baseball, a book, and my lunchbox.

REPRODUCIBLE PAGE

Unit 5, Week 2

The boy can either eat an apple or drink a bottle of milk.
This puzzle has several hundred little parts.
You're going to startle the kitten if you jiggle that rattle.

Unit 5, Week 3

Long ago, towns were probably not as crowded as they are now.
If you suddenly drop that houseplant, the pot is certain to break.
Since the brown pup is so playful, I will crouch down and pet it gently.

Unit 5, Week 4

This has been a special afternoon, but I'm unable to stay all night.
The unlucky boy had to reheat a whole plate of cool food.
Of course, my brother will replace the balloons he popped!

Unit 5, Week 5

I'm sorry that boy hurt his wrist, thumb, and knee.
We have a choice of writing or playing for an hour.
When you watch noisy lambs, you can't leave them even
for a minute!

Unit 6, Week 1

The visitor will buy a good book at the gift shop.
After we won the game, our coach bought each player ice
cream.
The worst rainstorm in March got my clothes all wet.

Unit 6, Week 2

Our new fan blew cool air until you disconnected it.
I think America is the most beautiful place in the world.
The space crew is due to return to Earth after their preflight
check.

REPRODUCIBLE PAGE

Unit 6, Week 3

Steph said she'd play dodgeball with everybody.
I believe they're having lots of company at Ralph's party.
We've saved enough money to buy a fudge cake for the young boy.

Unit 6, Week 4

The baker had a question about reusing the bread pan.
Did you notice that the woman untied her boots?
Instead of sitting alone, Jo sat between her pals on the leather couch.

Unit 6, Week 5

Miss Paul finally taught us the new spelling words.
The cold weather was displeasing because the ice wouldn't thaw.
Luckily, Dawn saved half of the sausages to cook for lunch tomorrow.

Unit 4 Sentence Reading Chart

	Phonics		High-Frequency Words			Reassess
	Total Words	Words Correct	Total Words	Words Correct	Reteach ✓	Words Correct
Week 1 *When Things Change*						
Sound of *a* in *ball, walk*	5					
Compound Words	4					
High-Frequency Words			5			
Week 2 *From Seed to Plant*						
Long *a: ai, ay*	6					
Long *e: e, ee, ea*	6					
High-Frequency Words			5			
Week 3 *Animals*						
Endings *-er, -est*	2					
Long *o: o, oa, ow*	5					
High-Frequency Words			5			
Week 4 *What Changes Are Hard?*						
Long *i: igh, ie*	5					
High-Frequency Words			5			
Week 5 *Weather Changes*						
Syllables VCV	7					
High-Frequency Words			5			
Unit Scores	40		25			

- **RECORD SCORES** Use this chart to record scores for the Day 5 Sentence Reading Assessment.

- **RETEACH PHONICS SKILLS** If the child is unable to read all the target phonics words, then reteach the phonics skills using the Blending Strategy lessons.

- **PRACTICE HIGH-FREQUENCY WORDS** If the child is unable to read all the target high-frequency words, then provide additional practice for the week's words, using the Tested Vocabulary Cards.

- **REASSESS** Use the same set of sentences or an easier set for reassessment.

Child's Name _____

Unit 5 Sentence Reading Chart

	Phonics		High-Frequency Words			Reassess
	Total Words	Words Correct	Total Words	Words Correct	Reteach ✓	Words Correct
Week 1 *Good Job!*						
Compound Words	7					
High-Frequency Words			5			
Week 2 *Taking Care of Animals*						
Syllables Consonant + *le*	7					
High-Frequency Words			5			
Week 3 *Family Jobs*						
Diphthongs *ou, ow*/ou/	7					
Suffixes *-ly, -ful*	3					
High-Frequency Words			5			
Week 4 *My Neighbors, My Friends*						
Sound of *oo* in *moon*	4					
Prefixes *un-, re-*	4					
High-Frequency Words			5			
Week 5 *Doing the Right Thing*						
Diphthongs *oi, oy*/oi/	3					
Silent Consonants *kn*/n/, *wr*/r/, *mb*/m/	5					
High-Frequency Words			5			
Unit Scores	40		25			

- **RECORD SCORES** Use this chart to record scores for the Day 5 Sentence Reading Assessment.

- **RETEACH PHONICS SKILLS** If the child is unable to read all the target phonics words, then reteach the phonics skills using the Blending Strategy lessons.

- **PRACTICE HIGH-FREQUENCY WORDS** If the child is unable to read all the target high-frequency words, then provide additional practice for the week's words, using the Tested Vocabulary Cards.

- **REASSESS** Use the same set of sentences or an easier set for reassessment.

Child's Name _____

Unit 6 Sentence Reading Chart

	Phonics		High-Frequency Words			Reassess
	Total Words	Words Correct	Total Words	Words Correct	Reteach ✓	Words Correct
Week 1 *Sports*						
Sound of *oo* in *book*	2					
Suffixes *-er, -or*	2					
High-Frequency Words			5			
Week 2 *The American Flag*						
Vowel Patterns *ew, ue*	4					
Prefixes *pre-, dis-*	2					
High-Frequency Words			5			
Week 3 *Family Celebrations*						
Contractions *'re, 've, 'd*	3					
ph/f/, *dge*/j/	4					
High-Frequency Words			5			
Week 4 *A Cowboy's Life*						
Short *e: ea*	2					
Base Words and Affixes	4					
High-Frequency Words			5			
Week 5 *Celebrations for Everyone*						
Vowel patterns *aw, au, au(gh)*	6					
Base Words and Affixes	5					
High-Frequency Words			5			
Unit Scores	34		25			

- **RECORD SCORES** Use this chart to record scores for the Day 5 Sentence Reading Assessment.

- **RETEACH PHONICS SKILLS** If the child is unable to read all the target phonics words, then reteach the phonics skills using the Blending Strategy lessons.

- **PRACTICE HIGH-FREQUENCY WORDS** If the child is unable to read all the target high-frequency words, then provide additional practice for the week's words, using the Tested Vocabulary Cards.

- **REASSESS** Use the same set of sentences or an easier set for reassessment.

Using End-of-Unit Assessment Results

To make instructional decisions at the end of each unit, consider scores for

- Unit Sentence Reading (Day 5 Assessments)
- Unit Test
- Benchmark Reader reading

Record Scores

Several forms are provided for recording children's progress across the year.

- Sentence Reading Charts: Record results of the weekly Day 5 assessments. See pp. 252–254.
- Record Chart for Unit Tests: Record scores for each Unit Test. See the Assessment Book, p. 16.
- Fluency Progress Chart: Record each child's WCPM across the year. See p. 245.
- Retelling Charts: Record the child's retelling scores for each unit. See the Assessment Book, pp. 12–14.

Questions to Consider

- Has the child's performance met expectations for daily lessons?
- What can the child read alone? What can the child read with supervision?
- Is the child progressing toward grade-level goals?

Evaluate Student Progress

To move into the next unit of *My Sidewalks*, the child should

- score 80% or better on cumulative Unit scores for Sentence Reading for phonics and high-frequency words
- score 80% or better on the Unit Test
- be able to read and retell the end-of-unit Benchmark Reader accurately
- be capable of working in the Level B group based on teacher judgment

If . . . the child scores below 80% on the tested phonics words,
then . . . reteach the phonics skills and reassess following the reteaching.

If . . . the child scores below 80% on the tested high-frequency words,
then . . . provide additional practice for the words and reassess.

If . . . the child's scores indicate a specific weakness in one area of literacy, such as fluency or comprehension,
then . . . focus the child's instruction and practice on that area.

If . . . the child has not met the fluency benchmarks for the unit,
then . . . consider that the benchmark WCPM at the high end of a range is more typical of on-level students, and children in intensive intervention may be progressing well even if they are not meeting fluency benchmarks.

The child may be more appropriately placed in *My Sidewalks*, Level A if the child

- scores 60% or lower on Unit Tests
- is struggling to keep up with the Level B group
- is unable to decode the simplest word types

Exiting the MY SiDEWALKS Intervention Program

In Level B of *My Sidewalks,* there are two opportunities for children to exit the program—at midyear and at the end of the year. Many factors govern decisions concerning instruction for individual children. Understandably, guidelines in your school or district regarding adequate yearly progress, in addition to processes such as Individualized Education Plans, will influence each child's placement in or exit from any intervention program.

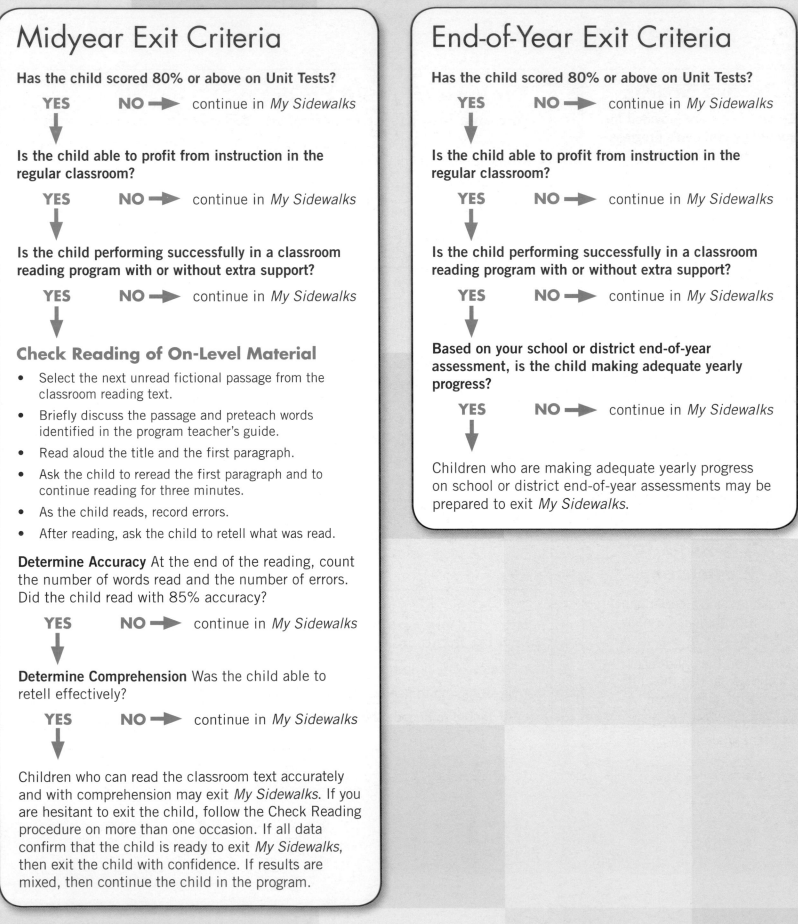

Midyear Exit Criteria

Has the child scored 80% or above on Unit Tests?

YES   NO ➡ continue in *My Sidewalks*

Is the child able to profit from instruction in the regular classroom?

YES   NO ➡ continue in *My Sidewalks*

Is the child performing successfully in a classroom reading program with or without extra support?

YES   NO ➡ continue in *My Sidewalks*

Check Reading of On-Level Material

- Select the next unread fictional passage from the classroom reading text.
- Briefly discuss the passage and preteach words identified in the program teacher's guide.
- Read aloud the title and the first paragraph.
- Ask the child to reread the first paragraph and to continue reading for three minutes.
- As the child reads, record errors.
- After reading, ask the child to retell what was read.

Determine Accuracy At the end of the reading, count the number of words read and the number of errors. Did the child read with 85% accuracy?

YES   NO ➡ continue in *My Sidewalks*

Determine Comprehension Was the child able to retell effectively?

YES   NO ➡ continue in *My Sidewalks*

Children who can read the classroom text accurately and with comprehension may exit *My Sidewalks.* If you are hesitant to exit the child, follow the Check Reading procedure on more than one occasion. If all data confirm that the child is ready to exit *My Sidewalks,* then exit the child with confidence. If results are mixed, then continue the child in the program.

End-of-Year Exit Criteria

Has the child scored 80% or above on Unit Tests?

YES   NO ➡ continue in *My Sidewalks*

Is the child able to profit from instruction in the regular classroom?

YES   NO ➡ continue in *My Sidewalks*

Is the child performing successfully in a classroom reading program with or without extra support?

YES   NO ➡ continue in *My Sidewalks*

Based on your school or district end-of-year assessment, is the child making adequate yearly progress?

YES   NO ➡ continue in *My Sidewalks*

Children who are making adequate yearly progress on school or district end-of-year assessments may be prepared to exit *My Sidewalks.*

D'Nealian™ Alphabet

a b c d e f g h i

j k l m n o p q r s t

u v w x y z

A B C D E F G

H I J K L M N O

P Q R S T U V

W X Y Z . , ' ?

1 2 3 4 5 6

7 8 9 10

Manuscript Alphabet

a b c d e f g

h i j k l m n

o p q r s t u

v w x y z

A B C D E F G

H I J K L M N

O P Q R S T U

V W X Y Z , ' . ?

1 2 3 4 5 6

7 8 9 10

D'Nealian™ Cursive Alphabet

a b c d e f g
h i j k l m n
o p q r s t u
v w x y z

A B C D E F G
H I J K L M N
O P Q R S T U
V W X Y Z . , ' ?

1 2 3 4 5 6
7 8 9 10

Matching Students to Text

Providing children with reading materials they can and want to read is an important step toward developing fluent readers. A fluency test allows you to determine each child's instructional and independent reading level. Information on how to take a fluency test is provided on pp. 262–263.

Instructional Reading Level

Only approximately 1 in 10 words will be difficult when reading a selection from the Student Reader for children in the *My Sidewalks* intervention program. Children reading at their instructional level need teacher support and will benefit from guided instruction.

Independent Reading Level

Children should read regularly in independent-level texts in which no more than approximately 1 in 20 words is difficult for the reader. Other factors that make a book easy to read include the child's interest in the topic, the amount of text on a page, how well illustrations support meaning, and the complexity and familiarity of the concepts.

Guide children in learning how to self-select books at their independent reading level. As you talk about a book with children, discuss the challenging concepts in it, list new words children find in sampling the book, and ask children about their familiarity with the topic. A blackline master to help children evaluate books for independent reading is provided on p. 261.

Self-Selected/Independent Reading

While oral reading allows you to assess children's reading level and fluency, independent reading is of crucial importance to children's futures as readers and learners. Children need to develop their ability to read independently for increasing amounts of time.

- Specify the amount of time you wish children to read independently each week. During the year, gradually increase the amount of time devoted to independent reading.

- Encourage children to read to a partner, to a stuffed animal, or to a family member.

- Help children track the amount of time they read independently. Tracking will help motivate them to gradually increase their duration and speed. A blackline master for tracking independent reading is provided on p. 261. Check it on a regular basis to monitor progress.

Name _____   Date _____

Choosing a Book to Read by Yourself

These questions can help you pick a book to read.

_____ 1.   Is this book about something that I like?

_____ 2.   This book may be about a real person, about facts, or a made-up story.
            Do I like reading this kind of book?

_____ 3.   Have I read other things by this author? Do I like the author?

If you say "yes" to question 1, 2, or 3, go on.

_____ 4.   Were there fewer than 5 hard words on the first page?

_____ 5.   Does the number of words on a page look about right to me?

If you say "yes" to questions 4 and 5, the book is right for you.

Independent Reading

Write the date, the title of the book, and the number of minutes you read.

Date	Title	Minutes

Matching Students to Text

Taking a Fluency Test

A fluency test is an assessment of a child's oral reading accuracy and oral reading fluency. Reading accuracy is based on the number of words read correctly. Reading fluency is based on the reading rate (the number of words correct per minute) and the degree to which a child reads with a "natural flow."

How to Measure Reading Accuracy

1. Choose a text of about 60 to 100 words that is unfamiliar to the child.

2. Make a copy of the text for yourself. Make a copy for the child or have the child read aloud from a book.

3. Give the child the text and have the child read aloud. (You may wish to record the child's reading for later evaluation.)

4. On your copy of the text, mark any miscues or errors the child makes while reading. See the fluency test sample on p. 263, which shows how to identify and mark miscues.

5. Count the total number of words in the text and the total number of errors made by the child. Note: If a child makes the same error more than once, such as mispronouncing the same word multiple times, count it as one error. Self-corrections do not count as actual errors. Use the following formula to calculate the percentage score, or accuracy rate:

$$\frac{\text{Total Number of Words} - \text{Total Number of Errors}}{\text{Total Number of Words}} \times 100 = \text{percentage score}$$

Interpreting the Results

- A child who reads 95–100% of the words correctly is reading at an independent level and may need more challenging text.

- A child who reads 90–94% of the words correctly is reading at an instructional level and will likely benefit from guided instruction.

- A child who reads 89% or fewer of the words correctly is reading at a frustrational level and may benefit most from targeted instruction with lower-level texts and further intervention.

How to Measure Reading Rate (WCPM)

1. Follow Steps 1–3 above.

2. Note the exact times when the child begins and finishes reading.

3. Use the following formula to calculate the number of words correct per minute (WCPM):

$$\frac{\text{Total Number of Words Read Correctly}}{\text{Total Number of Seconds}} \times 60 = \text{words correct per minute}$$

Interpreting the Results

An appropriate reading rate for an on-level second-grader is 90–100 WCPM.

Matching Students to Text

Fluency Test Sample

Fluency Test Sample

> "In that case, can you help make my lunch?" Curtis asked.
> *(me inserted)*
>
> Yelp clapped her hands (twice). Then she handed Curtis a card filled with notes.
>
> "Crackers with butter and jam," Curtis read. "Yum. Let's try it." But when Curtis turned, he didn't ~~spot~~ Yelp. *(stop)*
>
> After class, both tires on Curtis's *(H)* bike were flat. "Yelp! Help!" Curtis cried.
>
> Along came Yelp. She clapped her hands twice, and a pump landed next to Curtis. */tĭ/*
>
> Then Curtis pumped up his tires. *(sc)*
>
> Curtis had to admit that Yelp's pump helped.
>
> —From *Yelp! Help!*
> *My Sidewalks* Student Reader, Level B

Miscues

Insertion
The child inserts words or parts of words that are not in the text.

Omission
The child omits words or word parts.

Substitution
The child substitutes words or parts of words for the words in the text.

Hesitation
The child hesitates over a word, and the teacher provides the word. Wait several seconds before telling the child what the word is.

Mispronunciation/Misreading
The child pronounces or reads a word incorrectly.

Self-Correction
The child reads a word incorrectly but then corrects the error. Do not count self-corrections as actual errors. However, noting self-corrections will help you identify words the child finds difficult.

Fluency Test Results	▶	Reading Accuracy	▶	Reading Rate—WCPM
Total Number of Words: **86** Number of Errors: **5**		$\dfrac{86-5}{86} = \dfrac{81}{86} = .9418 = 94\%$		$\dfrac{81}{64} \times 60 = 75.9 = 76$ words correct per minute
Reading Time: **64 seconds**		Accuracy Percentage Score: **94%**		Reading Rate: **76** WCPM

Scope and Sequence

Concepts of Print and Print Awareness	Level A	Level B	Level C	Level D	Level E
Develop awareness that print represents spoken language and conveys and preserves meaning	●				
Identify parts of a book and their functions (front cover, title, page numbers)	●				
Understand the concept of letter and word (including constancy of words and word boundaries)	●				
Track print (front to back of book, top to bottom of page, left to right on line, sweep back left for next line)	●				
Match spoken to printed words	●				
Know capital and lowercase letter names and match them	●				
Write capital and lowercase letters	●				

Phonemic Awareness	Level A	Level B	Level C	Level D	Level E
Identify sounds that are the same or different	●				
Identify and isolate initial, final, and medial sounds	●				
Blend sounds orally	●	●			
Segment a word into sounds	●	●			
Add or delete phonemes	●	●			

Phonics	Level A	Level B	Level C	Level D	Level E
Understand and apply the *alphabetic principle* that spoken words are composed of sounds that are represented by letters	●				
Know letter-sound relationships	●	●	●		
Blend sounds of letters to decode					
Consonants	●	●			
Consonant blends	●	●	●		

Consonant digraphs	•	•	•		
Vowels					
Short	•	•	•	•	•
Long	•	•	•	•	•
r-Controlled	•	•	•	•	•
Digraphs	•	•	•	•	•
Diphthongs		•	•	•	•
Other vowel patterns	•	•	•	•	•
Phonograms/word families	•	•	•		
Decode words with common word parts					
Base words and inflected endings	•	•	•	•	•
Contractions	•	•	•	•	•
Possessives	•	•			
Compounds	•	•	•	•	•
Suffixes and prefixes		•	•	•	•
Blend syllables to decode words					
VC/CV	•	•	•	•	•
Consonant + *le*	•	•	•	•	•
VC/V and V/CV	•	•	•	•	•
VCCCV			•	•	•
V/V			•	•	•

Spelling					
Use sound-letter knowledge to spell	●	●	●	●	●
Use knowledge of word structure to spell	●	●	●	●	●
Blend multisyllabic words	●	●	●	●	●

Reading Fluency	**Level A**	**Level B**	**Level C**	**Level D**	**Level E**
Read aloud fluently with accuracy, comprehension, and appropriate pace/rate	●	●	●	●	●
Practice fluency in a variety of ways, including choral reading, partner/paired reading, repeated oral reading, tape-assisted reading, and Readers' Theater	●	●	●	●	●
Work toward appropriate fluency goals	40–60 WCPM	70–90 WCPM	100–120 WCPM	110–130 WCPM	120–140 WCPM

Vocabulary (Oral and Written)	**Level A**	**Level B**	**Level C**	**Level D**	**Level E**
Recognize regular and irregular high-frequency words automatically	●	●			
Recognize and understand lesson vocabulary	●	●	●	●	●
Develop vocabulary through direct instruction, concrete experiences, reading, and listening to text read aloud					
Use concept vocabulary	●	●	●	●	●
Use speaking vocabulary	●	●			
Use knowledge of word structure to figure out word meaning		●	●	●	●
Use context clues					
to confirm word identification	●	●	●		
to determine word meaning of multiple-meaning words, homonyms, homographs			●	●	●
to determine word meaning of unfamiliar words			●	●	●
Understand synonyms and antonyms			●	●	●

Text Comprehension	Level A	Level B	Level C	Level D	Level E
Comprehension Strategies					
Preview the text	●	●	●	●	●
Set and monitor purpose for reading	●	●	●	●	●
Activate and use prior knowledge	●	●	●	●	●
Make predictions	●	●	●	●	●
Ask and answer questions	●	●	●	●	●
Look back in text for answers			●	●	●
Recognize story structure: characters, plot, setting	●	●	●	●	●
Summarize text by retelling stories or identifying main ideas	●	●	●	●	●
Use graphic and semantic organizers			●	●	●
Comprehension Skills					
Compare and contrast	●	●	●	●	●
Draw conclusions		●	●	●	●
Main idea and supporting details	●	●	●	●	●
Sequence of events	●	●	●	●	●
Write in response to text	●	●	●	●	●

Unit 1 Word List

The words listed below are read and practiced each week in the *My Sidewalks* Student Readers and/or in practice activities.

Unit 1 Week 1 Neighborhoods

Short *a*			Final *ck*		Sounds Reviewed		High-Frequency Words
am	had	pass	back	pick	b/b/*	r/r/*	
an	has	quack	black	quack	c/k/*	s/s/*	always
as	hat	rack	block	rack	d/d/*	s/z/*	laugh
at	Jack	ran	check	Rick	e/e/*	t/t/*	only
back	jam	rap	chick	rock	f/f/*	u/u/*	told
bad	Jan	rat	clock	sack	g/g/*	v/v/*	
bag	jazz	sack	deck	sick	h/h/*	w/w/*	
bat	lap	sad	duck	sock	i/i/*	z/z/*	
black	mad	sat	Jack	tack	j/j/*	th/th/*	
cab	man	tack	kick	thick	k/k/*	ch/ch/*	
can	mat	tan	lick	truck	l/l/*	bl/bl/*	
cap	nap	that	lock	Zack	m/m/*	cl/cl/*	
cat	pack	van	luck		n/n/*		
Dad	pal	wag	neck		o/o/*		
fat	pals	Zack	Nick		p/p/*		
gab	pan		pack		qu/kw/*		

Unit 1 Week 2 Outer Space

Short *i*			*ng*/ng/	*nk*/ngk/	Sounds Reviewed		High-Frequency Words
big	Jill	ring	bang	bank	a/a/	t/t/*	
bit	kick	rink	gang	Frank	b/b/*	u/u/*	afraid
did	kid	rip	hang	ink	ck/k/	v/v/*	so
dig	king	sick	king	junk	d/d/*	w/w/*	surprise
fig	lick	sing	Ling	mink	e/e/*	x/ks/*	worry
fish	Ling	sink	lung	pink	f/f/*	th/th/*	
fit	lip	sit	rang	rink	g/g/*	sh/sh/*	
fix	lit	thick	ring	sank	h/h/*	fr/fr/*	
give	mink	thing	sang	sink	j/j/*		
hill	mix	think	sing	sunk	k/k/*		**Selection Words**
him	pick	tick	song	tank	l/l/*		
his	pig	Tim	thing	thank	m/m/*		astronaut
hit	pill	wig	wing	think	o/o/*		space
in	pin	will		wink	p/p/*		
ink	pink	win			r/r/*		
is	pit	wing			s/s/*		
it	Rick	wink			s/z/*		

Unit 1 Week 3 Out in the Woods

Short *o*			Consonant Blends			Sounds Reviewed		High-Frequency Words
block	lock	spot	band	green	spot	a/a/	s/s/*	
Bob	lots	stomp	best	hand	spring	b/b/*	s/z/*	answer
box	mom	stop	block	land	stamp	c/k/*	t/t/*	different
clock	mop	Tom	brick	lost	stand	ck/k/	u/u/*	ever
cost	nod	top	camp	mask	stick	d/d/*	v/v/*	learn
cot	not	tromp	clap	plant	stomp	e/e/*	w/w/*	
dock	ox	trot	clock	plants	stop	f/f/*	x/ks/*	
dot	plop		drag	plop	strap	g/g/*	ng/ng/	
drop	pond		drink	pond	string	h/h/*	nk/ngk/	
flock	pop		drop	print	strip	i/i/		
flop	pot		fast	ramp	swim	j/j/		
fog	rob		flip	rocks	tromp	k/k/*		
frog	rock		flock	scrap	trot	l/l/*		
got	rocks		flop	shop	twig	m/m/*		
hop	shop		frog	snack	twin	n/n/*		
hot	sob		grab	splash	wind	p/p/*		
job	sock		grass	split		r/r/*		

***= letter-sounds reviewed from Level A**

Unit 1 Word List

Unit 1 Week 4 Sand All Around

Short e

bed	help	sled
beds	helps	slept
beg	hen	smell
bell	hens	smells
bells	jet	spell
belt	left	stem
belts	leg	stems
bends	legs	step
best	let	steps
bet	melts	Ted
blend	men	tell
Clem	mess	tells
Deb	neck	ten
den	nest	tent
dens	nets	tents
desk	next	test
dress	pecks	web
egg	Peg	webs
eggs	pet	well
fed	pets	wet
fell	red	yells
Fred	rest	yes
get	sells	
Greg	set	

Inflected Ending -s

asks	picks
bends	sells
claps	sings
drinks	sips
fills	smells
grabs	sobs
helps	spins
hits	stops
melts	taps
nods	tells
packs	yells
pecks	

Plural -s

bags
beds
bells
belts
crops
dens
eggs
hands
hens
hills
legs
maps
mats
nets
pets
rats
stems
steps
tents
webs

Sounds Reviewed

a/a/	t/t/*	pt/pt/
b/b/*	w/w/*	sk/sk/
c/k/*	y/y/*	sl/sl/
ck/k/		sm/sm/
d/d/*	ng/ng/	sp/sp/
f/f/*	nk/ngk/	spr/spr/
g/g/*	cl/kl/	st/st/
h/h/*	cr/kr/	
i/i/	dr/dr/	
j/j/*	fr/fr/	
l/l/*	ft/ft/	
m/m/*	gr/gr/	
n/n/*	lp/lp/	
o/o/	lt/lt/	
p/p/*	mp/mp/	
r/r/*	nd/nd/	
s/s/*	nt/nt/	
s/z/*	pl/pl/	

High-Frequency Words

draw
eye
picture
read /red/

Selection Words

bird
desert
rain

Unit 1 Week 5 Who Can We Ask?

Short u

brush	jumps	shush
bug	junk	shut
buns	just	slug
bus	luck	slush
club	lump	stuck
crush	lunch	stump
cup	mud	stung
cups	mush	suds
cut	plucks	sun
drums	plus	thud
duck	pup	thump
flush	pups	truck
fun	rugs	tub
grunt	run	up
gum	rush	
hunt	scrub	
hush	shrub	
hut	shrunk	

sh/sh/

brush	shop
cash	shush
crash	shut
crush	slush
dash	splash
dish	trash
fish	wish
flash	
flush	
fresh	
hush	
mush	
rush	
shed	
shell	
shells	
shin	
ship	

th/th/

bath
math
moth
path
Seth
than
thank
that
them
then
thick
thin
thing
this
thud
thump
with

Sounds Reviewed

a/a/	s/z/	pl/pl/
b/b/*	t/t/*	scr/scr/
c/k/*	w/w/*	shr/shr/
ck/k/	ch/ch/	sl/sl/
d/d/*	ng/ng/	spl/spl/
e/e/	nk/ngk/	st/st/
f/f/*	th/th/	thr/thr/
g/g/*	sh/sh/	tr/tr/
h/h/*		
i/i/	br/br/	plural -s
j/j/*	cl/cl/	-s
l/l/*	cr/cr/	
m/m/*	dr/dr/	
n/n/*	fl/fl/	
o/o/	fr/fr/	
p/p/*	gr/gr/	
r/r/*	mp/mp	
s/s/	nt/nt/	

High-Frequency Words

also
among
early
today

Selection Words

coin

*= letter-sounds reviewed from Level A

Unit 2 Word List

Unit 2 Week 1 Danger!

Consonant Digraphs ch/ch/, tch/ch/, wh/hw/

bench	rich	patch
branch	such	pitch
bunch	which	pitching
check		scratch
chests	catch	scratching
chick	catching	sketching
chimp	crutch	stitch
chin	ditch	
chip	fetch	whacking
Chuck	fetching	when
chunk	hatch	which
crunching	hitching	whip
lunch	itch	whisk
munch	match	Whit
munching	Mitch	whiz

Inflected Ending -ing

asking	stamping
boxing	standing
buzzing	stinging
catching	swinging
crunching	whacking
drilling	yelling
fetching	
helping	
hitching	
lifting	
munching	
pinching	
pitching	
scratching	
sketching	
splashing	

Sounds Reviewed

a/a/	s/s/*	scr/skr/
b/b/*	t/t/*	sk/sk/
c/k/*	u/u/	spl/spl/
ck/k/	w/w/*	st/st/
d/d/*	x/ks/*	plural -s*
e/e/	y/y/*	
f/f/*	z/z/*	
h/h/*	ng/ng/	
i/i/	nk/ngk/	
k/k/*	sh/sh/	
l/l/*	br/br/	
m/m/*	cr/cr/	
n/n/*	dr/dr/	
o/o/	mp/mp/	
p/p/*	nd/nd/	
r/r/*		

High-Frequency Words

around
eight
enough
nothing

Selection Words

danger
fire

Unit 2 Week 2 Team Spirit

Inflected Ending -ed

added	grinned	rubbed
banged	hatched	rushed
batted	helped	scrubbed
bragged	hopped	shopped
chatted	hugged	slipped
checked	hunted	smelled
chipped	jogged	sobbed
clapped	kicked	spilled
dashed	limped	spotted
dragged	melted	stacked
dusted	petted	stepped
ended	pinched	stopped
filled	planned	tripped
fixed	rested	yelled
grabbed	rocked	

Inflected Ending -ing

batting	ripping
chipping	running
clapping	scrubbing
dragging	shopping
dropping	skipping
getting	slipping
grabbing	sobbing
grinning	spinning
helping	spotting
hopping	stopping
hunting	swimming
jumping	tripping
licking	winning
petting	
planning	

Sounds Reviewed

a/a/	p/p/*	dr/dr/
b/b/*	r/r/*	gr/gr/
ck/k/	s/s/*	mp/mp
d/d/*	t/t/*	nd/nd/
e/e/	u/u/	nt/nt/
f/f/*	v/v/*	pl/pl/
g/g/*	w/w/*	sc/sk/
h/h/*	x/ks/*	scr/skr/
i/i/	y/y/*	sk/sk/
j/j/*	ch/ch/	sl/sl/
k/k/*	ng/ng/	sm/sm/
l/l/*	sh/sh/	sp/sp/
m/m/*	tch/tch/	st/st/
n/n/*	br/br/	sw/sw/
o/o/	cl/cl/	tr/tr/

High-Frequency Words

build
carry
heavy
water

Selection Words

team

Unit 2 Week 3 Sharing

Long a (CVCe)

ace	lace	sale
age	lake	same
bake	late	save
cage	made	shade
cake	male	Shane
came	name	shape
cape	pace	space
case	page	stage
date	place	take
Dave	plane	tame
face	plate	tape
game	quake	trace
Grace	race	wade
grade	rage	wage
grapes	safe	wave
Jane	Sage	

c/s/

ace
face
Grace
lace
pace
place
race
space
trace

g/j/

age
cage
page
rage
Sage
stage
wage

Sounds Reviewed

a/a/	v/v/*
b/b/*	w/w/*
c/k/*	sh/sh/
d/d/*	th/th/
f/f/*	bl/bl/
g/g/*	gr/gr/
j/j/*	pl/pl/
k/k/*	pr/pr/
l/l/*	sp/sp/
m/m/*	st/st/
n/n/*	tr/tr/
p/p/*	
qu/kw/*	
r/r/*	
s/s/*	
t/t/*	

High-Frequency Words

another
enjoy
few
toward

Selection Words

share
tree

*= letter-sounds reviewed from Level A

Unit 2 Word List

Unit 2 Week 4 Side by Side

Long *i* (CVCe)

bike	ride
bite	ripe
bride	shine
dime	side
dive	slice
fine	slide
five	slime
hide	smile
kite	stripe
line	tile
miles	time
nice	vine
nine	vines
pine	while
pride	white
prize	wide
prizes	wipe
rice	wise

Inflected Endings *-ed, -ing*

baked	smiled	riding
biked	spilled	rising
chased	thrilled	shining
chimed	waved	skating
drilled	wiped	slicing
faced	wished	sliding
filled		smiling
fixed	biking	spilling
hiked	chasing	striking
kicked	drilling	thrilling
liked	filling	trading
missed	fixing	wiping
named	hiking	wishing
piled	kicking	
placed	making	
shined	missing	
skated	naming	
sliced	racing	

Sounds Reviewed

a/ā/	v/v/*	thr/thr/
b/b/*	w/w/*	tr/tr/
c/s/	x/ks/*	plural -s
ck/k/	z/z/*	
d/d/*	ch/ch/	
e/e/	ng/ng/	
f/f/*	sh/sh/	
h/h/*	th/th/	
i/i/	wh/hw/	
k/k/*	dr/dr/	
l/l/*	pl/pl/	
m/m/*	pr/pr/	
n/n/*	sk/sk/	
p/p/*	sl/sl/	
r/r/*	sm/sm/	
s/s/*	sp/sp/	
s/z/*	str/str/	
t/t/*		

High-Frequency Words

across
instead
moon
through

Unit 2 Week 5 Let's Celebrate

Long *o* (CVCe)

choke	pose
close	robe
cone	rode
drove	rope
froze	rose
globe	slope
hole	smoke
home	spoke
hope	stole
hose	stone
joke	stones
jokes	stove
moles	those
nose	throne
note	votes
poke	
pole	

Possessive Nouns

apes'	frogs'
bat's	hen's
bike's	hens'
bride's	hill's
bugs'	kid's
can's	kids'
cat's	king's
cats'	man's
chicks'	Mike's
crab's	moles'
dad's	mom's
dog's	mother's
dogs'	pals'
duck's	pig's
father's	rat's
fire's	snake's
friend's	vets'
frog's	

Sounds Reviewed

a/a/	p/p/*	nd/nd/
a/ā/	r/r/*	sl/sl/
b/b/*	s/s/*	sm/sm/
c/k/*	s/z/*	sn/sn/
ck/k/	t/t/*	sp/sp/
d/d/*	u/u/	st/st/
e/e/	v/v/*	thr/thr/
f/f/*	z/z/*	plural -s
g/g/*	ch/ch/	-s
h/h/*	th/th/	
i/i/	ng/ng/	
i/ī/	br/br/	
j/j/*	cl/cl/	
k/k/*	cr/cr/	
l/l/*	dr/dr/	
m/m/*	fr/fr/	
n/n/*	gl/gl/	
o/o/		

High-Frequency Words

father
mother
remember
touch

Selection Words

balloon

*= letter-sounds reviewed from Level A

Unit 3 Word List

Unit 3 Week 1 Ideas Become Inventions

Long *u* (CVCe)	Long *e* (CVCe)
cube	Eve
cute	Gene
duke	Pete
dune	Steve
flute	theme
huge	these
Luke	Zeke
mule	
prune	
rude	
rule	
tube	
use	

Contractions *'s, n't*

aren't	that's
can't	there's
couldn't	wasn't
didn't	weren't
don't	what's
hasn't	where's
haven't	
he's	
here's	
isn't	
it's	
let's	
she's	

Sounds Reviewed

a/a/	o/ō/	sh/sh/
b/b/*	p/p/*	wh/hw/
c/k/*	r/r/*	
d/d/*	s/s/*	
e/e/	s/z/	
e/ē/	t/t/*	
g/j/	v/v/*	
i/i/	w/w/*	
k/k/*	z/z/*	
l/l/*	pr/pr/	
m/m/*	st/st/	
n/n/*	th/th/	
o/o/		

High-Frequency Words

house
idea
machine
sign

Selection Words

invention
wheel

Unit 3 Week 2 Ways to Communicate

Vowel Sound of *y* (/ī/)

by	my
cry	sky
fly	spy
fry	try
shy	why

Vowel Sound of *y* (/ē/)

Andy	nanny
Benny	puppy
buddy	Sandy
bunny	silly
candy	skinny
fancy	sunny
funny	tummy
happy	

Ending *-es*, Plural *-es*

boxes	foxes	tummies
branches	glasses	wishes
buddies	hatches	
bunnies	hobbies	
buses	kisses	
buzzes	lunches	
candies	misses	
catches	nannies	
classes	pennies	
cries	presses	
dishes	puppies	
dries	rushes	
fixes	scratches	
fizzes	switches	
flies	tries	

Sounds Reviewed

a/a/	s/s/*	scr/skr/
b/b/*	s/z/	sk/sk/
c/k/*	t/t/*	sp/sp/
d/d/*	u/u/	sw/sw/
e/e/	w/w/*	tr/tr/
f/f/*	x/ks/*	ch/ch/
h/h/*	z/z/*	ch/tch/
i/i/	br/br/	sh/sh/
k/k/*	cl/kl/	th/th/
l/l/*	cr/kr/	wh/hw/
m/m/*	dr/dr/	-ed
n/n/*	fl/fl/	-es
o/o/	fr/fr/	-ing
p/p/*	gl/gl/	-s
r/r/*	pr/pr/	

High-Frequency Words

against
found
stood
wild

Selection Words

communicate
computer
letter
secret

Unit 3 Week 3 What a Smart Idea!

r-Controlled *ar*

art	jar
bark	march
barn	mark
car	park
card	scarf
charm	shark
chart	sharp
dark	smart
dart	
far	
farm	
hard	
harm	
harp	

r-Controlled *or, ore*

bore	north
born	or
chore	porch
cord	score
cork	shore
corn	short
for	sore
fork	sort
form	
fort	
forth	
horn	
more	
Norm	

Sounds Reviewed

a/ā/	o/ō/	rp/rp/
ar/är/	or/ôr/	rt/rt/
b/b/*	p/p/*	sc/sk/
c/k/	r/r/*	sm/sm/
d/d/*	s/s/*	sp/sp/
e/ē/	u/ū/	st/st/
f/f/*	rd/rd/	ch/ch/
h/h/*	rf/rf/	sh/sh/
i/ī/	rk/rk/	th/th/
i/i/*	rm/rm/	
m/m/*	rn/rn/	
n/n/*		

High-Frequency Words

become
even
front
thought

Selection Words

apple
crow
spider

*= letter-sounds reviewed from Level A

Unit 3 Word List

Unit 3 Week 4 Figure It Out

Syllables VC/CV

advice	forget	mittens
attic	garden	muffin
basket	happen	napkin
Brandon	harvest	pencil
button	helmet	plastic
carpet	hidden	problem
chipmunk	hornet	reptile
compete	index	ribbon
consume	insect	rotten
costume	inside	tadpole
cotton	invent	tennis
cricket	invite	traffic
entire	kitten	trumpet
escape	market	
forgave	mistake	

Sounds Reviewed

a/a/	l/l/*	ct/kt/
a/ā/	m/m/*	st/st/
ar/ä/	n/n/*	nt/nt/
b/b/*	o/o/	pl/pl/
c/k/*	o/ō/	pr/pr/
c/s/	or/ôr/	tr/tr/
d/d/*	p/p/*	ch/ch/
e/e/	r/r/*	
e/ē/	s/s/*	-'s
f/f/*	s/z/*	-s'
g/g/*	t/t/*	
h/h/*	u/u/	
i/i/	u/ū/	
i/ī/	br/br/	
k/k/*	cr/cr/	

High-Frequency Words

easy
follow
knew
usual

Selection Words

seed
turnip

Unit 3 Week 5 Where Ideas Come From

Contractions 'll, 'm	r-Controlled ir	r-Controlled ur	Syllable er	r-Controlled er
he'll	bird	burn	after	clerk
I'll	birth	burst	better	fern
I'm	dirt	church	butter	her
it'll	first	curb	chapter	nerve
she'll	girl	curl	crackers	serve
they'll	shirt	curve	enter	swerve
we'll	sir	fur	letter	verb
you'll	skirt	hurry	matter	verse
	stir	hurt	thunder	
	third	nurses	under	
		purse		
		turn		

Sounds Reviewed

ar/är/	n/n/*	st/st/
a/a/	or/ôr/	sw/sw/
b/b/*	p/p/*	ch/ch/
c/k/*	r/r/*	sh/sh/
ck/k/	s/s/	th/th/
d/d/*	s/z/	
er/èr/	t/t/*	
e/e/	ur/èr/	
e/ē/	v/v/	
f/f/*	w/w/*	
g/g/*	y/ē/	
h/h/*	br/br/	
i/ī/	cl/kl/	
ir/èr/	cr/kr/	
l/l/*	nd/nd/	
m/m/*	sk/sk/	

High-Frequency Words

along
both
color
guess

*= letter-sounds reviewed from Level A

Unit 4 Word List

Unit 4 Week 1 When Things Change

Sound of *a* in *ball, walk*

all	sidewalk
bald	small
ball	stalk
baseball	stall
call	talk
called	talked
chalk	tall
crosswalk	walk
eyeball	walking
fall	wall
falls	
halls	
halt	
kickball	
mall	
salt	
scald	

Compound Words

anthill	himself	something
backpack	homemade	sunrise
barnyard	homework	sunset
baseball	inside	sunshine
bathtub	kickball	
blackbird	landform	
campfire	laptop	
classmate	lipstick	
classmates	lunchbox	
crosswalk	nickname	
cupcake	pancake	
dishpan	pancakes	
eyeball	pigpen	
fireplace	popcorn	
fishpond	pothole	
flagpole	sandbox	
granddad	sidewalk	

Sounds Reviewed

a/a/	n/n/*	cr/kr/
a/ā/	o/o/	lt/lt/
ar/är/	o/ō/	lf/lf/
b/b/*	or/ôr/	mp/mp/
c/k/*	p/p/*	nd/nd/
c/s/	r/r/*	nt/nt/
ck/k/	s/s/	sc/sk/
d/d/*	s/z/	sm/sm/
e/e/	t/t/*	st/st/
f/f/*	u/u/	's
g/g/*	w/w/*	n't
h/h/*	x/ks/*	'll
i/ī/	ch/ch/	'm
i/i/	th/th/	plural -s
ir/ėr/*	sh/sh/	-ed
k/k/*	bl/bl/	-ing
l/l/*	cl/cl/	-s
m/m/*		

High-Frequency Words

gone
group
move
neighbor
promise

Selection Words

camera
photo

Unit 4 Week 2 From Seed to Plant

Long *a: ai, ay*

brain	tail	say
frail	trail	spray
mail	trails	sprays
main	train	stay
nail	trained	stray
paid	waist	sway
pail	wait	tray
pain		way
plains	clay	
rain	day	
rains	gray	
rainy	hay	
sail	jay	
sails	lay	
snail	may	
strain	pay	
strained	play	

Long *e: e, ee, ea*

be	seem	neat
he	sheep	peach
me	sleep	reach
she	street	real
we	sunscreen	scream
	sweet	seal
cheek	teeth	seat
deep	tree	sneaky
feel	wheel	squeal
green		steal
jeep	beach	stream
keep	beans	teach
need	beat	treat
needs	dream	
queen	feast	
see	leaf	
seeds	meal	

Sounds Reviewed

b/b/*	y/ī/	str/str/
d/d/*	ch/ch/	sw/sw/
e/e/*	sh/sh/	tr/tr/
f/f/*	th/th/	plural -s
h/h/*	wh/hw/	-ed
j/j/*	br/br/	-s
k/k/*	cl/kl/	
l/l/*	dr/dr/	
m/m/*	fr/fr/	
n/n/	gr/gr/	
p/p/*	pl/pl/	
r/r/*	scr/skr/	
s/s/*	sl/sl/	
s/z/*	sn/sn/	
t/t/*	spr/spr/	
u/u/	squ/skw/	
w/w/*	st/st/	
y/ē/		

High-Frequency Words

above
almost
change
often
straight

Unit 4 Week 3 Animals

Endings *-er, -est*

bigger	slower	messiest
bumpier	smaller	muddiest
cleaner	stronger	rainiest
colder	sunnier	safest
dirtier	thinner	shiniest
drier	wetter	sleepiest
faster	wider	sloppiest
fluffier		slowest
friskier	biggest	smallest
funnier	bravest	snowiest
happier	bumpiest	soapiest
hotter	dirtiest	strongest
longer	driest	sunniest
messier	fastest	thinnest
sadder	fluffiest	wettest
safer	happiest	widest
sillier	hottest	
sloppier	longest	

Long *o: o, oa, ow*

go	loan	flow
no	moan	glow
so	oats	grow
	road	grown
boat	roam	low
coach	roams	mow
coal	roast	own
coat	soap	pillow
float	soapiest	row
foam	throat	show
goats	toad	shown
groan	toast	slow
groaned	toasty	slower
groaning		slowest
groans	blow	snow
Joan	bow	snowiest
load	crow	tow

Sounds Reviewed

a/a/	l/l/*	dr/dr/
a/ā/	m/m/*	fl/fl/
ai/ā/	n/n/*	fr/fr/
al/ȯ/	o/o/	gl/gl/
b/b/*	p/p/*	gr/gr/
c/k/*	r/r/*	mp/mp/
d/d/*	s/s/	sl/sl/
e/e/	s/z/	sm/sm/
ea/ē/	t/t/*	sn/sn/
ee/ē/	u/u/	st/st/
f/f/*	w/w/*	str/str/
g/g/*	ng/ng/	thr/thr/
h/h/*	sh/sh/	plural -s
i/ē/	th/th/	-ed
i/i/	bl/bl/	-ing
i/ī/	cl/kl/	-s
ir/ėr/*	cr/kr/	
j/j/*		

High-Frequency Words

animal
country
cover
field
warm

Selection Words

panda
pocket

*= letter-sounds reviewed from Level A

Unit 4 Word List

Unit 4 Week 4 What Changes Are Hard?

Long i: igh, ie

bright	sighing	lie
brighter	sighs	lied
fight	sight	lies
flight	slight	pie
flights	sunlight	pies
fright	thigh	skies
high	tight	spied
highest	tighter	spies
light		tie
lightest	cried	tied
might	cries	ties
mighty	die	tried
night	dies	tries
nights	dried	
right	dries	
sigh	flies	
sighed	fries	

Sounds Reviewed

ai/ā/	s/z/	sl/sl/
ay/ā/	u/u/	sp/sp/
c/k/*	t/t/*	spr/spr/
d/d/*	y/ē/	tr/tr/
ea/ē/	sh/sh/	plural -s
ee/ē/	ch/ch/	-er
f/f/*	th/th/	-est
h/h/*	br/br/	-ed
k/k/*	cr/kr/	-ing
l/l/*	dr/dr/	-s
m/m/*	fl/fl/	
n/n/*	fr/fr/	
oa/ō/	gr/gr/	
ow/ō/	pl/pl/	
p/p/*	scr/skr/	
r/r/*	sk/sk/	
s/s/		

High-Frequency Words

below
child
children
full
important

Selection Words

Chicago

Unit 4 Week 5 Weather Changes

Syllables VCV

acorn	lemon	project
babies	lemons	protect
bacon	lizard	rapid
cabin	lizards	river
camel	magic	robins
clever	major	robot
closet	melon	salad
comics	metal	seven
cozy	model	seventh
dragon	moment	shadow
fever	music	shadows
finished	never	shivered
flavor	open	shivers
frozen	opens	silent
habit	over	siren
hotel	paper	spiders
human	pilot	tiger
label	planet	travels
ladies	ponies	tulip
lady	pony	visit
lazy	present	visits

Sounds Reviewed

a/a/	o/o/	ct/kt/
a/ā/	o/ō/	dr/dr/
b/b/*	or/ôr/	fl/fl/
c/k/*	ow/ō/	fr/fr/
d/d/*	p/p/*	nt/nt/
e/e/	r/r/*	pl/pl/
e/ē/	s/s/	pr/pr/
f/f/*	s/z/	sp/sp/
g/g/*	t/t/*	plural -s
g/j/	u/u/	plural -es
h/h/*	u/ù/	-ed
i/i/	v/v/*	
i/ī/	y/ē/	
ee/ē/	z/z/*	
j/j/*	sh/sh/	
l/l/*	th/th/	
m/m/*	cl/kl/	
n/n/		

High-Frequency Words

head
large
poor
though
wash

Selection Words

cloud
umbrella

Unit 5 Word List

Unit 5 Week 1 Good Job!

Compound Words

anthill	flagpole	rainfall
backbone	flashlight	sailboat
backpack	grapevine	sandbox
backyard	hallway	sidewalk
barnyard	herself	snowball
baseball	highway	snowflake
bathtub	homemade	snowman
bedtime	inside	spaceship
beehives	kickball	sunburn
birthday	lunchbox	sunlight
blueprint	mailbox	sunrise
campfire	nighttime	sunscreen
cannot	nutshell	sunshine
catfish	oatmeal	tightrope
classmate	pancake	treetops
cupcake	popcorn	weekday
daylight	railroad	weekend
firefly	rainbow	
fireplace	raincoat	

Sounds Reviewed

a/a/	p/p/*	pl/pl/
a/ā/	r/r/*	scr/skr/
ay/ā/	s/s/	sn/sn/
b/b/*	s/z/	sp/sp/
c/k/*	t/t/*	tr/tr/
ck/k/	u/u/	
d/d/*	w/w/*	
e/e/	y/y/*	
ee/ē/	ch/ch/	
f/f/*	sh/sh/	
g/g/*	th/th/	
h/h/*	bl/bl/	
i/ī/	cl/kl/	
ir/ėr/*	fl/fl/	
k/k/*	gr/gr/	
l/l/*	mp/mp/	
m/m/*	nd/nd/	
n/n/*	nt/nt/	
o/o/		

High-Frequency Words

book
heard
hold
listen
piece

Selection Words

skyscraper
worker

Unit 5 Week 2 Taking Care of Animals

Syllables: Consonant + le

able	gentle	scramble
apple	giggle	scribble
beagle	handle	simple
beetle	jiggle	snuggle
bottle	juggle	sparkle
bottles	jungle	stable
bubble	little	startle
bugle	maple	struggle
candle	middle	table
candles	needle	tangle
cradle	nibble	title
cradles	paddle	turtle
cuddle	puddle	turtles
cuddles	purple	wiggle
eagle	rattle	wiggled
fable	riddle	
gable	sample	

Sounds Reviewed

a/a/	n/n/*	st/st/
a/ā/	o/o/	str/str/
b/b/*	p/p/*	plural -s
c/k/*	r/r/*	
ea/ē/	s/s/*	
ee/ē/	t/t/*	
f/f/*	u/u/	
g/g/*	u/ü/	
g/j/	ur/ėr/	
h/h/*	w/w/*	
i/i/	cr/kr/	
i/j/*	scr/skr/	
l/l/*	sn/sn/	
m/m/*	sp/sp/	

High-Frequency Words

boy
either
hundred
several
you're

Unit 5 Week 3 Family Jobs

Diphthongs ou, ow/ou/

bounds	south	powerful
cloud	sprout	shower
couch	town	
count		
found	chow	
house	cow	
loud	crowd	
mouth	down	
out	flower	
proud	growls	
proudly	how	
shout	howls	
shouts	now	
sound	owl	
sounds	powder	
	power	

Suffixes -ly, -ful

bravely	softly	thankful
correctly	sweetly	useful
easily	tightly	
gladly		
happily	frightful	
loudly	graceful	
neatly	harmful	
nicely	hopeful	
perfectly	hurtful	
proudly	mouthful	
quickly	painful	
sadly	peaceful	
safely	playful	
shyly	powerful	
simply	skillful	

Sounds Reviewed

a/ā/	l/l/*	th/th/
ay/ā/	m/m/*	br/br/
b/b/*	n/n/*	cl/kl/
c/s/	o/o/	cr/kr/
c/k/*	or/ôr/	fl/fl/
ck/k/	p/p/*	fr/fr/
d/d/*	qu/kw/*	gl/gr/
e/e/*	r/r/*	gr/gr/
ea/ē/	s/s/*	pl/pl/
ee/ē/	s/z/	pr/pr/
er/ėr/	t/t/*	sk/sk/
f/f/*	u/u/*	spr/spr/
g/g/*	ur/ėr/	sw/sw/
h/h/*	ch/ch/	plural -s
i/ī/	sh/sh/	

High-Frequency Words

ago
break
certain
probably
since

Selection Words

tool
vacuum

*= letter-sounds reviewed from Level A

Unit 5 Word List

Unit 5 Week 4 My Neighbors, My Friends

Sound of oo in moon

afternoon	loop	tool
balloons	moon	tooth
bedroom	noon	zoo
bloom	poodle	zoom
boo	pool	
boost	raccoon	
boot	room	
booth	scoop	
broom	scoot	
cool	smooth	
droop	smoothly	
food	snoops	
fool	soon	
gloomy	spooky	
goofy	spoons	
hoop	too	

Prefixes un-, re-

unable	recheck
unbutton	reheat
unclean	remake
uncommon	repack
unhappy	repaint
unlike	replace
unload	replant
unlock	replay
unlucky	reread
unpack	resend
unsafe	restart
unspoken	retell
untangle	rethink
untie	reuse
unwell	revisit
unzip	

Sounds Reviewed

a/a/	n/n/*	plural -s
a/ā/	o/o/	-ing
b/b/*	p/p/*	bl/bl/
c/k/*	r/r/*	cl/kl/
c/s/	s/s/*	br/br/
ck/k/*	s/z/	dr/dr/
d/d/*	t/t/*	gl/gl/
e/e/	u/u/	nd/nd/
er/ėr/	w/w/*	nt/nt/
f/f/*	x/ks/*	pl/pl/
g/g/*	y/ē/	sc/sk/
h/h/*	z/z/	sm/sm/
k/k/	ch/ch/	sn/sn/
l/l/*	sh/sh/	sp/sp/
m/m/*	th/th/	st/st/

High-Frequency Words

been
brother
course
special
whole

Selection Words

neighborhood

Unit 5 Week 5 Doing the Right Thing

Diphthongs oi, oy

boil	pointing	joy
boiling	poison	joyful
choices	soil	joystick
coin	spoil	loyal
coins	spoiled	oyster
foil	voice	Roy
join	voices	soybean
joint		toy
joints	boy	toys
noise	boys	
noisy	cowboy	
oink	enjoy	
point	enjoys	

Silent Consonants kn/n/, wr/r/, mb/m/

knapsack	wrap	crumb
knee	wreath	crumbs
kneel	wreck	lamb
knife	wriggle	limb
knight	wrist	limbs
knights	write	plumber
knit	writing	thumb
knitting	wrong	thumbs
knob	wrote	
knock		
knocked		
knot		
know		
knuckle		
knuckles		

Sounds Reviewed*

b/b/*	l/l/*	th/th/
c/k/*	m/m/*	ng/ng/
c/s/*	n/n/*	plural -s
ck/k/	o/o/	-ing
d/d/*	ow/ō/	cr/kr/
e/e/	p/p/*	nt/nt/
ee/ē/	r/r/*	pl/pl/
f/f/*	s/s/*	sp/sp/
g/g/*	t/t/*	st/st/
i/ī/	v/v/*	
j/j/*	y/ē/	
k/k/*	ch/ch/	

High-Frequency Words

hour
leave
minute
sorry
watch

✻= letter-sounds reviewed from Level A

Unit 6 Word List

Unit 6 Week 1 Sports

Sound of oo in book

bookmark	shook
books	soot
brook	stood
brooks	took
cook	wood
cookbook	woodpecker
cooking	woof
crook	wool
foot	
football	
good	
hood	
hoof	
hook	
hooks	
look	
looking	
looks	

Suffixes -or, -er

actor	printer
baker	racer
batter	reader
buzzer	reporter
collector	runner
conductor	sailor
director	singer
driver	speaker
editor	swimmer
farmer	teacher
gardener	toaster
helper	visitor
inspector	winner
inventor	writer
kicker	
leader	
pitcher	
player	

Sounds Reviewed

a/a/	l/l/*	cr/kr/
ai/ā/	m/m/*	dr/dr/
al/ò/	n/n/*	lp/lp/
ar/är/	o/o/	ng/ng/
ay/ā/	oa/ō/	nt/nt/
b/b/*	p/p/*	pl/pl
c/k/*	r/r/*	pr/pr/
c/s/*	s/s/	rd/rd/
ck/k/	t/t/*	rm/rm/
d/d/*	u/u/*	rt/rt/
e/e/	v/v/*	sp/sp/
e/ē/	w/w/*	st/st/
ea/ē/	wr/w/	sw/sw/
f/f/*	z/z/*	
g/g/*	ch/ch/	plural -s
h/h/*	tch/tch/	-s
i/i/	sh/sh/	-ing
i/ī/	br/br/	
k/k/*		

High-Frequency Words

bought
buy
clothes
won
worst

Unit 6 Week 2 The American Flag

Vowel Patterns ew, ue

blew	blue
chew	bluebird
crew	clue
drew	clues
few	due
flew	glue
grew	Sue
knew	true
new	
news	
newt	
screw	
stew	
threw	
unscrew	

Prefixes pre-, dis-

disconnect	preheat
disgrace	preheating
disinfect	prepaid
dislike	prepay
disloyal	prepays
disorder	preschool
displace	preteen
displease	pretest
displeased	
disrespect	
distaste	
distrust	
precooked	
precut	
preflight	
pregame	

Sounds Reviewed

a/a/	l/l/*	cl/kl/
a/ā/	m/m/*	cr/kr/
ai/ā/	n/n/*	dr/dr/
ay/ā/	o/o/	fl/fl/
c/k/*	oo/ù/	gl/gl/
c/s/*	oo/ü/	gr/gr/
d/d/*	or/ôr/	nt/nt/
e/e/	ou/ou/	pl/pl/
e/ē/	oy/oi/	pr/pr/
ea/ē/	p/p/*	scr/skr/
ee/ē/	r/r/	sp/sp/
f/f/*	s/s/	st/st/
g/g/*	s/z/	thr/thr/
h/h/*	t/t/*	tr/tr/
i/i/	u/u/	
i/ī/	ch/ch/	plural -s
igh/ī/	th/th/	-ed
ir/ėr/	bl/bl	-ing
kn/n/		-s

High-Frequency Words

air
America
beautiful
Earth
world

Selection Words

colonies

Unit 6 Week 3 Family Celebrations

Contractions 're, 've, 'd

he'd	they're	you'd
I'd	they've	you're
I've	we'd	you've
she'd	we're	
they'd	we've	

ph/f/   dge/j/

dolphin	badge	porridge
gopher	badger	ridge
gophers	badges	smudge
graph	bridge	wedge
Joseph	dodgeball	
nephew	edge	
orphan	fridge	
phase	fudge	
Phil	hedge	
phone	hedgehogs	
phoned	judge	
Ralph	ledge	
Steph	lodge	
trophies	Madge	
trophy	Midge	
	pledge	

Sounds Reviewed

a/a/	mb/m/	y/y/*
a/ā/	n/n/*	sh/sh/
al/ò/	o/o/	th/th/
b/b/*	o/ō/	br/br/
d/d/*	or/ôr/	fr/fr/
e/e/	ou/ou/	gr/gr/
e/ē/	ow/ō/	pl/pl/
ew/ü/	p/p/*	sm/sm/
g/g/*	r/r/	st/st/
h/h/*	s/s/*	tr/tr/
i/i/	s/z/	
i/ī/	u/u/	plural -s
j/j/*	v/v/*	-ed
kn/n/	w/w/*	-es
l/l/*	wr/r/	
m/m/*	y/ē/	

High-Frequency Words

believe
company
everybody
money
young

*= letter-sounds reviewed from Level A

Unit 6 Word List

Unit 6 Week 4 A Cowboy's Life

Short e: ea

bread	sweat
breath	sweater
dead	thread
deaf	tread
dread	unhealthiest
dreadfully	unsteadily
feather	unsteady
head	weather
health	wealthier
healthy	
Heather	
heavier	
heaviest	
heavy	
instead	
leather	
meadow	
meant	
read	
ready	
spread	
steady	

Base Words and Affixes

baker	precooked	retrimming
careful	prefaded	reused
disconnecting	preheated	reusing
discovered	prejudging	rewrapped
dislike	premixes	rewrapping
disliked	preordered	rewriting
dislikes	preplanning	sitting
disliking	presetting	thankfully
dismounted	pretreated	uneasily
displeased	prewrapped	unhappier
disregarded	rechecked	unhappily
disrespectful	remodeled	unhealthiest
distrustful	remover	unhelpful
explorer	repacking	unkindly
freezing	replaced	unluckiest
gardener	replacing	unsaddled
healthy	replanning	unsteadily
heavier	replaying	unsteady
heaviest	resaddled	untied
inventor	rescrubbed	unzipping
luckily	retied	wealthier
powerfully	retraced	

Sounds Reviewed

a/a/	n/n/*	nk/ngk/
a/ā/	o/o/	br/br/
ar/är/	oo/ù/	ct/kt/
b/b/*	or/ôr/	dr/dr/
c/k/*	ou/ou/	fr/fr/
ck/k/	ow/ō/	nd/nd/
d/d/*	ow/ou/	nt/nt/
dge/j/	p/p/*	pl/pl/
e/e/	r/r/*	pr/pr/
e/ē/	s/s/*	rd/rd/
ea/ē/	s/z/*	sp/sp/
ee/ē/	t/t/*	spr/spr/
f/f/*	u/u/	st/st/
g/g/*	v/v/*	sw/sw/
h/h/*	w/w/*	thr/thr/
i/i/	wr/r/	tr/tr/
i/ī/	x/ks/*	
j/j/*	y/ē/	
k/k/*	z/z/*	
l/l/*	th/th/	
m/m/*	ch/ch/	

High-Frequency Words

alone
between
notice
question
woman

Selection Words

barrel
bull

Unit 6 Week 5 Celebrations for Everyone

Vowel Patterns aw, au, au(gh)

August	pause
author	paused
awful	pausing
because	pawn
caught	predawn
cause	redrawing
daughter	retaught
daughters	sausage
dawn	saw
drawn	scrawnier
fault	scrawny
haul	straw
hauling	taught
lawn	thawed
naughtiest	yawn
naughty	
Paul	

Base Words and Affixes

dirtiest	remaking	unplanned
discovered	retried	unplugging
disliking	replaced	unsaddled
displease	replay	unsteadily
expected	retaught	
funniest	rethinking	
hauling	rewrap	
luckily	rewrapping	
naughtiest	scrawnier	
paused	sleepier	
pausing	smelliest	
pinning	surprising	
precooked	thankfully	
predawn	undecided	
preplan	unexpected	
preset	unhappily	
redrawing	unhelpful	

Sounds Reviewed

a/a/	ir/ėr/	th/th/
a/ā/	k/k/*	nk/ngk/
ay/ā/	l/l/*	dr/dr/
b/b/*	m/m/*	lp/lp/
c/k/*	n/n/*	lt/lt/
c/s/*	or/ôr/	pl/pl/
ck/k/	oo/ù/	pr/pr/
d/d/*	p/p/*	rt/rt/
e/e/	r/r/*	scr/skr/
e/ē/	s/s/*	st/st/
ea/ē/	s/z/*	str/str/
ee/ē/	t/t/*	tr/tr/
f/f/*	u/u/	
g/g/*	v/v/*	
g/j/	wr/r/	
h/h/*	x/ks/*	
i/i/	y/y/*	
i/ī/	y/ē/	

High-Frequency Words

cold
finally
half
tomorrow
word

Selection Words

celebrate

Phonological Awareness

Many of the following activities can be used at any grade level by adapting the element being practiced and the degree of difficulty.

Activity Bank

Rhyming Words

Poems and Chants

Read a poem or chant to children. Emphasize the rhymes by whispering all except rhyming words. Have children say the poems with you in the same way to help them hear the rhyming words.

Did You Ever See . . . ?

Invent rhymes and sing them to the tune of "If You're Happy and You Know It."

> Did you ever see a <u>fly</u> with a <u>tie</u>?
>
> Did you ever see a <u>fly</u> with a <u>tie</u>?
>
> Did you ever? No, I never. Did you ever? No, I never.
>
> No, I never saw a <u>fly</u> with a <u>tie</u>.

Rhyme Book

Read children a book that uses rhyme. Ask them to identify rhyming word pairs. Distribute paper and have children fold it in half width-wise. Have them draw rhyming word pairs (one in each half) from the book or that they thought of themselves.

Initial Sounds

Picture Card Sound Match

Pass out five picture cards to each child. In turn each child shows a card, telling the beginning sound and asks another player if he or she has a picture card beginning with the same sound. If the player has a picture with the same beginning sound, he or she gives it to the child who asked. When a match is made, the player shows the cards, repeats the initial sound requested, and names the two pictures.

Same Sound Silly Sentences

Display a picture card—*dog.* Guide children to identify the initial sound: This is *dog.* The first sound in dog is /d/. What is the first sound in dog? Let's say other words that begin with /d/. Take four or five suggestions; then guide children to make a potentially silly sentence. For example *dog, dinosaur, dinner,* and *dark* could be used in the sentence:

> *The dog and the dinosaur ate dinner in the dark.*

Counting Words in a Sentence

How Many Words?

Say a simple sentence. (Use monosyllabic words at first.) Move tokens for every word you hear in the sentence. Count your tokens. Confirm by saying the sentence again and moving tokens while you say each word.

Counting Syllables in a Word

Clapping Names

Ask a child to say his or her first name. Repeat it, clapping once for each syllable as you say it. Have children say and clap the name with you. How many syllables (claps) did you hear? Repeat, substituting each child's name.

Phonemic Awareness

Many of the following activities can be used at any grade level by adapting the element being practiced and the degree of difficulty.

Blending and Segmenting Sounds

What Am I?

Play a riddle game with sounds.
Use items such as these:

/g/ /ā/ /t/ You open me. (gate)

/k/ /ā/ /v/ Bears sleep in me. (cave)

I Spy Some Phonemes

Choose an object in the classroom. Ask students to guess the name of your object by the clues you give them. Use clues such as these: *I spy an object with four sounds. The first sound is /t/. The last sound is /l/. The second sound is /ā/. The third sound is /b/.* Continue to provide clues until students can name the object. Repeat with other objects around the room. You may wish to have students take turns providing clues for the class.

Sound Count

Make a copy of the five-sound boxes pattern on p. 283 for each student. Supply markers, such as erasers, buttons, or checkers. Slowly say a word that has up to five sounds in it. Have each student put a marker in a box for each sound in the word.

Say the Sounds

Have a student show a picture card to another student. Ask the student to name the picture and then segment the sounds in the name of the picture (for example, *tent*, /t/ /e/ /n/ /t/).

For students who need more support with this activity, provide the appropriate number of sound boxes for the word and have students move a marker into a box for each sound.

Working with Vowels

Say a one-syllable word with a short vowel. Have students change the vowel sound to another short vowel to make a new word. Work with words such as *cab, bet, sit, log,* and *bug.* Use the Word Lists on pp. 268–279 of this book for more words.

Bubble Gum Words

Tell students you are going to slowly pull words out of your mouth, as you would pull out bubble gum. Have them identify each word as you "pull it out." Model sounding out the word *him*, /hhh/ /iii/ /mmm/, as you slowly say its sounds. Have students repeat after you as you pull other words out.

Substituting Sounds

Switcheroo

Give each student letter cards for *c, m, p, n, t,* and *a* in an envelope. Guide students in making new words by changing the letters. You may wish to begin with directions such as these:

Find the letters that make these sounds, /k/ /a/ /t/.

Blend the sounds together. What word did you spell? (cat)

Change the /k/ sound to /m/.

Blend the sounds together. What word did you spell? (mat)

Change the /t/ to /p/.

Blend the sounds together. What word did you spell? (map)

Continue substituting different sounds until you have made all of the following words: *nap, tap, cap, can, tan, man, pan,* and *pat.*

Make New Words

Have students make words that end with /t/ by changing the initial sound of *sit.* Model how to change the beginning sound and blend it with the middle and end sounds: /s/ *it* becomes /h/ *it.* Ask students to join you as you make other words, such as *pit, bit, wit, kit, lit, fit.*

This activity can be adapted for other consonant sounds by referring to the Word Lists on pp. 268–279 of this book.

Sound Switching

Tell students you will say a word. Ask them to listen carefully because you are going to switch one of the sounds and make a new word. Ask them to tell you which sound, beginning, middle, or end, was switched. For example, say *bat* and *bag,* and ask students which sound was switched. Continue the activity with these word pairs: *tab, tag; hot, hat; rake, wake; dad, sad; mad, made; red, read; page, cage; cap, cape; miss, mess; fan, fat; met, men; bug, rug.*

Name _____

Sound Boxes

Oral Vocabulary Words

UNIT 1	UNIT 2	UNIT 3	UNIT 4	UNIT 5	UNIT 6
Exploration	**Working Together**	**Creative Ideas**	**Our Changing World**	**Responsibility**	**Traditions**

DEVELOP LANGUAGE

avenue	courageous	construct	familiar	career	athlete
investigate	hazard	contraption	keepsake	community	challenge
rural	prevent	project	preserve	employee	champion
suburb	rescue	sidekick	represent	responsible	effort
urban	wildfire	unique	valuable	teamwork	rival
ascend	ability	conversation	adapt	concern	anthem
descend	compete	correspond	annual	growth	history
journey	contribute	postage	nutrients	litter	independence
orbit	recreation	reply	soil	protection	patriotic
universe	victory	transport	sprout	veterinarian	symbol
camouflage	conflict	brainstorm	appearance	assign	celebration
galaxy	greedy	brilliant	nursery	behavior	custom
mammal	inhabit	consume	stage	cooperate	occasion
tranquil	portion	prey	tend	obedient	sibling
wildlife	resolve	shrewd	transform	properly	tradition
arid	companion	abundant	adjust	acquaintance	climate
cactus	independent	assist	ancestor	appreciate	herd
dune	partnership	baffle	courage	communicate	livestock
landform	solution	generous	landmark	local	occupation
precipitation	survival	struggle	unexpected	respect	rodeo
curious	decorate	accomplish	blizzard	apologize	ceremony
delicate	dine	excel	condition	citizen	culture
information	float (n.)	inspiration	forecast	judgment	festival
inquire	holiday	process	predict	law	international
sturdy	participate	research	terrifying	scold	regional

My Sidewalks provides direct instruction and daily practice in the oral vocabulary words listed above. Children learn five words per week that develop a weekly concept related to grade-level science and social studies content. These words are beyond children's reading ability but are used to expand their understanding of the concept and their ability to discuss it.

Child's Name _____ Date _____

Level B *My Sidewalks*
Observation Checklist

Use this checklist to record your observations of children's reading skills and behaviors.

	Always (Proficient)	Sometimes (Developing)	Rarely (Novice)
Identifies and isolates initial sounds in words			
Identifies and isolates final sounds in words			
Blends sounds to make spoken words			
Segments one-syllable spoken words into individual phonemes			
Knows letter-sound correspondences			
Uses word structure to identify longer words			
Reads simple sentences			
Reads simple stories			
Understands simple story structure (character, setting, plot)			
Reads at an appropriate reading rate			
Reads with appropriate intonation and stress			
Summarizes plot or main ideas accurately			
Recognizes main ideas			
Recognizes sequence			
Makes comparisons and contrasts			
Draws conclusions to understand text			

Bookmarks

Fiction

- Who are the characters?

- Where does the story take place?

- When does the story take place?

- What happens . . .
  - in the beginning?
  - in the middle?
  - at the end?

Nonfiction

- What did I learn?

- What is this mainly about?

Connections Between *My Sidewalks* and Scott Foresman *Reading Street*

My Sidewalks is designed to parallel essential elements in *Scott Foresman Reading Street*. Connections between the two programs are reflected in the indexes of the Teacher's Guides.

- Corresponding **priority skills** ensure that students receive instruction in the critical elements of reading—phonemic awareness, phonics, fluency, vocabulary, and comprehension.

- Parallel **concepts and themes** enable smooth transitions between *My Sidewalks* and *Reading Street*.

- Consistency of **scaffolded instruction** promotes familiarity with routines and terminology.

- Alignment of **before, during, and after reading strategies** reinforces successful reading habits.

- **Comprehension** skill links provide Tier III readers with additional instruction and practice with main idea, compare/contrast, sequence, and drawing conclusions.

- **Vocabulary** links provide Tier III readers with additional instruction and practice with oral vocabulary.

- Consistent procedures for **corrective feedback** promptly reveal and address student needs, providing guidance for error correction.

- Connected **writing** modes offer student opportunities to respond to literature.

- **Cross-curricular** links lay out the same science and social studies foundations for Tier III readers as for students in the core program.

Index

ask questions, *V1* 6, 9, 12, 22, 25, 28, 38, 44, 54, 57, 60, 70, 73, 76, 86, 89, 92, 102, 105, 108, 118, 121, 124, 134, 137, 140, 150, 153, 156, 166, 169, 172, 182, 185, 188, 198, 201, 204, 214, 217, 220, 230, 233, 236; *V2* 6, 9, 12, 22, 28, 38, 41, 44, 54, 57, 60, 70, 73, 76, 86, 89, 92, 102, 105, 108, 118, 121, 124, 134, 137, 140, 150, 153, 156, 166, 169, 172, 182, 185, 188, 198, 201, 204, 214, 217, 220, 230, 233, 236

concept development. *See* Concept development.

fix-up strategies, *V1* 9, 12, 25, 28, 44, 57, 60, 73, 76, 89, 92, 105, 108, 121, 124, 137, 140, 153, 156, 169, 172, 185, 188, 201, 204, 217, 226, 233, 236; *V2* 6, 9, 12, 22, 28, 38, 41, 44, 54, 57, 60, 70, 73, 76, 86, 89, 92, 102, 105, 108, 118, 121, 124, 134, 137, 140, 150, 153, 156, 166, 169, 172, 182, 185, 188, 198, 201, 204, 214, 217, 226, 230, 233, 236

graphic sources. *See* Graphic sources.

paired reading, *V1* 7, 13, 23, 29, 39, 45, 55, 61, 71, 77, 87, 93, 103, 109, 119, 125, 135, 141, 151, 157, 167, 173, 183, 189, 199, 205, 215, 221, 231, 237; *V2* 7, 13, 23, 29, 39, 45, 55, 61, 71, 77, 87, 93, 103, 109, 119, 125, 135, 141, 151, 157, 167, 173, 183, 189, 199, 205, 215, 221, 231, 237

picture clues, *V1* 9, 12, 25, 28, 41, 44, 57, 60, 73, 76, 89, 92, 105, 108, 121, 124, 137, 140, 153, 156, 169, 172, 185, 188, 201, 204, 217, 220, 233, 236; *V2* 9, 12, 25, 28, 41, 44, 57, 60, 73, 76, 89, 92, 105, 108, 121, 124, 137, 140, 153, 156, 169, 172, 185, 188, 201, 204, 217, 220, 233, 236

picture walk, *V1* 9, 12, 25, 28, 41, 44, 57, 60, 73, 76, 89, 92, 105, 108, 121, 124, 137, 140, 153, 156, 169, 172, 185, 188, 201, 204, 217, 220, 233, 236; *V2* 9, 12, 25, 28, 41, 44, 57, 60, 73, 76, 89, 92, 105, 108, 121, 124, 137, 140, 153, 156, 169, 172, 185, 188, 201, 204, 217, 220, 233, 236

predict, *V1* 14, 30, 62, 78, 94, 126, 142, 158, 174, 190, 206, 238; *V2* 14, 30, 46, 78, 94, 126, 142, 158, 174, 206, 222, 238

preview, *V1* 6, 22, 38, 54, 70, 86, 102, 118, 134, 150, 166, 182, 198, 214, 230; *V2* 6, 22, 38, 54, 70, 86, 102, 118, 134, 150, 166, 182, 198, 214, 230

reader response. *See* Reader response.

recall and retell, *V1* 6, 9, 22, 25, 38, 41, 54, 57, 70, 73, 86, 89, 102, 105, 118, 121, 134, 137, 150, 153, 166, 169, 182, 185, 198, 201, 214, 217, 230, 233; *V2* 6, 9, 22, 25, 38, 41, 54, 57, 70, 73, 86, 89, 102, 105, 118, 121, 134, 137, 150, 153, 166, 169, 182, 185, 198, 201, 214, 217, 230, 233

self-monitor, *V1* 9, 12, 25, 28, 44, 57, 60, 73, 76, 89, 92, 105, 108, 121, 124, 137, 140, 153, 156, 169, 172, 185, 188, 201, 204, 217, 226, 233, 236; *V2* 6, 9, 12, 22, 28, 38, 41, 44, 54, 57, 60, 70, 73, 76, 86, 89, 92, 102, 105, 108, 118, 121, 124, 134, 137, 140, 150, 153, 156, 166, 169, 172, 182, 185, 188, 198, 201, 204, 214, 217, 226, 230, 233, 236

set purpose for reading, *V1* 6, 22, 38, 54, 70, 86, 102, 118, 134, 150, 166, 182, 198, 214, 230; *V2* 6, 22, 38, 54, 70, 86, 102, 118, 134, 150, 166, 182, 198, 214, 230

story structure,

character, *V1* 9, 33, 76, 92, 105, 108, 124, 188, 217; *V2* 28, 54, 76, 124, 140

plot, *V1* 92, 108, 217, 220, 236; *V2* 44, 140

setting, *V1* 38, 54, 60, 92; *V2* 28, 60

summarize, *V1* 6, 9, 22, 25, 38, 41, 54, 57, 70, 73, 86, 89, 102, 105, 118, 121, 134, 137, 150, 153, 166, 169, 182, 185, 198, 201, 214, 217, 230, 233; *V2* 6, 9, 22, 25, 38, 41, 54, 57, 70, 73, 86, 89, 102, 105, 118, 121, 134, 137, 150, 153, 166, 169, 182, 185, 198, 201, 214, 217, 230, 233

text features, *V1* 30, 70, 78, 86; *V2* 121, 126, 142, 174, 214

think alouds. Think alouds and teacher modeling are demonstrated throughout weekly lessons as a basic teaching strategy.

Concept development

concept definition mapping, *V1* xxiv–xxvi; *V2* xxiv–xxvi

concept vocabulary, *Welcome to My Sidewalks,* 23; *V1* 5, 6, 9, 11, 12, 14, 16, 21, 22, 25, 27, 28, 30, 32, 37, 38, 41, 43, 44, 46, 48, 53, 54, 57, 59, 60, 62, 64, 69, 70, 73, 75, 76, 78, 80, 85, 86, 89, 91, 92, 94, 96, 101, 102, 105, 107, 108, 110, 112, 117, 118, 121, 123, 124, 126, 128, 133, 134, 137, 139, 140, 142, 144, 149, 150, 153, 155, 156, 158, 165, 166, 169, 171, 172, 174, 176, 181, 182, 185, 187, 188, 190, 197, 198, 201, 203, 204, 206, 208, 213, 214, 217, 219, 220, 222, 224, 229, 230, 233, 235, 236, 238, 240; *V2* 5, 6, 9, 11, 12, 14, 16, 21, 22, 25, 27, 28, 30, 32, 37, 38, 41, 43, 44, 46, 48, 53, 54, 57, 59, 60, 62, 64, 69, 70, 73, 75, 76, 78, 80, 85, 86, 89, 91, 92, 94, 96, 101, 102, 105, 107, 108, 110, 112, 117, 118, 121, 123, 124, 126, 128, 133, 134, 137, 139, 140, 142, 144, 149, 150, 153, 155, 156, 158, 165, 166, 169, 171, 172, 174, 176, 181, 182, 185, 187, 188, 190, 197, 198, 201, 203, 204, 206, 208, 213, 214, 217, 219, 220, 222, 224, 229, 230, 233, 235, 236, 238, 240

oral vocabulary. *See* Oral vocabulary.

Sing with Me Big Book, *V1* 5, 21, 37, 53, 69, 85, 101, 117, 133, 149, 165, 181, 197, 213, 229; *V2* 5, 21, 37, 53, 69, 85, 101, 117, 133, 149, 165, 181, 197, 213, 229

think alouds. Think alouds and teacher modeling are demonstrated throughout weekly lessons as a basic teaching strategy.

Concepts of print

letter recognition, *V1* 13, 29

track print, *V1* 15, 31, 47, 63, 79, 95, 111, 127, 143, 159, 175, 191, 207, 223, 239; *V2* 15, 31, 47, 63, 79, 95, 111, 127, 143, 159, 175, 191, 207, 223, 239

Conclusions, draw. *See* Comprehension, Skills.

Connections, make

text to self, *V1* 14, 15, 25, 31, 33, 47, 54, 62, 63, 79, 95, 111, 117, 121, 123, 124, 127, 128, 133, 134, 139, 142, 143, 149, 155, 158, 159, 166, 175, 187, 191, 207, 208, 214, 223, 230, 239; *V2* 14, 15, 31, 47, 53, 59, 62, 63, 64, 78, 79, 86, 95, 111, 118, 121, 126, 127, 143, 150, 153, 159, 165, 175, 176, 190, 191, 198, 207, 223, 239

text to text, *V1* 17, 33, 49, 65, 81, 97, 113, 129, 145, 161, 177, 193, 209, 225, 241; *V2* 17, 33, 49, 65, 81, 97, 113, 129, 145, 161, 177, 193, 209, 225, 241

text to world, *V1* 12, 59, 73, 76, 78, 81, 85, 86, 89, 91, 97, 185, 191, 192; *V2* 25, 48, 54, 81, 91, 95, 96, 112, 117, 139, 155, 166, 171, 182, 185, 187, 197, 219

Content-area texts

art, *V1* 9, 158, 230, 233; *V2* 9, 28

health, *V1* 70

math, *V1* 134

music, *V1* 142; *V2* 12, 14, 190

science, *V1* 22, 25, 28, 30, 38, 41, 54, 94, 121, 134, 137, 198; *V2* 22, 25, 38, 41, 70, 73

social studies, *V1* 6, 57, 86, 89, 102, 110, 118, 126, 134, 150, 174, 182, 217; *V2* 86, 105, 118, 121, 134, 137, 140, 142, 150, 153, 158, 169, 182, 188, 190, 214, 217, 230

technology, *V1* 70, 188, 230; *V2* 9

Contractions. *See* Word structure.

Contrast. *See* Comprehension, Skills, compare and contrast.

Corrective feedback

fluency, *V1* 6, 7, 10, 13, 22, 23, 26, 29, 38, 39, 42, 45, 54, 55, 58, 70, 71, 74, 77, 86, 87, 90, 93, 102, 103, 106, 109, 118, 119, 122, 125, 134, 135, 138, 141, 150, 151, 154, 157, 166, 167, 170, 173, 182, 183, 186, 189, 198, 199, 202, 205, 214, 215, 218, 221, 230, 231, 234, 237; *V2* 6, 7, 10, 13, 22, 23, 26, 29, 38, 39, 42, 45, 54, 55, 58, 61, 70, 71, 74, 77, 86, 87, 90, 93, 102, 103, 106, 109, 118, 119, 122, 125, 134, 135, 138, 141, 150, 151, 154, 157, 166, 167, 170, 173, 182, 183, 186, 189, 198, 199, 202, 205, 214, 215, 218, 221, 230, 231, 234, 237

phonics, *V1* 4, 8, 20, 24, 36, 40, 52, 68, 72, 84, 116, 120, 132, 148, 164, 180, 196, 200, 216, 232; *V2* 4, 20, 24, 40, 52, 56, 58, 116, 132, 148, 152, 164, 180, 200, 212, 228

word structure, *V1* 56, 88, 100, 104, 136, 152, 168, 184, 212, 228, 232; *V2* 8, 36, 68, 72, 84, 88, 100, 104, 120, 136, 168, 184, 196, 216, 232

See also Fluency; Phonics.

Critical thinking. *See* Comprehension, Skills.

Cultures, appreciating. *See* Multicultural connections.

Differentiated instruction, *Welcome to My Sidewalks,* 10–11; *V1* xiv–xv; *V2* xix–xv

Directions, *V1* 46, 94, 158; *V2* 126, 236

Discussion. *See* Oral Language.

Draw conclusions. *See* Comprehension, Skills.

During reading comprehension strategies. *See* Comprehension, Strategies.

ELL

English Language Learners, *V1* xvi–xvii; *V2* xvi–xvii

Emergent literacy. *See* Concepts of print; Handwriting; Listening Comprehension.

Emerging reading/writing skills. *See* Concepts of print; Handwriting; Listening Comprehension.

Endings. *See* Word structure.

Error correction. *See* Corrective feedback.

ESL (English as a Second Language). *See* ELL.

Evaluation. *See* Assessment.

Expository nonfiction. *See* Genres.

Fable. *See* Genres.

Fairy tale. *See* Genres.

Family involvement. *See* School-home connection.

Fantasy. *See* Genres.

Fix-up strategies. *See* Comprehension, Strategies.

Flexible grouping. *See* Differentiated instruction.

Fluency

accuracy, *V1* 16, 32, 48, 64, 80, 96, 112, 128, 144, 160, 176, 192, 208, 224, 240, 244–245; *V2* 16, 32, 48, 64, 80, 96, 112, 128, 144, 160, 176, 192, 208, 224, 240, 244–245

assessment (WCPM), *V1* 16, 32, 48, 64, 80, 96, 112, 128, 144, 160, 176, 192, 208, 224, 240, 244–245; *V2* 16, 32, 48, 64, 80, 96, 112, 128, 144, 160, 176, 192, 208, 224, 240, 244–245

audio-assisted reading, *V1* 10, 13, 26, 29, 42, 45, 58, 61, 74, 77, 90, 93, 106, 109, 122, 125, 138, 141, 154, 157, 170, 173, 186, 189, 202, 205, 218, 221, 234, 237; *V2* 10, 13, 26, 29, 42, 45, 58, 61, 74, 77, 90, 93, 106, 109, 122, 125, 138, 141, 154, 157, 170, 173, 186, 189, 202, 205, 218, 221, 234, 237

automaticity, *V1* 16, 32, 48, 64, 80, 96, 112, 128, 144, 160, 176, 192, 208, 224, 240, 244–245; *V2* 16, 32, 48, 64, 80, 96, 112, 128, 144, 160, 176, 192, 208, 224, 240, 244–245

choral reading, *V1* 14, 30, 46, 62, 94, 110, 126, 142, 158, 174, 206, 222, 238; *V2* 14, 30, 62, 78, 94, 110, 126, 142, 158, 174, 190, 206, 222, 238

corrective feedback, *V1* 6, 7, 10, 13, 22, 23, 26, 29, 38, 39, 42, 45, 54, 55, 58, 70, 71, 74, 77, 86, 87, 90, 93, 102, 103, 106, 109, 118, 119, 122, 134, 135, 138, 141, 150, 151, 154, 157, 166, 167, 170, 173, 182, 183, 186, 189, 198, 199, 202, 205, 214, 215, 218, 221, 230, 231, 234, 237; *V2* 6, 7, 10, 13, 22, 23, 26, 29, 38, 39, 42, 45, 54, 55, 58, 61, 70, 71, 74, 77, 86, 87, 90, 93, 102, 103, 106, 109, 118, 119, 122, 125, 134, 135, 138, 141, 150, 151, 154, 157, 166, 167, 170, 173, 182, 183, 186, 189, 198, 199, 202, 205, 214, 215, 218, 221, 230, 231, 234, 237

echo reading, *V1* 78; *V2* 46

expression/intonation (prosody), *V1* 14, 110, 126, 142, 206, 238; *V2* 62, 78, 110, 190, 206

fluency probes. *See* Fluency, assessment.

modeling by teacher, *Welcome to My Sidewalks,* 28; *V1* 11, 14, 27, 30, 43, 46, 59, 62, 75, 78, 91, 94, 107, 110, 123, 126, 139, 142, 155, 158, 171, 174, 187, 190, 203, 206, 219, 222, 235, 238; *V2* 11, 14, 27, 30, 43, 46, 59, 62, 75, 78, 91, 94, 107, 110, 123, 126, 139, 142, 155, 158, 171, 174, 187, 190, 203, 206, 219, 222, 235, 238

oral reading, *V1* 7, 13, 23, 29, 39, 45, 55, 61, 71, 77, 87, 93, 103, 109, 119, 125, 135, 141, 151, 157, 167, 173, 183, 189, 199, 205, 215, 221, 231, 237; *V2* 7, 13, 23, 29, 39, 45, 55, 61, 71, 77, 87, 93, 103, 109, 119, 125, 135, 141, 151, 157, 167, 173, 183, 189, 199, 205, 215, 221, 231, 237

paired reading, *V1* 7, 13, 23, 29, 39, 45, 55, 61, 71, 77, 87, 93, 103, 109, 119, 125, 135, 141, 151, 157, 167, 173, 183, 189, 199, 205, 215, 221, 231, 237; *V2* 7, 13, 23, 29, 39, 45, 55, 61, 71, 77, 87, 93, 103, 109, 119, 125, 135, 141, 151, 157, 167, 173, 183, 189, 199, 205, 215, 221, 231, 237

punctuation, attention to, *V1* 14, 30, 62, 78

rate/pace, *V1* 46, 94, 158, 174, 222; *V2* 94, 126, 158, 222, 238

repeated reading, *Welcome to My Sidewalks,* 28–29; *V1* 6, 7, 10, 13, 17, 22, 23, 26, 29, 33, 38, 39, 42, 45, 49, 54, 55, 58, 61, 65, 70, 71, 74, 77, 81, 86, 87, 90, 93, 97, 102, 103, 106, 109, 113, 118, 119, 122, 125, 129, 134, 135, 138, 141, 145, 150, 151, 154, 157, 161, 166, 167, 170, 173, 177, 182, 183, 186, 189, 193, 198, 199, 202, 205, 209, 214, 215, 218, 221, 225, 230, 231, 234, 237, 241; *V2* 6, 7, 10, 13, 17, 22, 23, 26, 29, 33, 38, 39, 42, 45, 49, 54, 55, 58, 61, 65, 70, 71, 74, 77, 81, 86, 87, 90, 93, 97, 102, 103, 106, 109, 113, 118, 119, 122, 125, 129, 134, 135, 138, 141, 145, 150, 151, 154, 157, 161, 166, 167, 170, 173, 177, 182, 183, 186, 189, 193, 198, 199, 202, 205, 209, 214, 215, 218, 221, 225, 230, 231, 234, 237, 241

word reading, *Welcome to My Sidewalks,* 20; *V1* 10, 26, 42, 58, 74, 90, 106, 122, 138, 154, 170, 186, 202, 218, 234; *V2* 10, 26, 42, 58, 74, 90, 106, 122, 138, 154, 170, 186, 202, 218, 234

Folk tale. *See* Genres.

Generate questions. *See* Comprehension, Strategies, ask questions.

Genres

animal fantasy, *V1* 12, 44; *V2* 44

biographical sketch, *V1* 238

biography, *V1* 25, 185, 233; *V2* 217

comic strip, *V2* 62, 206

directions, *V1* 94, 158; *V2* 126, 236

expository nonfiction, *V1* 22, 38, 41, 54, 70, 102, 118, 121, 134, 169, 182, 198, 214, 230; *V2* 9, 22, 25, 38, 73, 86, 89, 102, 153, 166, 169, 182, 214, 230

fable, *V2* 76

fairy tale, *V2* 92

Graphic and semantic organizers

Grouping students for instruction. *See* Differentiated instruction.

Guided oral reading. Guided oral reading is part of every lesson plan.

Handwriting, *V1* 257–259; *V2* 257–259

Health. *See* Content-area texts.

High-frequency words

base words. *See* Word structure.

Higher-order thinking skills. *See* Comprehension, Skills.

Home-school connection. *See* School-home connection.

Homework. *See* School-home connection.

How-to article. *See* Genres.

Illustrations. *See* Comprehension, Strategies, picture walk; Graphic sources.

Immediate corrective feedback. *See* Corrective feedback.

Inferences. *See* Comprehension, Skills, draw conclusions. Inferential thinking questions appear throughout each lesson.

Inflected endings. *See* Word structure, endings, inflected.

Informal assessment. *See* Assessment, classroom-based.

Informational text. *See* Genres.

Instructional routines. *See* Daily Plans for lessons; Routine Cards at the back of this Teacher's Guide.

Judgments, make. *See* Comprehension, Skills, draw conclusions.

L

Language, oral. *See* Oral Language.

Letter recognition. *See* Concepts of print.

Letter-sound correspondence. *See* Phonics.

Listening comprehension

Literal comprehension. Literal comprehension questions appear throughout each lesson.

Literary devices. *See* Sound devices and poetic elements.

M

Main idea and supporting details. *See* Comprehension, Skills.

Make judgments. *See* Comprehension, Skills, draw conclusions.

Map. *See* Graphic sources.

Math. *See* Content-area texts.

Metacognition. *See* Comprehension, Strategies, self-monitor.

Monitor progress. *See* Assessment, progress monitoring.

Multicultural connections, *V1* 25, 57, 150; *V2* 38, 230, 238

Multisyllabic words. *See* Word structure, syllable patterns.

Mystery. *See* Genres.

Music. *See* Content-area texts.

Narrative nonfiction. *See* Genres.

New literacies. *See* Content-area texts, technology.

Nonfiction. *See* Genres.

Nonfiction narrative. *See* Genres.

Oral language

Oral reading. *See* Fluency.

Oral vocabulary

Paired reading. *See* Comprehension, Strategies; Fluency.

Parts of a book

Phonemic awareness. *See* Phonological and phonemic awareness.

Phonics

vowel diphthongs

oi, *V2* 148, 154, 157

ou, *V2* 116, 122, 157

ow, *V2* 116, 122, 157

oy, *V2* 148, 154, 157

vowel patterns, less common

a, al, *V2* 4, 10

au, aw, au(gh), *V2* 228, 234

ew, ue, *V2* 180, 186, 189

vowels, long

a, *V1* 116, 122, 125, 205

e, *V1* 164, 170, 173, 205; *V2* 26

i, *V1* 132, 138, 141, 205; *V2* 56

o, *V1* 148, 154, 157, 205; *V2* 40, 42

u, *V1* 164, 170, 173, 205

y, *V1* 180, 186; *V2* 29

vowels, r-controlled

ar, *V1* 196, 202, 237

er, *V1* 232, 234, 237

ir, *V1* 232, 234, 237

or/ore, *V1* 200, 202, 237

ur, *V1* 232, 234, 237

vowels, short

a, *V1* 4, 10, 42, 45, 77, 125

e, *V1* 52, 58, 77, 173

i, *V1* 20, 26, 45, 77, 141

o, *V1* 36, 42, 45, 77, 157

u, *V1* 68, 74, 77, 173

Phonological and phonemic awareness

add initial and final sounds, *V1* 39, 55, 100, 103, 106, 135, 138, 154, 183, 196, 199, 202, 231, 234

add sounds (phonemes), *V1* 100, 106, 151, 154, 183, 196; *V2* 36, 119, 135, 167, 183, 215, 218, 231, 234

blend sounds (phonemes), *V1* 4, 7, 10, 20, 23, 26, 36, 42, 167, 170, 228

count syllables, *V1* 215, 216, 280; *V2* 280

delete ending sounds (phonemes), *V1* 87, 90; *V2* 36, 196, 202

segment and blend sounds, *V1* 119, 122, 180, 186; *V2* 20, 23, 26, 39, 42, 116, 122, 132, 138, 148, 154, 164, 170, 180, 186, 212, 228

segment and count sounds, *V1* 68, 71, 74, 84, 116, 132, 148, 164, 180; *V2* 4, 10, 52, 55, 58, 151, 199

segment words into sounds (phonemes), *V1* 52, 58; *V2* 84

segment words into syllables, syllables into sounds, *V1* 212, 215, 218; *V2* 7, 68, 71, 74, 84, 87, 90, 100, 103, 106

Sound Pronunciation Guide, *Welcome to My Sidewalks,* 31–32

substitute sounds (phonemes), *V1* 13, 29; *V2* 189

Picture clues. *See* Comprehension, Strategies.

Picture walk. *See* Comprehension, Strategies.

Pictures. *See* Comprehension, Strategies, picture clues; Graphic sources, illustration.

Plot. *See* Comprehension, Strategies, story structure.

Poetic devices. *See* Sound devices and poetic elements.

Poetry. *See* Genres.

Predict. *See* Comprehension, Strategies.

Prefixes. *See* Word structure.

Prereading strategies. *See* Comprehension, Strategies, for specific strategies; Concept development.

Preview. *See* Comprehension, Strategies.

Prior knowledge. *See* Comprehension, Strategies.

Progress monitoring. *See* Assessment.

Prosody. *See* Fluency, expression/intonation (prosody).

Punctuation. *See* Fluency.

Purpose for reading. *See* Comprehension, Strategies, set purpose for reading.

Questions, answer. *See* Comprehension, Strategies.

Questions, ask. *See* Comprehension, Strategies.

Rate. *See* Fluency.

Reader response, *V1* 6, 9, 12, 14, 22, 25, 28, 30, 38, 41, 44, 46, 54, 57, 60, 62, 70, 73, 76, 78, 86, 89, 92, 94, 102, 105, 108, 110, 118, 121, 124, 126, 134, 137, 140, 142, 150, 153, 156, 158, 166, 169, 172, 174, 182, 185, 188, 190, 198, 201, 204, 206, 214, 217, 222, 220, 230, 233, 236, 238; *V2* 6, 9, 12, 14, 22, 25, 28, 30, 38, 41, 44, 46, 54, 57, 60, 62, 70, 73, 76, 78, 86, 89, 92, 94, 102, 105, 108, 110, 118, 121, 124, 126, 134, 137, 140, 142, 150, 153, 156, 158, 166, 169, 172, 174, 182, 185, 188, 190, 198, 201, 204, 206, 214, 217, 220, 222, 230, 233, 236, 238

Reading levels, *Welcome to My Sidewalks,* 14–15; *V1* xii–xiii; *V2* xii–xiii

Reading rate. *See* Fluency.

Realistic fiction. *See* Genres.

Recall and retell. *See* Comprehension, Strategies.

Recipe. *See* Genres.

Reference sources, *V1* 70, 190, 230

Repeated reading. *See* Fluency.

Research

bibliography, *Welcome to My Sidewalks,* 30

research base for My Sidewalks, *Welcome to My Sidewalks,* 6, 18–29, 30

Respond to literature. *See* Reader response.

Response to literature, *V1* 9, 15, 17, 25, 31, 33, 41, 47, 49, 57, 63, 65, 73, 79, 81, 89, 95, 97, 105, 111, 113, 121, 127, 129, 137, 143, 145, 153, 159, 161, 169, 175, 177, 185, 191, 193, 201, 207, 209, 217, 223, 225, 233, 239, 241; *V2* 9, 15, 17, 25, 31, 33, 41, 47, 49, 57, 63, 65, 73, 79, 81, 89, 95, 97, 105, 111, 113, 121, 127, 129, 137, 143, 145, 153, 159, 161, 169, 175, 177, 185, 191, 193, 201, 207, 209, 217, 223, 225, 233, 239, 241

Retelling. *See* Comprehension, Strategies, recall and retell.

Rhyme. *See* Genres.

Rhythm. *See* Sound devices and poetic elements.

Riddle. *See* Genres.

Routines. Instructional routines provide the framework for lessons. *See also* Routine Cards at the back of this Teacher's Guide.

W

Word reading. *See* Fluency.

Word structure

base words

without spelling changes, *V1* 56, 58, 88, 90, 100, 109; *V2* 45, 120, 141

with spelling changes, *V1* 104, 106, 109, 136, 138, 184, 189; *V2* 45, 120, 216, 218, 221, 232, 234

blending strategy, *V1* 56, 88, 100, 104, 136, 152, 168, 184, 212, 216, 228; *V2* 8, 36, 68, 72, 84, 88, 100, 120, 136, 168, 196, 216, 218, 221, 232

compound words, *V2* 8, 10, 84, 88, 90, 173

contractions, *V1* 168, 170, 228, 234; *V2* 13, 93, 196, 202

corrective feedback, *V1* 56, 88, 100, 104, 136, 152, 168, 184, 212, 228, 232; *V2* 8, 36, 68, 72, 84, 88, 100, 104, 120, 136, 168, 184, 196, 216, 232

cumulative review, *V1* 109, 189, 221; *V2* 13, 45, 77, 93, 109, 125, 141, 173, 221, 237

endings, comparative, superlative, *V2* 36, 42, 45, 125, 221

endings, inflected, *V1* 56, 58, 88, 90, 100, 104, 106, 109, 136, 138, 184, 186, 189; *V2* 45, 125, 141, 216, 221, 232

plurals, *V1* 56, 58, 184, 186

possessives, *V1* 152, 154, 221

prefixes, *V2* 136, 138, 141, 184, 186, 216, 218, 221, 232, 234

suffixes, *V2* 120, 122, 125, 141, 168, 170, 216, 218, 221, 232, 234

syllable -er, *V1* 232, 234

syllable patterns *V2* 237

consonant + *le*, *V2* 100, 104, 106, 109, 237

syllable *er*, *V1* 232, 234

VC/CV, *V1* 212, 216, 218; *V2* 77, 109, 237

VC/V, *V2* 68, 72, 74, 77, 109, 237

V/CV, *V2* 68, 72, 74, 77, 109, 237

Word study. *See* Phonics; Word structure; Vocabulary.

Word Wall, *V1* 5, 21, 37, 53, 69, 85, 101, 117, 133, 149, 165, 181, 197, 213, 229; *V2* 5, 21, 37, 53, 69, 85, 101, 117, 133, 149, 165, 181, 197, 213, 229

Writing

independent writing, *V1* 15, 17, 31, 33, 47, 49, 63, 65, 79, 81, 95, 97, 111, 113, 127, 129, 143, 145, 159, 161, 175, 177, 191, 193, 207, 209, 223, 225, 239, 241; *V2* 15, 17, 31, 33, 47, 49, 63, 65, 79, 81, 95, 97, 111, 113, 127, 129, 143, 145, 159, 161, 175, 177, 191, 193, 207, 209, 223, 225, 239, 241

interactive writing, *V1* 15, 31, 47, 63, 79, 95, 111, 127, 143, 159, 175, 191, 207, 223, 239; *V2* 15, 31, 47, 63, 79, 95, 111, 127, 143, 159, 175, 191, 207, 223, 239

journal writing, *V1* 15, 31, 47, 63, 79, 95, 111, 127, 143, 159, 175, 191, 207, 223, 239; *V2* 15, 31, 47, 63, 79, 95, 111, 127, 143, 159, 175, 191, 207, 223, 239

response to literature, *V1* 9, 15, 17, 25, 31, 33, 41, 47, 49, 57, 63, 65, 73, 79, 81, 89, 95, 97, 105, 111, 113, 121, 127, 129, 137, 143, 145, 153, 159, 161, 169, 175, 177, 185, 191, 193, 201, 207, 209, 217, 223, 225, 233, 239, 241; *V2* 9, 15, 17, 25, 31, 33, 41, 47, 49, 57, 63, 65, 73, 79, 81, 89, 95, 97, 105, 111, 113, 121, 127, 129, 137, 143, 145, 153, 159, 161, 169, 175, 177, 185, 191, 193, 201, 207, 209, 217, 223, 225, 233, 239, 241

sentence frames, *V1* 9, 25, 41, 57, 73, 89, 105, 121, 137, 153, 169, 185, 201, 217, 233; *V2* 9, 25, 41, 57, 73, 89, 105, 121, 137, 153, 169, 185, 201, 217, 233

sentence stems. *See* Writing, sentence frames.

shared writing, *V1* 9, 25, 41, 57, 73, 89, 105, 121, 137, 153, 169, 185, 201, 217, 233; *V2* 9, 25, 41, 57, 73, 89, 105, 121, 137, 153, 169, 185, 201, 217, 233

Writing elements

conventions, *V1* 17, 33, 47, 49, 65, 81, 95, 97, 111, 113, 127, 129, 145, 161, 177, 193, 209, 223, 225, 241; *V2* 17, 33, 49, 65, 81, 97, 113, 127, 129, 145, 161, 177, 193, 209, 225, 241

focus, *V1* 33, 65, 81, 241; *V2* 65, 145, 225

organization, *V1* 97, 113, 193, 225; *V2* 33, 49, 65, 81, 97, 129, 209,

support, *V1* 17, 49, 65, 81, 97, 113, 129, 145, 161, 177, 193, 209, 241; *V2* 17, 33, 49, 97, 113, 145, 177, 193, 209, 225, 241

Writing purpose

expository writing, *V1* 49, 65, 97, 129, 177, 193, 241; *V2* 33, 81, 97

descriptive writing, *V1* 17, 161, 209; *V2* 17, 49, 113, 145, 177, 225

narrative writing, *V1* 33, 81, 113, 145, 225; *V2* 65, 209

personal narrative, *V2* 129, 161, 193, 241

Teacher Notes

Teacher Notes

Teacher Notes

Blending Strategy

Teach children to blend words using this Routine.

1 Connect Relate the new sound-spelling to previously learned sound-spellings.

2 Use Sound-Spelling Card Display the card for the sound-spelling. Say the sound. Have children say it.

3 Listen and Write Have children write the letter(s) as they say the sound.

4 Model Demonstrate how to blend words with the sound-spelling. Have children blend a word with you.

5 Group and Individual Practice Have children work together to segment and blend several words with the sound-spelling. Then have each child blend two words individually. Provide corrective feedback.

Comprehension Strategy: Ask Questions

During reading, teach children to ask themselves these questions:

- **Nonfiction**

Before	What do I think this is mostly about? What do I already know about this?
During	What have I read so far? Do I understand what I've read?
After	What did I find out that I didn't know before?

Monitor Word and Story Reading

Use these approaches to monitor children's decoding and use of context as they read.

If... children come to a word they don't know, **then...** prompt them to blend the word.

1 Look at each letter and think of its sound.

2 Blend the sounds.

3 Read the new word.

4 Is the new word a word you know?

5 Does it make sense in the story?

Fluency Practice

Use one of these Routines for fluency practice. Provide corrective feedback as you listen to each child read.

- **Oral Reading** Have children read a passage orally. To achieve optimal fluency, children should reread the text three or four times.

- **Paired Reading** Reader 1 begins. Children read, switching readers at the end of each page. Then Reader 2 begins, as the partners reread the passage. For optimal fluency, children should reread three or four times.

- **Audio-Assisted Reading** The child reads aloud while listening to the recording. On the first reading, children point to words while they listen. On subsequent readings, they read along with the recording.

Routine Card 1

Use immediate corrective feedback to help children blend words.

If... children pause between sounds,
then... model blending the word without pauses. Then have children blend it again.

If... children say the wrong sound,
then... keep your finger on the missed sound, model it correctly, and have children repeat the sound. Then have them blend the word again.

If... children say the wrong sound when they say the word quickly,
then... model the correct word and have children repeat it. Have children say the sounds again slowly and then quickly to make it sound like a real word.

Routine Card 2

• Fiction

Story Questions

Who is in this story?

Where/When does this story take place?

What happens in this story?

Making Connections

Have I ever read a story like this before?

Has anything like this happened to me before?

Do any of the characters remind me of someone I know?

Routine Card 3

If... children have difficulty reading a story,
then... read a sentence aloud as children point to each word. Then have the group reread the sentence as they continue pointing. Continue reading in this way before children read individually.

If... children cannot read a high-frequency word,
then... tell them the word and have them repeat it. Have children spell the word and tell what word they spelled. Have them practice in pairs with word cards,
or... mark the missed word on a high-frequency word list and send the list home for additional practice, or have children practice with a fluent reader.

If... children have trouble reading words with the letter-sound patterns taught this week,
then... reteach the blending strategy lessons for the week.

Routine Card 4

Use these strategies to help children develop fluency.

• **Model Fluency** Model reading "as if you were speaking," attending to punctuation and phrasing and reading with expression (prosody).

• **Provide Corrective Feedback** Provide feedback on oral reading.

If... children misread a word,
then... help them decode it and have them reread the sentence.

If... children read at an inappropriate or unsteady pace,
then... model an appropriate pace, having children echo.

If... children lack oral expression,
then... model how to read based on the meaning of the passage. Tell children that their expression should show their understanding.

• **Monitor Fluency** See pp. 244–245 for assessment options.

Oral Vocabulary Routines

Use this Routine to teach each Amazing Word and any other oral vocabulary you may wish to introduce.

1 Introduce the Word Relate the word to a song or story children are learning. Supply a child-friendly definition. Have children say the word.

2 Demonstrate Provide several familiar examples to demonstrate meaning. When possible, use gestures or sketches to help convey meaning.

3 Apply Have children demonstrate understanding with a simple activity.

4 Display the Word Write the word on a card and display it in the classroom. Have children identify familiar letter-sounds or word parts.

Picture Walk Routine

To build concepts and vocabulary, conduct a structured picture walk before reading.

1 Prepare Preview the selection and list key concepts and vocabulary you wish to develop.

2 Discuss As children look at the pages, discuss illustrations, have children point to pictured items, and/or ask questions that target key concepts and vocabulary.

3 Elaborate Elaborate on children's responses to reinforce correct use of the vocabulary and to provide additional exposure to key concepts.

4 Practice For more practice with key concepts, have each child turn to a partner and do the picture walk using the key concept vocabulary.

Comprehension Strategies

Before, During, and After Reading strategies should be reinforced daily. Use the Routine on the back of this card to teach

- **Previewing Text** What do the title and pictures tell about the text?
- **Setting a Purpose for Reading** What do I want to find out?
- **Using Prior Knowledge** Does the selection remind me of anything I already know?
- **Making, Modifying, and Confirming Predictions** What do I think will happen next? Did it happen as I predicted?
- **Recognizing Story Structure** Who is in the story? Where/ When does it take place? What happens at the beginning? in the middle? at the end?
- **Summarizing Text** What are the main ideas?

Reading Long Words

Model these strategies to teach children to read long words.

Syllable Patterns

VC/CV as in *mit/ten, nap/kin*
V/CV (open) as in *pi/lot, o/pen*
VC/V (closed) as in *sev/en, fin/ish*
C+le as in *tum/ble, ca/ble*

1 Look for Chunks Divide the word into syllables, or chunks.

2 Blend Sound out each syllable, or chunk.

3 Say Chunks Slowly Slowly say each syllable from left to right.

4 Say It Fast Say the chunks fast to make a word.

Routine Card 5

Use this Routine to monitor understanding of concepts and vocabulary taught each week.

1 Display the week's background-building passage (*Let's Find Out*) in the Student Reader.

2 Remind the child of the concept that the class has been talking about that week.

3 Ask the child to tell you about the *Let's Find Out* passage and illustrations using some of the week's Amazing Words.

4 Ask questions about the passage and illustrations using the Amazing Words. Note which questions the child can respond to. Reteach unknown words using the Oral Vocabulary Routine.

Routine Card 6

Routine Card 7

1 Teach Describe each strategy explicitly, explaining when and how to use it.

2 Model Think aloud to model applying the strategy with different selections.

3 Practice Have children practice using the strategy, with support and prompting.

4 Apply Independently Expect children to begin using these strategies independently.

Routine Card 8

Base Words and Affixes

1 Look for Word Parts Figure out if the word has prefixes, endings, or suffixes.

2 Take Off Parts Take off the prefixes, endings, or suffixes.

3 Figure Out the Base Word Read the base word or sound it out.

4 Say Parts Slowly Slowly say each word part from left to right.

5 Say It Fast Say the word parts fast to make a word.